The Age of Intelligent Cities

This book concludes a trilogy that began with *Intelligent Cities: Innovation, Knowledge Systems and Digital Spaces* (Routledge, 2002) and *Intelligent Cities and Globalisation of Innovation Networks* (Routledge, 2008). Together, these books examine intelligent cities as environments of innovation and collaborative problem-solving. In this final book, the focus is on planning, strategy, and governance of intelligent cities.

Divided into three parts, each section elaborates on complementary aspects of intelligent city strategy and planning. Part I is about the drivers and architectures of the spatial intelligence of cities, whereas Part II turns to planning processes and discusses top-down and bottom-up planning for intelligent cities. Cities such as Amsterdam, Manchester, Stockholm, and Helsinki are examples of cities that have adopted bottom-up planning through the gradual implementation of successive initiatives for regeneration. On the other hand, Living PlanIT, Neapolis in Cyprus, and Saudi Arabia intelligent cities have started with the top-down approach, setting up urban operating systems and common central platforms. Part III focuses on intelligent city strategies: how cities should manage the drivers of spatial intelligence, create smart environments, mobilise communities, and offer new solutions to address city problems.

The main findings are related to a series of models which capture fundamental aspects of intelligent cities making and operation as environments enabling innovation-for-all. These models consider structure, function, planning, strategies toward intelligent environments, and a model of governance based on mobilisation of communities, knowledge architectures, and innovation cycles.

Nicos Komninos is Professor of Urban Development, Planning and Innovation Policy at the Aristotle University of Thessaloniki, Greece.

Regions and Cities

Series Editor in Chief
Susan M. Christopherson, *Cornell University, USA*

Editors
Maryann Feldman, *University of Georgia, USA*
Gernot Grabher, *HafenCity University Hamburg, Germany*
Ron Martin, *University of Cambridge, UK*
Martin Perry, *Massey University, New Zealand*

In today's globalised, knowledge-driven and networked world, regions and cities have assumed heightened significance as the interconnected nodes of economic, social and cultural production, and as sites of new modes of economic and territorial governance and policy experimentation. This book series brings together incisive and critically engaged international and interdisciplinary research on this resurgence of regions and cities, and should be of interest to geographers, economists, sociologists, political scientists and cultural scholars, as well as to policymakers involved in regional and urban development.

For more information on the Regional Studies Association visit www.regional studies.org

There is a **30 percent discount** available to RSA members on books in the ***Regions and Cities*** series, and other subject related Taylor and Francis books and e-books including Routledge titles. To order just e-mail alex.robinson@tandf.co.uk, or phone on +44 (0) 20 7017 6924 and declare your RSA membership. You can also visit www.routledge.com and use the discount code: **RSA0901**

78. **The Age of Intelligent Cities**
    Smart environments and
    innovation-for-all
    strategies
    Nicos Komninos

77. **Space and Place in Central and Eastern Europe**
    Historical trends and
    perspectives
    Gyula Horváth

76. **Territorial Cohesion in Rural Europe**
    The relational turn in rural
    development
    Edited by Andrew Copus and Philomena de Lima

75. **The Global Competitiveness of Regions**
    Robert Huggins, Hiro Izushi, Daniel Prokop and Piers Thompson

74. **The Social Dynamics of Innovation Networks**
Edited by Roel Rutten, Paul Benneworth, Dessy Irawati and Frans Boekema

73. **The European Territory**
From historical roots to global challenges
Jacques Robert

72. **Urban Innovation Systems**
What makes them tick?
Willem van Winden, Erik Braun, Alexander Otgaar and Jan-Jelle Witte

71. **Shrinking Cities**
A global perspective
Edited by Harry W. Richardson and Chang Woon Nam

70. **Cities, State and Globalization**
City-regional governance
Tassilo Herrschel

69. **The Creative Class Goes Global**
Edited by Charlotta Mellander, Richard Florida, Bjørn Asheim and Meric Gertler

68. **Entrepreneurial Knowledge, Technology and the Transformation of Regions**
Edited by Charlie Karlsson, Börje Johansson and Roger Stough

67. **The Economic Geography of the IT Industry in the Asia Pacific Region**
Edited by Philip Cooke, Glen Searle and Kevin O'Connor

66. **Working Regions**
Reconnecting innovation and production in the knowledge Economy
Jennifer Clark

65. **Europe's Changing Geography**
The impact of inter-regional networks
Edited by Nicola Bellini and Ulrich Hilpert

64. **The Value of Arts and Culture for Regional Development**
A scandinavian perspective
Edited by Lisbeth Lindeborg and Lars Lindkvist

63. **The University and the City**
John Goddard and Paul Vallance

62. **Re-framing Regional Development**
Evolution, innovation and transition
Edited by Philip Cooke

61. **Networking Regionalised Innovative Labour Markets**
Edited by Ulrich Hilpert and Helen Lawton Smith

60. **Leadership and Change in Sustainable Regional Development**
Edited by Markku Sotarauta, Ina Horlings and Joyce Liddle

59. **Regional Development Agencies: The Next Generation?**
Networking, knowledge and regional policies
Edited by Nicola Bellini, Mike Danson and Henrik Halkier

58. **Community-based Entrepreneurship and Rural Development**
Creating favourable conditions for small businesses in Central Europe
Matthias Fink, Stephan Loidl and Richard Lang

57. **Creative Industries and Innovation in Europe**
Concepts, measures and comparative case studies
Edited by Luciana Lazzeretti

56. **Innovation Governance in an Open Economy**
Shaping regional nodes in a globalized world
Edited by Annika Rickne, Staffan Laestadius and Henry Etzkowitz

55. **Complex Adaptive Innovation Systems**
Relatedness and transversality in the evolving region
Philip Cooke

54. **Creating Knowledge Locations in Cities**
Innovation and integration challenges
Willem van Winden, Luis de Carvalho, Erwin van Tujil, Jeroen van Haaren and Leo van den Berg

53. **Regional Development in Northern Europe**
Peripherality, marginality and border issues
Edited by Mike Danson and Peter De Souza

52. **Promoting Silicon Valleys in Latin America**
Luciano Ciravegna

51. **Industrial Policy Beyond the Crisis**
Regional, national and international perspectives
Edited by David Bailey, Helena Lenihan and Josep-Maria Arauzo-Carod

50. **Just Growth**
Inclusion and prosperity in America's metropolitan regions
Chris Benner and Manuel Pastor

49. **Cultural Political Economy of Small Cities**
Edited by Anne Lorentzen and Bas van Heur

48. **The Recession and Beyond**
Local and regional responses to the downturn
Edited by David Bailey and Caroline Chapain

47. **Beyond Territory**
Edited by Harald Bathelt, Maryann Feldman and Dieter F. Kogler

46. **Leadership and Place**
Edited by Chris Collinge, John Gibney and Chris Mabey

45. **Migration in the 21st Century**
Rights, outcomes, and policy
Kim Korinek and Thomas Maloney

44. **The Futures of the City Region**
Edited by Michael Neuman and Angela Hull

43. **The Impacts of Automotive Plant Closures**
A tale of two cities
Edited by Andrew Beer and Holli Evans

42. **Manufacturing in the New Urban Economy**
Willem van Winden, Leo van den Berg, Luis de Carvalho and Erwin van Tuijl

41. **Globalizing Regional Development in East Asia**
    Production networks, clusters, and entrepreneurship
    Edited by Henry Wai-chung Yeung

40. **China and Europe**
    The implications of the rise of China as a global economic power for Europe
    Edited by Klaus Kunzmann, Willy A Schmid and Martina Koll-Schretzenmayr

39. **Business Networks in Clusters and Industrial Districts**
    The governance of the global value chain
    Edited by Fiorenza Belussi and Alessia Sammarra

38. **Whither Regional Studies?**
    Edited by Andy Pike

37. **Intelligent Cities and Globalisation of Innovation Networks**
    Nicos Komninos

36. **Devolution, Regionalism and Regional Development**
    The UK experience
    Edited by Jonathan Bradbury

35. **Creative Regions**
    Technology, culture and knowledge entrepreneurship
    Edited by Philip Cooke and Dafna Schwartz

34. **European Cohesion Policy**
    Willem Molle

33. **Geographies of the New Economy**
    Critical reflections
    Edited by Peter W. Daniels, Andrew Leyshon, Michael J. Bradshaw and Jonathan Beaverstock

32. **The Rise of the English Regions?**
    Edited by Irene Hardill, Paul Benneworth, Mark Baker and Leslie Budd

31. **Regional Development in the Knowledge Economy**
    Edited by Philip Cooke and Andrea Piccaluga

30. **Regional Competitiveness**
    Edited by Ron Martin, Michael Kitson and Peter Tyler

29. **Clusters and Regional Development**
    Critical reflections and explorations
    Edited by Bjørn Asheim, Philip Cooke and Ron Martin

28. **Regions, Spatial Strategies and Sustainable Development**
    David Counsell and Graham Haughton

27. **Sustainable Cities**
    Graham Haughton and Colin Hunter

26. **Geographies of Labour Market Inequality**
    Edited by Ron Martin and Philip S. Morrison

25. **Regional Innovation Strategies**
    The challenge for less-favoured regions
    Edited by Kevin Morgan and Claire Nauwelaers

24. **Out of the Ashes?**
    The social impact of industrial contraction and regeneration on Britain's mining communities
    Chas Critcher, Bella Dicks, David Parry and David Waddington

23. **Restructuring Industry and Territory**
    The experience of Europe's regions
    Edited by Anna Giunta, Arnoud Lagendijk and Andy Pike

22. **Foreign Direct Investment and the Global Economy**
    Corporate and institutional dynamics of global-localisation
    Edited by Jeremy Alden and Nicholas F. Phelps

21. **Community Economic Development**
    Edited by Graham Haughton

20. **Regional Development Agencies in Europe**
    Edited by Charlotte Damborg, Mike Danson and Henrik Halkier

19. **Social Exclusion in European Cities**
    Processes, experiences and responses
    Edited by Judith Allen, Goran Cars and Ali Madanipour

18. **Metropolitan Planning in Britain**
    A comparative study
    Edited by Peter Roberts, Kevin Thomas and Gwyndaf Williams

17. **Unemployment and Social Exclusion**
    Landscapes of labour inequality and social exclusion
    Edited by Sally Hardy, Paul Lawless and Ron Martin

16. **Multinationals and European Integration**
    Trade, investment and regional development
    Edited by Nicholas A. Phelps

15. **The Coherence of EU Regional Policy**
    Contrasting perspectives on the structural funds
    Edited by John Bachtler and Ivan Turok

14. **New Institutional Spaces**
    TECs and the remaking of economic governance
    Edited by Martin Jones and Jamie Peck

13. **Regional Policy in Europe**
    S. S. Artobolevskiy

12. **Innovation Networks and Learning Regions?**
    James Simmie

11. **British Regionalism and Devolution**
    The challenges of state reform and European integration
    Edited by Jonathan Bradbury and John Mawson

10. **Regional Development Strategies**
    A European perspective
    Edited by Jeremy Alden and Philip Boland

9. **Union Retreat and the Regions**
    The shrinking landscape of organised labour
    Ron Martin, Peter Sunley and Jane Wills

8. **The Regional Dimension of Transformation in Central Europe**
   Grzegorz Gorzelak

7. **The Determinants of Small Firm Growth**
   An inter-regional study in the United Kingdom 1986–90
   *Richard Barkham,
   Graham Gudgin, Mark Hart and Eric Hanvey*

6. **The Regional Imperative**
   Regional planning and governance in Britain, Europe and the United States
   Urlan A. Wannop

5. **An Enlarged Europe**
   Regions in competition?
   Edited by Louis Albrechts, Sally Hardy, Mark Hart and Anastasios Katos

4. **Spatial Policy in a Divided Nation**
   Edited by Richard T. Harrison and Mark Hart

3. **Regional Development in the 1990s**
   The British Isles in transition
   Edited by Ron Martin and Peter Townroe

2. **Retreat from the Regions**
   Corporate change and the closure of factories
   Stephen Fothergill and Nigel Guy

1. **Beyond Green Belts**
   Managing urban growth in the 21st century
   Edited by John Herington

The Age of Intelligent Cities
Smart environments and
innovation-for-all strategies

Nicos Komninos

Routledge
Taylor & Francis Group
LONDON AND NEW YORK

First published 2015
by Routledge
2 Park Square, Milton Park, Abingdon, Oxon OX14 4RN

and by Routledge
711 Third Avenue, New York, NY 10017

Routledge is an imprint of the Taylor & Francis Group, an informa business

© 2015 Nicos Komninos

The right of Nicos Komninos to be identified as author of this work has been asserted by him in accordance with the Copyright, Designs and Patents Act 1988.

All rights reserved. No part of this book may be reprinted or reproduced or utilised in any form or by any electronic, mechanical, or other means, now known or hereafter invented, including photocopying and recording, or in any information storage or retrieval system, without permission in writing from the publishers.

Trademark notice: Product or corporate names may be trademarks or registered trademarks, and are used only for identification and explanation without intent to infringe.

British Library Cataloguing in Publication Data
A catalogue record for this book is available from the British Library

Library of Congress Cataloging-in-Publication Data
Komninos, Nicos.
 The age of intelligent cities : smart environments and innovation-for-all strategies / Nicos Komninos. — First Edition.
   pages cm — (Regions and cities)
 1. City planning—Environmental aspects. 2. City planning—Technological innovations. 3. Information networks—Social aspects. I. Title.
 HT166.K62595 2014
 307.1'216—dc23
 2014004114

ISBN: 978-1-138-78219-8 (hbk)
ISBN: 978-1-315-76934-9 (ebk)

Typeset in Times
by Apex CoVantage, LLC

Printed and bound in Great Britain by
CPI Group (UK) Ltd, Croydon, CR0 4YY

To my family, Elena and Alex

Contents

Acknowledgements	xvii
List of figures	xix
List of tables	xx

Introduction: the age of intelligent cities   1

   1. Intelligent cities for global challenges 1
   2. A trilogy on intelligent cities: twelve years of research 3
   3. Main ideas and contents of the third book 4

PART I
What makes cities intelligent? drivers of spatial intelligence of cities   11

1 Intelligent cities – smart cities: the landscape   13

   1. The rise of a new planning paradigm 13
   2. Movements shaping the intelligent city paradigm 16
   3. Intelligent city: a new reality – multiple concepts 19
   4. Structure: city, innovation, and smart environments 24
   5. Outcomes: city domains for smart systems application 27
   6. The landscape of intelligent cities 31

2 Intelligent city strategies: innovation through multi-layer knowledge functions   38

   1. Intelligent cities for innovation 38
   2. Two literatures shaping intelligent cities 39
   3. Towards user-driven, glocal innovation ecosystems 41
   4. Strategies for intelligent cities: profiles and innovation paths 44
   5. Strategies introducing multi-layer knowledge functions 51
   6. Intelligent city strategies: innovation by a mix of knowledge functions 57

xiv *Contents*

3 Smart cities, smart environments, and big data: innovation ecosystems of embedded spatial intelligence 61

  1. Smart environments and embedded spatial intelligence 61
  2. Milestones towards embedded spatial intelligence of cities 63
  3. Internet of Things, sensor networks, and smart cities 67
  4. Semantic Web, future media, and smart cities 69
  5. Cloud computing and smart cities 70
  6. From technologies to smart city services: user-driven innovation 72
  7. Innovation ecosystems of embedded spatial intelligence 73

4 Alternative architectures of spatial intelligence of cities: pathways to innovation 79

  1. What makes cities intelligent? 79
  2. Spatial intelligence of cities 80
  3. Baseline: agglomeration intelligence though connected variety 83
  4. Orchestration intelligence: Bletchley Park, the first intelligent community 85
  5. Empowerment intelligence: Cyberport, Hong Kong up-skilling platforms 88
  6. Instrumentation intelligence: Amsterdam and Santander smart-metering projects for environmental sustainability 91
  7. Towards a universal architecture of spatial intelligence 93

PART II
Planning for intelligent cities: connecting bottom-up and top-down perspectives 99

5 Intelligent cities and the bottom-up regeneration of metropolitan areas 101

  1. Intelligent city planning and the regeneration of metropolitan cities in Europe 101
  2. Planning for intelligent Thessaloniki 105
  3. Broadband networks 107
  4. City-wide applications and e-services 109
  5. Planning for smart city-districts 114
  6. Intelligent city planning in old metropolitan areas 118

6 Top-down planning for new intelligent cities and city-districts 124

  1. Top-down planning for new intelligent cities 124

2. *New economic cities in Saudi Arabia 125*
3. *Setting up smart city complexes in Saudi Arabia 133*
4. *A critical appraisal of top-down intelligent city planning 135*

7 **Strategic planning for intelligent cities: a roadmap across spaces and stages** 144

1. *Cities: from masterplans to strategic planning 144*
2. *Intelligent city planning: a connectionist model 145*
3. *Step one. The city: defining problems and communities 147*
4. *Step two. Defining innovation ecosystems driving urban change 148*
5. *Step three. Digital space: horizon scan of technologies and smart environments 150*
6. *Step four. Strategy: communities, knowledge functions, and circuits of innovation 154*
7. *Step five. Development of applications and platforms 157*
8. *Step six. Selecting business models of sustainability 160*
9. *Step seven. Documenting spatial intelligence 162*

PART III
Strategies and governance: innovation-for-all into smart environments 169

8 **Toward intelligent clusters and city-districts: platforms for self-organising growth** 171

1. *New growth conditions 171*
2. *Clustering for growth 175*
3. *Toward smart clusters: top-down thrust from smart specialisation 178*
4. *Cluster needs for intelligence: bottom-up demand 180*
5. *A strategy for intelligent clusters 185*
6. *Consensus space: foundations of an innovation community 186*
7. *Digital platforms for self-organising innovation 187*
8. *Resource efficiency innovations: green clusters and eco-districts 191*
9. *The G component 193*

9 **Toward smarter companies: building innovation ecosystems with smart environments** 196

1. *New trends: individual empowerment and big data 196*
2. *Innovation-for-all companies into smart environments: building own innovation ecosystems 199*

3. Market discovery using smart environments 201
4. Technology discovery using smart environments 205
5. Business model re-discovery using smart environments 213
6. BOWIE: an individual innovation trajectory 217

10 Smart city infrastructure: applications and solutions every city should have — 220

1. Infrastructure and applications every city should have 220
2. Broadband city: networks, sensors, and open data 221
3. Smart economy: city branding, marketplaces, and crowdfunding 224
4. Quality of life: environment, safety, and health care 229
5. Smart city networks and utilities 232
6. Intelligent city governance 235
7. Optimising smart city infrastructure 238

11 The governance of intelligent city ecosystems: communities, knowledge architectures, and innovation cycles — 243

1. Toward a generic model of intelligent city governance 243
2. A step forward: insights from big data 246
3. Governance of intelligent city ecosystems 249
4. Learning from the PEOPLE smart city pilots 250
5. Governance of actors: the art of community 255
6. Governance of assets: knowledge architectures 258
7. Governance of activities: collaborative innovation cycles 260
8. Intelligent ecosystems in the near future 262

Index — 267

Acknowledgements

The third book in the trilogy on Intelligent Cities presents ideas, models, and methodologies for strategic planning and governance. It gathers most of my academic activity over the period 2009–2013 on the design and creation of intelligent cities, presented at conferences and in working papers and research reports.

The book owes much to surveys, discussions, and the conclusions of research carried out during this period, and especially to the contribution of colleagues and researchers involved in the following projects:

- FIREBALL: Hans Schafffers (Alto University), Marc Pallot (Nottingham University), Michael Nilsson (Luleå University of Technology), Annika Sallstrom (Centre for Distance-Spanning Technology), Roberto Santoro (ESoCe-Net and ENoLL), Dave Carter (Manchester Digital Development Agency), Alvaro Oliveira and Jean Barocca (Alfamicro).
- PEOPLE: Eva García Muntión (RTDI Madrid), María Eugenia Ortiz Montalbán (ANOVA Consulting), Lorena Bourg (Ariadna Servicios Informáticos), Yannis Tsamboulatidis (Information Technologies Institute, CERTH), and Rapolas Lakavicius (European Commission).
- MEDLAB: Jesse Marsh (Atelier Studio).
- INNOSEE: Ivan Stoytchev (University of National and World Economy), Ludmil Kovachev (ITPIO Institute), and Kennet Lindquist (Swedish TelePedagogic Knowledge Centre).
- CROSS-INNO-CUT: Sotiris Zygiaris (PMU University, Saudi Arabia), Maria Schoina, Isidoros Passas and Elena Sefertzi, all at Urenio Research, and
- Individual research by my PhD students who have concluded or are near to submitting their thesis on intelligent cities, Panagiotis Tsarchopoulos, Nancy Martzopoulou, Christina Kakderi, Margarita Anngelidou, and Luca Mora.

I have enjoyed the cooperation of all, and I wish to acknowledge their contribution to the ideas that are presented here. I am really indebted to all of them.

I am thankful to John A. O'Shea who, for the third time, undertook the editing of this book, as he has done with the previous books in the Intelligent Cities trilogy, and who looked meticulously at the manuscript and substantially improved the syntax and meaning.

I would like also to thank Rob Langham, editor for the Regions and Cities series, as well as Natalie Tomlinson and Lisa Thomson at Routledge for their guidance and support in the publication of this book.

31 January 2014

Figures

1.1	Wordle cloud of intelligent city and smart city definitions	23
1.2	Intelligent city structure	24
1.3	Intelligent city application domains	30
4.1	Cyberport empowerment circuit	91
4.2	Generic dimensions of spatial intelligence of cities	94
5.1	Smart city-districts for the regeneration of Thessaloniki	115
5.2	Collaboration networks into the Port community	117
5.3	Digital space of cities – four rings and three gaps	119
7.1	A roadmap for intelligent city strategic planning: three stages and seven steps	146
7.2	Intelligent city strategy – three innovation circuits	155
7.3	Intelligent city scoreboard structure	165
9.1	Components and gates of the INTERVALUE platform	208
9.2	INTERVALUE technology exploitation process	211
9.3	Business models building blocks	214
10.1	Improve-my-city	237
10.2	ICOS – Intelligent Cities Open Source Community	239
11.1	Thermi pilot: a portfolio of smart city applications	253
11.2	User involvement into innovation cycles	261
11.3	A three-stage governance model	262

Tables

1.1	Smart city application domains and metrics	29
1.2	Intelligent city landscape	32
2.1	Layers of collective information intelligence	53
2.2	Layers of technology learning and absorption	54
2.3	Layers of knowledge creation and collaborative innovation	55
2.4	Layers of information dissemination and product promotion	57
3.1	A selection of smart city technologies based on Gartner's hype cycles	68
5.1	City-wide applications and e-services in the agglomeration of Thessaloniki	110
7.1	Smart city software development of applications and solutions	158
8.1	Key elements of smart specialisation strategy	179
8.2	Most-sought-after competences for cluster development	183
8.3	Knowledge-sharing platforms and Web-based innovation tools	188
9.1	Changing business models by using smart environments	215
10.1	Applications and solutions every city should have	221
11.1	Intelligent cities structural layers and elements	244

Introduction
The age of intelligent cities

> For each age is a dream that is dying or one that is coming to birth.
> – Arthur O'Shaughnessy

1. Intelligent cities for global challenges

Globalisation, urbanisation, and climate change have emerged as important challenges of the twenty-first century. The exponential growth of the urban population, which is expected to double within the next 40 years, is creating unprecedented socio-economic and environmental pressures. These are not, however, the only important trends that are shaping the new century. Debt crisis has become a permanent feature of the advanced economies of the EU and the USA; most dynamic growth regions are now to be found in China, India, and other developing Asian economies, and globalisation is channelling innovation investments into China and Southeast Asia. The narrative on the crisis that is gaining momentum defines its causes as lying in the production capabilities and low competitiveness of advanced economies, arguing that "advanced economies' fundamental capacity to grow by making useful things has been declining for decades, a trend that was masked by debt-fuelled spending" (Rajan 2012). New countries are dynamically entering the world scene, and the G20 is replacing the G7 as the primary venue for economic co-operation. A new world is rising, challenging the established order and hegemony of the West; a global world not only fuelled by information technologies, intense competition, and global knowledge flows, but also shaped by local creativities and user-driven innovation.

A new generation of cities and a new city-planning paradigm are also emerging: knowledge-intensive, innovative, and intelligent cities, which are driving and being driven by the above global changes. The contribution of cities to the innovation-led global economy is tied into their power to create synergies between technologies, knowledge, and skills scattered across populations and organisations. Every resident of a city and every organisation located there – be it a business, research centre, or university – are agents of codified and tacit knowledge. Relationships of cooperation and competition shape how information and knowledge flow among them, how technologies are transferred and exchanged, and how synergies are forged. Digital spaces and smart environments are facilitating and strengthening such information and knowledge flows. On the ground of innovative agglomerations and digital spatialities, the 'Intelligent City' is becoming the dominant urban development and planning paradigm of the twenty-first century, connecting urban, innovation, and digital environments and setting in motion powerful socio-technological engines for change and sustainable growth.

Leaders and governments all over the world consider innovation systems and information technologies to be critical drivers for addressing the fight against poverty and the challenges of competitiveness, employment, sustainable environments, and development. A sea of Web-based applications and information networks are already available to strengthen the ability of cities and citizens to manage information, knowledge transmission, technology learning, and innovation. These include wired and wireless broadband networks, metropolitan-area networks, fibre-optic cables linking the various organisations of a city, websites and portals for city branding, virtual cities, social media for online communities, city guides, professional directories of businesses and organisations, local marketplaces, e-commerce applications, digital spaces for education and research, environmental monitoring and alert, digital representations of sites and districts, virtual tours of monuments and cultural heritage, applications for city management such as automated budgeting, automated property registers, integrated personnel management tools, automated social security applications, thematic databases and open datasets, e-government city clouds, applications for journey planning and way-finding, smart energy and water grids, sensors embedded into buildings, and many others. These infrastructures and applications advance the innovation potential of cities offering better communication, online spaces of collaboration, real-time information, and knowledge-management tools. An extremely rich digital spatiality over the cities has given birth to a family of new concepts, such as cyber cities, digital cities, smart cities, and intelligent cities, all placing emphasis on relationships of collaboration between citizens, innovation actors, and digital agents.

Within this landscape, *The Age of Intelligent Cities* describes new ways for dealing with city development, innovation, and smart infrastructure in cities and regions. It focuses on strategies for intelligent cities, the deployment of digital technologies mobilising communities and creating innovative solutions to problems of competitiveness, social cohesion, safety, energy saving, environmental sustainability, and governance. It is expected that intelligent cities will lead to more efficient cities and more competitive innovation ecosystems, enabling a global extension of collaboration networks and new solutions created by users and citizens. These two novel elements – global innovation networks and local user-driven innovation – become feasible within the digital spatiality of cities. Some good examples illustrating such *glocal* innovation ecosystems can be found in cities that have received awards from the Intelligent Community Forum, in the European Network of Living Labs (ENoLL), and the CONCERTO cities for energy and environmental efficiency.

The subtitle of the book *Smart Environments and Innovation-for-All Strategies* emphasises a key function of intelligent cities: the setting of smart environments that enhance collaboration within ecosystems of innovation, engaging innovators, entreprises, institutions, citizens, and end-users. Digital networking at local and global levels and large-scale data collection and processing, as well as smart environments, enable individualised strategies adapted to needs and aspirations of every city actor. Within smart city environments, citizens, companies, clusters, districts, utility organisations, and the public administration can find resources that allow them to organise their own ecosystems, discover know-how and partners for producing innovative products and services, and reach customers from around the world.

2. A trilogy on intelligent cities: twelve years of research

The Age of Intelligent Cities is the third book in a trilogy that started with *Intelligent Cities: Innovation, knowledge systems and digital spaces* (Routledge, 2002), followed by *Intelligent Cities and Globalisation of Innovation Networks* (Routledge, 2008). All three books describe intelligent cities as ecosystems of innovation and collaborative problem-solving enabled by digital spaces and smart environments.

The focus of the first book was the genesis of intelligent cities via evolutionary processes leading towards open innovation systems and physical-digital ecosystems, which took place during the last decades of the twentieth century. This evolution commenced with the formation of localised systems of innovation, such as clusters, industrial districts, and innovative agglomerations, where spatial proximity and inter-firm collaboration spread out knowledge spillovers and created trust and risk-sharing attitudes. Diversification and networking of these focal localities was the basis for the creation of larger regional systems of innovation and learning regions, where institutional settings enhanced innovation through joint projects, learning infrastructures, triple-helix alliances, innovation funding mechanisms, and targeted innovation policies. Then, in the third stage, local and regional systems of innovation came into contact with the digital world and the World Wide Web, giving birth to intelligent districts, cities, and regions. This meeting between innovation and digital systems that created environments of learning and innovation across real and virtual spaces was further strengthened by Web 2.0 platforms and participatory practices of user-driven innovation.

The second book moved from evolution to structure and examined the structuring of intelligent cities and the spatial expansion from isolated clusters to multi-cluster systems and networks with global dimensions. This expansion from local to global innovation systems was made possible by a three-layer structure composed of physical, institutional, and digital spaces. Knowledge and innovation networks at the local level acquire global dimensions through digital networking and virtual innovation environments, while institutions for innovation channel collaborations and partnerships locally and globally. Within such glocal, but also physical-digital, innovation systems, four fundamental knowledge functions emerge: collective intelligence, learning and technology acquisition,

4 *Introduction*

collaborative innovation, and global information dissemination and product promotion. Thus, the architecture of intelligent cities was defined by three spatial layers (physical, institutional, digital) and four knowledge functions (gathering of intelligence, technology learning, innovation, and information dissemination) emerging from collaborative networks across the three spatial layers. Based on this structure, intelligent cities were conceived of as innovation territories with developed knowledge-intensive activities, institutions, and routines for cooperation in knowledge creation and innovation, advanced broadband infrastructure, digital spaces and e-services, and a proven ability to innovate and resolve problems collaboratively.

Now, this, the third book in the trilogy, takes a step from structure to strategy. It focuses on the drivers of the spatial intelligence of cities, the fundamental processes that make cities intelligent, and new capabilities of distributed intelligence offered by recent technological developments. It looks at different terms used, such as 'cyber', 'digital', 'smart', and 'intelligent' cities, which denote different aspects of the same reality, and attempts to bridge the gap between intelligent and smart cities by pointing out the processes of city intelligence or city smartness. It also looks at the operational level of planning for intelligent cities and how planners can connect city challenges, intelligent city strategies, and implementation approaches by bottom-up and top-down procedures. It describes core strategies to be followed by clusters and city districts, individual companies, and city authorities wishing to sustain spatial intelligence and distributed problem-solving. As the subtitle suggests, this book is particularly concerned with smart environments that enable innovation strategies for all, offering opportunities to every person, company, and organisation of a city to become more intuitive and innovative by using digital technology, and by mobilising communities and collaboration networks.

3. Main ideas and contents of the third book

Intelligent cities and smart cities are now not only a core topic in the literature of urban planning and development, but are also of interest to many other fields of the social sciences, engineering, and management, dealing as they do with smart environments, energy optimisation, environmental protection, intelligent transportation systems, socio-technical systems engineering, innovation management, knowledge management, e-government, and so on. It is truly an interdisciplinary field, gathering know-how and expertise from the social sciences, city planning, engineering, information sciences. This subject area has emerged over the last 15 years and the number of publications has been increasing exponentially since 2009. As an interdisciplinary field, the subject is now taught in many different university departments and schools at MSc and PhD levels.

Quite simply, *The Age of Intelligent Cities* is an inquiry into the making of intelligent cities, the management of drivers of spatial intelligence, strategic planning processes, and strategies for all city actors. The vision is about the making of territories (districts, cities, other localities, regions) that prosper through human skills, knowledge capabilities, collaborative innovation, information networks, and digital agendas; how this vision can be achieved; and which strategies can turn it into reality.

The book has a clear structure divided into three parts which elaborate on complementary aspects of intelligent city strategy, and especially how smart environments and digital city applications can be used to enable innovation by citizens, communities, stakeholders, companies, and public authorities. The core argument running through the chapters is that smart environments and online networks within intelligent cities enable a wide range of diversified and innovation-for-all strategies. In this sense, the book also contains a strong argument about innovation, describing a discrete stage in the evolution of the innovation paradigm, from linear to systemic, open, user-driven, and now 'innovation-for-all into smart environments'.

Part I is about the drivers and architectures of the spatial intelligence of cities. We start with the foundations, the building blocks of intelligent cities, and the pathways that infuse intelligence into innovation ecosystems. A fundamental question to start with concerns, What happens to an innovation ecosystem when it is placed into the context of the Internet and online communication networks? This is followed by other considerations: How do components, architecture, network geometry, hierarchy, and clustering within the ecosystem change? How do performance and resilience change? We know that cities are composed of smaller innovation ecosystems, and when these ecosystems start working in smart environments new capabilities emerge from the widening of collaboration, user-driven innovation, crowdsourcing, and real-time data streams. These enabling conditions offered by smart environments are primary fields and objects of strategy and planning.

Drivers of spatial intelligence can be found in different forms of distributed cognition which is organised across the physical, institutional, and digital space of cities. Such drivers include knowledge processes, large data sets capturing the working of urban systems, architectures of distributed know-how held by individuals, tools, learning environments, symbolic representations, digital assistants, and other components of distributed intelligence. The simplest form of such intelligence is representational intelligence (as the saying goes, a picture is worth a thousand words) offered by mirror-type digital cities. More-advanced forms of spatial intelligence that are discussed are 'orchestration intelligence', 'empowerment', and 'instrumentation intelligence' to be found in cities. Instrumentation intelligence becomes possible thanks to recent Internet technologies based on sensor networks and the Semantic Web, as a new form of collective intelligence captured by devices embedded into the physical space of cities. All forms of spatial intelligence are based on multi-level knowledge functions related to information collection, technology dissemination, and new knowledge creation that flourish within smart environments.

Part I starts with an overview of the literature on intelligent and smart cities in Chapter 1, a state-of-the-art account that sheds light on different concepts (cyber, digital, smart, intelligent) and different perspectives proposed by key authors and

6 *Introduction*

large information technology (IT) and consulting companies. It continues with three chapters focusing on different drivers of the spatial intelligence of cities, such as knowledge functions (Chapter 2),[1] smart systems and embedded spatial intelligence (Chapter 3), and alternative architectures of networking and operation (Chapter 4).[2]

In Part II, we turn to planning processes and discuss top-down and bottom-up planning for intelligent cities. As city authorities are becoming increasingly aware of the intelligent city–smart city paradigm, they are taking initiatives to more efficiently manage infrastructures and resources for addressing challenges of competitiveness, environmental sustainability, and social inclusion. In these endeavours, city managers and planners are more and more concerned with methodological and procedural issues: How to achieve city smartness? How can a city organise spatial intelligence? How can cities become more effective in solving urban problems? How can they make more with less, and increase competitiveness, sustainability, and inclusion?

Referring to cases from all over the world, we examine intelligent city formation processes and strategic planning steps: environment scanning, analysis, objectives setting, strategy design, implementation, launch and operation, monitoring, and assessment. Living PlanIT, Neapolis in Cyprus, Saudi Arabia intelligent cities, and other cities have started with a top-down approach, setting up urban operating systems that enable connecting devices (sensors, smart meters, QR codes, actuators), applications, and processes over a common central platform. On the other hand, metropolitan agglomerations and larger cities are adopting the intelligent city paradigm through the selection and gradual implementation of applications, with each one focusing on a specific problem of city growth, environment, transport, government, and so on. A series of case studies on smart city planning in Barcelona, Helsinki, Manchester, Oulu, and Thessaloniki are discussed to show how these efforts combine urban regeneration with the intelligent city planning paradigm.[3]

In terms of planning, the main challenge is to identify the best possible way of linking top-down and bottom-up initiatives; activating communities and stakeholders in defining distributed problem-solving strategies; and creating digital applications and solutions, operation models, and impact assessment methodologies. Our main contribution here is a planning roadmap for intelligent cities and districts, composed of three stages and seven steps. From the strategic planning perspective comes the division of the roadmap into three stages: analysis, strategy development, and implementation. From the standard model of intelligent cities come the three components of analysis, namely, the city, the innovation system, and the digital space. From smart environments come the components of implementation, such as software development, business models, and measurement. The roadmap starts by defining the problems that need to be addressed, then takes into account the physical, institutional, and digital structure of intelligent cities, and concludes with applications and solutions, business models for sustainability, and methods for measuring innovation and efficiency. It establishes a collaborative framework among the city's resources, its innovation institutions, and its digital spaces, which generates solutions with the involvement of citizens, companies, and public authorities.

Part II starts with bottom-up planning experiences from different intelligent / smart city initiatives in Europe (Chapter 5),[4] continues with top-down approaches in the Middle East (Chapter 6), and concludes with the planning roadmap connecting bottom-up and top-down perspectives (Chapter 7).

In Part III, having discussed the drivers of intelligence and planning processes, we focus on strategy: how cities can manage the drivers of spatial intelligence, formulate strategies, create smart environments, mobilise communities, and offer new solutions to city problems. The challenge here is diversity. Cities are agglomerations of 'related varieties', which feed innovation by bridging knowledge fields. Strategy and governance are examined from the perspective of diversity: how smart environments enable custom pathways and collaboration strategies for different city actors to be developed.

Initially, strategies are examined from the perspective of city districts and clusters comprising a city (Chapter 8). Each district (central business / financial district (CBD), historic centre, shopping centre and peripheral mall, industrial zone, technology district, university campus, port and airport district, recreation area, etc.) is treated differently because problems, functions, communities, and governance differ from one to the other. Within each and every district or cluster, problems and efforts for improvement are related to *innovation and competitiveness* of economic activities; *infrastructure and utility networks* for transport, energy, water, waste, and broadband; *quality of life*, well-being, social and digital divides, pollution, safety in public spaces, health and social care services; and *governance*, decision-making, democracy, administration services offered to citizens, and monitoring and measurement of performance.

We then look at strategies that are meaningful for individual companies (Chapter 9). Based on experiences and pilots from a number of research projects, we describe how companies can use smart environments to Build Their Own Innovation Ecosystem (BOWIE). BOWIEs are custom innovation ecosystems made by physical-virtual networks connecting actors along a value chain. They combine capabilities for market intelligence and discovery, technology development and use, and platform-based business models for collaboration and alliances. This is an extremely promising field, especially for smaller companies that enable them to take advantage of external knowledge and capabilities through digital collaboration.

From the perspective of city authorities, we discuss smart infrastructure, applications, and solutions that every intelligent city should have (Chapter 10). We also present a disruptive business model for intelligent cities based on open-source software, open data, and cloud technologies, which can offer enormous advantages to cities, breaking market and technology barriers by minimising smart city development costs and increasing the quality of e-services in terms of installation, update, instant scalability, trust, and reliability.

Part III – and the book – concludes with a chapter (Chapter 11) on governance of intelligent city ecosystems, in which we present a generic model of governance for actualising communities, defining architectures of knowledge, and undertaking activities for innovation based on cycles of user engagement. Overall, the book introduces readers to the fundamentals of intelligent city strategy, starting with strategy drivers, those factors and functions that generate spatial intelligence, going through strategic planning and operation, and concluding with strategies and disruptive business models that offer increased competitiveness and sustainability.

To date, intelligent cities offer an attractive prospect, a strategy and a vision for the future for sustaining islands of innovation in metropolitan agglomerations, rather than an urban pattern that has already been implemented. There is a long way to go before this planning vision is turned into urban reality. The intelligent city as an agglomeration of communities fully connected and instrumented, in which knowledge flows of learning, collective intelligence, and creativity enable all members to address their individual or communal problems and fulfil their aspirations remains a long-term vision.

Putting aside for the moment the intense wave of publication over recent years about intelligent and smart cities, especially after 2009, our knowledge of such innovative environments is still quite limited. The ability to create truly intelligent environments that open minds and empower citizens and producers to innovate is limited, as well. This is a weakness both in terms of understanding the complexity of intelligent environments and in terms of strategic planning and management of the drivers of spatial intelligence. This challenge is guiding the present book, and the aim of the 11 chapters is to enlighten fundamental aspects of intelligent cities by describing five interrelated models of their making and operation: (1) a model of structure, (2) a model of spatial intelligence, (3) a model of function, (4) a model of strategic planning, and (5) a model of governance.

Notes

1 An earlier version of Chapter 2 was published in Komninos, N. (2009). Intelligent cities: Towards interactive and global innovation environments. *International Journal of Innovation and Regional Development*, Vol. 1, No. 4, 337–355. Permission granted by Inderscience, which retains copyright of the original paper.
2 Chapter 4 is based on two previous publications: Komninos, N. (2011). Intelligent cities: Variable geometries of spatial intelligence. *Journal of Intelligent Buildings International*, Vol. 3, No. 3, 172–188; and Komninos, N. (2013). What makes cities intelligent? In M. Deakin (ed.) *Smart Cities: Governing, modelling and analysing the transition* (pp. 77–95). London and New York: Routledge. Permission granted by Taylor & Francis.
3 These case studies were published in the special issue: Komninos, N. and Schaffers, H. (eds) (2013). Smart cities and the Future Internet in Europe. *Journal of the Knowledge Economy*, Vol. 4, No. 2, 119–134.
4 Another version of this chapter was published as Komninos, N. and Tsarchopoulos, P. (2013). Towards intelligent Thessaloniki: From agglomeration of apps to smart districts. *Journal of the Knowledge Economy*, Vol. 4, No. 2, 149–168. Permission granted by Springer.

References

Komninos, N. (2009). Intelligent cities: Towards interactive and global innovation environments. *International Journal of Innovation and Regional Development*, Vol. 1, No. 4, 337–355.

Komninos, N. (2011). Intelligent cities: Variable geometries of spatial intelligence. *Journal of Intelligent Buildings International,* Vol. 3, No. 3, 172–188.

Komninos, N. (2013). What makes cities intelligent? In M. Deakin (ed.) *Smart Cities: Governing, modelling and analysing the transition* (pp. 77–95). London and New York: Routledge.

Komninos, N., and Schaffers, H. (eds) (2013). Smart cities and the future Internet in Europe. *Journal of the Knowledge Economy,* Vol. 4, No. 2, 119–134.

Komninos, N., and Tsarchopoulos, P. (2013). Towards intelligent Thessaloniki: From agglomeration of apps to smart districts. *Journal of the Knowledge Economy*, Vol. 4, No. 2, 149–168.

Rajan, R. (2012). *A crisis in two narratives*. Project Syndicate. www.project-syndicate.org/commentary/a-crisis-in-two-narratives.

Part I
What makes cities intelligent?
Drivers of spatial intelligence of cities

1 Intelligent cities – smart cities
The landscape

1. The rise of a new planning paradigm

A short article by Haya El Nasser (2011) in *USA TODAY* titled "Will 'intelligent cities' put an end to suburban sprawl?" received considerable attention on the Internet, resulting in hundreds of references to it on social media. The argument made by El Nasser is that 'smart growth' is near the end of its shelf-life, concluding a 20-year cycle as a major urban planning paradigm, and now 'intelligent cities' has become the new "darling lingo of planners" as it captures the essence of twenty-first-century technology that can help track how people use cities and live within them. This does not mean, El Nasser argues, that the sustainability principles of Smart Growth and New Urbanism – the design movement driving sustainable growth with compact cities, multiple transport choices, natural ecosystem preservation, passive architecture, and green energy solutions – has become obsolete, but rather that intelligent cities as a new planning paradigm can more efficiently drive urban renewal towards sustainability. Connecting the concept of intelligent cities with urban renewal opens up a new path that allows us to view every city and city-district from a new perspective and consider how intelligent city planning principles and strategies can sustain urban regeneration in terms of competitiveness, as well as social and environmental sustainability.

The new planning paradigm of intelligent cities (although 'smart cities' is the term mostly used in Europe) has been forged by academic research and experimental city projects. A series of publications that has appeared since 2000 reflects the evolution in thinking in this field and discusses the contribution of information technologies and the Internet to city development and planning, the city and the digital space, and the role of virtual spaces and digital ecosystems in enhancing innovation within twenty-first-century cities. This literature clearly shows how open digital platforms are used to empower citizens, enterprises, and organisations in developing innovative, open, and collaborative solutions to make cities more efficient and sustainable.

Among the first publications that opened up this new field was the book by Ishida and Isbister (2000) on technologies, experiences, and future prospects of digital cities, which focused on the way in which the information society, the Internet, and mobile computing were creating a virtual space over cities. This was

14 *What makes cities intelligent?*

a book devoted to digital cities and contained experimental city projects that were using platforms for communication, city representation, and city management. Based on the proceedings of an international symposium in Kyoto, Japan, this collection of papers made clear the interdisciplinary perspective that is needed for making digital cities. The digital cities symposium series provided material for another two publications with similar titles, *Digital Cities II* (Tanabe et al., 2005), and *Digital Cities III* (Van den Besselaar and Koizumi, 2005), which discussed the concept of the digital city, politics, knowledge and data modelling, design, monitoring and evaluation, and technologies and architectures, while presenting case studies and city experiments. The social, class, power, gender, and ethnicity impact of information and communication technologies on cities and how new media in cities shape societies, economies, and cultures was the focus of another influential publication on digital city spaces. *The Cybercities Reader* (Graham, 2003) contained case studies from all over the world such as Amsterdam, Lima, Jamaica, and Melbourne, and highlighted different ways in which the digital space affected all aspects of city life, economy, commerce, (tele)working, community, urban surveillance, and control. Digital cities were also discussed in Aurigi (2005), which focused on economic regeneration and place promotion strategies sustained by electronically distributed services and participatory decision-making. Case studies of European cities were presented, where urban processes were interwoven with front-end information sites, digital spaces, and digital networks. Laguerre (2006) explored the digitisation of the American city, and how information technology practices in the Silicon Valley and San Francisco metropolitan area were re-organising social relations, global interactions, and workplace environments.

However, the creation of digital spaces was not the only driver of current developments in the field. Another set of processes, equally important, fed urban change and new planning concepts. At the turn of the century, some cities and regions in Europe, Japan, and the USA displayed an exceptional capacity for developing new knowledge and innovation. They offered a favourable environment for research, technology, and innovation based on proximity, knowledge spillovers, institutions for learning, social capital, and digital collaborative spaces. *Intelligent Cities: Innovation, Knowledge Systems and Digital Spaces* (Komninos, 2002) analysed three different spatial models for creating environments of innovation, based on spatial proximity and knowledge spillovers (industrial districts and clusters), learning institutions (innovating regions), and physical-digital innovation ecosystems (intelligent cities). A follow-up publication (Komninos, 2008) explained the rise of intelligent cities with respect to the spread of global information and technology supply networks and user-driven innovation processes. The distinctive characteristic of intelligent cities was attributed to the integration of three types of intelligence: human intelligence of the population, collective intelligence of institutions for collaboration, and machine intelligence of digital networks and applications. The book also described the building blocks of intelligent cities with respect to collaborative physical-digital platforms sustaining networks for strategic intelligence, technology learning and acquisition, innovation, and product marketing and promotion. The same concerns were reflected in *Broadband Economies* (Bell et al., 2008), which looked at how city information and communication infrastructure and digital services sustain the innovation economy of cities. Based on experiences from the Intelligent Community Forum (ICF), the authors told the story of 'intelligent communities' around the world: cities that deployed broadband networks to build local prosperity, improve global competitiveness, and promote social inclusion. The work of Yigitcanlar, Velibeyoglu, and Baum (2008) also explored similar initiatives for sustaining knowledge cities and processes for the successful integration of information technologies and urban knowledge-based development. Within the same strand of works, publications on the "knowledge city" (Carillo, 2006; Edvinsson, 2008) outlined the contribution of learning institutions and knowledge-based networks to the wealth of cities.

Another strand of publications looked towards a more extended digital space, which is being created by wireless broadband networks, mobile devices, open platforms, and systems embedded into the physical space of cities. Aurigi and De Cindio (2008) discussed augmented urban spaces created by ubiquitous computing, mobile devices, and wireless connectivity. This new intersection of physical and digital environments is reshaping cities and has implications for the public sphere, community empowerment, and people-led urban planning. Leach (2009) looked at computer-aided techniques for experimental use of generative design tools and parametric design, and how cities might gain insights from digital platforms like the iPhone and offer open-innovation environments to citizens and organisations.

More recent publications revisit smart cities from a novel perspective. Deakin (2013) and Deakin and Al Waer (2012) see a transition from intelligent to smart cities, and reinterpreted W. Mitchell's (2007) analysis from the city of bits to e-topia as transition from intelligent to smart cities. Hatzelhoffer et al. (2012) looked at the practical issues of smart cities and the ingredients for converting innovative ideas into reality. Townsend (2013) wrote about the great challenges of urbanisation, the need for thinking cities and technologies used in future cities in the long rather than the short term, and the "birth of a new civic movement as the smartphone becomes a platform for reinventing cities from the bottom-up." Greenfield and Kim's (2013) *Against the Smart City* presents a critical account of top-down ambitious projects such New Songdo, Masdar City, and PlanIT Valley, "interventions of incremental enhancement-of off-the-shelf products acquired through existing procurement channels, services via conventional contracts, tacked onto spatial and institutional arrangements that already exist" (Greenfield and Kim, 2013, n.p.). Another strand of literature evolving in parallel discuss sentient or sensing cities, urban informatics and ubiquitous computing, city infrastructures, and technologies embedded into a continuum of places that are seemingly coherent (Wood, 2009) that support citizen engagement (Foth et al., 2011; Shepard, 2011) with real-time data (Capelli, 2013).

This cited literature (though very selective and referring only to some of the major books out of a large number of publications) offers a summary account of the evolving thinking about intelligent cities. It is clear that a new paradigm of city planning and development has emerged from the convergence of globalisation, user-driven innovation, information technologies and the Internet, the widespread use of social media, and the collective intelligence of the Web. A radical turn towards the intelligent city paradigm is taking place as information and communication technologies meet with innovation-led urban and regional economies. Intelligent cities are part of the efforts being made to create environments that improve our cognitive skills, as well as our ability to learn, foresee, innovate, and produce more with less. They achieve it by creating smart environments that enable the engagement of citizens with innovation, while also promoting the integration of skills and competences scattered spatially on a global scale. In such territories, local systems of innovation are placed into digital collaboration spaces, interactive tools are offered, and sensors and systems feed the system with real-time data. The latent and explicit promise of the intelligent city paradigm is to set out the conditions conditions for more effectively addressing the great contemporary challenges of urbanisation, growth, sustainability, and inclusion.

2. Movements shaping the intelligent city paradigm

Major contributions that shape the paradigm of intelligent cities have come from academic research, city planning initiatives, policies of international organisations, and solutions offered by large multinational companies.

Academic research has been very active in defining the overall landscape. The first academic paper on intelligent cities appeared in 1990 (Batty, 1990), and the first academic paper on smart cities was published in 1992 (Gibson et al., 1992). These forerunner publications were not related to the World Wide Web that was still being set up at that time, and which a few years later would become the main driver of intelligent city thinking. A good number of university research labs in the EU and the USA focus exclusively on this field, including the pioneering lab of William Mitchell at the MIT Smart Cities Research Group; the Centre for Advanced Spatial Analysis (CASA) at UCL; URENIO Research at Aristotle University of Thessaloniki; MIT Senseable City Lab; the Centre of Regional Science at the Vienna University of Technology; and the Centre for Learning Communities at Edinburgh Napier University. However, high-level research is being carried out by individual researchers or groups in laboratories active in related fields, such as collective intelligence, intelligent environments, living labs, environment and energy optimisation, intelligent transportation systems, innovation management, knowledge management, and e-government.

City planning initiatives in Europe, the USA, and Asia contributed enormously in scaling up the discourse and practice of intelligent city planning, by undertaking initiatives and implementing pilot projects. Well-known cases include Smart Amsterdam with a large number of digital spaces for green mobility, environmental protection, and energy savings; Smart Santander, with thousands of sensors embedded into the city and experimental applications related to the environment, noise, traffic, and parking; Barcelona's innovation clusters, innohubs, open Wi-Fi, and open data initiatives; Zaragoza's Milla Digital; Manchester's IT-based urban regeneration; Stockholm's public fiber-to-the-home (FTTH) broadband network and e-services for education, social care, and inclusion; Singapore's iN2015 Masterplan to sustain information and communications technologies (ICT) and innovation in every economic sector of the city (logistics, health, banking, tourism, manufacturing, education); Malaysia Multimedia Super Corridor (MSC Malaysia); Seoul Digital Media City (DMC); New Songdo in Korea; New Economic Cities of Saudi Arabia; New York City's digital city (NYC Digital) with 311 government information and non-emergency service; and many others.

An extremely valuable source of information about local experimentation in the field is to be found in the Intelligent Community Forum (ICF) and in the cities that have received awards from the ICF since 2001, either as Smart21, Top7, or intelligent communities of the year. Many cities and regions appear on this list, covering a variety of sizes and roles: small cities such as Pirai, Brazil, with 23,000 residents to multi-million-population cities like Tianjin, China, with a population of 11 million; a global metropolis like New York City and small rural communities like Bario, Malaysia; and industrial cities and city suburbs. Among them, awards for the most advanced intelligent communities were given to LaGrange, USA (2000); New York, USA (2001); Calgary, Canada (2002); Glasgow, UK (2004) Mitaka, Japan (2005); Taipei, Taiwan (2006); Waterloo, Ontario, Canada (2007); Gangnam District-Seoul, South Korea (2008); Stockholm, Sweden (2009); Suwon, South Korea (2010); Eindhoven, the Netherlands (2011); Riverside, California, USA (2012); and Taichung City, Taiwan (2013). These cities were deemed to be the most intelligent communities with respect to five criteria of excellence in ICT, knowledge, and innovation, which capture efforts in *broadband infrastructure* and the local capacity for digital communication, k*nowledge workforce* and the capability of the population for qualified work in knowledge-intensive activities, *innovation* and innovation-friendly environment that attracts creative people and businesses, *digital democracy* and policies to bridge digital divides, and *marketing* to strengthen the attractiveness of communities with respect to other cities and regions.

International organisations, such as the EU, the Organisation for Economic Co-operation and Development (OECD), the World Bank, the Rockefeller Foundation, and the US National Building Museum, also gave an important push to the intelligent city agenda. Most relevant is EU research from the 7th Frame Programme for Research and Technological Development (FP7), the Competitiveness and Innovation Framework Programme (CIP), and now the EU Horizon 2020 programme, which aim at stimulating a wider uptake of innovative ICT-based services for smart cities, linking smart cities with user-driven innovation, future Internet technologies, and experimental facilities for testing applications.

A major initiative in the EU in promoting the same agenda of locality, ICT, and innovation is also the European Network of Living Labs (ENoLL). The definition of Livings Labs given by ENoLL is, "a Living Lab is an open innovation environment in a real-life environment in which user-driven innovation improves services, products and societal infrastructures" (Bergvall-Kåreborn and Ståhlbröst, 2009). A Living Lab can be a city district where a full-scale urban laboratory exists, providing ground for inventing, prototyping, and marketing of new technology applications; it may include interactive testing, but is managed as an innovation environment well beyond the test bed functions. As a city-based innovation environment, the Living Lab takes advantage of pools of creative talent, the affluence of socio-cultural diversity, and the unpredictability of inventiveness and imagination in the urban setting. Living Labs contribute to advances in the telecom and digital services of cities with a view of making these cities significant transaction points for global flows of goods, services, people, and ideas. Infrastructures are improved, public policies are adapted to firm-specific assets, and clusters of competencies are maintained and advanced by applied research and experimental development. The entire urban environment becomes an intelligent environment and a living laboratory for prototyping and testing new technology applications and new methods of generating and fostering innovation.

Multinational companies from the ICT, engineering, and consulting sectors have also contributed enormously to the intelligent city paradigm. Large companies such as IBM, CISCO, and Microsoft are strongly involved in and are contributing to shaping this research and planning agenda, to developing solutions and applications, and to providing support grants for smart city projects.

In 2009, CISCO launched the global "Intelligent Urbanisation" initiative from Bangalore and signed a Memorandum of Understanding (MoU) with the local government to develop a roadmap for an intelligent and sustainable Bangalore City. The global "Intelligent Urbanisation" initiative was designed to help cities around the world use the network as the fourth utility (along with electricity, natural gas, and water) for integrated city management, better quality of life for citizens, and economic development. Bringing together a broad portfolio of products, services, partners, and solutions across CISCO, the initiative was initially focused on intelligent, sustainable solutions for public safety and security, transportation, buildings, energy, health care, and education. As an example of how technology can be used to improve security operations, CISCO proposed its own internal Security Operations Centre: real-time security monitoring and alerts, video surveillance tools, acoustic sensors, card-readers with biometric recognition, and automatic alerts and security activation systems were the highlights of this environment.

Microsoft collaborated with Coventry University and Birmingham City Council to establish Birmingham as the first UK intelligent city and showcase new and innovative applications. The "Intelligent City Proof of Concept" was about an interoperable technology platform focusing on transport. The objectives included demonstrating the intelligent city vision for Birmingham and creating a service layer platform integrated with existing data and services that would manage journeys across devices and modes of transport; empower individuals to make more informed, smarter choices; and describe the impact of travel patterns on economic and environmental conditions.

IBM announced its *Smarter Cities* programme as part of the company's initiative for an *Intelligent Planet*. The programme was created to stimulate economic growth and quality of life in cities and metropolitan areas with the activation of new approaches to thinking and acting in the urban ecosystem. Interconnected and instrumented smart technologies offer a real-time integrated view of complex city systems, enabling administrators to monitor operations, improve performance, and respond to the needs of their jurisdictions each day. IBM's initiative focuses on nine areas: smarter buildings and urban planning, environment, energy and water, transportation, education, healthcare, social programmes, public safety, and government and administration – in each of which the company proposed a series of best practices, strategies, technologies, and applications (IBM, n.d.). The approach is comprehensive, as the problems are addressed not only in terms of technology, but also in terms of management practices and institutional arrangements. The company also introduced the "Smarter Cities Challenge," a three-year programme of support to 100 cities around the world to become smarter by enhancing their capacity to collect, analyse, and act on information across multiple channels.

3. Intelligent city: a new reality – multiple concepts

In the wider cyber-digital-smart-intelligent cities literature, these concepts refer to the digital dimension of cities, but with different meaning and connotations. Cybercities and cyberspace highlight either the early wave of e-government applications for city management or more recent technologies for security and control over the urban space (Graham, 2003). Digital cities are more oriented towards the representation of the city, the way that a digital metaphor of the city is constructed, and how we can learn more about the physical city through its virtual representation (Ishida and Isbister, 2000; Besselaar and Koizumi, 2005).

'Intelligence' comes with the understanding that digital city applications can improve innovation ecosystems because of their ability to acquire and process information, as well as sustain learning, experimentation, problem-solving, and the collective intelligence of a human community. From this perspective, an intelligent city is a multi-layer territorial innovation system based on knowledge-intensive activities, institutions for co-operation and learning, communication infrastructure, and digital tools that maximise the problem-solving capabilities of city communities (Komninos, 2002; Komninos, 2008; Mitchell, 2007).

The smart city literature seems to focus more on the latest advancements in mobile and pervasive computing, wireless networks, and agent technologies as they become embedded into the physical spaces of cities. It is estimated that smart city applications – with the help of instrumentation and interconnection of mobile devices, sensors, and actuators that allow real-world data to be collected and analysed with computational models – improve the ability to forecast and manage urban flows and push city intelligence forward (Chen-Ritzo et al., 2009; Deakin, 2013).

20 *What makes cities intelligent?*

> **A new spatiality of cities – multiple concepts**
>
> *Cyber cities*, from cyberspace, cybernetics, governance and control spaces based on information feedback, and city governance; but also meaning the negative / dark sides of cyberspace, cybercrime, tracking, identification, and military control over cities.
>
> *Digital cities*, from digital representation of cities, virtual cities, digital metaphor of cities, cities of avatars, second-life cities, and simulation (sim) cities.
>
> *Intelligent cities*, from the new intelligence of cities, collective intelligence of citizens, distributed intelligence, crowdsourcing, online user collaboration, broadband for innovation, social capital of cities, collaborative learning and innovation, and people-driven innovation.
>
> *Smart cities*, from smart phones, mobile devices, smart meters, sensors and sensor networks, smart systems, embedded systems, smart environments, and instrumentation sustaining the intelligence of cities.

Reference to intelligence is to be found in both literatures of intelligent cities and smart cities. The term 'intelligence' comes from the Latin verb *intellegere*, which means to understand, and describes the capacity to acquire, create, and apply knowledge. Human intelligence is a property of the mind to reason and solve problems based on capacities to communicate, to learn, to create new ideas, to plan, and to foresee. Legg and Hutter (2007) gatheted an inventory of definitions of intelligence, which is the largest and most well-referenced collection, according to the authors. They list 18 definitions of intelligence that have been proposed by groups or organisations; 35 definitions from psychologists; and 18 definitions from researchers in artificial intelligence. They then scanned these definitions, pulling out commonly occurring features and concluding that intelligence has three key attributes which occur simultaneously. These include the ability of an individual agent, human or non-human, to interact with the environment; the ability to succeed or profit with respect to some goal or objective; and the ability to adapt to adapt to different objectives and environments.

The term 'Intelligent city' has been used in various ways to denote the capacity of certain environments and communities to collect and process information, nurture knowledge, innovate, plan, and resolve problems. This understanding of intelligent cities, as intelligent communities, reflects all traits of intelligence proposed by Legg and Hutter (2007), because they use broadband networks for online communication and interaction, deploy e-services to attain objectives and goals, and adapt to different challenges by developing knowledge skills and innovations.

However, in the intelligent city literature, we find many different ways in which intelligent cities are described both literally and metaphorically: with respect to skills, knowledge and creativity of the population; with respect to advances in broadband infrastructure and communication services; with respect to efficiency in addressing challenges of employment, the environment, wealth creation, and cohesion; with respect to innovation performance and collaborative problem-solving; or in combinations of the above.

'Smart city' is an equivalent concept. The term was coined in 1992 to signify urban development's turn towards technology, innovation, and globalisation (Gibson et al., 1992). In urban development, the term 'smart growth' has been used extensively by the Congress for the New Urbanism (CNU) to denote anti-sprawl principles that are environmentally and economically smart, promoting mixed-use neighbourhoods, compact cities for low energy consumption, smart location, and sustainable communities. Closer to the current meaning, the World Foundation for Smart Communities used the term in the mid-1990s to motivate communities to use information technology to meet the challenges of a global knowledge economy. More recent uses of the term refer to participatory action and engagement, and investments in human and social capital, traditional and modern communication infrastructure for sustainable development, and high quality of life (Caragliu et al., 2009). For many organisations, the term is also used to capture the deployment of new Internet technologies, smartphones and mobile devices, the Internet of Things (IoT) for promoting real-world user interfaces, and more connected cities. Overall the emphasis on smart embedded devices represents a distinctive characteristic of smart cities compared to intelligent cities (Belissent, 2010; Deakin and Al Waer, 2012).

A collection of formal definitions of 'intelligent city' and 'smart city' concepts by different organisations and authors is presented below, which reveals that the two concepts converge around the same understanding of city intelligence.

MIT Smart Cities Group: "The new intelligence of cities, resides in the increasingly effective combination of digital telecommunication networks (the nerves), ubiquitously embedded intelligence (the brains), sensors and tags (the sensory organs), and software (the knowledge and cognitive competence). This does not exist in isolation from other urban systems, or connected to them only through human intermediaries. There is a growing web of direct connections to the mechanical and electrical systems of buildings, household appliances, production machinery, process plants, transportation systems, electrical grids and other energy supply networks, water supply and waste removal networks, systems that provide life safety and security, and management systems for just about every imaginable human activity. The cross-connections among these systems – both horizontal and vertical – are growing" (Mitchell, 2007).

URENIO Research: "The term 'intelligent city' describes a territory (community, district, cluster, city, and city-region) with four main characteristics: (1) a creative population and developed knowledge-intensive activities or clusters of such activities; (2) embedded institutions and routines for cooperation in knowledge creation allowing one to acquire, adapt, and advance knowledge and know-how; (3) a developed broadband infrastructure, digital spaces, e-services, and online knowledge management tools; and (4) a proven ability to innovate, manage and resolve problems that appear for the first time, since the capacity to innovate and to manage uncertainty are the critical factors for measuring intelligence" (Komninos, 2008).

Smart Cities project: "The concept of the 'smart city' has recently been introduced as a strategic device to encompass modern urban production factors in a common framework and, in particular, to highlight the importance of Information and Communication Technologies (ICTs) in the last 20 years for enhancing the competitive profile of a city" (Caragliu et al., 2009).

European Smart Cities: "A Smart City is a city well performing in 6 characteristics, built on the 'smart' combination of endowments and activities of self-decisive, independent and aware citizens. Smart Cities can be identified (and ranked) along six characteristics: (1) Smart economy (competitiveness), (2) Smart people (social and human capital), (3) Smart governance (participation), (4) Smart mobility (transport and ICT), (5) Smart environments (natural resources), and (6) Smart living (quality of life)" (Giffinger, 2007).

IBM Smart Planet Initiative: "A smarter city is one that uses technology to transform its core systems and optimise the return from largely finite resources. By using resources in a smarter way, it will also boost innovation, a key factor underpinning competitiveness and economic growth. Investment in smarter systems is also a source of sustainable employment. Smarter cities make their systems instrumented, interconnected and intelligent" (IBM, 2010).

Forrester Research: Smart cities are "using information and communications technologies to make the critical infrastructure components of a city – which include healthcare, education, real estate, transportation, utilities, and city administration and public safety – more intelligent, interconnected, and efficient" (Washburn and Sindhu, 2009).

Eurocities: "In broad terms a 'Smart City' is understood to mean a city that makes a conscious effort to innovatively employ information and communication technologies (ICT) to support a more inclusive, diverse and sustainable urban environment" (Eurocities, 2009).

European Innovation Partnership on Smart Cities and Communities: "Smart cities should be regarded as systems of people interacting with and using flows of energy, materials, services and financing to catalyse sustainable economic development, resilience, and high quality of life; these flows and interactions become smart through making strategic use of information and communication infrastructure and services in a process of transparent urban planning and management that is responsive to the social and economic needs of society" (European Innovation Partnership on Smart Cities and Communities, 2013).

Smart Cities Background Paper: "The concept of a Smart City goes way beyond the transactional relationships between citizen and service provider. It is essentially enabling and encouraging the citizen to become a more active and participative member of the community, for example, providing feedback on the quality of services or the state of roads and the built environment, adopting a more sustainable and healthy lifestyle, volunteering for social activities or supporting minority groups. Furthermore, citizens need employment and 'Smart Cities' are often attractive locations to live, work and visit. But the concept is not static: there is no absolute definition of a smart city, no end point, but rather a process, or series of steps, by which cities become more 'liveable' and resilient and, hence, able to respond quicker to new challenges. Thus, a Smart City should enable every citizen to engage with all the services on offer, public as well as private, in a way best suited to his or her needs. It brings together hard infrastructure, social capital including local skills and community institutions, and (digital) technologies to fuel sustainable economic development and provide an attractive environment for all" (UK Government, 2013).

FIREBALL Smart Cities White Paper: "The smart city concept is multidimensional. It is a future scenario (what to achieve), even more it is an urban development strategy (how to achieve it). It focuses on how (Internet-related) technologies enhance the lives of citizens. This should not be interpreted as drawing the smart city technology scenario. Rather, the smart city is how citizens are shaping the city in using this technology, and how citizens are enabled to do so. The smart city is about how people are empowered, through using technology, for contributing to urban change and realising their ambitions. The smart city provides the conditions and resources for change. In this sense, the smart city is an urban laboratory, an urban innovation ecosystem, a living lab, an agent of change. Much less do we see a smart city in terms of a ranking. This ranking is a moment in time, a superficial result of underlying changes, not the mechanism of transformation. The smart city is the engine of transformation, a generator of solutions for wicked problems, it is how the city is behaving smart" (Schaffer et al., 2012).

Figure 1.1 gives the cloud of terms used in the above definitions. It was made with Wordle and clearly denotes the three building blocks or layers of intelligent or smart cities: (1) the city, citizen, and activities block; (2) the knowledge, intelligence, and innovation block; and (3) the smart systems and urban technologies block.

Based on the evidence of these definitions, our understanding is that 'intelligent city' and 'smart city' correspond to the same planning concept, a form of strategic planning based on the use of smart systems and new services (e-services) to support collaborative innovation processes and citizens' engagement in addressing the city challenges of urbanisation, sustainable growth, and globalisation. The

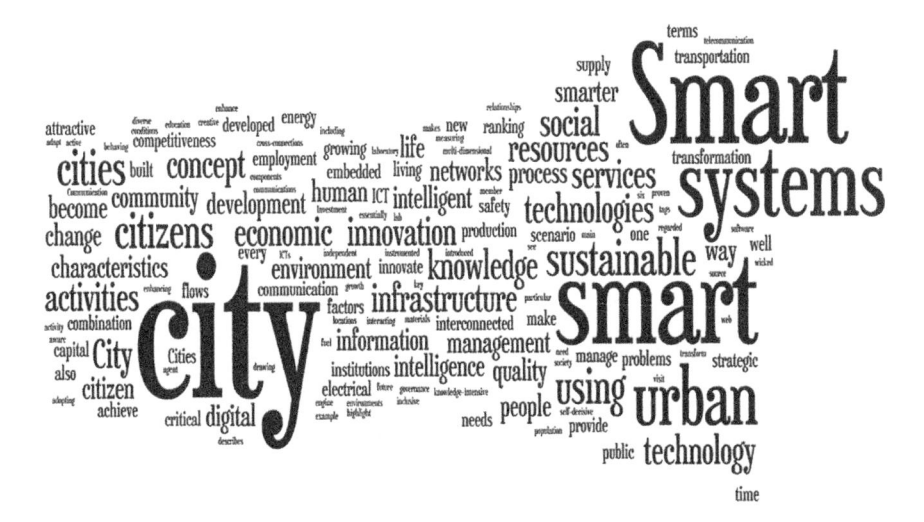

Figure 1.1 Wordle cloud of intelligent city and smart city definitions

24 *What makes cities intelligent?*

concepts differ in connotation in relation to novelty, with intelligent cities pointing towards collective intelligence and user collaboration based on the introduction of new e-services, and smart cities pointing towards the latest developments in smart technologies and embedded systems.

Actually, Future Internet research brings those concepts further closer within an integrated smart environment of multiple 4G broadband networks, Internet of Things (IoT) solutions, virtualisation of infrastructure, smart mobile devices, the Semantic Web, and extended user-driven experimentation and participatory use cases (European Commission, DG INFSO, 2010).

It should be stressed that smart and intelligent cities are not events in the cybersphere, but integrated social, physical, institutional, and digital spaces in which the digital components facilitate and improve the functioning and management of socio-economic activities taking place in the actual, physical space of cities. The variation of meaning corresponds to multiple ways in which the digital spatiality of cities is connected to spatialities of agglomeration, innovation, and governance.

4. Structure: city, innovation, and smart environments

Intelligent cities are structured as multi-layer territorial systems of innovation, bringing together and connecting: knowledge-intensive activities, innovation institutions, and digital spaces (Figure 1.2). These layers reflect both the elements found in definitions of intelligent and smart cities and the fundamental dimensions of intelligence (human, collective, artificial) to be found in cities.

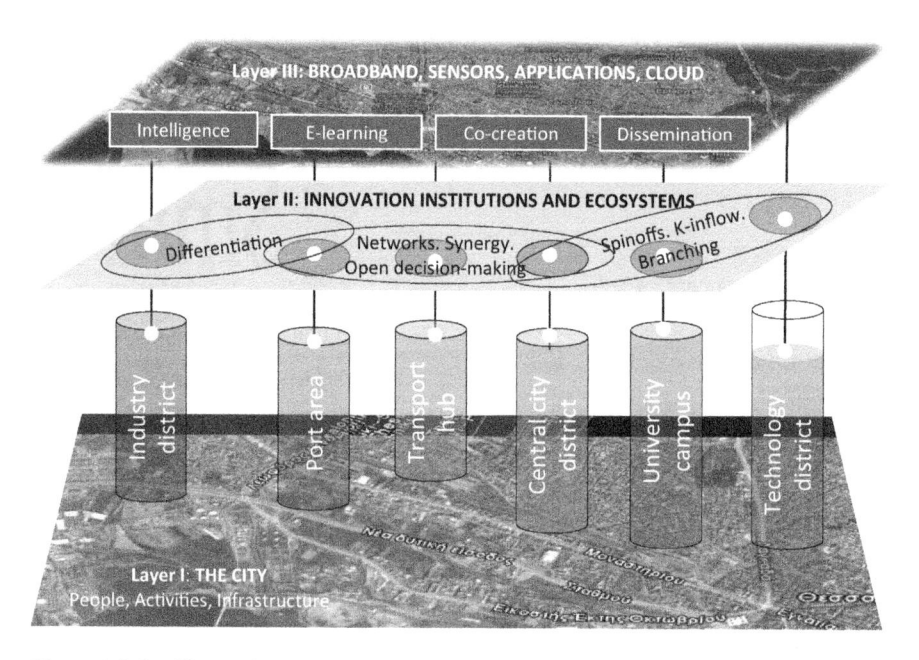

Figure 1.2 Intelligent city structure

Layer I, the city: The first layer includes the city's resources, population, knowledge-intensive activities in manufacturing and services, and city infrastructure. The population of the city, knowledge workers, and innovative companies, clusters, and districts are the fundamental elements on which intelligent cities are erected. Proximity in physical space is important, integrating enterprises, production facilities, and service providers into coherent urban systems. Critical factors in this layer are the spatial concentration of human intelligence and the intellectual capital of the city's population.

Layer II, the innovation system: The second layer includes institutional settings for knowledge creation and co-operation in technology and innovation. Key institutions are those supporting R&D, collective intelligence, innovation funding, technology transfer, and collaborative innovation. These are pillars that promote knowledge and innovation systems within the clusters comprising the city, between different clusters in the city, and between innovation processes taking place in physical and digital space. Critical factors at this level are 'institutional thickness' and collaboration, trust, and knowledge spillovers within the community.

For more than 20 years, innovation has been a central driving force of urban and regional development. A rich literature corroborates this orientation. Innovation-led or knowledge-based development of cities and regions has become the model which most cities and regions try to adopt and adapt to their particular conditions. A central element in linking innovation and regional development is the concept of 'system of innovation,' which denotes the co-operation nexus among R&D, technology institutions, innovation funding, and production organisations located in close proximity, as a driving force of innovation and development. However, recent trends reveal a profound transformation of systems of innovation towards more open and global profiles. Several factors have contributed to this change: a new geographical mobility of R&D, offshoring, new supply chain architectures shaped by flagship networks of multinational companies, the rise of global clusters of excellence, people-led product innovation, Web 2.0, and participatory product development. Altogether, these changes create a 'glocal' spatiality of innovation, shaped by the combination of local participatory and user-driven innovation processes linked to global innovation networks enabled by digital collaboration and virtual spaces for innovation.

Layer III, smart environments: The third layer includes broadband networks and e-services that strengthen and enhance collaboration and the functioning of cities. These hard and soft infrastructures create smart environments based on multimedia tools, sensors, and interactive technologies, which make the innovation ecosystems of cities more open and participatory, and the functioning of cities more efficient due to streams of data, real-time information, and automated control. Critical factors at this level are content management, information processing, intelligent agents, virtual networking, Web 2.0 technologies, sensors and other devices of machine-to-machine communication and intelligence.

The digital space of smart cities can be conceived of as an array of concentric circles of broadband networks infrastructure, data compilation and analysis technologies, web-based applications, and e-services. Broadband networks – both wired and wireless – together with access and communication devices – PCs, mobile phones, sensors, RFIDs, public e-blackboards and displays – provide a unified communication space over the cities. Sensors for monitoring air pollution, fire detection, the structural heath of buildings, perimeter access control, radiation levels, electromagnetic levels, traffic congestion, smart roads, smart parking, smart lighting, intelligent shopping, noise mapping, water quality, water leaks, waste management, item locations, and many others are already available (Libelium, n.d.). Networks are supported by technologies that offer security for data and access, privacy protection, authentication, Web service management, and routing. Over this core circle run a series of data-management technologies, such as intelligence gathering, data processing, data analytics, Web-collaboration, and 3D visualisation, which enable the creation of Web applications and e-services for businesses, citizens, and the government.

Computer Aided Design (CAD) and Geographical Information Systems (GIS) are major technologies enabling the digital management of urban space. Intelligent cities, however, rely on a different set of technologies, Web-based applications, virtual collaboration tools, and ubiquitous communities. The main difference between these Web-based tools and CAD and GIS is that they help in creating digital spaces where activities take place instead of representing digitally the urban space. A collection of representative collaborative tools for intelligent cities can be found at the URENIO site (URENIO, 2014), including tools for supporting innovation ecosystems (content management, collaborative innovation, digital marketing), for improving infrastructures and utilities with sensors and embedded systems, for e-governance, and monitoring and benchmarking. Web 2.0 offered additional means for mobilising and organising collective intelligence with applications such as Innocentive, iBridge, CrowdSpirit, IdeaScale, Peer-to-Patent, and many others.

A dominant software stack used for creating intelligent environments is the open-source Linux, Apache, MySQL, and PHP/Perl / Python (LAMP) stack, which is a preferred platform for building and deploying Web applications and e-services. An equivalent stack of cloud computing is OpenStack, a cloud operating system that controls large pools for computing, storing, and networking resources, all managed through a dashboard that offers control via the Web.

Today, cloud computing is adding a new level of efficiency and economy to these virtual environments, delivering IT resources on demand and opening up new business models and market opportunities. In some ways, cloud computing is a metaphor for Internet-based services and the increasing movement of virtual computing and data-hosting resources onto the Web. It effectively removes the software application platform from the underlying hardware infrastructure, freeing developers and users from the need to possess the hardware. In cloud computing, the user's data is held and software executed on the cloud (the Internet) and the network becomes the computer, while the use of resources follows the utility pricing model (Sun Microsystems, 2009). By delivering higher efficiency, massive scalability, and faster, easier software development with lower costs, cloud computing opens new prospects for the massive involvement of people and authorities in the creation of digital spaces and e-services, and the further development of intelligent cities as collaborative environments.

A major challenge for building intelligent cities is integrating the three layers mentioned above and building 'bridges' that connect the physical, institutional, and digital spaces of intelligent cities. Analysis of intelligent places shows that most 'bridges' are organisational and institutional in nature and highly dependent on the digital technologies implemented. Each layer has a different role within intelligent city integration. Cities offer skills, resources, infrastructure, governance, and management capacities. Digital spaces (broadband + applications + e-services) offer information processing, and make cities interactive and capable of gathering, storing, and disseminating information. Innovation defines how solutions to city challenges are produced, how cities and organisations respond to challenges, and how new products and services are created and adapted to external conditions.

Integration offers the true advantages of intelligent cities by actualising a series of innovation circuits and improvements to the city. Digital spaces make cities interactive, reduce the needs for physical space and for traffic and energy; enable real-time response to emergencies; dematerialise cities; and remove density and constructions. Digital spaces make innovation more efficient, thus facilitating collaboration, involving more people, and widening innovation networks. Innovation makes cities more competitive, sustains new industries, and increases the wealth of cities.

5. Outcomes: city domains for smart systems application

The most urgent challenge of smart city environments is to address the current problems and sustainable development priorities of cities within a global and innovation-led world. A public consultation held by the European Commission (2008) on the major urban and regional development challenges in the EU identified three main priorities for the policy after 2013. It appears that competitiveness will remain at the heart of urban and regional policy, and in particular research, innovation, and upgrading of skills to promote the knowledge economy. Active labour market policy is a top priority to sustain employment, strengthen social cohesion, and reduce the risk of poverty. Another hot societal issue is sustainable development, reducing greenhouse gas emissions and improving the energy efficiency of urban infrastructure.

Smart city solutions are expected to deal with these challenges, sustain the innovation economy and wealth of cities, and maintain employment and fight against poverty through employment generation by optimising energy and water usage and savings, and ensuring safer cities. However, to achieve these goals, city authorities and stakeholders must undertake initiatives and strategies that create the physical–digital environment of intelligent cities, actualising useful applications and e-services, and assuring the long-term sustainability of smart systems and applications through viable business models.

The first priority that cities must address on this path towards intelligence is to create a rich environment of broadband networks and digital applications. This includes: (1) the development of broadband infrastructure combining cable, optical fibre, and wireless networks to offer high connectivity and bandwidth to citizens and organisations located in the city; (2) the enrichment of the physical space and infrastructures of cities with embedded systems, smart devices, sensors, and actuators, and offering real-time data management, alerts, and information processing; and (3) the creation of applications enabling data collection and processing, Web-based collaboration, and actualisation of the collective intelligence of citizens. The latest developments in cloud computing and the emerging Internet of Things, open data, Semantic Web, and future media technologies have much to offer. These technologies can assure economies of scale in infrastructure and turnkey solutions for Infrastructure as a Service (IaSS) and Software as a Service (SaaS), that dramatically decrease the development costs while accelerating the learning curve for operating smart systems.

The second priority consists of initiating large-scale participatory innovation processes and competitions for the creation of applications and e-services that will run and improve every sector of activity, cluster, and piece of city infrastructure. All city economic activities and utilities can be seen as fields of innovation in which citizens and organisations participate in the development of new e-services. Demand for e-services is increasing, but not at a disruptive pace. There is a critical barrier between software applications and the provision of e-services in terms of sustainability and financial viability. Not all applications are turned into e-services. Those that succeed in bridging the gap rely on successful business models that turn technological capabilities into innovations, secure a continuous flow of data and information, and offer useful services.

Here the third priority of city authorities comes into play: creating business models that sustain the long-term operation of e-services. To date, the environment of e-services and their business models has been very complex, with limited solutions available 'off-the-shelf,' a lot of experimentation, and many failures.

Cities currently face problems of standardisation of the main building blocks of intelligent city solutions in terms of applications, business models, and e-services. There is a group of applications that all cities should have, but that need to be adapted to and customised in each city. Open-source software communities can contribute substantially to avoiding 'smart city in a box' solutions. Cloud computing could also dramatically decrease the costs and accelerate the learning curve for the operation of smart cities. Standardisation would dramatically reduce the development and maintenance costs of e-services due to cooperation, exchange, and sharing of resources among localities.

The taxonomy of domains of applications and solutions has been a subject of extensive discussion among smart city developers and vendors. Standardisation is missing. Many different categories and taxonomies have been proposed by organisations and research institutes. The most representative follow.

The Vienna Centre for Regional Science (Giffinger, 2007) has proposed a rather holistic smart city development view with six domains for smart city solutions and optimisation. Table 1.1 presents these domains, together with key performance indicators per domain.

The IBM Institute for Business Value analysis (IBM, 2010) has defined six domains for smart city applications and services through e-government and use of ICT for service delivery and management by local governments: citizens who use ICT for human and social services related to education, health, housing and social aspects; businesses that make use of an efficient business system with a high level of innovation and creation; transport systems and accessibility to and from cities;

Table 1.1 Smart city application domains and metrics

Smart economy *(Competitiveness)*	Smart people *(Social and human capital)*
• Innovative spirit • Entrepreneurship • Economic image and trademarks • Productivity • Flexibility of labour markets • International embeddedness • Ability to transform	• Level of qualification • Affinity of lifelong learning • Social and ethnic plurality • Flexibility • Creativity • Cosmopolitanism / Open-mindedness • Participation in public life
Smart governance *(Participation)*	Smart mobility *(Transport and ICT)*
• Participation in decision-making • Public social services • Transparent governance • Political strategies and perspectives	• Local accessibility • (Inter-)national accessibility • Availability of ICT infrastructure • Sustainable, innovative, and safe transport systems
Smart environment *(Natural resources)*	Smart living *(Quality of life)*
• Attractivity of natural conditions • Pollution • Environmental protection • Sustainable resource management	• Cultural facilities • Health conditions • Individual safety • Housing quality • Education facilities • Tourism attractivity • Social cohesion

Source: Based on Giffinger (2007)

communication through ICT infrastructures such as high-speed broadband and Wi-Fi; energy and the presence of smart grids and use of smart metering for energy management; and water and the use smart technologies for water management and regulation.

Accenture (2011) in the report entitled *Building and Managing an Intelligent City* has described an open interoperable platform with intelligent infrastructure functionality over which seven domains of services are offered: office and residential building management, natural resource management, transportation, health and safety, waste management, education and culture, and public administration services.

Apps for Smart Cities (2012) outlines smart city applications that enable better and participatory governance. The city should become a platform enabling creativity and applications to empower citizens. Applications should address the following themes: smart manufacturing, new production tools (home-produced food, energy, micro-manufacturing, 3D printing); collaboration and sharing of resources via the Internet; urban farming; apps relating to open data; apps relating to smart energy; apps for smart transportation and smart health; and technology for open source-culture, sustainability, and art.

CISCO's Smart + Connected Communities solutions focus on personalised spaces, and residential and government services. The Intelligent X Platform described smart

30 What makes cities intelligent?

city services in building management, home, sports and leisure, education, administration services, safety, security and emergency response, transport, and energy.

The EU Smart City stakeholders platform (Smart Cities and Communities, n.d.), created by the European Commission to share smart city solutions, best practices, and project ideas, has identified four domains for solutions on the platform: end-use energy efficiency, energy supply and smart grids, transport and mobility, and ICT.

Given the above diversity of views, we suggest describing the fields for intelligent / smart city applications with respect to the fundamental building blocks of every city: those of production, consumption, infrastructure networks, and government. From this perspective, the following taxonomy of applications and solutions, illustrated in Figure 1.3, offers a holistic view of applications domains:

- *Innovation economy:* Applications focusing on production sectors or production clusters, such as manufacturing, logistics, financial services, commerce, tourism, education, health, and others.
- *City infrastructure / utilities:* Applications focusing on networks and services for transport and mobility, energy, water, and waste management.
- *Quality of life—living in the city:* Applications focusing on consumption and well-being: improving the quality of life, bridging the social and digital

Innovation economy
- Investment and entrepreneurship
- Creativity, research, and innovation
- Work and labour markets
- Products and services markets
- Collaboration and supply chains

Living in the city – quality of life
- Housing
- Health and social care
- Education
- Recreation and sports
- Environment, safety and security

City infrastructure and utilities
- Mobility, transport and parking
- Energy saving, smart grid, and renewable energy
- Water management and saving
- Waste management and valorisation
- Broadband, wired and wireless

City governance
- Decision making / citizen participation / democracy
- Government services to citizens
- City planning / city management
- Monitoring and benchmarking

Figure 1.3 Intelligent city application domains

divides, monitoring the environment, offering safety in the public space, and facilitating social care services.
- *City governance:* Applications focusing on city management and operation facilitating decision-making and democracy, city planning, administration services to citizens, and monitoring and measurement of city performance.

In these domains, applications and e-services can cover the entire city or a city-district. City vs. city-districts, the classical dichotomy of city planning, is a key dimension that differentiates applications. Typical city-districts to be found in most cities are the central business / financial district (CBD), historic centre, shopping centre, shopping malls, industrial areas, technology and business parks, university campus, port area, and airport area, as well as housing, sports, and recreation areas. At the district level, applications are more specialised, targeted on the functional and physical characteristics of the district, and mainly managed by decentralised authorities and public-private coalitions specific to the district.

The positive impact of available smart city solutions on cities has not yet been fully demonstrated, nor have the necessary funding mechanisms and business models for their sustainability been adequately developed. Creating the market for applications and solutions is the first priority. Estimations about the smart city market are very optimistic, but vary considerably. The innovation ecosystem of intelligent cities has to be defined in terms of applications, e-services, and financial engineering, thereby helping cities to make better decisions, find funding, identify revenue sources, develop private-public partnerships, and open up public data for commercial use.

6. The landscape of intelligent cities

Thinking about cities from the perspective of intelligent city planning is not about building or expanding the actual city, but about making the existing city more efficient, more competitive, less energy consuming, and safer, by infusing technology and innovation. It is about reorganising the city.

A key issue in making such environments is to understand and manage the linkages between the physical, institutional, and digital aspects of cities and how these interconnections activate knowledge functions, release creativities, and transform knowledge into innovation. Intelligent cities can achieve more global and interactive systems of innovation, and through digital interaction can enable an extension of innovation collaboration networks and user participation. However, the precise way in which digital collaboration enables the participation of suppliers, innovators, customers, and end-users in innovation processes has to be defined with respect to the functional differentiation and complexity of each city. Different forms of digital applications, virtual spaces, and novel e-services have to be offered in different city districts. Intelligent cities are emerging from a dynamic re-arrangement of city clusters, institutions, and networks.

The previous sections have highlighted key elements of this large emerging landscape revealed by a literature growing at exponential rate. Table 1.2 attempts codifying this discussion and indicates a series of related topics organised along two axes, vertically, from intelligent city concept to strategy, and horizontally, from intelligent city genesis to impact.

Table 1.2 Intelligent city landscape

	Genesis	Concept	Structure / Building blocks	Impact
Concept and structure	• A digital space over the urban agglomeration, urban planning and governance • Innovation-driven cities: ecosystems of innovation, global innovation networks, user-driven innovation, cities as Living Labs	• Digital cities: Virtual representation of cities • Cyber cities: Governance / control • Smart cities: Sensors / real world UI • Intelligent cities • Integration of human, collective, and AI	• Layer 1: Physical space, agglomeration, clusters, people (human intelligence) • Layer 2: Innovation space, innovation system and drivers (collective intelligence) • Layer 3: Digital space, broadband, virtual / smart environments, apps, Web-based collaboration (artificial intelligence)	• More competitive cities: Smart growth cities, global cities, high-income cities • Quality cities: Inclusive cities, social care, safe cities, environmental sustainable • Sustainable cities: Infrastructure saving, e-services for traffic, energy, and utilities • Good governance of cities
	Innovation drivers	Innovation ecosystems	Fundamental knowledge functions	Innovation architectures in smart environments
Innovation ecosystems	• R&D / technology development • University–industry collaboration • Foresight, forecasting, futures • Co-design / co-innovation • User-driven innovation • Innovation incubation / funding	• Clusters and districts • Regional systems / Triple-helix • Open innovation • Glocal and interactive systems • Living Labs • Smart specialisation ecosystems-RIS3	• Information collection and processing • Technology learning, technology transfer, technology absorption • Innovation, R&D, co-development • Information dissemination, product promotion, marketing	• Innovation circuits • Agglomeration of smart solutions • Orchestration • Empowerment • Instrumentation

	Broadband networks and sensors	Data management – intelligence	Collaboration Web / applications	Location aware technologies
Smart environments	• Wired and wireless networks • Sensors and sensor networks • Smart meters • Internet of Things • Urban operating systems	• OLAP – Business intelligence • Gigabit datasets / distributed systems • Data mining • Open data / linked data • Semantic technologies – Ontologies • Cloud-based solutions	• Content Management Systems • Online collaboration spaces • Web based co-design • Web 2.0 product development • Crowdsourcing platforms • Mashups, content syndication	• Location aware technology • Smart objects • Augmented reality • Street view – 3D visualisation • Mobile applications • Active reporting – instant mapping
	Intelligent / smart cities governance	Intelligent city strategy profiles	Strategic planning process	Metrics and assessment
Strategies and planning	• Actualising communities and networks • Distributed knowledge architectures • Innovation cycles	• Infrastructure-based strategies • Sector-based strategies • Cluster-based strategies • Strategies for districts and neighbourhoods • Agglomeration of multiple cores and sectors	• Planning process and roadmap • Planning methodologies and toolbox • Setting objectives and priorities • Applications / solutions / FOSS • Business model selection	Population, education, skills Knowledge creation, innovation institutions, social capital Broadband networks, smart environments, e-services Impact: Innovation, wealth of cities, improvement

(*Continued*)

Table 1.2 (Continued)

	Domain 1: Innovation Economy	Domain 2: Quality of Life, Living in the City	Domain 3: City Infrastructure and Utilities	Domain 4: City Governance
Applications, smart city solutions	• Investment • Innovation • Work • Markets • Collaboration and supply chains	• Housing • Health and social care • Education • Recreation • Environment • Safety and security	• Mobility and transport • Energy saving, smart grid • Water management • Waste collection and management • Broadband, wired and wireless	• Decision making / e-democracy • Planning and city management • Administration services to citizens • Monitoring, measurement, and benchmarking

References

Accenture (2011). *Building and managing an intelligent city.* Accenture Management Consulting.
Apps for Smart Cities (2012). The Apps for Smart Cities manifesto. Retrieved, 2 January 2014, from www.appsforsmartcities.com/?q=manifesto.
Aurigi, A. (2005). *Making the digital city: The early shaping of urban Internet space.* London: Ashgate.
Aurigi, A. and De Cindio, F. (2008). *Augmented urban spaces.* Aldershot, UK: Ashgate.
Batty, M. (1990). Intelligent cities: Using information networks to gain competitive advantage. *Environment and Planning B: Planning and Design,* Vol. 17, No. 3, 247–256.
Belissent, J. (2010). *Getting clever about smart cities: New opportunities require new business models.* Forrester for Ventor Strategy. Available at http://goo.gl/fLKUen.
Bell, R., Jung J. and Zacharilla, L. (2008). *Broadband economies: Creating the community of the 21st century.* New York: Intelligent Community Forum.
Bergvall-Kåreborn, B. and Ståhlbröst, A. (2009). Living Lab: an open and citizen-centric approach for innovation. *International Journal for Innovation and Regional Development,* Vol. 1, No. 4, 356–370.
Besselaar, P. and Koizumi, S. (eds) (2005). *Digital Cities III: Information technologies for cocial capital – Cross-cultural perspectives.* Berlin: Springer-Verlag.
Capelli, L. (ed.) (2013). *City sense: Shaping our environment with real-time data.* Catalonia, Spain: Actar, IaaC.
Caragliu, A., Del Bo, C. and Nijkamp, P. (2009). *Smart cities in Europe.* Series Research Memoranda 0048, VU University Amsterdam, Faculty of Economics, Business Administration and Econometrics.
Carillo, F. (2006). *Knowledge cities. Approaches, experiences and perspectives.* Oxford, UK: Butterwoth-Heinemann.
Chen-Ritzo, C. H, Harrison, C., Paraszczak, J. and Parr, F. (2009). Instrumenting the planet. *IBM Journal of Research & Development,* Vol. 53, No. 3, 338–353.
Deakin, M. (ed.) (2013). *Smart cities: Governing, modelling and analysing the transition.* New York, NY: Routledge.
Deakin, M. and Al Waer, H. (eds) (2012). *From intelligent to smart cities.* New York, NY: Routledge.
Edvinsson, L. (2008). Knowledge navigation and the cultivating ecosystem for intellectual capital. In G. Ahonen (ed.) *Inspired by Knowledge in Organisations.* Swedish School of Economics and Business Administration, No. 182.
El Nasser, H. (2011). Will 'intelligent cities' put an end to suburban sprawl? *USA TODAY.* Retrieved 2 January 2014, from http://usatoday30.usatoday.com/news/nation/2011-01-28-cities28_ST_N.htm.
Eurocities (2009). Smart cities. In Smart Cities Workshop. Brussels, 16 and 17 November 2009. Retrieved 2 January 2014, from www.majorcities.eu/generaldocuments/pdf/eu_smart_city_initiative_workshop_report.pdf.
European Commission (2008). *Growing regions, growing Europe.* Communication from the Commission to the European Parliament and the Council. Fifth progress report on economic and social cohesion. COM(2008) 371 final. Luxembourg: Office for Official Publications of the European Communities.
European Commission, DG INFSO (2010). *Future Internet research and experimentation.* Retrieved 2 January 2014, from http://cordis.europa.eu/fp7/ict/fire/docs/fire-presentation-2011-en.pdf.

European Innovation Partnership on Smart Cities and Communities (2013). Strategic Implementation Plan. Retrieved 2 January 2014, from http://ec.europa.eu/eip/smartcities/files/sip_final_en.pdf.
Foth, M., Forlano, L., Satchell, C. and Gibbs, M. (eds) (2011). *From social butterfly to engaged citizen: Urban informatics, social media, ubiquitous computing, and mobile technology to support citizen engagement.* Cambridge, MA: MIT Press.
Gibson, D. V., Kozmetsky, G. and Smilor, R. W. (eds) (1992). *The technopolis phenomenon: Smart cities, fast systems, global networks.* New York, NY: Rowman & Littlefield.
Giffinger, R. (2007). *Smart cities. Ranking of European medium-sized cities.* Vienna, Austria: Centre of Regional Science (SRF), Vienna University of Technology.
Graham, S. (2003). *The cybercities reader.* London, UK: Routledge.
Greenfield, A. and Kim, N. (2013). *Against the smart city.* New York, NY: Kindle Edition.
Hatzelhoffer, L., Humboldt, K., & Lobeck, M. (2012). *Smart city in practice: Converting innovative ideas into reality.* Berlin, Germany: Jovis Verlag.
IBM (2010). *A vision of smarter cities: How cities can lead the way into a prosperous and sustainable future.* New York, NY: IBM Institute for Business Value.
IBM (n.d.). Smarter cities. Retrieved 2 January 2014, from www.ibm.com/smarterplanet/us/en/smarter_cities/overview/.
Ishida, T. and Isbister K. (eds) (2000). *Digital cities: Technologies, experiences, and future perspectives.* Berlin, Germany: Springer-Verlag.
Komninos, N. (2002). *Intelligent cities: Innovation, knowledge systems and digital spaces.* London and New York: Taylor & Francis.
Komninos, N. (2008). *Intelligent cities and globalisation of innovation networks.* London and New York: Routledge.
Laguerre, M. (2006). *The digital city: The American metropolis and information technology.* Basingstoke, UK: Palgrave Macmillan Press.
Leach, N. (ed) (2009). Digital cities. *Architectural Design*, Vol. 79, No. 4, 6–13.
Legg, S. and Hutter, M. (2007). A collection of definitions of intelligence. In B. Goertzel and P. Wang (eds) *Advances in artificial general intelligence: Concepts, architectures and alglorithms.* Amsterdam, the Netherlands: IOS Press.
Libelium (n.d.). 50 sensor applications for a smarter world. Retrieved 2 January 2014, from www.libelium.com/top_50_iot_sensor_applications_ranking/.
Mitchell, W. (2007). Intelligent cities. *E-Journal on the Knowledge Society*, UOC Papers. Retrieved 2 January 2014, from www.uoc.edu/uocpapers/5/dt/eng/mitchell.html.
Schaffers, H., Komninos, N. and Pallot, M. (eds) (2012). *Smart cities as innovation ecosystems sustained by the Future Internet.* FIREBALL White Paper. Retrieved 2 January 2014, from www.urenio.org/2012/04/23/smart-cities-fireball-white-paper.
Shepard, M. (ed.) (2011). *Sentient city: Ubiquitous computing, architecture, and the future of urban space.* Cambridge, MA: MIT Press.
Smart Cities and Communities (n.d.). Solutions proposals. Retrieved 2 January 2014, from http://eu-smartcities.eu/.
Sun Microsystems (2009). *Open source and cloud computing: on-demand, innovative IT on a massive scale.* Retrieved 2 January 2014, from www.newformat.se/documents/ose/sun-open-source-and-cloud-computing-white-paper-2009-06.pdf.
Tanabe, M., Van den Besselaar, P. and Ishida, T. (2005). Digital cities II. Computational and sociological approaches. *Lecture Notes in Computer Science*, Vol. 2.
Townsend, A.M. (2013). *Smart cities: Big data, civic hackers, and the quest for a new Utopia.* New York, NY: W.W. Norton & Company.

UK Government (2013). *Smart cities background paper*. Dept for Business Innovation and Skills. Retrieved, 2 January 2014, from www.gov.uk/government/uploads/system/uploads/attachment_data/file/246019/bis-13-1209-smart-cities-background-paper-digital.pdf.

URENIO (2014). Applications and tools for intelligent cities. Retrieved 2 January 2014, from www.urenio.org/digital-collaboration-tools/.

Van den Besselaar, P. and Koizumi, S. (2005). *Digital cities III. Information technologies for social capital: Cross-cultural perspectives*. Amsterdam and Berlin: Springer-Verlag.

Washburn, D. and Sindhu, U. (2009). *Making sense of smart city initiatives*. Forrester Research.

Wood, A. (2009). *City ubiquitous: Place, communication, and the rise of Omnitopia*. New York, NY: Hampton Press.

Yigitcanlar, T., Velibeyoglu, K. and Baum, S. (2008). *Creative urban regions: Harnessing urban technologies to support knowledge city initiatives*. Hershey, PA: IGI Global.

2 Intelligent city strategies
Innovation through multi-layer knowledge functions

1. Intelligent cities for innovation

This chapter connects the rise of intelligent cities to innovation on local and global scales, related to information, technology learning, knowledge creation, and dissemination networks, and the subsequent needs for online management, communication, and collaboration environments. By developing sector-focused, cluster-based, or more complex intelligent city strategies, territories can set in motion multi-layer knowledge functions and innovations that make cities more competitive, inclusive, and sustainable.

We develop this argument in five sequential steps. The first section of the chapter is an introductory note on the formation of the intelligent city planning paradigm based on the convergence of the 'digital city' and 'innovation ecosystems' literatures. Section two discusses current trends and causes that drive innovation towards glocal systems. It is common knowledge now that innovation springs from networks and systems which help transform inputs (funds, ideas, patents, technologies, skills) into marketable outputs (exports, new products, jobs, new companies, profits, etc.). The literature on innovation over the last 30 years, starting from Nelson & Winters' (1982) evolutionary metaphor, has revealed the spatial enlargement of innovation and the different environments that mediate between innovation inputs and outputs. Today, the globalisation of innovation networks and the involvement of users are changing these environments (clusters, alliances, company networks, supply architectures), forging new types of ecosystems, such as global innovation clusters, intelligent hubs, intelligent agglomerations, and Living Labs experimenting for product development. Innovation ecosystems that emerge have the capacity to integrate knowledge distributed on different spatial scales (thanks to digital communication) and skills dispersed to the population (thanks to Web 2.0 participatory media). Intelligent cities are born from these new possibilities of innovation within smart environments. Section three examines fundamental profiles of intelligent city strategies, connecting them with different types of ecosystems related to city sectors, clusters and districts, city infrastructure, and networks. Representative cases of strategies discussed come from Singapore to Stockholm, Living Labs in Europe, and more mixed approaches in Taipei. These cases show that the key added value of intelligent city strategies is in the setting up of advanced knowledge functions developed at physical, institutional, and digital spaces. Section four looks at these knowledge functions in detail, and at how multi-layer networks of direct and virtual communication sustain information intelligence, technology learning, new knowledge creation, and information dissemination. The chapter concludes by considering intelligent city strategies as a combinatory set of knowledge functions, which lead to more interactive, efficient, and globally open systems of innovation, much needed in contemporary cities and regions.

2. Two literatures shaping intelligent cities

Intelligent cities constitute a new planning paradigm pertinent for both the fields of urban development and innovation management. In the field of urban development, intelligent cities sustain the rise of knowledge-based local and regional economies. In the field of innovation development, they introduce a new type of innovation ecosystem combining the creativity of the local population with global innovation networks and the consequent opening up of innovation on a global scale. Connecting local resources and global innovation networks, intelligent cities can effectively address the challenges of growth, competition, and sustainability. The literature on intelligent cities reflects the gradual shaping of this planning paradigm and the way its technological base (telecoms, sensors, and virtuality) was enriched with various forms of networking and social intelligence and an innovative functionality allowing the environments produced to be characterised as 'intelligent.'

Mitchell (2007) argued that the new intelligence of cities resides in the increasingly effective combination of digital telecommunication networks, ubiquitously embedded intelligence, sensors and tags, and knowledge management software. This technological construction, he argued, did not appear all at once, but came as a result of continuous evolution, starting with the development of the theory of digital interaction, the invention of packet switching, the Arpanet, Ethernet, the Internet, the World Wide Web, the rapid expansion of wired and wireless communications, the appearance of laptop computers and other end-user communication devices, mobile phones, Blackberries and iPods, tiny embedded microprocessors, digital sensors and tags, minuscule digital cameras and microphones, radio-frequency identification (RFID) tags, and global positioning systems (GPS) and other location aware devices. Then large-scale software appeared. Take for example Google, which ties all these pieces together, and social media that enable and sustain social and cultural connections through the operation of software. This narration of evolution towards intelligent cities changes the older arguments about telecommunications in the city, cybercities, and digital cities (Graham, 2003; Graham and Marvin, 1996; Horan, 2000; Isida and Insbister, 2000; Van den Besselaar and Koizumi, 2005), taking into account recent contributions from the field of intelligent environments, social media, and ambient intelligence. The fact that digital intelligence is now ubiquitously present throughout urban environments makes the old metaphors of cyberspace and virtual worlds quite outmoded. However, the intelligence of the world of devices and Internet of Things (IoT) is limited by the artificial intelligence available, while underestimating the fact that the strengths and wealth of cities have always been found in two other forms of intelligence, human and collective, stemming from the agglomeration of skills and the institutions of cooperation.

In contrast to this technology-driven understanding, the work of social scientists placed intelligent cities in the context of knowledge, creativity, and intellectual capital. Florida wrote extensively about creative cities in the USA and Europe (Florida, 2002; Florida, 2005; Florida, 2010). The propensity of cities to generate prosperity, he argues, depends on their creative class, knowledge workers, scientists, artists, engineers, lawyers, entrepreneurs, and innovators. They produce new ideas, new products, new strategies, and new theories. People and collaboration are the main assets of cities. "Companies cluster in order to draw from concentrations of talented people who power innovation and economic growth" (Florida, 2005, p. 29). However, talent and education that allow knowledge to be transformed into innovation need an appropriate environment of tolerance and experimentation to flourish. Talent, technology, and tolerance connected together shape creative environments. "Cities need a people climate even more than they need a business climate" (Florida, 2010, p. 345). Social capital for cooperation, open societies, and social networks enable cities to address their problems more intelligently. The same importance is attached to people and collaboration by theories on intellectual capital for communities and cities (Bounfour and Edvinsson, 2005; Edvinsson, 2006; Edvinsson and Malone, 1997). Intellectual capital is the set of intangible assets of an organisation, the collective experience and knowledge distributed among in-house employees and external experts, suppliers, and customers' confidence. What makes cities more intelligent is the intellectual capital of their organisations. The system of territorial knowledge and creativity is also structured by the same capital.

Within the intelligent city literature, we also witness the permanent concern about building bridges between the technological base of intelligent cities and social objectives, and innovation objectives in particular. In one of the oldest references to the concept, Batty (1990) makes a clear connection between intelligent cities and competitive advantage. Collective intelligence (Levy, 1997), distributed intelligence and problem-solving (Kuhlmann et al., 1999), and regional intelligence (Komninos, 2004) outline how information technologies and virtual environments enable communities to channel individual practice into social projects addressing the complexity and challenges of the modern world (Noubel, 2004). Bridging innovation and broadband, intelligent cities create multi-level systems of innovation where the knowledge functions of innovation are deployed in physical, institutional, and digital spaces. What intelligent cities offer are skills, institutions, and virtual spaces of cooperation sustaining the creation of new knowledge (research), monitoring knowledge flows (intelligence), disseminating existing knowledge (technology transfer), applying knowledge (innovation), developing new activities based on knowledge (incubation), and managing knowledge remotely (e-government) (Komninos, 2008).

The link between intelligent cities and innovation has been a major factor throughout this literature; though there are diverging views about the type of intelligence (human, organisational, artificial) that drives innovative behaviour. For instance, the initiative for *Smart Communities* (SC) clearly intended "to help communities worldwide better understand the important role of technology, economic development and importantly, creativity and innovation to success and survival in the new global economy" (Smart Communities, 2008). The concept of 'smart community' was used to describe a community that makes an effort to use information technology and fundamentally change life and work conditions; the concept is an attempt that goes far beyond the mere use of information technology, to preparing a community to tackle the challenges of a global, knowledge economy. This becomes clear in the setting of such communities. One starting point for setting up a SC is leadership by key individuals or institutions who share authority, risk, and responsibility, forming a partnership that guides the strategy and the business plan of the community. This is followed by the setting up of a coalition and development of the SC's vision; undertaking a preliminary assessment of needs and opportunities; developing an action plan; shaping the personality of the community; determining the infrastructures; and laying down the rules of governance (Smart Communities, 2002).

However, in some cases an unsophisticated connection between intelligent cities and broadband networks has only led cities to invest heavily in communication infrastructure (cable and wireless), assuming that broadband is a sufficient window to innovation and competitiveness. Broadband is necessary, but is not enough; intelligent cities are equally about ICT and knowledge exchange, human skills, and innovation support institutions. Instead of putting information technology first, intelligent city planning aims to put smart innovation environments and services in place to manage knowledge networks, resources, and capabilities with the help of digital technology.

3. Towards user-driven, glocal innovation ecosystems

The survey by Jaruzelki, Loeher, and Holman (2013) on largest companies globally reveals how virtual environments and e-tools can be used by those companies to produce innovations, thus improving speed and lowering cost, enhancing quality and reducing complexity, and engaging customers in innovation. They have plotted a diagram of 35 innovation tools, from customer immersion labs to social media dashboards, falling into the areas of customer insight, ideation, product development, and launch; they indicate the most efficient and the least efficient tools, the level of use by companies, and tools enabling productivity or market and customer insight. A part of digital innovation tools used by individual companies, digital platforms and digital commons enable groups of companies and local ecosystems of innovation to develop networks at a global scale and use competences and markets from around the world. This 'glocalisation' of innovation has now become a dominant trend. Digital interaction extends collaboration networks and the participation of suppliers and users globally.

It is well documented that innovation activities tend to cluster. In Europe, for instance, R&D laboratories and companies active in R&D are concentrated to a

42 *What makes cities intelligent?*

great extent in a series of islands of innovation and innovative regions in northwest Europe and Scandinavia. This spatial polarisation of innovation is explained by the horizontal and vertical knowledge interaction within the clusters, local knowledge spillovers, and the 'embedded tacit knowledge' thesis (Edquist, 1997; Keeble et al., 1998; Malmberg and Maskell, 2002). Because innovation activities rely on tacit knowledge networks, they have location-specific dimensions and tend to cluster. Tacit knowledge is spatially immobile and not easily communicated other than through personal interaction (Morgan, 2004). Clustering becomes inevitable in innovation in order to materialise innovative behaviour based on tacit knowledge and interdisciplinary exchanges and spillovers.

Recent evidence, however, maintains that international relationships and global knowledge flows are crucial sources of creativity and innovativeness within local innovation clusters. Successful clusters are building and managing resources from around the globe (Bathelt et al., 2004; Owen-Smith and Powell, 2004). There is growing evidence that even in the most innovative clusters, an important proportion of their knowledge and customer bases are not local (Gertler and Wolfe, 2005). Local clusters and innovative cities are going global to take advantage of external resources (suppliers and technology providers), market opportunities (customers), and global funds and investments (Uhlmann, 2008). In developing countries, innovation offshoring tends also to cluster. Intense offshoring takes place in a limited number of cities and regions in India, China, and Malaysia, and in global city-regions such as Singapore and Hong Kong, giving birth to agglomerations of high-tech activities and innovative clusters.

The globalisation of innovation networks is a contemporary trend that deeply influences innovation clusters and local systems of innovation. Globalisation, as the "intensification of worldwide social relations which link distant localities in such a way that local happenings are shaped by events occurring many miles away and vice versa" (Giddens, 1990, p. 64), has now extended to an even larger range of activities including R&D and innovation. Information technology enables coordinating networks and transactions in real time on a planetary scale. Decentralising business units and operations to every corner of the world has become routine practice, but now companies are also redistributing their product innovation, even basic and applied research, across global R&D networks (Economist Intelligence Unit, 2004; United Nations, 2005).

The trend is relevant for both large and small innovative companies. Large global corporations are setting up massive innovation facilities and cooperation networks in the developing countries of Asia. CISCO already has R&D facilities in Bangalore, India; Toyota in Thailand; Nokia operates nine satellite design studios located in India (Bangalore), China (Beijing), and Brazil, where researchers and designers work to customise products to each market (Business Week, 2007). The United Nations Conference on Trade and Development (UNCTAD) survey on the internationalisation of R&D shows that China has become the most attractive destination for non-equity R&D collaboration (United Nations, 2005). The majority of the new R&D centres that multinational companies plan to open during the next years are to be located in India and China. This R&D relocation has taken multiple forms: 'Satellite R&D' labs located in developing countries focus on the exploitation and adaptation of 'home R&D,' which have relatively low strategic importance and are vulnerable to budget cuts decided on by headquarters. 'Contract R&D' labs are a pure form of innovation offshoring confined to the provision of lower-cost skills, capabilities, and infrastructure. Knowledge exchange remains very limited in this case, too. 'Equal Partnership' labs are the most advanced but also the most limited form, and concern those multinational labs that are charged with a regional or global product mandate. Knowledge exchange is higher here and, eventually, there is mutual knowledge exchange (Ernst, 2006).

Innovation offshoring is also becoming important for smaller companies. Venture capital funds in Silicon Valley, for instance, require startup businesses to plan offshore outsourcing as a precondition for funding, imposing a business model which keeps strategic management functions on site (customer relations, marketing, finance, and business development), while moving product development and research work to offshore locations (Ernst, 2006).

As a result of these trends, innovation spending and performance in Asia is growing rapidly. In the previous decade (from 2000 to 2005), while business R&D expenditure rose by 5.2 percent in North America, 2.3 percent in Europe, and 3.8 percent in Japan, it rose by 17 percent in India and China, and by 19.7 percent in Australia, Brazil, Singapore, South Korea, and Taiwan combined. Actually, the Innovation Union Scoreboard 2013 documents that the USA, Japan, and South Korea have a performance lead, with South Korea joining the USA as the most innovative country. China's lead over the EU27 can be found in R&D expenditure in the business sector, and China has also decreased its gap in international co-publications, public-private co-publications, and patents (Hollanders and Es-Sadki, 2013).

These are just a few facts from a sea of evidence demonstrating the rise of Asia as an important location for R&D and innovation. Innovation offshoring follows the intense relocation of production activities to Asia in diverse industry sectors, such as textiles and footwear, electronics, automotive components, machine tools, software, and IT-based business services. Innovation offshoring goes beyond the relocation of routine activities, such as quality control, call centres, and 24/7 business support services. Strong technology-led clusters and hubs have emerged all over Asia: for broadband technology in South Korea and Singapore; for mobile communications and digital consumer devices in South Korea, Taiwan, and China; and for software engineering in India (Ernst, 2006).

The survey conducted by the Economist Intelligence Unit (2004) documented that the main causes that drive the relocation of R&D toward Southeast Asia are the search for reduced R&D costs and the ability to tailor goods and services to particular markets. However, new factors have also appeared alongside the classical factors of foreign direct investment (FDI) attraction (proximity to local markets and bypassing of tariff barriers), such as tapping into pools of local know-how, taking advantage of local creativity, avoiding relocation expenses, and shrinking of R&D budgets. The *Global Innovation 1000* report by Booz-Allen-Hamilton has documented that the largest R&D-spending companies in the world have demonstrated both rising revenues and rising innovation spending. However, the

44 *What makes cities intelligent?*

ratio between these two measures (R&D spending per sale) is declining: revenues are rising faster than innovation spending. The authors argue that this trend can be attributed to the increasing globalisation of R&D, which is outsourced to facilities in lower-cost regions of the world (Jaruzelski et al., 2006).

The global decentralisation of R&D and innovation mobility has a direct impact on innovation clusters and other territorial innovation systems, as well. The most innovative cities and clusters to be found in Silicon Valley, Seattle, Austin, Raleigh, and Boston in the USA, in Stockholm, Munich, and Helsinki in the EU, and in Bangalore, Beijing, Shanghai, Seoul, Singapore, Taiwan, and Tokyo in Asia take on board this new local–global innovation dynamics. Public authorities in the USA, Europe, and Asia and most major cities are deploying strategies to address these new challenges to make their cities more innovative, open, global, and intelligent.

4. Strategies for intelligent cities: profiles and innovation paths

Intelligent cities are a response to these trends towards user-driven and global innovation. The 'innovation clustering–global innovation' geography has become possible thanks to digital collaborative environments and information communication infrastructure. A new type of urbanity is taking shape, as innovative clusters extend their cooperation networks virtually, into those of intelligent cities. The development of intelligent cities enables the global reach of local innovation clusters, innovation poles, and other innovative agglomerations. Intelligent cities offer the capability of online knowledge processing and exchange: faster and more direct communication, high capacity for information storage and processing, online knowledge management, agent-based knowledge assessment, 24/7 real-time communication, virtual cooperation, and so on. Key practices in the overall innovation cycle, such as information provision, technology transfer, product development, partnership, and so on, can now be performed collaboratively over digital space and be distributed to various localities around the globe.

Most intelligent city strategies document the structural relationship between innovation, digital interaction, and the global market. However, all intelligent city strategies are not the same. There are important differences in terms of geographical area, focus, and the way in which relationships between locality, innovation, and information technology are organised and implemented.

Four broad strategy profiles are presented below, together with representative cases, focusing on city sectors, clusters or districts, infrastructure, and the holistic approach.

Sector-focused strategies

Many intelligent city strategies clearly aim to transform specific sectors of the city, be it the manufacturing, services, or social sectors. The geography of sectors within the city is not an issue or critical factor, compared to their growth and networking with activities inside and outside the city. The objective here is to sustain glocal and user-driven innovation within the most important sectors of the city.

A good illustration of this approach is "iN2015" (Intelligent Nation 2015), the strategy and programme for turning Singapore into an intelligent island. The strategy is guided by the vision of "an intelligent island, a global city, powered by Infocomm" (IDA, 2007). Information and communication technologies (infocomm) will be harnessed to strengthen the fundamental ingredients of city development: innovation (the capacity to create new products or new ways of doing something), integration (the ability to harness resources and capabilities across diverse organisations and geographies), and internationalisation (the need to be well plugged into the globalised economy).

Implementation of the strategy relies on the transformation of ten major activity sectors of Singapore through infusion of information technology and learning:

- The digital media and entertainment sector, establishing a digital marketplace for the creation and commercialisation of content and services;
- The education and learning sector, delivering more engaging services and allowing students and teachers to use interactive learning resources and applications;
- The financial services sector, allowing Singapore to become an innovative hub offering front-end wealth management services;
- The healthcare and biomedical sciences sector, providing personalised services, exchange of data across providers, and offering a holistic view of patients' medical needs;
- Manufacturing and logistics, entrenching Singapore's position as a high-value manufacturing hub and supply chain centre, offering platforms for trade documentation and services for trading and logistics;
- The tourism, hospitality, and retail sectors, mainly through the digital concierge programme that allows visitors to access personalised, location-aware information and to carry out transactions;
- The government sector, offering a wide range of services and access channels using a standard operating environment across the entire public sector, allowing inter-agency and inter-personal collaboration; and
- The development of infocomm infrastructure and services; enterprise development for infocomm companies; and infocomm manpower.

In each sector, a planning committee has been set up, which in consultation with the public has elaborated a ten-year plan that reaffirms the strategic role of information technology as a differentiator and enabler of innovation and globalisation. The plans foresee the implementation of projects that introduce new products and services in each sector, establishing a pervasive and intelligent infrastructure, going beyond user-inputs with intelligent data collection and mining, offering personal digital assistants to every citizen, and advanced services in collaborative product design and intelligent supply chain management, turning companies into 'techno-strategists' that have the ability to combine technical know-how with domain experience for innovative products and solutions.

The central objective of the sectoral plans is to integrate R&D, commercialisation, and IT. The plan for the digital media and entertainment (DME) sector, for instance, puts forward a series of resource centres providing DME firms with technology tools and training, such as the DME technology creation and commercialisation initiative; the digital asset management programme with the Digital Vault (a digital content bank); the Digital Key (safe trading of content); and the Digital Courier (end-to-end sales, payment, and delivery of digital assets). All in all, these initiatives intend to create strong sectoral systems of innovation, combining R&D, product development capability, and wide marketing and product promotion.

Cluster or district-focused strategies

Other intelligent city strategies focus on city districts and clusters. There are two main reasons for this. In metropolitan areas and larger cities, a functional specialisation of city districts takes place as the activities and the physical space of districts – central business district, industrial areas, port areas, university districts, recreation areas, and housing districts – differentiate substantially. On the other hand, governance also becomes fragmented as the aforementioned districts develop their own administration and decision-making capacity, relying on various forms of public, private, and public-private coalition.

Representative cases of this type of strategy can be found in many cities in Europe where intelligent city strategies are connected to urban regeneration objectives. Chapter 5 discusses the regeneration of Europen cities with respect to district-based smart systems and innovative communities. Living Labs (LLs) also create collaboration bonds between localities, innovation, and ICTs into selected city districts or clusters. LLs are targeted at city districts or clusters, with the aim of becoming significant testing beds for new products, services, and new ideas. The concept takes advantage of fundamental qualities of the urban environment (agglomeration, infrastructure, collaboration), moving research out of laboratories into a real-life context, allowing citizens to participate in research, product design, and product testing. Users are invited to cooperate with researchers, product designers, and developers to test and improve innovative ideas and R&D outcomes. Through the LLs, the city infrastructure is improved; public policies are adapted to firm-specific assets; and clusters of competencies are maintained and advanced by applied research and experimental development, education, and training. The city district becomes a 'living laboratory' for prototyping and testing new technology applications and new methods of generating and fostering innovation.

LLs offer original ways to create urban clusters that are experimenting with innovative products and global markets. The cluster-based approach is strong in most ongoing initiatives. For instance:

- The Normandy LL relies on the skills, networks, and resources of the Secure Electronic Transactions Competitiveness Cluster (TES) managed by this cluster. It tests innovative products and services using mobile communication technology in the fields of logistics, health, tourism, marketing, and

citizenship, involving the end user in the product development and innovation processes. The Normandy LL combines three operational units: the *Usage Observatory* involved in the institutional aspects of secure electronic transactions, the *Innovation Institute* elaborating new product concepts, and the *Experimental Centre* assessing product prototypes with the aid of end users (Pole TES, n.d.).
• The Forum Virium Helsinki is another LL based on a cluster developing new customer-driven digital services and content. Many significant companies, R&D organisations, and public sector organisations located in the Helsinki region are taking part. In a series of domains (metropolitan traffic, healthcare, education, retail, digital home, and culture), the activities of the LL encompass typical cluster activities, such as cooperation in new product development, internal and external networking, creation of an environment favourable to innovation, and even the development of the region (Forum Virium, n.d.).

The LL movement appeared at the end of 2006 as part of the official programme of the Finnish presidency of the EU, and the concept has proven to be extremely popular. Since then, seven successive waves of expansion have increased membership of the European Network of Living Labs (ENoLL) to 320 members from EU countries, North and South America, Australia, Africa, and Asia.

Smart infrastructure-focused strategies

Some cities, typically the most affluent ones, follow an infrastructure-led development, considering that other initiatives will join and populate an underlying structural framework. Very popular in top-down planning has been the idea of an urban operating system, a common infrastructure of communication and data management that integrates information which comes from many and diverse sources. A Forrester report on smart city business models stresses that technology push is still dominant in the actual smart city agenda. Smart city solutions are currently more vendor push than city government pull based, beside the evident priority that "smart city solutions must start with the city not the smart" (Belissent, 2010).

Stockholm is a representative case of this type of strategy, of a very balanced development between infrastructure, applications, and e-services. In June 2009, the city of Stockholm received the ICF prize as the most intelligent community of the year. The evaluation was based on data that demonstrated that the city had combined dynamic growth, globalisation, innovation, broadband infrastructure, and digital services (ICF, 2009).

Historically speaking, Stockholm has been an open city, with large influxes of individuals settling there to study or work. However, it was not just job positions that were attracting the population. Many young people preferred the faster pace of life, the city's cultural diversity and the large range of activities it offered. In 2007, the city's population was 795,000 but that figure is expected to reach

1 million by 2030, with the population in the Stockholm / Mälaren Valley area expected to rise to 3.5 million. Stockholm is a very important centre for innovation. In the innovation scoreboard rankings for Europe's regions, Stockholm came in first, with a combined ratio of 0.90/1.00 and with very high scores in specific innovation indicators, such as knowledge-intensive workers, life-long learning, public and private R&D, patents, and high-tech services. It has held first place since 2003. It had been in second place up until 2002 (Hollanders et al., 2012).

The city's growth has been based on knowledge-intensive services, the financial sector, service enterprises such as legal and accounting services, trade, and technical consultancy services. Most of the country's central services and one in three foreign companies have their headquarters there. The population is educated to a high level, with 51 percent of the city's residents being university graduates. Stockholm has a very high percentage of new businesses and almost one in three new businesses started up in the Stockholm region. The organised clusters of innovative undertakings, as well as the establishment of Kista Science City, which is a major ICT centre, have all contributed to the city's innovation-driven growth and development.

Kista began in the mid-1970s as a satellite town for Stockholm, located just 15 km northwest of the city. In 1975, Ericsson relocated to Kista; three years later, IBM followed, and after 1985 many SMEs set up there. The City of Stockholm set up the Electrum Foundation, along with private undertakings and universities that were interested in the venture, with the aim of improving knowledge transfer from universities and promoting partnership between research and industry. This 'triple helix' innovation model led to the development of a complex of ICT activities, and the establishment of undertakings, research institutes, and the University of Stockholm's Computer Science School and incubators, as well as the city's urban management agencies at Kista. Today, some 31,000 people work at Kista Science City, which houses 1,400 enterprises and businesses of all sizes. The cluster is also highly active in the environment and clean-technologies sector.

Apart from Kista, Stockholm's development and growth has been based on the biosciences, and the city holds an important place in the European clean technologies industry. The city authorities and Swedish government are the leading clean technologies customers, having made major investments in the energy-savings and equipment sectors. In 2009, the City of Stockholm was also selected by the European Commission as Europe's first Green Capital for its holistic approach to growth. which includes an ambitious target of making the city totally non-reliant on fossil fuels by 2050.

In parallel with the innovation economy, Stockholm has also created a strong local broadband economy. Stokab, a company founded in 1994, lies at the core of the broadband economy. It is owned by Stockholms Stadshus AB, which in turn is owned by the City of Stockholm. Stokab's objective is to promote economic growth by stimulating the ICT market in the Stockholm area. Stokab builds, runs, and maintains a fibre optic network in the Stockholm area and leases fibre optic connections. Based on the logic of telecom market liberalisation, the company provides a network open to all interested parties under the same terms and conditions. The company also runs the City of Stockholm's intranet covering both administrative functions and the needs of the public in the education / training, childcare, leisure, and culture sectors. The network consists of 5,600 km of cables and a total of 1.2 million km of fibre optics. Customers who rent the network can use it to provide services in line with their own business model. The business cluster thereby created includes the network owners, telecom providers, Internet service providers and other service providers, and property owners / developers, and the end recipients are the city's residents and businesses. Ninety-eight per cent of the population has a broadband connection, and 95 percent of buildings meet the basic conditions for broadband network access.

Four hundred and fifty enterprises and 90 public organisations offer services over that network. The city is developing e-services in line with a governance model that includes online services for citizens, transparent public administration, and effectively organised public services. In addition to providing certificates and other standard municipal services, illustrative examples of the types of digital services on offer include *childcare* (users can request, compare and obtain information about kindergartens and crèches, and submit applications online), *parent–pupil dialogue* (better information about schools and courses), *accommodation finding services* (rental of vacant properties in the city), *digital libraries* (the ability to search for books, films, and music, and receive e-books and e-music), *telemedicine*, and *care of the elderly at home,* as well as *traffic management* (information about the current traffic situation and promotion of alternative forms of getting around using bicycles, public transport or foot).

Stockholm's long-term plan published in Vision 2030 (City of Stockholm, 2006) identifies the key characteristics of the city as a global metropolis, at the heart of an internationally competitive and innovative region, and a place where citizens can enjoy a rich urban experience and a wide range of high-quality social services. The city uses Web-based tools to monitor the progress being made in achieving the plan's objectives and targets, and also publishes best practices as examples that could inspire other regions.

Agglomeration of smart ecosystems

Intelligent city strategies may also extend to entire cities and regions, engaging multiple innovation ecosystems, clusters, and industry sectors. The environment that emerges is highly complex, created by the juxtaposition of smaller innovation ecosystems. Furthermore, each company has the possibility to create its own innovation ecosystem by combining elements of the physical, social, and digital resources to be found in the agglomeration.

Such decentralised, bottom-up strategies for innovation development, broadband networks, and digital services can lead to highly-complex intelligent agglomerations. If successful, a global networked intelligence emerges from local knowledge, skills, and competences distributed across many organisations located in the agglomeration. However, the movement from low-level rules to higher-level organisation, which is usually called 'emergence,' cannot be truly described

50 *What makes cities intelligent?*

as emergent until the local interactions result in some kind of organised macro-behaviour. The state of emergence commences when a higher-level pattern arises out of interactions between local actors (Johnson 2004, pp. 18–19). Furthermore, in such systems that learn from the ground level, macro-intelligence and adaptability emerge from accumulation of local knowledge. Gordon's research has shown five fundamental principles shape the emerging systemic behaviour: large numbers of operating units are needed; operation rules should be simple enough to avoid actors being misled; random interactions and encounters are important; individual behaviour should lead to larger patterns; and the primary mechanism of the swarm logic is interaction between neighbours (Gordon cited by Johnson 2004, pp. 78–79).

The development of Taipei as an intelligent community is close to this perspective. In 2006, the ICF announced Taipei as the top intelligent community of the year. The rationale behind this selection highlights the creation of multiple innovative clusters, broadband networks, and electronic services. Among the achievements of Taipei, cited by the ICF, were Taipei's 88 technology incubators, which continue to produce new businesses, products, and technologies for the global market; its 45 R&D centres and technology parks for software, data communications, mobile communications; the highly skilled knowledge workers; the large number of spinoffs and startups; and the growing capability for ubiquitous broadband, m-government, e-government, e-schools, and the creation of e-communities initiatives, equal access to Internet services for all, and the cyber-city initiative, which are all together are transforming an innovative agglomeration into a "high-tech city of the digital future" (ICF, 2006).

Intelligent city strategies implemented by cities can be placed between two opposite profiles. On the one hand, a profile created by a strong IT identity, whose core elements are 'broadband,' 'IT training,' and 'e-services.' Close to this profile are Singapore, Seoul, and most new smart city districts, such as New Songdo in South Korea and PlanIT Valley in Portugal. On the other hand, a profile shaped by the objectives of knowledge-based development, whose core elements are 'regeneration,' 'clusters,' 'innovative districts,' and broadband services to citizens. Close to this profile are New York, Florida, Manchester, Stockholm, and most bottom-up initiatives for intelligent cities.

Regardless of the profile, the above reference to strategies that focus on sectors, clusters, infrastructure, and agglomeration shows that intelligent city strategies combine locality, innovation, and smart environments in many diverse and creative ways. What locality has to offer to systems of innovation is the simultaneous presence and operation of all the system's components: external economies related to the reduction of cooperation costs within the system, tacit knowledge flows, and above all the creation of local communities of trust and the social capital needed for innovation. On the other hand, what smart environments have to offer to local systems of innovation is better communication, rapid transmission of explicit knowledge, the opening up of participative processes, and the global extension of networking. Forms of e-cooperation, e-technology, e-innovation, and e-marketplace offer important enhancements to local innovation ecosystems.

Critiques of intelligent city strategies do not question their effectiveness in transforming local knowledge and innovation activities. On the contrary, what is questioned is the justice and equality they bring to the city. For instance, critiques of Malaysia's Multimedia Super Corridor (MSC) and the Putrajaya and Cyberjaya projects (the flagship intelligent cities in Prime Minister Mahathir's vision to transform Malaysia into a fully developed nation by the year 2020) have shown that such high-tech developments may perpetuate existing patterns of social and spatial inequality if specific action to redistribute wealth is not taken. These large-scale investments in information infrastructure are concentrated in the main city-region of Malaysia and have further polarised the national spatial structure, while marginal groups and individuals are subjected to new forms of social and spatial exclusion because their participation is dependent on the possession of skills required for an emerging knowledge economy (Bunnell, 2002). Neither do intelligent city strategies escape the usual financial risks of large-scale urban development projects. The MSC has suffered from Malaysia's economic woes and the lack of interest from foreign corporations, leading the Multimedia Development Corporation into substantial debt.

5. Strategies introducing multi-layer knowledge functions

A key question to answer is what is 'behind' those strategies that are diversified per sector, cluster, or infrastructure? What are the mechanisms that drive succeess to innovation, sustainability, and development goals?

Our understanding is that intelligent city strategies, beside their diversity, introduce and enhance key knowledge functions within the respective urban systems and innovation ecosystems. A key feature of intelligent clusters, Living Labs, and sector-driven strategies is that they all develop innovation through sustaining knowledge in their area of reference. It makes no difference whether the level of implementation is the entire city, a city cluster, a network, or a sector of activity. They achieve this innovation role in two ways:

- On the one hand, by enabling user-driven innovation, involving citizens, customers and user, and opening up the innovation ecosystems to collaboration with suppliers, researchers, and innovators from within and outside the city. Deploying digital collaboration tools and e-services, more people, more suppliers, and more customers and consumers can join in innovation activities.
- On the other hand, by enriching the urban system with smart environments, sensors, devices, and digitally augmented spaces, strengthening information flows, real-time alert and response, and forecasting capabilities, and making the urban activities more interactive and efficient.

Key objective behind any type of intelligent city strategy it is to create physical, institutional, and digital spaces that enhance distributed knowledge functions of the respective ecosystems. Applications for virtual networking, virtual clustering, virtual product co-development, virtual technology exchange, virtual order placing, and virtual follow-up of processes, etc., have greatly amplified

52 *What makes cities intelligent?*

the ability of organisations to co-operate, learn, and innovate. In intelligent cities, these entities of cyberspace acquire links to relevant physical practices and institutional agreements, creating multi-layer knowledge functions.

Different intelligent cities strategies actualise different combinations of the four fundamental knowledge functions of gathering intelligence, technology learning, new knowledge creation, and information dissemination. For each function, specific e-tools and platforms are used, based on information management applications, intelligent agents for alert, search, information classification, processing, and dissemination. At the end of the day, these multi-layer knowledge functions improve the operation of urban systems and innovation ecosystems.

Collective information intelligence

This is a field with enormous potential within intelligent cities and clusters. Collective information intelligence is about collaboration in gathering and processing information; it is not reinventing the wheel, but rather getting a strategic view on markets, technologies, and innovation. Business intelligence, which has set the stage for collective intelligence, is defined as an activity to overview the internal and external environment of an organisation, with the intention of finding information that can be incorporated into decision-making processes. It relates to the exploitation of information gathered from suppliers and customers; it uses data from enterprise resource planning (ERP) and customer relationship management (CRM), applies data mining and data compilation techniques, and produces online analytical processing (OLAP) reports elucidating hidden aspects of the business environment and activity. Informed action is then taken (Enterweb, 2006).

Digital spaces of collaboration and intelligent cities sustain a particular form of information intelligence, in which information collection, assessment, and dissemination are based on the combined action of a group of people, a community, or a network of organisations. In collective strategic intelligence, data comes from a network of actors that disclose and share information. This multi-layer network of information intelligence produces a distributed system based on collective wisdom, collaboration, and interaction. The collection of information is distributed within the community, and the assessment of information is also distributed and based on agreed criteria.

Many vendors and platforms support this kind of intelligence. They use tools such as weblogs, wikis, social media, RSS, and portals, but above all visualisation tools. A common characteristic is that they provide intelligence by delimiting fields of observation, because information search, collection, and analysis are more effective if performed by thematic field.

Collective information intelligence needs three conditions to converge: (1) a network of actors who provide continuous information inputs; (2) an institutional agreement about the rules of cooperation in information collection, analysis, and disclosure; and (3) a virtual cooperation platform containing the depository of data and the e-tools for analysis and dissemination (Table 2.1). The virtual space mediates both global networking and end-user participation. Global information

Table 2.1 Layers of collective information intelligence

Urban space: communities and users	Institutional space: agreements and processes	Digital space: platforms and applications
• City or city-district • Group of users • Communities • Cluster of companies • Information networks • Associations • Other grouping of actors	• Identification of data sources • Information collection • Validation procedures • Information processing • Data model • Users' rights and privileges • Information disclosure rules	• Data sources: the Web, sensors, social media, open data • Business intelligence apps • Search algorithms • Semantic search • Data mining • Visualisation • Inference • Foresting

is customised to reflect the needs and perspective of individual users. The intelligence of the system is human, organisational and artificial, compilation of information from multiple sources, distributed information processing, and adaptation of information to individual profiles and needs.

Technology learning and absorption

Technology learning in intelligent cities is the capacity provided to organisations to acquire knowledge and skills from external sources. The concept refers to absorptive capacity (AC), which was first proposed by Cohen and Levinthal (1990) in line with the firm's ability to identify, assimilate, and exploit knowledge from external environment. AC includes three procedures: search, assimilation of knowledge identified, and commercial exploitation and use. In geographical terms, technology absorption is conditional on the region's human potential, research and development, and finance and governance institutions, linked with all aspects of the local innovation system and the way businesses operate in this system. From the perspective of the innovation system, the institutional dimension is dominant, as the capacity to assimilate technology is not only determined by internal factors within the organisation, but also by the external environment and the institutional arrangements that facilitate collaboration, the flow of knowledge therein, and the mechanisms for knowledge transfer involved (Cohen and Levinthal, 1990).

R&D exploitation and technology transfer are major mechanisms of technology learning, connecting technology-led companies with organisations performing R&D. The technology supply building blocks keep pace with the way companies innovate and create value. Until recently, innovation was driven by internal R&D of companies and was protected through patents, trademarks, and copyrights. However, as science and technology evolve at great speed and delve into ever more complex domains, innovation increasingly becomes dependent on external sources, dense networks of collaboration, the involvement of customers and end users, and technology transfer via multi-layer networks.

54 *What makes cities intelligent?*

Table 2.2 Layers of technology learning and absorption

Urban space: communities, districts, users	Institutional space: agreements and processes	Digital space: platforms and applications
• Communities of technology providers • Technology districts • University labs • Cluster of technology providers • Technology recipients • Other groupings of technology organisations	• Technology learning processes • Technology transfer / licensing agreements • R&D valorisation and commercialisation agreements • Spinoffs • Technology dissemination rules • Intelectual property rights agreements	• R&D valorisation and commercialisation platforms • Patent scanning platforms • Technology transfer spaces • Technology collaboration spaces • Virtual learning environments • Virtual class • Technology demonstration spaces

In intelligent cities various digital applications and tools can be used to support technology acquisition and learning, creating multi-layer collaboration networks among communities, institutions, and digital assistants (Table 2.2), including:

- *R&D databases:* The most important research outcomes, especially those that lead to the development of new products, new production processes, and new services, can be listed in such databases. Technology providers, from universities and other R&D institutions, submit information about research, expertise, and technology services offered, while technology users, from both the private and public sector, can access this information over the Web.
- *Virtual technology learning:* Technology training and learning are based on roadmaps that guide the development of skills and the usage of technology. Self-training modules can help users to accomplish any task related to technology use and innovation, such as new product development, spinoff company creation, IP management, management of quality, cost-reduction practices, and others.
- *Technology collaboration spaces:* Collaboration between technology providers and users, and between academia and businesses can be facilitated by digital spaces and online communication tools, such as technology-matching, interaction simulation, technology demonstration, protected discussion forums, and others. On such digital spaces, entrepreneurs and public organisations can post their technology needs, which are then communicated to technology providers in order to open dialogue and find technologies and solutions.

Acquisition of state-of-the-art technology is an area that is substantially enhanced by online platforms. It is true that global technology e-marketplaces have been in operation for some years now, such as Yet2com, offering intellectual property from multinational companies, universities, and research centres. In these platforms, technology offers are stored in databases, following agreement by the organisation holding the intellectual property rights (IPR). Users seeking solutions to their technology needs search the database and may then contact the technology provider online. The virtual technology marketplace is coupled with other online services related to technology transfer, such as consulting services for assessing a portfolio of intellectual property, evaluation of better solutions to a given problem or need, legal assistance through the deal-making process.

Such soft infrastructures facilitate the dissemination, marketing, and promotion of R&D and technology. They may be useful to universities and research organisations in making known their intellectual property and technological achievements. They also enable open innovation to be widely practiced in both directions of acquiring external technology and offering technologies to other organisations.

New knowledge creation and innovation

A prime objective for intelligent cities city strategies, particularly those focused on production clusters or sectors, is collaborative innovation, the co-operation of a group of actors in the development of a new product or service. Radjou (2004) described collaborative innovation as a network composed of four types of actors: (1) inventors – creative agents who conduct basic research and design new products and services resulting in the patenting of inventions; (2) transformers – multifunction production and marketing services that convert inputs from inventors into new products and sell them to their internal or external customers; (3) financiers – funding innovation for intellectual property; and (4) brokers – market makers who find and connect service providers with the network, buying or selling services, and enriching the capabilities of the network.

Virtual collaboration is a substantial component for this type of networking. Product developers can use Web applications, platforms, and e-tools to facilitate co-operation among spatially distributed organisations. In intelligent cities, a multi-layer network of actors, agreements, and digital tools can help distributed product development and innovation (Table 2.3).

Table 2.3 Layers of knowledge creation and collaborative innovation

Urban space: communities and users	Institutional space: agreements and processes	Digital space: platforms and applications
• Innovation communities • Living Labs • R&D performers • Global technology providers • Customers • Citizens and end users • Government institutions • Other grouping of innovation developers	• Co-creation, bringing together technology push and application pull • Exploration, engaging stakeholders and users at the earliest stage of co-creation • Experimentation and live scenarios with users • Evaluation of new ideas, innovative products	• Crowdsourcing platforms • Living Labs platforms • Collaborative innovation platforms • Ideation and idea capture tools • Customer immersion labs • Virtual prototyping • Digital focus groups • Virtual experimentation and testing tools

InnoCentive is a good example of such large-scale global collaboration for innovation. It is a virtual network linking companies, contract research organisations, university labs, and freelance scientists; it uses the Internet to connect research-driven companies (seekers of know-how) and top scientists (solvers) worldwide. "Seeker" companies anonymously announce scientific problems (as challenges) and the award that they intend to pay in the case of resolution. "Solver" scientists are registered scientists and labs that attempt to provide a solution to such posted problems. InnoCentive is the broker that facilitates the collaboration process, defines the intellectual property rights relating to collaboration, and guarantees payment of the award (InnoCentive, n.d.).

Virtual collaborative environments like Crowdspirit and IdeaStorm are examples of virtual spaces that help create Web-based product development communities. Crowdspirit operated until 2010 in a four-step process: innovators sent ideas and contributors fine-tune them and vote for the best one; a core team defined the product specifications with partners; the first prototype was tested and then further improved by the community; and users could purchase products from the CrowdSpirit partners and the community recommended products to new partners (Chanal and Caron-Fasan, 2010). IdeaStorm developed by Dell also operates in four steps: people post ideas about Dell products and services; the community votes on ideas; popular ideas float to the top via the selection by the crowd; and Dell respond with implementing ideas most relevant to the public (Killian, 2009). Both platforms materialise the concept of crowdsourcing, the act of taking a job traditionally performed by a designated agent and outsourcing it to a large group of people through an open call (Howe, 2006).

The challenge of setting up such virtual collaboration spaces for technology transfer is organisational and technological. This is the main lesson we learned after years of experimentation in this field. It is highly demanding to sustain a continuous flow of technology offers, avoid discontent from the terms of exploitation, and keep alive a vigorous network of technology providers and users. The virtual space assists technology exchange and builds on market relations or social networks of trust and cooperation. Virtuality *per se* is not sufficient for or capable of replacing real-world cooperation and exchange. Relations of exchange and trust remain the bottom-line of innovation. The virtual space adds content broadness, transparency, systematisation, and openness, while making innovators aware of external technology capabilities and ideas

Intelligent cities set the framework for developing both the organisational and digital aspects of such types of collaborative innovation. The reasons are well justified in the literature that analyses the geographic scales of technology co-operation and transfer, and the problems produced by the geographical, cultural, and linguistic distances between technology providers and users. Living Labs offer such collaborative environments, providing the local system of innovation with additional creativity and co-operation capacity. What happens in Living Labs is in fact crowdsourcing, with the population of the LL taking on the role of collective product designer and tester. The advantage of physical-virtual communities of innovation compared to just virtual ones is in the stronger social and institutional factors of innovation.

Information dissemination and marketplaces for global promotion

The announcement of new products and services, and the promotion and delivery of products and services can be considered the last mile of innovation. For intelligent cities, this field is particularly important, and most strategies develop applications and solutions for building local market identity, local market promotion, virtual marketplaces, and e-services provision (e-government). Virtual environments play an important role in this last mile. E-markets were among the earliest applications of digital technologies to business activities.

City-based virtual marketplaces, e-malls for businesses, and online marketing services created within intelligent cities differ substantially from company portals and privately owned e-stores and e-markets. Their distinctive characteristic is collectiveness and openness. They do not market products and services from a single organisation, but rather promote those of the city, the cluster, or the community. They create public digital marketplaces and digital commons in which all interested companies of a community can find a place to 'locate' and offer products and services. They do not operate for the profit of a particular organisation, but rather promote the interest of the community or city as a whole. They create multi-layer networks and synergies among communities of vendors that promote products and services collaboratively (Table 2.4).

Many platforms of this type are available: virtual tours of the city, presenting monuments, arts, and crafts, together with stores and products with the use of digital maps and panoramic photos; virtual marketplaces where companies can place their e-shop with information on products and services, present product offers and carry out e-commerce transactions; and e-government shops, with services from the public administration.

Table 2.4 Layers of information dissemination and product promotion

Urban space: communities and users	Institutional space: agreements and processes	Digital space: platforms and applications
• Commercial communities • Local vendor associations • Central city marketplaces • Peripheral marketplaces • End user / consumer networks • Other trade associations • Groups of citizens	• Information dissemination • Promotion of products and services • Promotion rules • Marketing plans • Marketing alliances • Global supply chains • Innovation diplomacy • Dispute resolution	• E-commerce platforms and applications • Online marketing tools • Social media marketing • Viral marketing • Virtual marketplaces • Analytics tools • City-branding apps

6. Intelligent city strategies: innovation by a mix of knowledge functions

Developing intelligent cities and augmented innovation environments, every district of a city – be it a productive cluster, a technology district, the central city area or other district – can improve its innovation capabilities through the use of broadband networks and online services. The objective is not broadband *per se*, but rather the opening up of the cluster or the district to extended collaboration and user participation. Broadband services and virtual environments are the medium for making systems of innovation more open and user responsive.

In intelligent cities, knowledge operations take place in three-layer systems, with layer 1 offering resources of the agglomeration, innovative clusters and companies, communities of organisations and users; layer 2 defining institutional agreements and processes information mastering, technology transfer, and innovationl and layer 3 offering virtual collaborative spaces and tools, such as portals, agents, content management systems, Web 2.0 platforms, and marketplaces enabling large-scale collaboration and user participation (Tables 2.1, 2.2, 2.3, and 2.4).

By deploying such multi-layer knowledge functions and intelligent environments, communities and cities create knowledge endowments and advantages. Within these environments, each company can build its specific physical-virtual innovation ecosystem, combining its internal knowledge capabilities with those of other companies and research organisations. In addition, the same endowments enhance distributed knowledge and innovation in every cluster and district of the city. However, this cannot be done via digital spaces alone. The distinctive attribute of intelligent cities compared to digital cities and cyberspaces is integration and networking across the digital, social, and physical spaces of cities.

References

Bathelt, H., Malmberg, A. and Maskell, P. (2004). Clusters and knowledge: local buzz, global pipelines, and the process of knowledge creation. *Progress in Human Geography*, Vol. 28, No. 1, 31–56.

Batty, M. (1990). Intelligent cities: Using information networks to gain competitive advantage. *Environment and Planning B: Planning and Design*, Vol. 17, No. 3, 247–256.

Belissent, J. (2010). *Getting clever about smart cities: New opportunities require new business models*. Forrester for Ventor Strategy. Available at http://goo.gl/fLKUen.

Bounfour, A. and Edvinsson, L. (eds) (2005). *Intellectual capital for communities: Nations, regions, and cities*. Oxford, UK: Elsevier, Butterworth Heinemann.

Bunnell, T. (2002). Multimedia Utopia? A geographical critique of high-tech development in Malaysia's Multimedia Super Corridor. *Antipode*, Vol. 34, No. 2, 265–295.

BusinessWeek (2007). Inside innovation – special report. *Business Week August 10, 2007*. Retrieved 2 January 2014, from www.businessweek.com/innovate/di_special/20070830insideinnov.htm.

Chanal, V. and Caron-Fasan, M. L. (2010). The difficulties involved in developing business models open to innovation communities: The case of a crowdsourcing platform. *M@n@gement*, Vol. 13, No. 4, 318–340.

City of Stockholm. (2006). Vision 2030. A world-class Stockholm. Retrieved 2 January 2014, from http://goo.gl/pQK2tF.

Cohen, W. and Levinthal, L. (1990). Absorptive capacity: A new perspective on learning and innovation. *Administrative Science Quarterly*, No. 35, No. 1, 128–152.

Economist Intelligence Unit (2004). Scattering the seeds of invention: The globalization of research and development. Retrieved 2 January 2014, from http://graphics.eiu.com/files/ad_pdfs/RnD_GLOBILISATION_WHITEPAPER.pdf.

Edquist, C. (ed.) (1997). *Systems of innovation: Technologies, institutions and organisations.* London, UK: Frances Pinter.
Edvinsson, L. (2006). Aspects on the city as a knowledge tool. *Journal of Knowledge Management,* Vol. 10, No. 5, 6–13.
Edvinsson, L. and Malone, M. S. (1997). *Intellectual capital: Realizing your company's true value by finding its hidden brainpower.* New York, NY: HarperBusiness.
Enterweb (2006). Competitive intelligence and strategic intelligence. Retrieved 2 January 2014, from www.enterweb.org/strategy.htm.
Ernst, D. (2006). *Innovation offshoring: Asia's emerging role in global innovation networks.* East-West Center Special Reports, No. 10, East-West Center. Retrieved 2 January 2014, from www.eastwestcenter.org/fileadmin/stored/pdfs/SR010.pdf.
Florida, R. (2002). *The rise of the creative class and how it's transforming work: Leisure, community and everyday life.* New York, NY: Basic Books.
Florida, R. (2005). *Cities and the creative class.* New York and London: Routledge.
Florida, R. (2010). Building the creative community. In J. Brown-Saracino (ed.) *The gentrification debates: A reader* (pp. 345–360). New York, NY: Routledge.
Forum Virium (n.d.). Members and co-operation partners. Retrieved 2 January 2014, from www.forumvirium.fi/en/introduction.
Gertler, M. and Wolfe, D. (2005). Spaces of knowledge flows: Clusters in a global context. *Dynamics of Industry and Innovation: Organizations, Networks and Systems.* Copenhagen, Denmark: DRUID Tenth Anniversary Summer Conference.
Giddens, A. (1990). *The consequences of modernity.* Stanford, CA: Stanford University Press.
Graham, S. (ed.) (2003). *The cybercities reader.* London, UK: Routledge.
Graham, S. and Marvin, S. (1996). *Telecommunications and the city: Electronic space, urban places.* London, UK: Routledge.
Hollanders, H., Rivera Léon, L. and Roman, L. (2012). *Regional innovation scoreboard 2012.* Brussels, Belgium: European Commission.
Hollanders, H. and Es-Sadki, N. (2013). *Innovation union scoreboard 2013.* Brussels, Belgium: European Commission.
Horan, T. (2000). *Digital places: Building our city of bits.* Washington, DC: ULI – the Urban Land Institute.
Howe, H. (2006). The rise of crowdsourcing. *Wired Magazine,* Issue 14.06, 1–5.
ICF (2006). Intelligent Community of the Year, 2006, Taipei, Taiwan. Retrieved 2 January 2014, from www.intelligentcommunity.org/index.php?submenu=Awards&src=gendocs&ref=ICF_Awards&category=Events&link=ICF_Awards.
ICF (2009). Intelligent Community of the Year, 2009, Stockholm, Sweden. Retrieved 2 January 2014, from www.intelligentcommunity.org/index.php?submenu=Awards&src=gendocs&ref=ICF_Awards&category=Events&link=ICF_Awards.
IDA (2007). *Innovation. Integration. Internationalisation – Singapore: An intelligent nation, a global city, powered by infocomm.* Singapore iN2015 Steering Committee.
InnoCentive (n.d.). *InnoCentive whitepaper: Adding value to stage-gate through the use of challenges.* Retrieved 2 January 2014, from http://pages.innocentive.com/whitepaper-stagegate.html.
Ishida, T. and Isbister K. (eds) (2000). *Digital cities: Technologies, experiences, and future perspectives.* Berlin, Germany: Springer-Verlag.
Jaruzelski, B., Dehoff K., and Bordia, R. (2006). Smart spenders: Global Innovation 1000. *Strategy and Business Magazine,* Winter, No. 45. Retrieved 2 January 2014, from www.strategy-business.com/article/06405?pg=all.

60 What makes cities intelligent?

Jaruzelki, B., Loeher, G. and Holman, R. (2013). Global Innovation 1000: Navigating the digital future. *Strategy + Business*, No. 73, 1–33.

Johnson, S. (2004). *Emergence: The connected lives of ants, brains, cities, and software*. New York, NY: Scribner.

Keeble, D., Lawson C., Moore, B. and Wilkinson, F. (1998). Collective learning processes, networking and institutional thickness in the Cambridge region. *Regional Studies*, Vol. 33, No. 4, 319–332.

Killian, V. (2009). IdeaStorm overview. Retrieved, 2 January 2014, from www.slideshare.net/Dell/ideastorm-overview.

Komninos, N. (2004). Regional intelligence: Distributed localised information systems for innovation and development. *International Journal of Technology Management*, Vol. 28, Nos. 3/4/5/6.

Komninos, N. (2008). *Intelligent cities and globalisation of innovation networks*. London and New York: Routledge.

Kuhlmann, S., Boekholt, P., Georghiou, L., Gyu, K., Heraud, J., Laredo, P., Lemola, T., Loveridge, D., Luukkonen, T., Polt, W., Rip, A. Sanz-Menendez, L. and Smits, R. (1999). *Improving distributed intelligence in complex innovation systems*. Final Report, TSER project, Fraunhofer Institute, Systems and Innovation Research, Karlsruhe.

Lévy, P. (1997). *Collective intelligence: Mankind's emerging world in cyberspace*. Cambridge, MA: Perseus Books.

Malmberg, A. and Maskell, P. (2002). The elusive concept of localization economies: Towards a knowledge-based theory of spatial clustering. *Environment & Planning A*, Vol. 34, No. 3, 429–49.

Mitchell, W. (2007). Intelligent cities. *E-Journal on the Knowledge Society*, UOC Papers. Retrieved 2 January 2014, from www.uoc.edu/uocpapers/5/dt/eng/mitchell.html.

Morgan, K. (2004). The exaggerated death of geography: Localised learning, innovation and uneven development. *Journal of Economic Geography*, Vol. 4, No. 1, 3–21.

Nelson, R. and Winters, S. (1982). *An evolutionary theory of economic change*. Cambridge, MA: Harvard University Press.

Noubel, J. F. (2006). *Collective intelligence: The invisible revolution*. Retrieved 2 January 2014, from http://goo.gl/c4RpYQ.

Owen-Smith, J. and Powell, W. W. (2004). Knowledge networks as channels and conduits: The effects of spillovers in the Boston biotechnology community. *Organisation Science*, Vol. 15, No. 1, 5–21.

Pole T.E.S (n.d.). *Join the cluster*. Retrieved, 2 January 2014, from www.pole-tes.com/web/portal/website/content/page/index.do?websiteId=2&navigableId=410.

Radjou, N. (2004). *Innovation networks: A new market structure will revitalise invention-to-innovation cycles*. Retrieved 2 January 2014, from http://goo.gl/oNdqfX.

Smart Communities. (2002). *Guide for creating a smart community*. Available at http://198.103.246.211/documents/SC-Guide.pdf.

Smart Communities (2008). *The concept of smart communities*. Retrieved 2 January 2014 from www.smartcommunities.org/concept.php.

Uhlmann, R. (2008). Global integration of regional clusters. *IRE conference*, Rennes June 2008.

United Nations (2005). *UNCTAD survey on the internationalization of R&D*. Retrieved 2 January 2014, from www.unctad.org/en/docs/webiteiia200512_en.pdf.

Van den Besselaar, P. and Koizumi, S. (2005). *Digital cities III. Information technologies for social capital: Cross-cultural perspectives*. Amsterdam and Berlin: Springer-Verlag.

3 Smart cities, smart environments, and big data

Innovation ecosystems of embedded spatial intelligence

1. Smart environments and embedded spatial intelligence

Intelligent cities rely on collaboration networks among human communities, innovation ecosystems, digital infrastructure, and e-services, which enable higher problem-solving and resource efficient practices. This urban paradigm is also characterised by continuous transformation, which is fuelled by changes in innovation ecosystems, broadband networks, and information technologies.

Cities change during periods of growth and periods of decline. In times of growth, changes are introduced by adding and expanding industrial zones, malls, universities, ports, central business districts, cultural amenities, housing districts, and infrastructure; in times of recession, by restructuring or closing manufacturing zones, shipbuilding sites, railway stations, wharfs, and degenerated districts.

In the paradigm of intelligent cities, changes are made primarily by renewal and regeneration, by developing and adopting more innovative methods of operation, using less energy and water, producing less waste in an intangible economy, becoming more open and efficient to global competition, and by arbitraging solutions globally. All districts of cities (central business district, housing, commerce, industry, education, and recreation), infrastructure, and utilities (transport, energy, buildings, water, and waste) benefit from the combined deployment of innovation and information technology. However, the objectives of competitiveness and sustainability – CO_2 reduction, low environmental footprint, energy savings, sustainable transport – are achieved because citizens, organisations, and governments develop innovative behaviour through the use of technology.

This chapter explores changes which are currently being introduced by Future Internet research and experimentation, outlining how cities are affected by emerging Internet technologies, smart environments, and user-driven innovation. The Internet of Things (IoT), networks of sensors and smart devices, embedded systems, the Semantic Web, the Internet of users and people, cloud computing, in two words the 'Future Internet,' mark a technological turn that produces a new type of spatial intelligence of cities, namely an embedded spatial intelligence. This form of intelligence is advancing the information and knowledge capabilities of cities which were previously just based on Web technologies (Web 2.0, social media, crowdsourcing platforms) and opens up a new cycle of innovation and e-services in cities.

Collective intelligence and social media have been major drivers of the spatial intelligence of cities. They offered the appropriate technology layer for organising the involvement of citizens in the creation and use of information on collaboration spaces, crowdsourcing platforms, mash-ups, and other means of online participation. Now, the turn towards smart environments and embedded systems offers a new type of spatial intelligence of cities – an embedded spatial intelligence – relying on sensors, real-time information, and gigabit data generated along the functioning of cities.

The concept of spatial intelligence of cities refers to the ability of a community to use its human capital, innovation institutions, physical space, and smart infrastructure to create environments that more efficiently address the challenges of competitiveness, sustainability, and inclusion (Deakin, 2011; Komninos, 2011). This concept allows the terms 'intelligent city' and 'smart city' to be unified into a common field of research focusing on the underlying cognitive processes that increase the problem-solving capability of communities and cities.

Embedded spatial intelligence has a direct impact on the services that cities offer to citizens and on the optimisation of urban infrastructure networks. It bring us closer to the way in which William Mitchell (2007) has described the intelligence of cities as an effective combination of digital telecommunication networks, ubiquitously embedded intelligence, and software for knowledge and cognitive competence. Future Internet technologies with instrumentation and interconnection of mobile devices and sensors can collect and analyse urban data in real-time, improve the ability to forecast and manage urban flows, and thus push city intelligence forward (Chen-Ritzo et al., 2009). In this context, new research questions have arisen concerning: (1) the technology drivers of embedded spatial intelligence, (2) the new e-services that can be offered in cities, and (3) the governance of innovation ecosystems based on smart environments embedded into the urban space.

The chapter discusses these questions and outlines the impact of Future Internet technologies on core knowledge functions of intelligent cities. It is based on a combination of literature about Future Internet research, cases studies on smart city projects and experimental facilities in smart cities, foresight exercises about the future of cities, and hype cycles of smart city technologies. The reference corpus that we have taken into account includes a variety of sources and documents:

- EU FP7 research on Future Internet technologies, Future Media Internet, Future Media Networks, and Future Internet experimental facilities; and research on smart cities in the context of the Competitiveness and Innovation Framework Programme (CIP) and the Strategic Energy Technology Plan (SET-Plan).
- OECD reports and governmental papers on the future of the Internet economy outlining strategic policy directions.

- Large corporate research programmes in the field of intelligent and smart cities and white papers by large consulting groups on smart city solutions.
- Gartner's Hype Cycles on emerging technologies and smart city technologies, which illustrate societal expectations and innovative technologies.
- Foresight exercises about the future of cities presented by academic institutions, the Institute for the Future (IFTF), and related academic literature.

This corpus can help in describing how intelligent cities are changing by the actual wave of Internet technologies, and how their internal mechanisms of information, innovation, and knowledge creation are affected by smart systems, smart-object-centred services, the Semantic Web, and cloud-based solutions.

2. Milestones towards embedded spatial intelligence of cities

We have argued that the paradigm of intelligent cities appeared as a fundamental component of the global knowledge economy and model for organising people-driven innovation and city-based global innovation hubs. By injecting information technologies and innovation capabilities into the ecosystems of cities, these become more open, innovative, efficient, and manageable. City infrastructure and utilities also benefit from the deployment of broadband networks because of lower operating costs, real-time alert and response, and better prediction of citizen demand. The entire urban system of products, services, and infrastructure becomes more sensitive to changing market conditions and needs, and adopts more intelligent ways of operation.

Since 2009, within this paradigm of urban development and planning, a new round of technologies has appeared, related to smart systems, embedded devices, sensor networks, and real-world user interfaces. These technologies. together with mobile smart devices, have become enablers of new e-services in areas such as transport, environment, energy, business, and government. Large companies in the ICT sector, such as IBM, CISCO, Microsoft, and Accenture, are involved to a considerable degree in and are contributing to shaping this new smart city agenda. EU research in the context of the FP7 and CIP is also stimulating a wider uptake of innovative ICT-based services for smart cities, linking smart city solutions with user-driven innovation and Future Internet research. Quite new fields of experimentation have opened up, redefining the way innovation ecosystems and smart environments are being combined to address urban challenges.

A major milestone in this turn towards an embedded intelligence of cities was the IBM initiative "Smarter Planet – Smarter Cities (SP-SC)," launched in 2009. Proposed as a central strategy for a sustainable future, this initiative was intended to stimulate economic growth and quality of life in cities and metropolitan areas with the activation of new technology systems and infrastructure. The SP-SC initiative sees the city as an agglomeration of ecosystems (a system of systems) and as a platform, which – more than states, provinces or even nations – can make twenty-first-century life more productive, efficient, and vibrant. The IBM model for making

64 *What makes cities intelligent?*

cities more efficient and sustainable is described as a combination of connectivity, instrumentation, and intelligence (IBM Institute for Business Value, 2009):

- Connectivity offers communication capability among a sea of networked things, buildings, cars, roadways, pipelines, appliances, infrastructure, and people.
- Instrumentation offers real-time information from all city sub-systems captured by smart meters, sensors, and embedded devices.
- Intelligence comes from algorithms, analytics, and visualisation that turn data into informed decisions and actions.

Cities – interconnected and instrumented with smart technologies – can offer real-time information, monitoring of operations, and direct response to the needs of citizens and organisations. These three components together pave the way for a more sustainable world. IBM's initiative is focusing on multiple areas of city life, and it has been estimated that using this type of embedded intelligence, urban systems can reduce traffic by 20 percent, save energy by 15 percent, lower healthcare cost by 90 percent, lower public safety costs, offer better education with fewer resources, and deliver better government services to citizens. The approach is comprehensive, as city challenges are not addressed in terms of technology only, but, instead, management practices and institutional arrangements are also taken into consideration along with technology solutions and citizen engagement.

In 2009, CISCO also launched the global Intelligent Urbanisation initiative from the city of Bangalore, India, and signed an MoU with the local government to develop a roadmap for an intelligent and sustainable Bangalore. Intelligent Urbanisation was designed to help cities around the world by using broadband networks as a utility for integrated city management, better quality of life for citizens, and economic development. Later, the company moved to the "Smart + Connected Communities" (S+CC) initiative to help communities transform themselves and realise sustainable economic growth, resource management, and enhanced quality of life. The broadband network was seen as a fourth utility and as a platform to connect everything. Areas of implementation include transportation, urban utilities, real estate, safety and security, and government. CISCO also endorsed the IDC concept of 'Intelligent X' as a technology ecosystem which integrates smart devices (involving machine-to-machine (M2M) and telemetry capabilities), high-speed ubiquitous communications networks, and intelligent software and services that can process, consolidate, and analyse data in order to support industry-specific business processes. At the core of Intelligent X solutions are three key enablers: (1) increased computational power available through high-performance chipsets and hardware and high-performance networks, (2) improved maturity in business intelligence and analytics, and (3) the introduction of new delivery models based on cloud computing (Carter et al., 2011).

Accenture, a global management consulting and technology services provider, presented a similar smart city concept focusing on city infrastructure and utilities. The company argued that rapid urbanisation and rising population place enormous pressures on ageing city infrastructure for gas and electricity, water supply, waste management, and transportation. In parallel, the mobility of populations and businesses, as the world is now more open, requires that cities remain globally attractive. Cities increasingly compete in four different arenas: for businesses that generate wealth; for public and private investments; for residents – mainly well-educated, entrepreneurial people; and for visitors. Intelligent infrastructure is the technological response to these challenges: "The intelligent infrastructure is both analogue and digital. That is, in addition to the physical infrastructure – roads, buildings, rail, and power and utility grids – an information and communications technology infrastructure serves as the basis for most of the monitoring and optimisation capabilities of an Intelligent City, and for the interaction between citizens and service providers" (Accenture, 2011, p. 14).

From this perspective, key characteristic of an Intelligent City are the delivery of services using advanced technologies, such as M2M communication, active sensors and RFID, smart grids for more efficient energy production and delivery, intelligent software and analytics, and broadband communications that serve as a core network for all related city administration, citizens, and businesses. The technology base of intelligent city infrastructure is accompanied by a set of other key enablers, such as strategy, management and governance, appropriate regulatory frameworks, financial incentives, and partnerships among the private and public sectors. For Accenture, the most important enabler for intelligent cities is an open, interoperable, and scalable platform that provides intelligent infrastructure-as-a-service for optimal resource management. Among the fundamental characteristics of this platform are the existence of an environment for partnering and cooperation, fully automated service via a central hub, efficient data exchange, flexibility for service and product combination, modular architecture, scalability, and Internet-based service; in effect, all the core features of cloud computing. The proposed platform makes the delivery of services feasible in seven key domains of cities: transportation, health and safety, waste management, education and culture, public administration, office and residential uses, and nature resource management. As technologies and solutions evolve, new components can be replaced and integrated on demand.

The European Commission has also been very active in this field, by setting up several funding lines for research and experimentation on smart cities in the context of Future Internet research, the Competitiveness and Innovation Programme (CIP), and the Strategic Energy Technology Plan (SET-Plan).

FP7-ICT projects focused on smart cities were primarily part of the *Future Internet Research and Experimental* (FIRE) action line. The most well known is the Smart Santander test bed facility currently composed of a large number of active and passive sensors deployed both at static locations (streetlights, facades, bus stops) and onboard mobile vehicles (buses, taxis). FIREBALL was another project in the FIRE action line that established a coordination mechanism among a network of cities across Europe engaging in long-term collaboration for user-driven open innovation to explore the opportunities of Future Internet in smart cities. FIREBALL's objectives were to bring together three European communities, those of Future Internet research, Living Labs, and smart cities, and to define modes of collaboration and alliance (Schaffers et al., 2012). Smart cities were considered to be key demand-side drivers of Future Internet innovation.

66 *What makes cities intelligent?*

In the context of the SET-Plan and SETIS (the SET Information System), the Directorate General of Energy introduced the "European Initiative on Smart Cities" to demonstrate the feasibility of implementing advanced energy and climate technologies at a local level. Through the Smart Cities Stakeholders Platform, the initiative fosters the dissemination of the most efficient models and strategies for a low-carbon and low-emissions future, systemic approaches and organisational innovations related to energy efficiency, and smart management of supply and demand (Smart Cities and Communities, n.d.). The platform supports cities and regions in ambitious and pioneering projects and cooperative schemes, such as an 80 percent reduction in greenhouse gas emissions through green energy by 2050. The Strategic Implementation Plan proposed by the European Innovation Partnership (EIP) on Smart Cities and Communities concentrates on three vertical areas: (1) sustainable urban mobility, alternative energies, public transport, efficient logistics, and planning; (2) sustainable districts and the built environment, improving the energy efficiency of buildings and districts, increasing the share of renewable energy sources used and the liveability of communities; and (3) integrated infrastructures and processes across energy, ICT, and transport, connecting infrastructure assets to improve the efficiency and sustainability of cities (EIP, 2013).

The Competitiveness and Innovation Programme (CIP) also has an action line for "Open innovation for future Internet-enabled services in smart cities", introducing three co-related perspectives: user-driven open innovation; innovative Internet-based services; and cross-border networks of smart cities. In the CIP perspective, smart cities offer a field for bridging the gap between Future Internet technologies and innovative e-services stemming from user-driven innovation. Technologies such as mobile and location-based services, broadband and high-speed networks, the Internet of Things, sensor networks and RFID, advanced communication protocols and standards, security and privacy management systems, and multimodal interfaces and 3D technologies are expected to create a wave of new services in cities related to smart living, the green digital agenda, and improved citizen involvement. In the first round of experimentation, seven smart city projects were funded by the CIP-ICT-PSP (Policy Support Program) – Epic, Life 2.0, Open Cities, People, Peripheria, Smart IP, and Smart Islands – with pilots in many cities in Europe. These pilot projects focused on accelerating the uptake of smart technologies in cities, creating user-driven innovation ecosystems, improving the capacities of small companies, and strengthening the role of the user and the citizen. The emphasis was on fostering innovation in services under realistic conditions, taking-up completed R&D work, extending tested prototypes, and combining partial solutions for an innovative outcome. Priority technology areas were those of real-time interaction, open-trusted service platforms, sensors and RFID, multimodal user interfaces, simulation, and location-based technologies and services. Priority domains for application were those of smart education, smart energy, e-participation, e-government, smart retail, well-being, and transportation (Pietrantonio, 2010). The CIP initiative for smart cities now continues under the Horizon 2020 programme.

The above initiatives show that both in large multinational companies and research institutions, the recent turn towards – and interest in – smart cities has been driven by two objectives. On the one hand, it is the use of new Internet technologies, such as sensor networks, smart devices, RFID, the Semantic Web and the Internet of Things, cloud computing for offering new e-services to citizens, and optimising the functioning of cities. On the other hand, it is the pursuit of sustainability, as cities search for a more inclusive and sustainable future, transforming themselves into green cities with less energy consumption and fewer CO_2 emissions.

3. Internet of Things, sensor networks, and smart cities

The social, economic, and technological perspectives of new Internet technologies and their potential impact on cities and spatial ecosystems were described in two foresight reports prepared by the Institute for the Future (FTF). The report entitled *Future Knowledge Ecosystems* identified 14 trends that will broadly set the context for technology-based cities and regions over the next five to 20 years (Townsend et al., 2009). Changes are described in three domains: economy and society, science and technology, and models and location sites for R&D. In each domain, weak signals and early indications of upcoming trends were identified, as well as the expected impact on technology-led urban spaces. In science and technology, most important trends were: (1) the spread of ubiquitous computing, which is expected to create massive streams of data, while simultaneously providing new tools for scientific collaboration in the lab; and (2) the shift from artificial intelligence to hybrid sensemaking and hybrid identities, which combine inputs from social networks and more limited forms of machine intelligence.

The second report entitled *A Planet of Civic Laboratories. The Future of Cities, Information and Inclusion* was a ten-year forecast covering the period up to 2020 that focused on the intersection between urbanisation and digitalisation and the massive stream of data generated within cities by IoT solutions, which is expected to turn every city into a unique civic laboratory, a place where innovations driven by citizens are born to meet local needs (Townsend et al., 2011). In both foresight reports, the technologies that mattered most for smart cities were those of sensors and smart devices, open data, and cloud computing.

The same group of technologies was also pointed out as main emerging technologies in Gartner Inc.'s future estimations. Gartner's analysts reviewed more than 1,800 technologies and highlighted a series of technologies relating to smart cities, such as cloud computing, sensor networks, consumer-generated media, location-aware applications, and predictive analytics. In this type of analysis, technologies are ranked at different stages of maturity on a 'Hype Cycle' composed of five stages representing the progression of technology from birth to mainstream use. The five Hype Cycles are:

1 'Technology Trigger' or technology breakthrough is the product launch stage of R&D, startup companies, the first round of venture capital, and the first generation of products;
2 'Peak of Inflated Expectations' is the phase of over-enthusiasm and eventually unrealistic expectations when mass media hype begins and activity moves beyond early adopters;

68 *What makes cities intelligent?*

3 'Trough of Disillusionment' is the stage of supplier consolidation and failures, the second and third round of venture capital, less than 5 percent adoption; press interest reduces because technologies fail to meet expectations and quickly become unfashionable;
4 'Slope of Enlightenment' is about experimentation and practical applications of the technology, second-generation products, methodologies and best practices standardisation, as well as third-generation products; and
5 'Plateau of Productivity' is the stage in which the benefits of technologies become widely demonstrated and accepted, there is high growth adoption, and 20–30 percent of the potential market has adopted the innovation. A graphic representation of maturity and adoption of technologies shows how they are relevant to solving real problems and opening opportunities.

According to technology hype cycles published by Gartner from 2009 to 2013, the Internet of Things (IoT) is among the most important component of the current technology shift in smart cities, combining active sensors and RFID for robust and cost-effective identification of many different objects in terms of functionality, technology, and application fields in cities. Sensor networks in cities can gather an enormous amount of information from connected smart objects and grids over utility networks. Real-time response to this data and prediction of behaviour patterns become possible with high-capacity processing and computing power. Also, the Web is progressing away from PCs, and user interfaces are becoming embedded into the physical space of cities. A new group of applications, such as location-aware applications, near-field communication, speech recognition, Internet micro-payment systems, and mobile application stores, which are close to mainstream market adoption, are expected to offer a wide range of new e-services via embedded systems. Augmented reality is also becoming a hot topic, enabled by smart phones and eyeglasses, and is creating next-generation location-aware information and services projected over the built space of cities (Gartner, 2010; Gartner, 2012a; Gartner, 2012b).

Table 3.1 A selection of smart city technologies based on Gartner's hype cycles

Technology trigger	Peak of inflated expectations	Trough of disillusionment	Slope of enlightenment	Plateau of productivity
• Cloud security integration • Information semantic services • Wi-Fi positioning systems • Smart government frameworks	• Internet of Things • Real-time infrastructure • Big-data management for government • Augmented reality • Information stewardship applications	• Cloud computing • Virtual assistants • Mesh networks • Consumer-generated media • Machine-to-machine communication • Advanced metering	• SaaS • Cloud advertisement • Security as a Service • Visualisation • Speech recognition • Idea management	• Location-aware technology • Predictive analytics

Data source: Gartner, 2012a; and Gartner, 2012b

The IoT is growing exponentially. Thomas Frey (2012) mentions an estimate from GSMA (Global System for Mobile Communications (GSM) Association) that 24 billion devices will be connected by 2020, while CISCO and Ericsson project the number to be 50 billion. In 2009, the number of connected devices exceeded the number of people on the planet; the number of connected devices per person reached 1.84 in 2010 and is expected to reach 3.47 by 2015, and 6.58 in 2020. This new infrastructure of IoT and sensors in cities paves the way for embedded spatial intelligence, further advancing the capabilities created by Web 2.0, social media, and crowdsourcing. A real-time spatial intelligence – based on automated information processing, M2M communication, and response – becomes available on smart phones and mobile devices. For this type of embedded spatial intelligence, an important issue is the development of urban IoT platforms over city clusters or districts, offering a common framework for ambient sensor networks such as intelligent information infrastructure and universal ubiquitous sensor network architectures (Hernández-Muñoz et al., 2011).

These technologies can overcome the fragmented market of smart city applications and provide generic solutions for cities. Examples of generic architectures include networked RFID tags (passive and active tags, mobile devices), sensor networks (multimodal sensors and actuators, built-in intelligent agents), and connected objects, such as distributed intelligent systems, intelligent objects, and biometrics (Lemke, 2010).

While the future uses of IoT technologies that will bridge the physical and virtual worlds are still largely a matter for speculation, there are estimations that they will bring significant economic benefits. OECD policy guidance encourages research in this field, investments in business R&D, technological neutrality, open global standards, and the harmonisation of frequency bands (OECD, 2008). There are, however, significant technological barriers to overcome. Sensor communication requires the cooperation of all devices over all communication technologies and different networks, including GSM and wireless local area networks (WLAN). However, Hildenbrand (2011) considers that this is not feasible with current networks, devices, and communication technologies, as technology cannot convert all devices operating on a certain communication technology or protocol. There is a need for a new technology that virtually overlays all others and allows communication between the different protocols.

4. Semantic Web, future media, and smart cities

Data-driven decisions, techniques for forecasting, and predictive analytics are a follow-up to the IoT and data generated by sensor networks. What is needed, however, is semantic M2M communication, as gigabit data generated by the functioning of cities can be processed and analysed only by machines. Use of ontologies and other semantic technologies opens up a new domain for smart city applications, as they can combine information from multiple sources and inform users when information matches their interests.

Semantic meaning provided by ontologies, like the Good-Relations annotator tool for creating rich RDF meta-data, can describe products and services more accurately. The introduction of HTML5 was also an important step. The cloud will offer additional opportunities for linked data, as any object can be related to other objects contained in the cloud. The Semantic Web is expected to break down barriers, merging data from different sources and presenting data in ways one has never thought of before. Social media collaboration and collective intelligence will be able to reach higher levels of efficiency and information accuracy.

Future media research and technologies are also expected to offer a series of solutions that might work in parallel with the Internet of Things and embedded systems, providing new opportunities for content management. Media Internet technologies at the crossroads of digital multimedia content and Internet technologies encompass media being delivered through Internet networking technologies and media being generated, consumed, shared, and experienced on the Web. Technologies enabled by the functionalities of the Future Media Internet, such as content and context fusion, immersive multi-sensory environments, location-based content dependent on user location and context, augmented reality applications, open and federated platforms for content storage and distribution, are expected to provide the foundations for new e-services within the ecosystems of cities (European Commission, 2010a; European Commission, 2010b).

The OVUM (2011) report on smart cities considers cloud computing and the IoT as fundamental layers of ubiquitous connectivity on which stands a layer of open public data and advanced analytics for fast-based decisions. Governments and many public agencies have started offering open data, providing access to datasets and stimulating the creation of applications for information retrieval and decision-making. Such data that come from various sources – the public administration, sensors, citizens, and businesses – create opportunities for advanced analytics, visualisation, and intelligence and enable users to detect patterns, generate alerts, and visualise information, and eventually predict trends.

Use cases and applications are built on this new technology layer. MIT's Serendipity project, for instance, facilitates the use of semantic sensing. Developed by the Human Dynamics Group at the Media Lab in order to advance corporate productivity and innovation, the goal is to match interests and skills among a community of workers. A hypothetical-use case is when persons meet accidentally in a public space, their smartphones communicate and if profiles of common interests and expertise are traced, then alerts are exchanged and people might stop and talk instead of walking by each other (Shepard, 2011).

5. Cloud computing and smart cities

Cloud computing offers advantages which are complementary to the Internet of Things. It is based on several technological and managerial advances related to high-speed networks, virtualisation, and standardisation of platforms and applications. However, "cloud computing is a new way of delivering computing resources, not a new technology," providing computer services through the Internet and new business models of outsourcing (Prasanth, 2012, p. 25). The cloud is another way to think of the Internet itself. People can access applications and software development tools, and store files remotely from a computer via the Internet. The cloud is Google's Gmail, Google Docs, and Dropbox. In these type of platforms, data are not stored on the user's own PC, but rather on servers and at massive data centres of the hosting company. In the case of iPhone applications, which million of users download, the platform and development tools to build these applications are also cloud based.

The US National Institute for Standards and Technology (NIST) gives a clear description of cloud computing as being composed of five essential characteristics – on-demand self service, ubiquitous network access, metered use, elasticity, and resource pooling; three service models – Software as a Service (SaaS), Platform as a Service (PaaS), and Infrastructure as a Service (IaaS); and four deployment modes of cloud – private, community, public, and hybrid (Mell and Grance, 2011).

Foresight estimations about developments in cloud computing were given by the Gartner Hype Cycle for Cloud Computing, which positioned 38 technologies from this field at different stages of the Hype Cycle (Fenn, 2010). Expectations are very high. Most technologies, however, were at the 'Technology Trigger' stage, and cloud computing overall was at the 'Peak of Expectations' stage. A few solutions were at the 'Experimentation' stage, and none were at the stage of demonstrated results. The timeframe for all solutions ranges from two to ten years, and only virtualisation and software-as-a-service are closer to mainstream adoption.

The impact of cloud computing on smart cities has been discussed in forecast studies for 2020 mentioned (Townsend et al., 2009; Townsend et al., 2011). While in the short term, cloud computing will be delivered by large commercial clouds, government G-clouds are promising models for (larger) cities, creating urban clouds that reduce IT costs, and offering platforms for small business applications and e-services. Fenn (2010) argues that governments are realising the benefits of cloud computing but are concerned about the level of security for their data in the private cloud. Cloud computing is also opening new possibilities in the virtualisation of physical spaces, and their substitution by digital ones. Already because of the global crisis since 2009, many urban activities relating to trade and services have gone virtual – killing their physical part – while allowing companies and organisations to maintain operations in times of austerity, gain flexibility, and lower fixed capital costs. Cloud computing is also expected to sustain new growth sectors of cities, which are now moving from manufacturing to services in the context of a wider movement from products to services, as material and intangible infrastructures start being provided by the cloud.

Equally important is the expected standardisation of smart city solutions, platforms, and applications, pre-installed on the cloud. Standardisation is necessary to provide on-demand self services and drop development cost. Standardisation will accelerate technology diffusion and learning curves as city administrations and their IT departments will become aware of proven solutions for all domains of the city. We expect a standardisation of platforms and applications in many different domains of cities related to economic activities (trade, manufacturing, services, logistics), quality of life (safety, environment, social care), utilities (transport, energy, water, broadband), and city management (administration, democracy, planning).

6. From technologies to smart city services: user-driven innovation

The engagement of users and user-driven innovation are important preconditions for turning Future Internet technologies into new services in smart cities. The Web 2.0 era has pushed cities to consider the Internet (including mobiles) as a more participative tool for engaging citizens and tourists. Many initiatives were launched by city-based Living Labs to investigate and anticipate how digital technologies will change the way people live in the city and their implications for urban dynamics. Future Internet, Living Labs, and smart cities together form a new innovation ecosystem comprising users, citizens, ICT companies, research scientists, and policymakers. In such ecosystems, Future Internet technologies are the technology push driver, smart cities represent the application pull demand, and Living Labs form the exploratory and participative playground in between.

Crowdsourcing is the usual form of citizen participation in smart cities. The word comes from the combination of 'crowd' and 'outsourcing and the main idea is to assign a task to a large group of people or a community' (Howe, 2006). It is an extreme form of open innovation in which tasks are not assigned to selected external providers, but rather to crowds. Crowdsourcing is also strongly related to online platforms and collaborative Web spaces, because the participation of large communities (crowds) presupposes the use of digital media. It is an online distributed problem-solving and production model. It also marks a distinctive stage in the evolution of the intelligent cities standard model during the first years of the twenty-first century.

The two cases that follow illustrate the contribution of crowdsourcing to smart cities: 'NYC Simplicity Idea Market' and 'Improve My City' are applications for citizen participation and city improvement relying on large-scale user involvement.

NYC Simplicity Idea Market was launched in February 2011 by the City of New York and remained in operation for about one year. Employees of all levels of administration and city agencies were invited to suggest and share ideas about improvements to city government. Each one could upload ideas, comment on the ideas of others, and vote for those considered best. Then, experts reviewed the most popular proposals and the city administration implemented the best ones (Barkat et al., 2011). A large community within the city, estimated at 300,000 employees, was invited to elaborate ideas about education, safety, and maintenance of the city's infrastructure. Innovation was based on the combination of ideas generated by employees, user-driven evaluation of ideas, feasibility assessment by experts, and solutions implemented by the city administration. A content management system and a crowdsourcing platform were used to enable employee participation and assessment through voting. Everything revolved around crowdsourcing, the engagement of a large community of the city, selecting ideas based on the preferences of the same community, and enabling participation through social media.

Improve My City (ImyC) was developed by URENIO in 2012 in the context of the PEOPLE project, a smart city project that formed part of the EU CIP-ICT-PSP. Improve My City is an open source application created under Affero General Public Licence (AGPL) V3 license. The platform of ImyC is a Joomla 2.5.x-compatible component to report, gather, present, comment on, vote for, and track demands on the map. Anyone can download the code from the GitHub for use or improvement. Because ImyC is a free application based on Joomla, it is widely used in many cities in Europe, Asia, and South America. It is already offered in more than 25 languages. Citizens can report local problems and suggest improvements, write comments on other posts, and vote to support suggestions and demands. Reported issues and citizen requests go directly into the city's government queue for resolution, and the responsible authority informs users about the progress of their request. Again, the main concept here is motivated crowdsourcing. The entire community of a city can be involved. Citizen reporting ideas and suggestions are listed in different categories related to improvement of the environment. Innovation is based on a combination of crowdsourcing about city problems and solutions, while implementation relies on institutional action from city hall. During a second cycle of crowdsourcing, communities of users and developers support customisation of the application for different environments and languages.

In such crowdsourcing and user-driven innovation, user involvement is the main driver of spatial intelligence. In the first step, the city, citizens, and communities define challenges that need to be addressed. Any form of intelligence starts by defining problems to be addressed, which also sets the metrics of success. Challenges are specific to each city, its sectors, districts, utilities, quality of life, and governance. From the open innovation–crowdsourcing perspective, challenges are defined collectively by aggregation and prioritisation of citizens' views and demands. Then a problem-solving roadmap is prepared. User-driven innovation is called on to provide ideas along the roadmap, in terms of information collection, use of proven solutions, inventing new solutions, and disseminating selected solutions. Digital media and open platforms facilitate the entire process by offering e-tools that help a large number of participants to become involved, share insights, combine skills, and aggregate resources. The outcome is urban empowerment and improvement: an increase of collective capability in defining problems and solutions, and implementation mechanisms through collaboration, institutions, and use of public resources.

7. Innovation ecosystems of embedded spatial intelligence

The instances of Future Internet described in the previous sections – Internet of Things, Semantic Web, cloud computing – are cornerstones of new innovation ecosystems that are emerging in smart environments. Within environments of embedded spatial intelligence, the building blocks of innovation – competences, products, markets, business models – take on new forms and new types of innovation ecosystems are formed. The nodes of ecosystems multiply geometrically, become sentient and interactive; hybrid identities are formed with semantically richer labels; all interactions become location aware; and the fundamental knowledge functions of intelligent cities are supported by real-time data. Smart environments alter all the building blocks of urban economic activities: capabilities, products, markets, and the business models.

Capabilities: The new technology stack of 'IoT' + 'Semantic Web' + 'Cloud' does not automatically lead to the development of new e-services. User involvement is necessary to provide skills and resources for new product / services designs and development. User-driven approaches, such as Living Labs and open innovation initiatives, promote a more proactive role for end users and citizens in service innovation, assuring good coordination between the technology offer from vendors and the service demand from citizens. In developing such smart city solutions, there are a number of methods for involving users which are described in abundant detail in the literature, such as Lead Users, User-Driven Innovation, User-Centred Design, User-Created Content, and User Co-Creation perspectives.

Crowdsourcing platforms can make citizen participation in innovation a reality. A large collection of platforms is presented on the 'Crowdsourcing Landscape' (Dawson and Bynghall, 2011) that can support the entire cycle of innovation: for innovation funding (Crowdfunding), ideas generation (Idea Platforms, Prediction Markets, Content Markets, Content Rating), collaborative innovation and product development (Distributed Innovation, Innovation Prizes, Cycle Sharing, Competition Platforms) and implementation (Crowdsourcing Aggregators, Microtasks, Service Marketplaces). However, before adopting crowdsourcing strategies, "companies need to carefully consider the strategic question of what could and should be done inside and outside the organization. In many cases there are good reasons to draw on local rather than global providers. Distinguishing between when commodity or talented providers are required allows use of the most relevant approaches. Protection of intellectual property is a significant consideration, but risks are often over-estimated and can be mitigated." (Dawson, 2011, p. 19).

Smart products – smart objects: Products and services based on Future Internet technologies are not standalone products. Complex systems are needed to offer them, composed of broadband infrastructure comprised of wired and wireless networks; embedded systems into the physical space of cities, sensors, smart devices and smart meters; APIs for interoperability and data integration; data hosting and security; predictive modelling; applications for optimisation of smart city utilities and activities; provision of e-services, and location-based services in particular. Layers of hardware, devices, and software are interwoven with the physical space, infrastructure, and functions of cities. Sensors, activators, RFID, smart meters, cameras, routers, switches, storage, authentication, and firewall servers have to work together in order to capture and process the information generated by the operation of cities and turn it to useful service.

To deal with such complex systems, leading ICT organisations have proposed the concept of 'Urban Operating Systems or Integrated Urban Infrastructure,' enabling all smart city components, applications, and services to run on a common system. The argument is that an urban operating system can provide the protocols for the operation of cities, collect data about everything going on in a city and respond in real time. CISCO, for instance, considers that unified network architecture will help service providers move away from individual computing clusters, create integrated operations centres, and enable to master rapid-changing services and utilities. The challenge of data integration is evident: "A couple of decades ago, the development of the Internet was hampered by disparate networks unable to interoperate. Urbanisation poses a similar challenge. Hundreds of different systems and protocol across an urban centre are not interoperable. The convergence of all kinds of data across a unified IP network makes it possible to develop new services to anyone, anywhere, and at anytime" (Pike Research, 2012).

While the concept of one common operating system integrating all devices and smart solutions is an exciting prospect offering potential economies of scale and scope, the structure and governance of cities does not endorse a unified architecture. Data integration seems more feasible at the level of city districts or smaller city clusters or at the level of utilities, which are endowed with governance and control capacity, but not at the level of the entire city. The reason is that, given the actual liberalisation and privatisation of local government, there is no overall authority with full control over cities. On the contrary, there are pockets of decentralised decision-making, exercising control over different city-districts and areas. Technology solutions should adapt to existing city governance instead of assuming an all-inclusive city administration and management. City-districts, clusters, and utility sectors are appropriate levels for organising smart infrastructures and services using Future Internet technologies rather than the entire city with its different subsystems and fragmented governance.

Smart city markets: Within this ecosystem of data generation and integration, products and services circulate with their virtual identities. The Internet of Things and smart objects blur the line between digital and physical worlds, making their distinction hard to define. In every vertical market, the aspects of product design, development, marketing, and exchange work primarily with the digital identities involved. Because of the priority of the virtual, the potential market of smart city solutions covers all vertical markets located within the city.

Estimations about the size of the smart city market vary considerably, but in all cases forecasts describe huge markets. ABI Research estimated the smart city market at $8 billion in 2010 and $39 billion in 2016, by Pike Research at $108 billion for the period 2010–2020, and by the Centre for Urban Science and Progress at $160 trillion for the next 30 years. Ovum predicted spending per city at $35–55 billion, of which 15 percent would be on software and 85 percent on hardware and services. Pike Research estimated that explosive urbanisation will create smart city markets covering the fields of sustainability, citizen well-being, and economic development: "The smart city technology market will surpass $20 billion in annual value by 2020. This represents a compound annual growth rate of 16.2 percent" (Pike Research, 2012). The report continues that many of the market drivers, technology innovations, and decision-making processes associated with smart cities are focused on existing industry and operational silos: energy, water, transportation, buildings management, and/or government services. Now, however, the smart city is also becoming a space for the testing and implementation of cross-functional technologies and solutions. The IDC Government Insights estimation for the smart city market in 2013 predicted that 70 percent of worldwide spending on smart city projects will be focused on energy, transportation, and public safety; smart city information challenges will begin to be framed as big-data cases, and cities with open data initiatives will drive 50 percent more private, citizen, and crowdsourced mobile applications (Clarke et al., 2013).

Business models: In creating smart city products and services, cloud computing offers significant advantages, such as external economies, lower capital entry requirements and maintenance costs, and security, while its scalability enables quick adjustment to changing demand. There are also technical advantages related to software updates and new version installations, which become easier if applications are maintained on the cloud. However, the transition to the cloud is done by cautious steps, because these technologies are still evolving and have not yet fully addressed the issues of service standardisation, security, and privacy. Policy White Papers provide valuable guidance to city authorities about the deployment of cloud-based services. An important source of advice is the report prepared by the Australian government, which provides information about public policies and programmes addressing the transition to cloud computing in the US, UK, EU, Canada, and Japan (Australian Government, 2011). The recommendation is for streams of consultation work, providing public agencies with guidance and documentation, cost-benefit analyses, testing of services in less important areas initially, and then moving on to full deployment of new cloud-based services, and eventually the creation of G-city clouds.

* * *

Future Internet technologies are generating new services in every domain of cities. All city districts, city utilities, and city government services can profit from the use of smart objects and smart environments. Mobile phones are becoming the main access point for services offered on a personal level. Cell phones are able to open the door to augmented reality applications, online payment, near field communication apps, and identity and passport apps, as well as unfettered access to the Internet. Journey planning and wayfinding enable one to locate and orient oneself in the city as if one had assistance from a person with the best knowledge of the city, along with all available information on public transport services and intermodal networks. Service discovery and the location of services of interest become available, as does real-time medical care, user review and assessment options, and real-time information to community groups. Reading ambient data in digital layers over the buildings can provide inform about traffic, crime, air quality, and many other areas of interest.

City authorities are gradually becoming aware of solutions, applications, and use cases based on the Future Internet technology stack. Moving toward such solutions, the demand for broadband connections substantially increases because of the transition from connecting people to connecting things. Network interoperability and merging of network and media technologies, as well as mobile-to-mobile communication, have become necessary to manage and give meaning to the streams of data generated. Policy and experimentation are needed to turn these possibilities into a reality. The OECD (2008) report on the Future Internet economy provides a series of policy recommendations to deal with these challenges, such as building next-generation network infrastructure, making Internet access available to everyone everywhere, promoting Internet-based innovation, competition and user choice, empowering consumers, creating public digital content and user-driven content, ensuring the protection of personal data, and intellectual property rights and trusted Internet-based services, as well as creating environments that encourage infrastructure investment, broadband connectivity, and innovative services and applications.

References

Accenture (2011). *Building and managing an intelligent city*. Accenture Management Consulting.

Australian Government (2011). *Cloud computing strategic direction paper*. Department of Finance and Deregulation.

Barkat, H., Jeaggli L. and Dorsaz P. (2011). *Citizen 2.0. 17 examples of social media and government innovation*. Retrieved 2 January 2014, from www.thinkinnovation.org/en/blog/2011/11/citizen-2-0-17-examples-of-social-media-and-government-innovation/.

Carter, P., Rojas, B., and Sahni, M. (2011). *Delivering next-generation citizen services: Assessing the environmental, social and economic impact of Intelligent X on future cities and communities*. IDC White Paper. Retrieved 2 January 2014, from www.cisco.com/web/strategy/docs/scc/whitepaper_cisco_scc_idc.pdf.

Chen-Ritzo, C. H., Harrison, C., Paraszczak, J. and Parr, F. (2009). Instrumenting the planet. *IBM Journal of Research and Development*, Vol. 53, No. 3, 338–353.

Clarke, R. Y., Yates, M., Chulani, M., Brooks, A. Wu L. and Sasahara, E. (2013). *Worldwide smart city 2013 top 10 predictions*. IDC Government Insights. Retrieved 2 January 2014, from www.idc-gi.com/getdoc.jsp?containerId=GI239209.

Dawson, R. and Bynghall, S. (2011). *Getting results from crowds*. San Francisco, CA: Advanced Human Technologies.

Deakin, M (2011). The embedded intelligence of smart cities. *Intelligent Buildings International*, Vol. 3, No. 3, 189–197.

European Commission (2010a). *Future media Internet: Research challenges and road ahead*. DG Information Society and Media. Luxembourg: Publications Office of the European Union.

European Commission (2010b). *Future media networks: Research challenges 2010*. DG Information Society and Media. Luxembourg: Publications Office of the European Union.

EIP (2013). *European innovation partnership on smart cities and communities. Strategic implementation plan*. Retrieved 2 January 2014, from http://ec.europa.eu/eip/smartcities/files/sip_final_en.pdf.

Fenn, J. (2010). *Emerging technology hype cycle 2010: What's hot and what's not*. Retrieved 2 January 2014, from http://blog.bimeanalytics.com/english/analysis-gartners-emerging-technology-hype-cycle-2010-hot.

Frey, T. (2012). *Empowering 'Things' for our Internet of Things*. Retrieved 2 January 2014, from www.wfs.org/blogs/thomas-frey/empowering-%E2%80%9Cthings%E2%80%9D-for-our-internet-things.

Gartner (2010). *Gartner's 2010 hype cycle. Special report evaluates maturity of 1,800 technologies*. Retrieved 2 January 2014 from www.gartner.com/newsroom/id/1447613.

Gartner (2012a). *Gartner's 2012 hype cycle for emerging technologies*. Retrieved 2 January 2014 from www.gartner.com/newsroom/id/2124315.

Gartner (2012b). *Hype cycle for smart city technologies and solutions, 2012*. Retrieved 2 January 2014 from www.gartner.com/doc/2098315.

Hernández-Muñoz, J. M., Vercher, J. B., Muñoz, L., Galache, J. A., Presser, M., Hernández Gómez L. A., and Pettersson, J. (2011). Smart cities at the forefront of the future Internet. In J. Domingue et al. (eds), *The Future Internet* (pp. 447–462). *Lecture Notes in Computer Science*, Vol. 6656, Springer.

Hildenbrand, D. (2011). *A world full of sensors*. Retrieved 2 January 2014, from www.vector1media.com/article/features/22047-a-world-full-of-sensors.html.

Howe, J. (2006). The rise of crowdsourcing. *Wired Magazine*, Vol. 14, No. 6, 1–4.

IBM Institute for Business Value (2009). *A vision of smarter cities: How cities can lead the way into a prosperous and sustainable future*. IBM Global Business Services Executive Report. Somers, NY: IBM.

Komninos, N. (2011). Intelligent cities: Variable geometries of spatial intelligence. *Intelligent Buildings International*, Vol. 3, No. 3, 172–188.

Lemke, M. (2010). *Open innovation for future Internet enables services in 'smart' cities*. CIP ICT-PSP Info Day, January 2010, European Commission, DG Information Society and Media.

Mell, P. and Grance, T. (2011). *The NIST definition of cloud computing*. US Department of Commerce: NIST Special Publication 800–145.

Mitchell, W. (2007). Intelligent cities. *E-Journal on the Knowledge Society*, UOC Papers. Retrieved 2 January 2014, from www.uoc.edu/uocpapers/5/dt/eng/mitchell.html.

OECD (2008). *Shaping policies for the future of the Internet economy*. Seoul, Korea: OECD Ministerial meeting on the Future of the Internet Economy.

OVUM (2011). *Is your city smart enough?* OVUM publications.

Pietrantonio, D. (2010). *ICT policy support programme*. Draft work programme 2010. Oeitas Workshop. Portugal, 27 November 2009, European Commission, DG Information Society and Media.

Prasanth, A., (2012). Cloud computing services: A survey. *International Journal of Computer Applications*. Vol. 46, No. 3, 25–29.

Pike Research (2012). *Smart cities: Infrastructure, information, and communications technologies for energy, transportation, buildings, and government: City and supplier profiles, Market Analysis, and Forecasts*. Retrieved 2 January 2014, from www.pikeresearch.com/research/smart-cities.

Schaffers, H., Komninos, N., Pallot, M. (eds) (2012). *Smart cities as innovation ecosystems sustained by the future Internet*. FIREBALL White Paper. Retrieved 2 January 2014, from www.urenio.org/2012/04/23/smart-cities-fireball-white-paper.

Shepard, M. (2011). Toward the sentient city. In M. Shepard (ed.) *Sentient city* (pp.15–36). Cambridge, MA: MIT Press.

Smart Cities and Communities. (n.d.) *Solution proposals*. Retrieved 2 January 2014, from www.eu-smartcities.eu/solution-proposals.

Townsend, A., Maguire, R., Liebhold, M. and Crawford, M. (2011). *A planet of civic laboratories. The future of cities, information and inclusion*. Palo Alto, CA: Institute for the Future.

Townsend, A., Soojung-Kim Pang, A., and Weddle, R. (2009). *Future knowledge ecosystems: The next twenty years of technology-led economic development*. Palo Alto, CA: Institute for the Future.

4 Alternative architectures of spatial intelligence of cities
Pathways to innovation

1. What makes cities intelligent?

The new interdisciplinary paradigm of 'intelligent cities' or 'smart cities' – bringing together theories, methodologies, and practices from diverse fields, such as urban development, strategic planning, Web and Internet technologies, knowledge and innovation management – is overturning established urban development and planning practices. The impact of this paradigm reaches far beyond the domain of cities as it influences the challenges of global competitiveness, sustainability and climate change, employment and inclusion.

A rich literature reflects the evolution of thinking and practice in the field of digital – intelligent – smart cities and outlines the contribution of information technologies and innovation processes to the development and planning of twenty-first-century cities. From Mitchell (1996), Ishida and Isbister (2000), and Graham (2003) focusing on technologies, experiences, and case studies of digital cities, to Komninos (2002 and 2008), Bell et al. (2009) on intelligent cities and the nexus of ICTs, collective intelligence and innovation, to Caragliu et al. (2009), Belissent (2010), Deakin (2011), Schaffers et al. (2011) on smart cities, embedded systems and the future Internet, this literature also highlights a trajectory of change. It describes the continuous evolution of digital technologies and innovation systems that feed intelligent cities and the creation of more open and innovative urban ecosystems deployed over the digital, social, and physical space of cities. Such ecosystems enable citizens, end users, enterprises, and organisations to develop innovative attitudes, to become more competitive and resource efficient, and to become more intelligent in decision-making.

Despite the great diversity of strategies and solutions that can be observed, intelligent and smart cities rely on a core of knowledge processes. We call this core 'spatial intelligence of cities.' Spatial intelligence is made by informational, cognitive, and innovation processes, which take place within cities and enable citizens and organisations to more efficiently address the challenges they face. It refers to the ability of a community or a city to combine its intellectual capital, institutions for collaboration, and smart infrastructure for setting up knowledge functions that optimise the use of resources in a wide range of fields and challenges.

80 *What makes cities intelligent?*

Spatial intelligence is the ingredient that makes cities intelligent. Having said this, the aim of this chapter is to discuss different architectures and trajectories that make spatial intelligence emerge. Furthermore, the aim is to describe the fundamental variables of spatial intelligence and how they change along the evolution that takes place in digital technologies and innovation systems.

In previous chapters, we have argued that the intelligence of cities is based on a series of knowledge functions which are collectively created and deployed, such as network-based information intelligence and forecasting, technology learning and acquisition, new knowledge creation and dissemination. Here, we extend these arguments by showing how different forms of spatial intelligence are activated by arrangements of knowledge functions, big data and infrastructure into cities.

We start from the concept of spatial intelligence of cities and a quick overview of the literature on cyber, digital, intelligent, and smart cities, which points to different types of spatial intelligence. We then describe four trajectories and architectures of spatial intelligence – agglomeration, orchestration, empowerment, and instrumentation – that can be found within cities. Cases studies from Bletchley Park, UK; Cyberport, Hong Kong; Smart Santander, Spain; and Amsterdam Smart City illustrate the above types of spatial intelligence. These socio-technological experiments highlight important efforts to create intelligent places and contribute to a better understanding of the many faces of spatial intelligence. In the last section, we attempt a synthesis of different types of spatial intelligence by defining a universal architecture, based on variables such as the type of knowledge functions activated (information gathering, technology learning, innovation, dissemination), the type of intelligence used (human, organisational, artificial), and the type arrangements within the urban space in which processes takes place.

2. Spatial intelligence of cities

The spatial intelligence of cities is based on informational and cognitive processes, such as information collection and processing, real-time alert, forecasting, learning, collective intelligence, distributed problem-solving, co-creation, and collaborative innovation that take place in cities. Pointing out the 'spatial' aspect denotes that space and agglomeration are preconditions of such intelligence.

Spatial intelligence emerges from the agglomeration of communication means and the integration of competences, know-how and heuristic strategies. It is a distributed intelligence that takes into account the environment in the development of cognitive processes. Opposed to the dominant cognitive approach, which focuses on individual agents (human or machine), distributed intelligence is concerned with the interaction of individuals with institutions and objects of their environment. Using such distributed intellectual capacities and infrastructures, cities can respond effectively to changing conditions, address challenges, plan their future, and sustain the well-being of citizens.

Collective intelligence has been a major driver of the spatial intelligence of cities. Partnerships, collaboration platforms, and social networks nurture the development of technologies, skills, and learning. Social media have contributed enormously via crowdsourcing platforms, mash-ups, Web-collaboration, and other means of participatory problem-solving. Media technologies and collaborative platforms remain a key instrument of spatial intelligence. However, the recent turn towards smart cities and embedded systems highlight other routes as well. The rise of new Internet technologies promoting cloud-based services, the Internet of Things, the use of smart phones and smart meters, networks of sensors and RFIDs, and more accurate semantic search open new ways to collective action and collaborative problem-solving.

The literature on digital, intelligent, and smart cities, which spans a period of 20 years, highlights different forms of spatial intelligence which appeared with respect to different Web technologies, knowledge and innovation processes, and forms of community engagement. Since the 1980s, urban development has been linked to innovation ecosystems, technology-driven localities, innovation clusters, and creative hubs, in which R&D, knowledge, and innovation were connected by agglomeration and locality. In the 1990s, a new digital spatiality started expanding over the physical and institutional space of cities. However, ICTs, the Internet and the Web alone would not have had a strong impact on cities if contemporary urban agglomerations were their development not rooted in knowledge and innovation. In the 2000s, digital spatiality joined the spatiality of cities in multiple ways, enhancing communication, city representation, virtualisation of infrastructures, transforming urban activities, optimisation of city functions, and more participatory governance. These different roles of the digital space and the different forms of integration between physical, institutional and digital spaces gave birth to different forms of spatial intelligence within 'cyber,' 'digital,' 'intelligent,' and 'smart' city environments.

Cyber-intelligence: The cyber literature marked the initial stage of the digital trajectory of cities. Cybercities and cyberspace refer to any type of virtual space generated by a collection of data within the Internet (Shiode, 1997), but the concept also contains the sense of inspection and control with communication and information feedback as preconditions of effective action. It carried some seeds from the ideas of cybernetics that appeared in the 1940s on communication with machines and feedback loops in decision-making. This perspective led to early e-government applications for city management and more recently to technologies for security and control over the urban space, and in some cases the transfer of military methods of tracking, identification, and targeting into the governance of urban civil society (Graham, 2010). In a broader sense, a cybercity is conceived as a Web-based city in which people interact with each other through and exclusively over cyberspace. Antorroiko (2005) points out that the 'cyber' prefix refers also to the dark side of the virtual space, to 'cyberterrorism' and 'cyborg' dimensions.

Representational intelligence: A more neutral discussion opened within the digital city literature with the extensive work of Ishida and Isbister (2000), Hiramatsu and Ishida (2001), and Van den Besselaar and Koizumi (2005). It concerned the representation of the city, in early forms via portal-type webpages, and panoramic and 3D representations of cities, and later with augmented reality

82 *What makes cities intelligent?*

technologies, and urban tagging. Digital cities are connected communities that combine "broadband communications infrastructure; a flexible, service-oriented computing infrastructure based on open industry standards; and innovative services to meet the needs of governments and their employees, citizens and businesses" (Yovanof and Hazapis, 2009). The digital city is a metaphor of the city: an understanding of the city through its virtual representation. Digital cities were accurately described as 'mirror-city metaphors,' as their logic was to offer "a comprehensive, web-based representation, or reproduction, of several aspects or functions of a specific real city, open to non-experts" (Couclelis, 2004). The spatial intelligence related to solutions of this type was based on advantages of representation and visualisation. "A picture is worth a thousand words" reflects this idea that complex environments can be described and understood better via a virtual representation or visual metaphor.

Collective intelligence: The discussion about city intelligence emerges at the crossroads between the knowledge-based development of cities (knowledge cities) and the digital cities of media. There are some quasi-similar understandings of city intelligence. Mitchell attributes city intelligence to a combination of telecommunication networks, sensors and tags, and software improving the knowledge and cognitive competences (Mitchell, 2007). City intelligence comes from partnerships and social capital in organising the development of technologies, skills, and learning, and engaging citizens to become involved in creative community participation (Deakin and Allwinkle, 2007). The intelligence of cities is based on a combination of the creative capabilities of the population, knowledge-sharing institutions, and digital applications organising collective intelligence, which altogether increase the ability to innovate that is the ultimate indication of intelligence. Therefore, it emerges within urban agglomerations from the integration of three types of intelligence: (1) the inventiveness, creativity and human intelligence of the city's population; (2) the collective intelligence of the city's institutions and social capital for innovation; and (3) the artificial intelligence of public and city-wide smart infrastructure, virtual environments, and intelligent agents (Komninos, 2008). In these perspectives, the spatial intelligence of cities builds on collective intelligence and social capital for collaboration. It is based on people-driven innovation and environments supporting the principles of openness, realism, and empowerment of users in the development of new solutions (Bergvall-Kåreborn and Ståhlbröst, 2009).

Intelligence into data: The recent turn towards – and interest in – smart systems and smart cities link city intelligence to the rise of new Internet technologies, smart phones, smart devices, sensors, RFIDs, the Semantic Web and the Internet of Things. Smart city solutions using sensors and smart devices improve the ability to gather information, forecast and manage urban activities and flows, and advance city intelligence (Chen-Ritzo et al., 2009). Within this group of technologies, spatial intelligence moves out of applications and enters into the domain of data: the meaning of data becomes part of data, data are provided just-in-time, and real-time data enable real-time response.

Critical questions within this large landscape of practices and transformations concern the sources of the spatial intelligence of cities: the structures, mechanisms, and architectures that sustain the problem-solving capability of cities. What makes a city intelligent or smart? Which type of spatial intelligence is activated within each district and sector of the city? Is it a spatial intelligence common to all districts or are different structuring patterns activated within different city districts depending on their functional characteristics and governance?

We discuss these questions with respect to case studies from Bletchley Park, UK; Cyberport, Hong Kong; and Smart Amsterdam, and the forms of spatial intelligence emerged in these places. We start from the baseline, the *agglomeration intelligence of cities*, and then we present three different forms of spatial intelligence that rely on different arrangements within the urban space. These case studies show that spatial intelligence of cities takes many different forms and follows diverse trajectories as well. The variable connections between the digital, social, and physical space of cities, and the large number of digital applications gathered over cities, actualise many mechanisms that both give structure to and sustain city intelligence. These forms are *orchestration intelligence*, which is based on collaboration and distributed problem-solving within a community having full control over information and knowledge processes; *empowerment intelligence,* which is based on people's competences through up-skilling provided by experimental facilities, open platforms, and city infrastructure; and *instrumentation intelligence*, based big data, real-time information, data analysis, and predictive modelling for better decision-making across city districts and utilities. These trajectories of spatial intelligence can work in isolation or in a complementary way. They provide different arrays of problem-solving capabilities, always working with networks and connections between the physical, institutional, and digital space of cities.

3. Baseline: agglomeration intelligence though connected variety

From the moment they emerged, cities were based on advantages created by spatial proximity, the division of labour and collaboration, use of common infrastructure, face-to-face communication, and the development of trust and alliance. The spatial agglomeration of people, activities, and buildings was driven by advances in the division of labour and exchange of goods, and, in turn, generated a series of positive social and economic externalities. Soja (2003), writing about the first urban settlements and cities, insists on "putting cities first," attributing to Synekism – the physical agglomeration of people with a form of political coordination – the capacity to advance creativity, innovation, territorial identity, and societal development which arise from living in dense and heterogeneous agglomerations.

Soja refers extensively to *The Economies of Cities* by Jane Jacobs (1969) and the findings at Catal Huyuk, the largest and most developed early city in southern Anatolia, where Jacobs located major innovations and transformations from hunting and gathering to agriculture, the first metallurgy, and weaving and crude pottery – which took place because of the existence of the city. These innovations, he argues, as well as every major innovation in human society, come from cooperation, synergy, and multiple savings obtained from living in dense urban settlements. The externalities of cities and the various types of agglomeration economies (external, scale, scope, location, urbanisation) stem, on the one hand, from savings in energy, time and materials, and on the other hand, from collaboration and the creation of synergies. The spatial agglomeration of people and activities produces both savings and synergies.

The new industrial geography has described how proximity generates additional externalities in the innovation economy because of informal collaboration, untraded interdependences, knowledge spillovers, trust, and diffusion of tacit knowledge. It is the diversity of cities, the connected variety of the urban agglomeration that increases individual intelligence by bridging fields of knowledge. 'Related variety' (Boschma and Frenken, 2011) has been an influential concept in innovation-led regional development over 20 years, sustained by studies on innovative industrial districts containing many and diverse skills, on high-technology regions with a variety of machinery and knowledge infrastructure, and on innovative cities with a variety of science and technology fields in world-class research institutes and universities. The industrial innovation literature uses also similar 'brokering' concepts to explain how innovation derives from connecting various fields of research and technology and insights from connecting different fields of science and technology (Hargadon, 2003).

When digital applications begin to concentrate over cities, collaboration and synergies scale up. As citizens come into the digital space and use applications, they share more and share it more quickly. Interaction becomes easier and synergy stronger. The holy triad of synergies (proximity, trust, communication) is strengthened: proximity increases because the 'other' is just a few clicks away; trust deepens because digital interaction leave traces; and communication intensifies because we have more means and tools to this end. Digital interaction enables wider collaboration, more extended supply chains, and more end-user participation. The agglomeration of digital applications and e-services, created by the engagement of the population of the city, scales-up collaboration with content management systems, co-design tools, collaborative work environments, crowdsourcing platforms, and content mash-ups.

As computers, devices, and information systems become embedded into cities, the collaboration patterns among citizens change substantially. Change does not concern scalability only, but above all the architectures of cooperation. New networking architectures emerge, involving both humans and machines. As digital technology transfers tasks from humans to machines, workflows become more complex, more tasks are performed in co-operation, machines inspect the workflow of collaboration, and storage capacity skyrockets. The city ends up with quicker responses, better-quality procedures, lower operation costs, and higher problem-solving capability – in other words, with higher spatial intelligence. This happens because machine intelligence is added to the human intelligence of citizens and to the collective intelligence of their community. The agglomeration of digital applications is the beginning of spatial intelligence, in the same way that the spatial agglomeration was the beginning of cities.

4. Orchestration intelligence: Bletchley Park, the first intelligent community

The first community that successfully practised a human–machine cooperation and integration of individual, collective, and machine intelligence was Bletchley Park in the UK. The story of Bletchley Park is well known in the WWII code-breaking literature. However, it was never referred as an intelligent city or intelligent community.

Bletchley Park is located 80 kilometres northwest of London. Bletchley is an ordinary town, a regional urban centre in the county of Buckinghamshire, at the intersection of London and North-Western Railway with a line linking Oxford to Cambridge. Just off the junction, within walking distance from the station, lies Bletchley Park, an estate of about 100 hectares with a grand Victorian mansion at the centre of the estate.

The development of Bletchley Park started in August 1939 when the Government Code and Cypher School moved from London to Bletchley Park to carry out their code-breaking work in a safer environment. A small group of people was initially settled at Bletchley, composed of code-breaking experts, cryptanalytic personnel, and university professors from the exact sciences and mathematics. Alan Turing arrived at Bletchley Park in 1939, together with other professors from Cambridge, to help set up the methods of analysis and workflow of cryptanalysis. Bletchley Park carries the mark of Turing and his ideas on intelligence, logic, and software priority over hardware, and solutions over a universal computing process.

The mission of Bletchley Park was to find the daily settings of the Enigma machines used by the German Army to encode all transmitted messages between the army headquarters, divisions, warships, submarines, port and railway stations, military installations, and other installations, and then decode all these messages. It is estimated that by 1942, the German Army had a least 100,000 Enigma machines, which produced an enormous traffic of codified messages of vital importance for the daily operation of all army units. The Enigma machine was an electro-mechanical device for encryption and decryption of messages based on polyalphabetic substitution. It relied on interchangeable rotors of 26 letters, initially three and later five, moving rings, and a plugboard which permitted variable electrical wiring connecting letters in pairs. Every key pressed on the keyboard caused one step on the first rotor – after a full rotation, the others rotors also moved – and then electrical connections were made that changed the substitution alphabet used for encryption. Decoding was symmetrical. The receiver had to settle the machine in its initial setting of rotors, rings, and plugging, type the coded message, and recover the original. The combination of rotor order, the initial position of rotors, and plug settings created a very large number of possible permutations. For each setting of rotors, there were trillions of ways to connect ten pairs of letters on the plugboard. It was practically impossible to break the encryption by hand.

The Park was an 'industry' for information collection, processing, decoding, and distribution. Thousands messages were intercepted daily, while overall 200,000–500,000 German messages were decoded between 1940 and 1945. The impact was also extremely high. The strategic role of Bletchley Park was in the battle for supplies, defeating the U-boats in the Atlantic, and securing the inflow of materials, foods, and ammunition to Britain. By the end of 1941, the British announced that the problem of maritime supplies had been solved. Historians estimate that the work done in Bletchley Park shortened the war by two to four years and saved millions of lives. The philosopher George Steiner described Bletchley Park as the greatest achievement of Britain during the war and perhaps during the whole twentieth century.

The amount of collaborative knowledge work carried out was enormous. That is important for Bletchley as an intelligent community. The work in Bletchley was done in wooden huts, designated by numbers, and brick-built blocks that were constructed after 1939 to house the different sectors of cryptanalysis. In the years thereafter, the personnel of Bletchley Park increased in number at a spectacular rate, and by the end of the war they numbered about 10,000. People came from all fighting services, and were seconded to Bletchley Park because of their skills: authors, diplomats, bankers, journalists, and teachers, and many women who received training in information-processing tasks.

The workflow at Bletchley Park in breaking German communications codes was based on a collaborative schedule between scientists, experts, trained workers, and machines that offered increased intelligence to deal with this challenge. The methodological solutions about how to break the Enigma ciphers were given by a group of British cryptanalysts and mathematicians at Bletchley Park who continued and enriched the methods devised by Polish mathematicians in previous and simpler models of Enigma machines. The wiring structure of the machines and some fundamental design flaws – no letter could ever be encrypted as itself – were exploited. The breaking of the codes was based on human factors and mistakes made by the Germans. Alan Turing and Cambridge mathematician Gordon Welchman, who also invented the method of perforated sheets, provided the designs for the new machine – the British Bombe – that could break any Enigma cipher, provided an accurate assumption could be made of about twenty letters in the message. Alan Turing contributed with several insights to breaking the Enigma cipher, while also somehow continuing his theoretical work on computable numbers and the universal Turing machine.

The key to the success of Bletchley Park was large-scale collaboration and an organised workflow that integrated a variety of information sources and processes. Cryptanalysts worked as a team. They had to analyse all the messages of the day to make assumptions from the basic setting of the rotors. Codebooks found in sunken submarines or captured ships were also very helpful and provided Enigma ground settings and abbreviations. They had to simulate the entire German classification system, mapping, and acronyms. Cryptanalysis acquired meaning only through the coordination of different activities across an extended workflow, and solving ciphers was only part of it. There was an organised division of labour and specialisation for different tasks along the process of intercepting the messages, transferring them to Bletchley Park, code breaking, verification, and dissemination of the information to recipients. The raw material came from a web of wireless intercept stations around Britain and overseas. Code-breakers based in the huts were supported by teams who turned the deciphered messages into intelligence reports. The letter from Turing, Welchman, Alexander, and Milner-Barry to Churchill in October 1941, asking for more resources at Bletchley Park, personnel, night shifts, interception stations, specialised decoders, support to the Bombes, shows this integrated large-scale functioning of the community.

When a cryptanalyst developed an assumption about a possible relationship between a portion of plaintext and the ciphertext in a message, he prepared a menu (called a crib – plain text that corresponded to the cipher text) which was sent to be tested on a 'Bombe' machine. This was an electromechanical machine used to discover the set of rotors, the settings of the alphabet rings, and the wiring of the plugboard. The machine would check a million permutations, exclude those containing contradictions, and finally reveal how the Enigma machine had been set in order to produce this crib. The 'Bombe' would then provide a solution by discounting every incorrect one in turn. The first 'Bombe' was based on Turing's design and was installed at Bletchley Park in 1940. Subsequent versions were equipped with Welchman's diagonal board, which could substantially decrease the number of possible rotor settings. In 1944, Colossus, the first digital electronic computer, became operational at Bletchley Park. Colossus was designed to break messages coded on Lorenz machines. The Lorenz machine created more-complex ciphers, using a code in which each letter of the alphabet was represented by a series of five electrical impulses. Obscuring letters were also generated by Lorenz's 12 rotors. The first Colossus arrived at Bletchley Park in December 1943. In practical terms, Bletchley Park used the world's first electronic computer and digital information processing machine.

Bletchley Park had all the four essential characteristics that we now attribute to intelligent cities: (1) a creative population working in information and knowledge-intensive activities; (2) institutions and routines for collaboration in knowledge creation and sharing; (3) technological infrastructure for communication, data processing and information analysis; and (4) a proven ability to innovate and solve problems that appear for the first time. Bletchley Park was the first intelligent community ever created.

Bletchley Park, as a prototype of an intelligent community, was an urban ecosystem in which the organised division of labour and the orchestration of distributed tasks based on institutional rules with the support of intelligent machines produced radical innovations. The military organisation in this district and the absence of the spontaneous complexity we usually find in cities should not lead us to undervalue the innovativeness of its design and its effectiveness in dealing with extremely complex problems. It represents a top-down solution that was feasible under extreme conditions when the social division of labour within cities becomes a technical division also.

88 *What makes cities intelligent?*

5. Empowerment intelligence: Cyberport, Hong Kong up-skilling platforms

There are, however, other routes to spatial intelligence, which stand on the contribution of city districts and urban infrastructure to knowledge and skills development.

The spatial structure of intelligent cities is actually taking the form of 'knowledge ecosystems' and 'innovative districts' over 'smart networks.' This form is produced by the decentralisation of urban management and the development of smart urban networks. The literature on the clustering of innovation has explained the causes of spatial gathering and the creation of islands of innovation (Morgan, 2004; Simmie, 1998). Many types of clusters, such as cohesion clusters, industrial districts, innovative milieu, and planned technology parks (Hart, 2000) with different sizes, activities, degrees of internal association, and input-output relationships operate over urban infrastructures. City networks for mobility, energy, and utilities, on the other hand, are becoming smarter in the pursuit of environmental sustainability and resource savings. It is estimated that smart infrastructure, smart grids, sensors, wireless meters, and actuators, might have a higher impact on energy savings and CO_2 reduction than the total positive effect from renewable energy sources.

Metropolitan strategic plans like the "Melbourne 2030 Plan" and Stockholm's "Vision 2030" have clearly adopted this strategy of organising innovation ecosystems and knowledge-intensive districts over advanced infrastructure, including broadband, telecommunications, energy, smart transport, and logistics. Melbourne has institutionalised this district-led development via 'knowledge precincts,' areas surrounding university campuses in which special land-use regulations favour the location of activities that link to university infrastructure and R&D, offering opportunities for technology diffusion and cross-fertilisation between high-tech businesses, academia, and public facilities (Yigitcanlar et al., 2008). This architecture is beneficial for all innovation ecosystems of a city, which profit from technology networking, knowledge spillovers, and knowledge transfer.

Furthermore, some urban ecosystems are pursuing conscious strategies for involving the wider population of the city, not just producers and technologists, and are creating large-scale up-skilling with education and learning on experimental facilities and ICT infrastructure. Living Labs, for instance, offer a good case of user involvement and large-scale creativity development. Users take part in new product development and testing within real urban environments and participatory innovation processes, integrating *co-creation* activities, bringing together technology push and application pull, *exploration* activities engaging user communities in an earlier stage of the co-creation process, *experimentation* activities, implementing the proper level of technological artefacts to experience live scenarios, and *evaluation* of new ideas and innovative concepts and technological artefacts in real-life situations (Pallot, 2009). Such open and user-centric innovation ecosystems operate in many and diverse sectors, such as mobile communications, media, agriculture, food industry, health, medicine, e-government services, smart cities, sports, education, and social work.

There are also city ecosystems that act as 'innovation universities' or 'intelligent campuses,' which use the built environment of the city and experimental facilities to disseminate learning and innovation. Large-scale up-skilling strategies thus become possible, thereby improving the creativity, intelligence, and inventiveness of the population, and introducing 'innovation-for-all' environments, in which every citizen or company can become a producer of services and active innovator.

Cyberport, Hong Kong, is an innovation ecosystem that has effectively advanced this strategy of up-skilling, using advanced telecommunication infrastructure and multimedia technologies organised into knowledge district. Cyberport is a new district located on the west side of Aberdeen Country Park on Hong Kong Island. The district has been developed as a government programme aimed at developing the knowledge economy of Hong Kong. As an autonomous technology district, Cyberport is focusing on professional and enterprise development, offering an open platform for innovative ideas to flourish and for start-ups in the field of media technologies. The district is wholly owned by the Hong Kong SAR Government and managed by Hong Kong Cyberport Management Company Limited.

Cyberport includes many different activities, land uses, and zones. Within a relatively small piece of land of 24 hectares, there is an enterprise zone with four quality buildings that host about 100 information technology and media companies, a research institute, business incubator, conference centre, shopping mall, five-star Le Meridien hotel, a huge housing complex, and a large park at the heart of Cyberport which extends along the coastline. The area is served by fibre optic and copper networks offering high-speed broadband connections and a wide range of digital services and laboratory equipment. Buildings in the technology zone are grade-A intelligent office buildings. All these activities are organised into four different zones: the technology zone with Cyberport 1, 2, 3, and 4 buildings; the commercial zone with the mall and the hotel; the residential zone; and the park and open green area zone. Despite this functional division, the relatively small surface of the district and the openness here create a continuum of uses, as all the spaces are accessible to the community of the district.

Activities and land uses have been selected to promote the mission of the district and to ensure its sustainability. Cyberport Phase I was developed on public land and the construction work took place from 2000 to 2008. The funding scheme foresaw a split into two parts, the Cyberport zone and the ancillary residential zone. The mission of the Cyberport zone was to create a strategic cluster of leading information technology and information services companies and a critical mass of professionals in these sectors. The mission of the residential zone was to generate revenue for the Cyberport project. A development company acquired part of the land (about 20 percent of the plot), together with the infrastructure already on site to build the residential zone. The developer (Cyber-Port Limited) was responsible for the total construction costs of both the Cyberport and the housing complex (Hong King Legislative Council, 2002). The residential zone includes eight 50-storey buildings and two lower complexes – two to five storeys – for high-income residences along the coast. Overall, 2,800 homes were built. In return for the concession of the land and infrastructure of the residential zone, the developer delivered the technology zone as a turnkey solution, with Cyberport 1, 2, 3, and 4, the shopping mall arcade, the five-star hotel operated by Le Meridien, and the central park. Revenues generated by the commercial zone – mall and hotel – go to the technology zone and cover training, learning, and incubation expenses. The district was publicly funded and serves the public interest. This genuine funding model contributes both to development and operation of Cyberport 1, 2, 3, 4, and to the public and open character of the district.

Cyberport should not be seen as usual technology district or a technology park. It is a community that nurtures talent in the media industry, turning skills and talent into start-ups. It amplifies the skills and creativities of the Hong Kong population using experimental digital infrastructure and open platforms. The objectives are technology diffusion, up-skilling, and the enhancement of human capabilities. Cyberport is a creative community supplied with advanced communication and media infrastructure and digital connectivity. "Cyberport identifies, nurtures, attracts and sustains talent so it is able mobilise ideas, talents and creative organisations. It is a creative milieu; a place that contains the necessary requirements in terms of hard and soft infrastructure to generate a flow of ideas and inventions" (Interview with CEO of Cyberport, N. Yang). The focus of the district is the IT and multimedia sector, where it sustains a creative community. Technologies and digital applications that have been developed in Hong Kong Universities or the Technology Park can be transferred to the younger generation though practical learning and experimental training. Training from the world's leading media and IT companies is provided together with the laboratory equipment and start-up funding for follow-up training that promotes entrepreneurship.

To achieve these objectives, Cyberport has developed state-of-the-art infrastructure, media equipment, and digital services which are organised as open technology learning platforms. Each platform serves a specific objective of training, creativity, and entrepreneurship:

- *The Entrepreneurship Centre* is a platform whose objective is to build and promote entrepreneurship and competence in the digital entertainment industry, focusing on business skills, games, animation and digital entertainment, by offering financial assistance, support and professional services for enterprise development.
- *The Technology Centre* (formerly the Digital Media Centre) is a state-of-theart digital multimedia creation facility, high-end production equipment and cloud SaaS, whose objective is to offer software and hadrware support to content developers, multimedia professionals, small- and medium-sized enterprises.
- *The iResource Centre* is a digital content storage platform, which serves as a trusted marketplace and clearing house for the aggregation, protection, license issuance and distribution of digital content.
- *The Testing and Certification of Wireless Communication Platform* provides continuous mobile communication services and coverage of mobile phone signals (3G, GSM, CDMA, and PCS) in both outdoor and indoor areas within Cyberport in cooperation with major mobile communications service operators.
- *The Knowledge Centre* invests in local talent by building up ICT knowledge through training students and young people, knowledge sharing programmes,

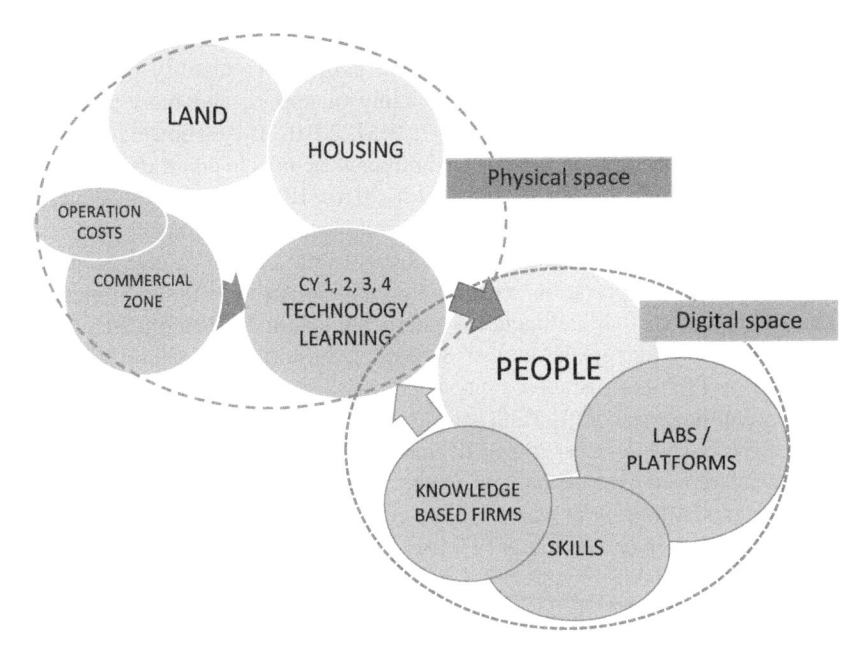

Alternative architectures of spatial intelligence 91

Figure 4.1 Cyberport empowerment circuit

and competitions. It supports also initiatives for ICT business development and adoption in Hong Kong.

These open technology platforms are operated in cooperation with industry leaders who are the founding industrial partners. CISCO, Hewlett Packard, IBM, Microsoft, Oracle, and PCCW have been involved through sponsorship programmes, while the students benefit from access to top-of-the-market technologies, scholarships, placement opportunities, and employment.

The dual mechanism described above – entailing (1) the open digital technology platforms, and (2) the real-estate based sustainability – provides an open-ended mechanism for professional training, learning, and up-skilling (Figure 4.1). Critical views to be found on the web concern mainly the urban characteristics of Cyberport, such as accessibility, liveability, how pleasant it is as place to work. The setting enhances human capabilities and intelligence by simultaneously providing hard urban infrastructure and soft digital technologies and services. Developed on public land, Cyberport is creating intelligence through up-skilling funded by real estate business models, and spreading out skills and capabilities into the entire urban system of Hong Kong.

6. Instrumentation intelligence: Amsterdam and Santander smart-metering projects for environmental sustainability

Among the most influential contributions to the creation of city intelligence has been the IBM Smart Planet – Smarter Cities (SP-SC) model based on the combination of broadband networks, smart meters, and predictive modelling. City intelligence is improved by making the city systems 'interconnected' and 'instrumented,' and by using the information gathered to identify patterns of behaviour, develop predictive models of likely outcomes, and more-informed decision-making (Dirks and Keeling 2009; IBM, 2010). It is estimated that this instrumentation intelligence might offer significant savings in city traffic, energy, health, and public safety costs (Kaiserswerth, 2010). IBM is testing this concept through partnerships with cities worldwide. In many cities, the company and local administrations work together to provide this type of solution in energy, water management, and transportation, reducing the city's footprint on the environment.

This concept of spatial intelligence is clearly applied in the experimental facility of Smart Santander in the city of Santander, in northern Spain. The facility, funded by FP7, has installed a city-wide network of sensors and devices to monitor pollution, noise, traffic, and parking. The test bed is composed of around 3,000 IEEE 802.15.4 devices, 200 GPRS modules and 2,000 joint RFID tag / QR code labels deployed over the built environment of the city and moving vehicles, buses, and taxis. A long-term plan envisions the deployment of about 20,000 sensors. Devices work over a common IP infrastructure using cellular, radio-meshed networks, and available broadband (Krco, 2010). The architecture supports a secure and open platform of heterogeneous technologies and the facility applies user-driven innovation methods (through competitive open calls) for the design of innovative applications and implements 'use cases,' such as bus tracking, air quality monitoring, urban waste management, and others. The facility is open to researchers and service providers to test architectures, enabling technologies, and pilot applications, the interaction and management of protocols, and support services such as discovery, identity management, and security, and the social acceptance of services related to the Internet of Things (Smart Santander, n.d.). The OSWINDS Group, for instance, run the SEN2SOC experiment over Smart Santander, connecting sensor measurements and social network interactions and producing new user-oriented services which can test and improve the infrastructure itself (Vakali et al., 2013).

Instrumentation intelligence is also widely implemented in Amsterdam Smart City. Smart devices and wireless meters transmit information over broadband networks and provide intelligence to citizens and organisations of the city to optimise energy-saving practices. Decisions can be made with respect to accurate and on-time information provided by smart devices or by the crowd. Many solutions for this type of logic are being implemented in different districts of the city: housing and living (West Orange, Geuzenveld, Haarlem, Onze Energie), working (ITO Tower, monumental buildings, employee contest), mobility (Ship to Grid, Moet je Watt), and public space (Climate Street, smart schools, ZonSpot, smart swimming) (Baron, 2011). Overall, 43 projects are being implemented in three areas (Ijburg, Nieuw West, Zuid Oost) and five themes (Living, Working, Mobility, Public Facilities, and Open Data) (Amsterdam Smart City, 2009).

In the Haarlem area, for instance, 250 users can test an energy management system and get insight into the energy consumption of appliances, enabling monitoring of energy usage and appliances to be remotely switched on and off. In the

Geuzenveld neighbourhood, 500 homes have been provided with smart metres and energy displays to become aware of energy consumption and discuss energy savings at brainstorming sessions. In the West Orange project, 500 households have been provided with smart metres and displays, and a personal energy-saving goal is set for every household. The overall goal is to save at least 14 percent on energy and reduce CO_2 emissions by an equal amount. The ITO tower, a large multi-tenant office building, is testing which smart building technologies, co-operative agreements, and practices can make office buildings more sustainable. Information gained by smart plugs and insight based on data analysis are used to provide more efficient solutions. In the Utrechtsestraat, a shopping street with numerous cafés and restaurants, 140 small enterprises are testing solutions for a more sustainable environment: logistics using electric vehicles, energy-saving lamps for street lighting dimmed during quiet times, solar-powered garbage compacters, smart metres and displays for energy consumption, and incentives and benefits arising from energy savings (Amsterdam Smart City, 2009). The city also is experimenting with crowdsourcing, co-creation, open data, and open innovation to involve citizens in finding better solutions for public space and mobility. Ambitious goals were set to reduce CO_2 emissions by 40 percent and achieve a 20 percent energy reduction in 2025 compared to a 1990 baseline. Key performance indicators show that these goals can be achieved. In the Climate Street, already more than 50 percent sustainable waste collection and 10 percent energy savings have been recorded.

7. Towards a universal architecture of spatial intelligence

Moving beyond the baseline of agglomeration intelligence, orchestration, empowerment, and instrumentation intelligence shows different architectures that cities can adopt to increase their problem-solving capability. Spatial intelligence actualises arrays of knowledge functions and smart systems to more efficiently manage available city resources and human capital. They articulate large-scale and city-wide endowments of different types of intelligence, namely collective (in some cases organisational), human, and machine intelligence. All architectures of spatial intelligence increase the efficiency of cities to address complex and non-linear problems, but they do it in very different ways.

Orchestration is based on the large-scale division of work and integration of knowledge tasks which are distributed among the members of a community. Each task may be simple, but the size of the collaboration defines the complexity of the entire knowledge process. The overall result may be truly innovative. Empowerment rests on improvements of individual skills and know-how. It is an individual learning process, but when practiced massively on the entire city can produce great results. Instrumentation intelligence replicates computer processes at city level, gathering information from sensors, social media, and urban activities, processing this information, and providing real-time information, alerts, hopefully forecasts, and wiser decisions.

A few variables, however, generate the above types of spatial intelligence:

- The knowledge functions involved, which might relate to information-in, learning, innovation, information-out;

94 *What makes cities intelligent?*

- The intelligence used, which might be primarily human, collective from collaboration, or machine intelligence relying on sensors, agents, and self-control processes;
- The workflow, infrastructure and arrays followed, which might entail different complementarities between the spatial, institutional, and digital dimensions of cities.

Clearly, orchestration, empowerment, and instrumentation are not the only feasible forms of spatial intelligence produced from these variables. Many more combinations are possible. Future Internet technologies and future media research, for instance, are bringing in new solutions in terms physical – digital relationships, with new infrastructure (cloud computing, RFIDs, sensors, real-world user interfaces, mobile devices), data (open data, linked data), and trusted services.

Such forms of spatial intelligence can be practiced in all domains of cities: the innovation economy of cities with different solutions for work and collaboration in city districts, sectors of economic activity, clusters and city ecosystems; the quality of life with e-services for social care, health, safety, environmental monitoring and alert; the utilities of cities with their different networks, flows and infrastructures; and the governance of cities with services to citizens, decision-making procedures, participation, and more direct democracy. At least 25 different domains of cities can be identified as potential fields for deploying spatial intelligence using hundreds of applications and e-services.

In each of city domains (district, sector or network), spatial intelligence emerges from the combination of knowledge processes, type of intelligence involved, and type of spatial arrangement deployed (Figure 4.2). Outputs and effectiveness in terms of city growth, employment, and environmental sustainability depend on how these variables are combined. It is a critical issue for smart city planning and governance to select the most effective combination of variables with respect to the character of the city and the problems in focus. Instrumentation, for instance,

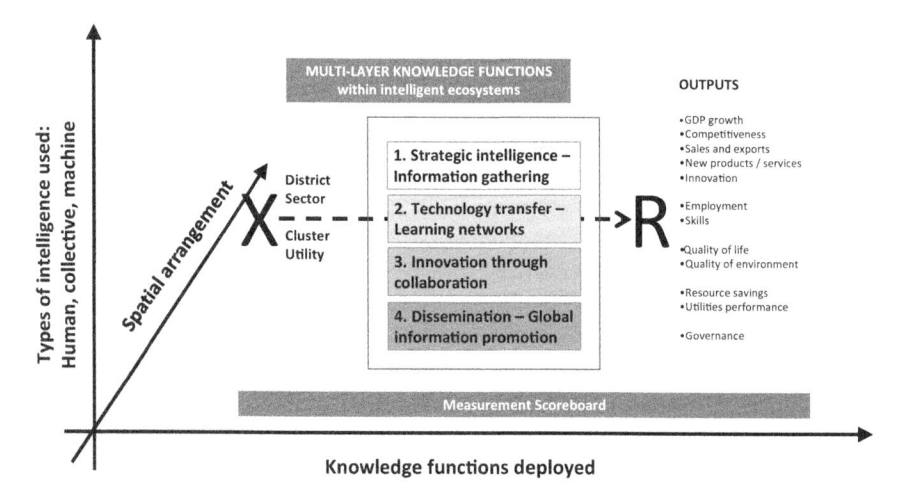

Figure 4.2 Generic dimensions of spatial intelligence of cities

seems suitable for providing resource efficient urban networks, and sustainable transport, energy, and environment; orchestration offers advantages in terms of quality of service and operation costs in well structured areas such as ports and technology districts; empowerment is a good solution for innovative clusters, start-ups, employment generation, leading to more competitive places.

Intelligent cities are expected to and have promised to more efficiently address contemporary urban challenges. However, to date, intelligent city strategies seem to have a rather limited impact on the great challenges of cities concerning competitiveness, employment, and environmental sustainability. This mismatch signifies several things: that smart environments are not well targeted at city challenges; that solutions are more technology push than need driven; or that cities have not developed sufficient spatial intelligence. All explanations can be true, and cities with all the technology and institutions they actually have are not yet sufficiently intelligent. By and large, contemporary solutions are lagging in terms of achievement and the social impact reached by Bletchley Park.

We are just entering the age of intelligent cities and we still lack a deeper understanding of the processes that create city intelligence. Most definitions of intelligent cities or smart cities stress the use of information and communications technologies to make cities more innovative and efficient. But, they do not equally stress other drivers of spatial intelligence and forms of integration among digital spaces and open connected communities, innovation institutions and networks, regeneration strategies, and measurement and assessment systems, which when take all together generate spatial intelligence. We have to engineer more integrated solutions for every sector, district, and innovation ecosystem of a city, as integration is the key to higher spatial intelligence and efficiency.

References

Amsterdam Smart City. (2009). Amsterdam, the Netherlands: Municipality of Amsterdam.
Amsterdam Smart City. (2009). *Projects*. Retrieved 2 January 2014, from http://amsterdamsmartcity.com/projects.
Antirroiko, A. V. (2005). Cybercity. *Encyclopedia of the city*. London, UK: Routledge.
Baron, G. (2011). *Amsterdam smart city*. Amsterdam, the Netherlands: Amsterdam Innovation Motor.
Belissent, J. (2010). *Getting clever about smart cities: New opportunities require new business models*. Forrester for Ventor Strategy Professionals. Retrieved 2 January 2014, from http://goo.gl/hnuuRo.
Bell, R., Jung, J. and Zacharilla, L. (2009). *Broadband economies: Creating the community of the 21st century*. New York, NY: Intelligent Community Forum Publications.
Bergvall-Kåreborn, B. and Ståhlbröst, A. (2009). Living Lab: An open and citizen-centric approach for innovation. *International Journal of Innovation and Regional Development*, Vol. 1, No. 4, 356–370.
Boschma, R. and Frenken, K. (2011). Technological relatedness and regional branching. In H. Bathelt, M. P. Feldman, and D. F. Kogler (eds), *Beyond territory: Dynamic geographies of knowledge creation, diffusion, and innovation* (pp. 64–81). London, UK: Routledge.
Caragliu, A., Del Bo, C. and Nijkamp, P. (2009). *Smart cities in Europe*. Amsterdam, the Netherlands: VU University Amsterdam, Faculty of Economics, Business Administration and Econometrics.

Chen-Ritzo, C. H, Harrison, C., Paraszczak, J. and Parr, F. (2009). Instrumenting the planet. *IBM Journal of Research and Development*, Vol. 53, No. 3, 338–353.

Couclelis, H. (2004). The construction of the digital city. *Environment and Planning B: Planning and Design*, Vol. 31, No. 1, 5–19.

Deakin, M. (2011). The embedded intelligence of smart cities. *Intelligent Buildings International*, Vol. 3, No. 3, 189–197.

Deakin, M. and Allwinkle, S. (2007). Urban regeneration and sustainable communities: The role networks, innovation and creativity in building successful partnerships. *Journal of Urban Technology*, Vol. 14, No. 1, 77–91.

Dirks, S. and Keeling, M. (2009). *A vision of smarter cities*. Dublin, Ireland: Centre for Economic Development.

Graham, S. (ed.) (2003). *The cybercities reader*. London, UK: Routledge.

Graham, S. (2010). *Cities under siege: The new military urbanism*. London, UK: Verso Books.

Hargadon, A. (2003). *How breakthroughs happen. The surprising truth about how companies innovate*, Boston, MA: Harvard Business School Press.

Hart, D. A. (2000). *Innovation clusters: Key concepts*. Working paper, Department of Land Management and Development, and School of Planning Studies, The University of Reading, United Kingdom.

Hiramatsu, K. and Ishida, T. (2001). An augmented web space for digital cities. *Applications and the Internet 2001 Proceedings*. Retrieved 2 January 2014, from http://ieeexplore.ieee.org/xpl/freeabs_all.jsp?arnumber=905173.

Hong King Legislative Council (2002). *Background brief on Cyberport*. Legislative Council Secretariat. Retrieved 2 January 2014, from www.legco.gov.hk/yr01-02/english/panels/itb/papers/itb0708cb1-2172-1e.pdf.

IBM (2010). *A vision of smarter cities: How cities can lead the way into a prosperous and sustainable future*. Somers, NY: IBM Global Services.

Ishida T. and Isbister K. (eds) (2000). *Digital cities: Technologies, experiences, and future perspectives*. Berlin, Germany: Springer-Verlag.

Jacobs, J. (1969). *The economy of cities*. New York, NY: Random House.

Kaiserswerth, M. (2010). *Creating a smarter planet: One collaboration at a time*. IBM Research Zurich. Retrieved 2 January 2014, from www.earto.eu/fileadmin/content/01_Seminars___Conferences/AC_2010/4-Matthias_Kaiserswerth.pdf.

Komninos N. (2002). *Intelligent cities: Innovation, knowledge systems, and digital spaces*. London, UK: Routledge.

Komninos, N. (2008). *Intelligent cities and globalisation of innovation networks*. London and New York: Routledge.

Krco, S. (2010). SmartSantander – a smart city example. *ICT event 2010*. Brussels: Belgium, 27–29 September.

Mitchell, W. (1996). *City of Bits: space, place and the infobahn*. Cambridge, MA: Massachusetts Institute of Technology.

Mitchell, W. (2007). Intelligent cities. *E-Journal on the Knowledge Society*, UOC Papers. Retrieved 2 January 2014, from www.uoc.edu/uocpapers/5/dt/eng/mitchell.html.

Morgan, K. (2004). The exaggerated death of geography: Localised learning, innovation and uneven development. *Journal of Economic Geography*, Vol. 4, No. 1, 3–21.

Pallot, M. (2009). *Engaging users into research and innovation: The Living Lab approach as a user centred open innovation ecosystem*. Retrieved 2 January 2014, from Webergence Blog. Available at www.cwe-projects.eu/pub/bscw.cgi/1760838?id=715404_1760838.

Schaffers, H., Komninos, N., Pallot, M., Trousse, B., Nilsson M. and Oliveira, A. (2011). Smart cities and the future Internet: Towards cooperation frameworks for open innovation. *The Future Internet, Lecture Notes in Computer Science*, Vol. 6656, 431–446.

Shiode, N. (1997). An outlook for urban planning in cyberspace: Toward the construction of cyber cities with the application of unique characteristics of cyberspace. *Online Planning Journal*, Oct. Nov. Retrieved 2 January 2014, from www.casa.ucl.ac.uk/planning/articles2/urban.htm.

Simmie, J.M. (1998). Reasons for the development of 'Islands of innovation'. Evidence from Hertfordshire. *Urban Studies*, Vol. 35, No. 8, 1261–1289.

Smart Santander. (n.d.) *SmartSantander Experimental Test Facilities*. Retrieved 2 January 2014, from www.smartsantander.eu/index.php/testbeds.

Soja, E. (2003). Writing the city spatially. *City*, Vol.7, No. 3, 269–280.

Vakali, A., Angelis, E. and Giatsoglou, M. (2013). Sensors talk and humans sense towards a reciprocal collective awareness smart city framework. *IEEE International Conference on Communications* (IEEE ICC). Retrieved 2 January 2014, from http://smartsantander.eu/index.php/sen2soc.

Van den Besselaar, P. and Koizumi, S. (2005). *Digital cities III. Information technologies for social capital: Cross-cultural perspectives*. Amsterdam and Berlin: Springer-Verlag.

Yigitcanlar, T., O'Connor, K. and Westerman, C. (2008). The making of knowledge cities: Melbourne's knowledge-based urban development experience. *Cities*, Vol. 25, No. 2, 63–72.

Yovanof, G.S. and Hazapis, G.N. (2009). An architectural framework and enabling wireless technologies for digital cities & intelligent urban environments. *Wireless Personal Communications*, Vol. 49, No. 3, 445–463.

Part II
Planning for intelligent cities

Connecting bottom-up and top-down perspectives

5 Intelligent cities and the bottom-up regeneration of metropolitan areas

1. Intelligent city planning and the regeneration of metropolitan cities in Europe

The regeneration of metropolitan cities of Europe in relation to intelligent city planning highlights how larger cities are adopting this new paradigm and how the deployment of broadband networks, smart spaces, Web applications, and e-services is helping every city to become more innovative and efficient in resources and environmental sustainability. The evolutionary course from digital to intelligent cities, which can be found in the literature, is also being replicated in the processes that are taking place in every city. The digital life of cities starts in hyperspace, but it soon becomes embedded into the social life and the physical environment of cities, empowering people and advancing innovation. An irreversible current is driving cities from digital applications to smart ecosystems and intelligent places.

Starting from this perspective, the purpose of this chapter is to bring to the surface how intelligent city planning is regenerating metropolitan cities in Europe. We start by offering a summary account of intelligent city planning in Barcelona, Manchester, and Helsinki, and then go on to discuss in more detail current developments in the city of Thessaloniki. These cities have been studied in the context of the FIREBALL project, which offered a good number of case studies and a realistic picture of European smart city strategies (Komninos et al., 2013). Narratives of smart city strategies analysed in the framework of FIREBALL are also available at Vimeo (http://vimeo.com/fireball4smartcities).

In discussing the regeneration of metropolitan cities in Europe in relation to intelligent city planning, we focus on three processes that usually shape metropolitan regeneration: (1) the creation of a backbone of broadband networks, (2) the creation and agglomeration of digital applications in every domain of the city life and activity, and (3) the renewal of city-districts through smart systems and innovative communities. We also discuss governance challenges related to gaps encountered as cities undergo this process of transformation, and the impact assessment of digital applications and e-services. However, in essence, we are describing how intelligent city planning principles and initiatives can contribute to the regeneration of old metropolitan areas and help larger cities address their own objectives: how to use broadband networks, smart spaces, Web applications, and e-services to create place-specific collective intelligence, collaborative innovation, and environmental sustainability.

Barcelona

Barcelona has implemented digital urban policies over a long period and has run numerous initiatives to promote smart city development. An extensive account of this development is given by Bakici et al. (2013). The city's general objective is to use ICTs in order to transform business processes and the public administration, both internally and externally. The main focus of the Barcelona Smart City throughout the last decade has been competitiveness and the development of a local smart economy built on collaboration networks between companies, institutions, citizens, and city hall. Other objectives relate to supporting innovation, creating new channels of communication, facilitating access to information both locally and internationally, and improving the efficiency of public services. Altogether, smart city initiatives in Barcelona can be placed under four headers: smart economy, smart living, smart people, and smart governance.

The city has invested heavily in extended broadband infrastructure, the creation of innovation clusters and districts, and e-services available to citizens. Broadband networks offer the backbone network for the installation of sensors and the provision of e-services. A corporate fibre optic network connects the main municipal buildings. A Wi-Fi mesh network provides wireless connection to those municipal services and employees working at street level. Networks comprised of multi-vendor and multipurpose sensors are configured to be used by services providers and a public Wi-Fi network offers open broadband access.

In terms of innovation cluster development, the flagship project has been the 22@Barcelona district, which has regenerated an old industrial area of 200 hectares into an innovative district gathering knowledge-intensive activities and offering new working spaces for government agencies, companies, and research institutes. 22@Barcelona combines the concern for science, technology, and competitiveness with spaces for companies and professionals, green infrastructure, and a housing component of 4,600 dwellings, as well as the pursuit of quality of life and identity. The district also supports a series of programmes aimed at creating new business opportunities such as the 22@urban Lab, 22@Synergys, and the Barcelona Urban Innovation Lab & Dev (BUILD), which encourages the participation of companies in the development of innovative products and services for urban management. The 22@Urban Lab offers infrastructure and services and public spaces in the city of Barcelona to carry out real environment tests on products and services for smart city infrastructure, such as outdoor public street lighting points with LED technology; charging points for electric cars; gas, electricity, and water smart meters; solar-powered motorbikes; traffic lights adapted to the blind that provide orientation, 'crossing,' and 'end crossing' sound signals; traffic-control cameras; fibre optic networks to the home; and much else besides.

Intelligent cities and the bottom-up regeneration 103

A large number of applications and platforms created by companies and organisations owned by the city enable e-services to be provided to citizens. FabLab Barcelona, a leading fabrication laboratory, offers digital fabrication machines and tools while Barcelona Urban Innovation Lab & Dev (BUILD) operates an open public–private platform that promotes the use of electric vehicles in the city. Other applications are based on sensors for parking, public lighting control, information panels, surveillance cameras, and municipal fleet management. Public data owned by the city is made accessible to the public through a portal that includes more than 300 categories of data in five areas related to territory, population, urban services, economy, and administration. Apart from promoting transparency, this open data provides opportunities for social innovation and private sector initiatives for public services.

Manchester

Manchester is another city with a long-term agenda for digital development linked to urban regeneration. The city has gradually developed and formulated smart city planning principles. In the mid-1980s, Manchester City Council adopted three thematic priorities for regeneration, (1) a focus on working with areas and neighbourhoods, (2) the development of a creative city strategy through arts and cultural industries, and (3) innovation and future economic growth, through the development of the Manchester Science Park and ICT infrastructure. In 2008, a digital strategy began to be prepared which introduced the concern for digital technologies and linked it to the regeneration agenda. In 2011, the launch of the EU's Digital Agenda for Europe provided further ground for policies and actions related to digital technologies and the user-driven innovation approach. A detailed description of this evolutionary course is given by Carter (2013).

The main themes highlighted in the Digital Strategy for Manchester are: (1) *digital inclusion,* in order to tackle the digital divide; (2) the development of *digital industries and clusters,* to overcome the lack of business finance and support new investment, start-ups, and better access to skills and employment in new sectors; and (3) *digital innovation,* in order to generate investments in innovation and new infrastructure in relation to the Future Internet research community. These orientations drive Manchester smart city initiatives in areas such as energy, cloud-based solutions, new high-speed infrastructure (fibre and wireless), networks and e-services. Flagship initiatives that implement them include the new generation access (NGA) networks, the East Manchester regeneration project, and the Eastserve Living Lab.

The Manchester City Region NGA initiatives are being developed in partnership with the Manchester Digital Development Agency (MDDA), which is part of Manchester City Council and the Commission for the New Economy. The main focus is the Corridor 'Living Lab NGA' pilot project, which aims to connect 500 businesses and 1,000 residential users through an FTTP network. The network is expected to work as a test bed for business-to-business transactions, business-to-consumer, and community-based applications; e-services that will be developed

104 *Planning for intelligent cities*

focus on innovation in public service delivery in areas such as telecare, health, energy efficiency, smart energy, e-learning, smart mobility, and flexible working (Carter, 2013).

The East Manchester Regeneration Project covers an area of 1,100 hectares situated immediately east of Manchester's City Centre, which had been the city's major industrial area in the past. Industrial restructuring brought factory closures, massive unemployment, and environmental degradation. Regeneration was planned in terms of opportunities for a knowledge-driven economy and support for digital competences. An online community network, run in partnership with local citizen organisations and representatives, known as 'Eastserve,' was established in 2001. Eastserve connected more than 2,000 homes with wireless broadband Internet connections, as well as 17 local schools, eight online community access centres, and ten public access points in libraries and other centres. All were connected to a 100Mbps wireless backbone linking four tower blocks around the East Manchester area, from where bandwidth is distributed over a wireless network. Schools and public buildings receive an online community service, developed by Eastserve, and relay it to other residential locations. In parallel, the provision of micro-loans through the local credit union has enabled people to buy computer equipment and use the e-services offered.

Other people-focused e-services include the Manchester Internet Hub that offers enhanced connectivity across the city, especially between Manchester Science Park, Sharp and Media City, UK; the 'Low Carbon Open Data Network' that collects real-time environmental data using low-cost, low-power sensors and provides open access to these data; 'Smart Innovation & People' for digitally supported community engagement; 'Green Digital Charter,' an initiative to reduce the environmental impact of digital technologies and to develop innovative smart energy project using smart meters; and 'Digital and Creative Skills,' which brings together businesses in the digital and creative sectors, offering education and training to develop more innovative ways for people to gain skills and get access to advanced learning.

Helsinki

Helsinki smart city initiatives are also multidimensional, but are mainly built on clusters and user-driven innovation. The strategy does not endorse solutions limited to municipal boundaries, but removes bureaucratic barriers, thereby enabling a competitive and agile smart region. Collaboration is high priority. The Helsinki Region is developing smart services that work as platforms for innovation, and are open to all parties and organisations. Smart Helsinki is part of the overall innovation strategy for the region that is aimed at developing strong clusters related to mobile technologies and at taking advantage of local favourable factors, such as high-quality research and education, continuous demand for innovative services, a highly competitive business environment, and quadruple-helix innovation networks.

Living Lab clusters are actively supported by local and regional governments through governmental funding for research and innovation. There is a strong tradition of Living Lab research in Finland, and various types of organisations, universities, large companies, and government agencies have established Living Labs in the Helsinki Region. Municipalities also promote Living Labs to sustain economic development and social innovation in the areas of energy, the provision of healthcare services, care for the elderly, preventive care and urban living. The Living Labs that have been established in and around the Helsinki Region, such as the 'Helsinki Living Lab,' 'Virium Forum,' and the 'Arabianranta Living Lab' contribute to smart city development.

With this strong orientation on Living Labs and innovation clusters, the City of Helsinki has contributed to the creation of a "Mobile Applications Cluster" by organising competitions for smartphone applications (Hielkemand and Hongisto, 2013). Competitions generate a stream of new mobile applications, which in many cases use open data provided by the Helsinki Region. In two competitions, the Helsinki Region made available public transportation data, and Apps4Finland made data available related to the environment and spatial information. This Porterian cluster of mobile technologies compliments Helsinki's Smart City strategy. The cluster benefits from local factors, such as the existence of broadband providers, telecommunication companies, NOKIA, the skilled workforce, and specialised startups; from demand conditions, such as government demand and demand from the banking and transportation sectors; firm strategies focused on global markets; and supporting infrastructure, 3G networks, and specialised service providers. Solutions created by the cluster benefit both the Mobile Application Cluster and Smart Helsinki. Competitive–collaborative processes within the cluster involve information technology providers, and media companies, as well as e-service and mobile applications providers. Creating a nucleus of innovative and competitive companies, the mobile applications cluster offers new competences, economic growth, and wealth to the region.

2. Planning for intelligent Thessaloniki

Similar initiatives to those found in smart Barcelona, Manchester, and Helsinki are also present in Thessaloniki, the second largest metropolitan city of Greece. In Thessaloniki, intelligent city projects are gaining momentum, sustained by the permanent concern for innovation-driven development of the city over the last 25 years.

Thessaloniki is a 2,300-year-old city, and over the course of its history has gone through a series of transformations and cultures. It has seen Hellenistic, Roman, Byzantine, Venetian, Ottoman, and again Greek periods, all of which have left their mark on the city. Mark Mazower reconstructed a more recent history of Thessaloniki from 1430 to 1950 in the book *Salonica City of Ghosts,* and explained how this Mediterranean port city nurtured a cosmopolitan blend of cultures and a mixture of Greek, Turkish, and Jewish populations (Mazower, 2004) for more than 500 years. As one might expect, this long history brings with it memories and landmarks of different visions and 'ghosts,' but every period has also created its own identity, laid over the memories of the previous ones. The vision that actually drives the city is innovation-led development and the strengthening of clusters, both in traditional manufacturing and knowledge-intensive services.

One landmark in the recent history of Thessaloniki was the new city plan, endorsed after the great fire of 1917 that destroyed most of the historic centre of Thessaloniki. The fire levelled almost the entire commercial district, all the shops, hotels and restaurants, and entertainment and business premises, and ruined the heart of the old Ottoman city. The new city plan was prepared by the Committee for the New Thessaloniki Town Plan, with significant input from the British landscape architect Thomas Mawson, and above all the French architect and urban planner Ernest Hébrard. Out of the fire's ashes a new city was created, founded on market principles rather than on ethnicity and religion. The new plan introduced a functional reorganisation of the city, with commercial and tertiary sector activities in the centre, manufacturing and logistics to the west, and housing and garden cities to the east. The city grid was aligned City Beautiful concepts and new infrastructure was built. Thus, a great socio-economic change took place based on the gentrification and occupation of the city centre by the most affluent residents, irrespective of nationality and religion. The Ottoman city, with its ethnic and religious divisions, was replaced by a Western city based on the principles of the market economy, the pursuit of productivity, and functional specialisation of city districts.

The post-war economic development of Thessaloniki was characterised by intense industrial development. A large manufacturing complex was created on the west side of the city composed of chemical, plastics, pulp, textile, and food industries. Housing sprawl took place in the eastern part, as foreseen by the Hébrard Plan. Internal migration inflows led to increases in the population, bringing the figure to close to 1 million inhabitants today. However, during the last decade, the industrial base of Thessaloniki has undergone major changes. The number of manufacturing establishments has decreased by 42.7 percent, employment by 17.8 percent, and added value by 3.1 percent. In contrast, the total value of production has increased by 17.9 percent and sales by 18.4 percent, as manufacturing has become more capital intensive and integrated into global supply chains (Georghiou et al., 2009). During the same period, a substantial growth in services was observed. The tertiary sector responded better to globalisation challenges, quickly integrating organisational innovations and increasing its share in terms of employment and GDP. Within the tertiary sector, a dynamic core has been created by outward-oriented services that characterise the current growth of Thessaloniki. These include sectors such as tourism, ICT, health, higher education and research, business services, transport, and international trade. These new sectors are now considered as growth engines contributing both to GDP and employment growth all around the EU (European Commission, 2008).

Since the 1990s, all city stakeholders think of innovation-led development as the top development priority. The concern for knowledge-intensive activities and new technology districts is all-inclusive in Thessaloniki, considering that knowledge and innovation can provide competitive advantages to counter-balance the decline of manufacturing. To date, the position of Thessaloniki as the second-most important innovation centre in the country has been due to higher education, public research, and knowledge-intensive services. The 2009 innovation data confirm that the innovation strengths of Thessaloniki lie in human resources, higher education, and public R&D (Pro Inno Europe, 2009).

Actually, the innovation economy of Thessaloniki is developing along two parallel pathways: it is developing on the one hand by setting up business clusters and new technology districts, such as the Technology Park and the Centre for Research and Technology, the Technopolis ICT business park, the Thermi and i4G incubators, the Alexander Innovation Zone; and on the other hand, it is developing thanks to the deployment of broadband networks and e-services for business, government, and citizens that are sustaining a new economy developing around the ICT sector. These two paths overlap but not coordinated, the first being supported by public research and technology policy, while the second is progressing thanks to private investments being made by large telecommunication companies, Internet Service Providers (ISPs), ICT companies, and more recently the city government.

3. Broadband networks

Broadband access in Thessaloniki is provided by private sector operators, such as OTEnet, Vivodi Telecom, Tellas, Hellas-On-Line (HOL), and Forthnet, with Asymmetric Digital Subscriber Line (ADSL) and Very-High-Bit-Rate Digital Subscriber Line (VDSL) being the main standards. Most Internet providers use OTE's Bit Stream Network, which is the most extensive privately owned fibre optic network. ISPs lease ADSL connections to offer online services, but they do not have access to OTE's network infrastructure. This is changing, thanks to the liberalisation of telecommunications, as part of the aforementioned network passes into the control of the ISPs. The typical download / upload speeds available over OTE's network are 4/1 Mbps and 24/1 Mbps for ADSL and 30–50 Mbps download for VDSL. The core of the city is covered with ADSL 14–24 Mbps and the metropolitan periphery with 9–16 Mbps. Internet access is available by first subscribing to the preferred ISP and then through this provider to OTE for a line. Broadband penetration is about 25 percent in the region of Central Macedonia and is assumed to be higher in the city of Thessaloniki.

Additional connectivity in academic districts is offered by the Greek Research and Technology Network (GRNET) fibre optic network that interconnects the city's universities and technical and research institutes to a wider academic and research institution network. Five points of presence (PoPs) are maintained within the context of the network: the Aristotle University of Thessaloniki, the University of Macedonia, the Thessaloniki Higher Educational Institute, the Centre for Research & Technology, the Center for Research and Technology – Hellas (CERTH), and the Informatics and Telematics Institute, which constitute secondary nodes that are equipped with switches or optical add-drop equipment, that aggregate customer traffic. The GRNET network, managed by the state-owned limited company GRNET S.A., supports the electronic interconnection of academic and research institutions with each other and with other academic networks through its upstream provider GÉANT (the pan-European communications infrastructure serving Europe's research and education community). It provides extensive coverage and much greater potential for the large number of students and researchers who use it. The GRNET backbone network of dark fibre optic cable (Wavelength Division Multiplexing – WDM technology at extra high speeds of 1–2.5 Gbps) covers a total length of more than 8,000 km. All the nodes are based on routers with Gigabit speeds and are interconnected with a network of 2.5 Gbps speeds over Dense Wavelength Division Multiplexing (DWDM) technology with leased wavelengths from the current provider (OTE).

3G and 4G coverage is very important and mobile broadband is developing at a rapid pace. It is offered by three mobile telecommunications service providers in Thessaloniki: Cosmote, Vodafone, and Wind. Speeds for both the Wind and Cosmote providers are up to 24 Mbps download (High-Speed Downlink Packet Access, HSDPA) and 5.72 Mbps upload, while Vodafone offers broadband speeds up to 42.2 Mbps download (HSDPA). An average 3G speed is 8Mbps. Recently, GSM providers started offering 4G broadband connections that are four times faster than the 3G network. The good level of coverage in the entire city, coupled with strong marketing by the mobile telecommunication companies, have resulted in diffusion of mobile Internet connections via smart phones and tablets at a very high rate, thereby increasing overall Internet penetration and accessibility.

Wireless broadband is offered by many public organisations covering local zones and city districts. These networks have been developed by local authorities, the Aristotle University, the Expo, the Port area, and other public or semi-public organisations. The access points are operated at 2.4–2.48 GHz and are compliant with the 802.11b standard, which has a maximum raw data rate of 11 Mbps, and the 802.11g standard, which extends the maximum raw data rate to 54 Mbps. A good example is the Wi-Fi network in the municipality of Thermi in the eastern part of metropolitan Thessaloniki. The municipality has installed 13 Wi-Fi hotspots and the wireless network consists of Point-to-Multipoint (PMP) and Point-to-Point (P2P) links, which enables wider areas which are characterised by either large numbers of visitors (commercial districts, archaeological sites, plazas, etc.) or areas not covered by the usual broadband infrastructure (ADSL). The wireless network offers free Internet access to citizens. It also supports the development of services and applications such as VoIP (Voice over Internet Protocol) and VoD (Video on Demand). The 13 Wi-Fi hotspots create small communication areas around localities of high accessibility, such as the town hall, the mall, the cultural centre, and the commercial street, as well as the cultural and community centres of adjacent smaller communities.

Non-profit initiatives operating on a community/collaborative basis also offer free wireless broadband connections, such as the Salonica Wireless Network (www.swn.gr/forum/index.php) and the Wireless Metropolitan Network of Thessaloniki (www.twmn.net/). Using cheap wireless equipment, they are removing the barriers that telecommunications companies erect, and offer a really open metropolitan network. They use antennas mounted on rooftops and windows and the free radio frequency of 2.4 GHz to create a free, locally owned, wireless backbone. The goal is to use open-source routing solutions and create an open, Wide Area Network (WAN) with metropolitan coverage.

4. City-wide applications and e-services

Using this broadband backbone, companies and organisations located in Thessaloniki are developing applications and online services related to the city's activities, digital presence, and functioning ranging from individual websites to more complex applications for content aggregation, location-based services, online administration services, and community services to citizens. Most applications come from bottom-up initiatives created out of the interest and concern of their developers. However, seen as a whole, they create a rich layer of digital services which is emerging from dispersed individual actions. The formation of this digital layer has characteristics similar to swarm intelligence and creativity (Gloor, 2006), a "movement from low-level rules to high-level sophistication" (Johnson, 2001, p. 18). It is a layer composed of applications which were given birth by the invisible hand of the digital market, and which are operated by developers, sellers, buyers, and citizens without central planning or coordination. A survey conducted within the context of the FIREBALL project helped describe the major components and characteristics of this Web-based Thessaloniki. The survey included three steps: definition of Web applications which concern the city; identification and listing of e-services offered; and interviews with selected e-service providers.

The first stage of the survey focused on defining applications which determine the Web presence and e-services of Thessaloniki. Here we have a problem similar to the 'building vs. city' duality. The city is composed of buildings, but 'buildings' and 'city' are different entities in terms of spatial attributes and functions. Relationships of proximity, agglomeration, collaboration, identity, and governance create cities and city-districts out of buildings and individual activities. Thus, the Web presence of a city is defined both by the sum (agglomeration) of Web applications related to its buildings, monuments, infrastructures, and activities, and by applications dealing with the city as a system of interconnected objects.

Bearing this in mind, the following types of Web applications and e-services are considered as characterising the city of Thessaloniki (and any city) as a whole, in contrast to applications related to its constituent objects:

- *City representations:* Applications and e-services which concern the digital representation of the city or serve as guides to the city.
- *City sectors:* Applications and e-services which concern an entire sector of activity within the city (all hotels in the city, entertainment in the city, etc.).
- *City districts:* Applications and e-services which concern the functioning or management of a city district (university campus, central business district, technology district, port area, etc.).

110 *Planning for intelligent cities*

- *Citizen aggregation:* Applications and e-services which rely on gathering data provided by citizens, leading to content aggregation and collective intelligence.
- *City services:* Applications that enable the provision of administration, social, community, safety, and environmental services to citizens by the authorities.
- *Location-based services:* Applications that enable the provision of services by relying on spatial identification and locality (i.e., location-based services, local offerings, and promotion of products and services).
- *City infrastructure and networks:* Applications and e-services which concern the use, functioning, and management of city infrastructure and utilities (transport, energy, water, waste).
- *City decision-making, planning and management:* Applications and e-services for mastering and managing the development of the city (city planning, consultation, and citizen engagement in decision-making).

Having defined this typology of city-related applications, the second stage of the survey concerned the identification of e-services in Thessaloniki that fall into the above eight categories. Identification was based on expert opinion from Web developers, IT experts, website administrators, city managers, and utility companies. A search on the Web also produced an additional yield. A large number of online services were identified in all domains of the city, from virtual guides of Thessaloniki to e-services for business, education, culture, utilities, transport, and city management. A representative sample is given in Table 5.1. Though their number is not as large as the number of all digital objects related to Thessaloniki (i.e., all the websites having an IP in the city), they represent a significant amount of Web and smart phone applications, which define the digital presence and online services offered in the city.

Table 5.1 City-wide applications and e-services in the agglomeration of Thessaloniki

Application domain	Number of services	Representative services	URL
The city			
Street view	N < 10	City street view	http://goo.gl/vsIsFs
		Thessaloniki 360^0	http://goo.gl/kaIugY
City guide	N < 10	Thessaloniki city guide	http://goo.gl/2hFNQe
		Location based services	smartphone apps
Urban economy			
City sectors	N > 30	Hotels in Thessaloniki	http://goo.gl/F3GH1C
		Virtual marketplace	http://goo.gl/rMZJBa
City clusters	N < 10	ICT market intelligence	http://goo.gl/wh8INF
		Organic products cluster	http://goo.gl/cW3SeI
City-districts	10 < N < 30	Thessaloniki Helexpo	http://goo.gl/UuLmjk
		Port – Container terminal	http://goo.gl/D19Qme

Application domain	Number of services	Representative services	URL
Quality of life			
Culture	10 < N < 30	Thessaloniki events	http://goo.gl/vaqccK
		Museums of Thessaloniki	http://goo.gl/OTEmsD
Education	N > 30	Aristotle University VPN library	http://goo.gl/7KYNKe
		Online research services	http://goo.gl/5T9DdS
Social care, health	10 < N < 30	Municipal social services	http://goo.gl/xu02zE
		City emergency services	http://goo.gl/TG1iD4
Environment	N < 10	AirThes: Air quality early warning	http://goo.gl/UWawDg
		Thermi air pollution alert	http://goo.gl/zvInrP
City infrastructure & utilities			
Mobility	N > 30	OASTH plan router	http://goo.gl/K3dZv0
		Ring road real-time monitoring	http://goo.gl/SxZv2x
Energy	N < 10	Thessaloniki natural gas	http://goo.gl/fa86bA
		Smart home solutions	http://goo.gl/niVeWA
Water, waste, recycling	N < 10	Water company –online payment	http://goo.gl/LyiU63
		Recycling of greater Thessaloniki	http://goo.gl/liI5O2
Broadband	N < 10	Wireless metropolitan network	http://goo.gl/22dRdw
		Thessaloniki wireless network	http://goo.gl/UUieG6
City governance			
Decision-making	N < 10	Municipal council live	http://goo.gl/E2hzz7
		Thermi, Improve-my-City	http://goo.gl/Wv7jQ9
Administration services	N > 30	Municipality electronic services	http://goo.gl/Ib8RIw
		Syzefxis telematic services	http://goo.gl/MxwCOh
City planning and management	N < 10	Thessaloniki geoportal	http://goo.gl/aeZB3u
		Cadastre electronic services	http://goo.gl/MMPA4M

Source: Field survey

Most known e-services to citizens are those related to administration services offered by public authorities, mobility and transport services, and local e-commerce, commercial advertisement, and marketing services. Those which are most technologically advanced and are best integrated into the physical space of Thessaloniki relate to mobility (public transport, fleet management, route planner, intelligent road monitoring). Interviews with managers of these systems provided information about how they were developed and how they actually operate.

112 *Planning for intelligent cities*

OASTH (www.oasth.gr) is the Organisation of Urban Transportation of Thessaloniki. It is a legal entity governed by private law, representing approximately 2,000 small shareholders. The organisation employs a staff of 2,400 who drive the organisation's buses on a daily basis, providing services to the wider metropolitan area of Thessaloniki via 68 bus lines.

OASTH has invested about €5 million in satellite fleet management and online services connecting all the 600 buses and 3,500 bus stops in its network. The system comprises many different digital services:

- GPS-based fleet management providing with real-time information about the position and working conditions of every bus. Every 20 seconds or 150 m, the bus sends its position traced by GPS.
- Acoustic information inside the buses informing the public about the next stop, which is activated automatically by GPS data.
- Digital displays at the 220 most-used bus stops, informing the public about the timing, direction, and arrival of buses. Displays are connected to fleet management and the information they provide is accurate and real-time.
- Route planner for selecting best routes in terms of distance covered or time spent with respect to the start and end points of a route. The user can find arrival times for routes at bus stops by selecting the route, the direction, and the bus stop of interest.

The development of this system was subcontracted out to external vendors. Data entry and route updates take place internally within the organisation. Data and applications are also maintained by the control centre on internal servers. The bus stops where displays were placed were selected by local authorities. Initially displays were supplied with power from photovoltaic panels, but these were vandalised or stolen. Bus stops also provide acoustic information for the blind. The system offers information to 500,000 people who use the services of the organisation daily. The added value to end users is in the form of better information on route (bus stops), inside the buses with acoustic updates about the next stop, and on the Web or smart phone with the route-planner application. Online fleet management is lowering maintenance costs for the fleet and ensuring a quicker response in the case of working failures or accidents.

The Eastern Ring Road Information System (http://155.207.18.200/ringroad/motion.html) is another e-service that provides real-time information about traffic conditions and incident detection and management on the city's ring road. The ring road is one of the most important parts of the urban infrastructure, with more than 100,000 journeys along the road taking place each day. The information system covers a length of about 12.5 km in each direction along the Eastern Ring Road of Thessaloniki. The system consists of three components:

- Wireless networks IEEE 802.11 (Wi-Fi) and IEEE 802.16 (Wi-Max) connecting smart devices placed on the Ring Road (cameras, sensors, displays), and transferring information about traffic conditions to the control centre.

Intelligent cities and the bottom-up regeneration 113

- Smart devices on the ring road, including five variable message signs and a closed television circuit with eight rotating cameras and nine fixed cameras. Cameras are equipped with image detection and processing hardware for recording and analysing traffic data on real-time.
- Traffic Control Centre where data are stored and validated before being public. The Advanced Transportation Management System (ATMS) software from NETworks© is used to support the operation of the system.

Data from cameras pictures, message signs, incidents, and traffic rates are made available via the Internet, and users have access through the Web or smart phone. Data are refreshed every two minutes, due to the bandwidth constraints of the wireless network. The control centre gathers information from cameras about traffic conditions and incidents; traffic loads are displayed with different colours for low (green), mid (yellow), and high (red) traffic. The system suggested messages to appear on the adjustable message signboards, but the controller has to validate these suggestions before they actually appear on the Ring Road displays.

Funding for the design and development of the system was provided by the Regional Authority and the Information Society Operational Programme, with a total budget of €1.4 million. The infrastructure, wireless network, and software were developed by a consortium of providers, including ICT companies, transport consultants, developers, and the academic research labs of the Aristotle University and the Institute of Transport – CERTH. However, due to failure of the business model for running and operating the system, its function is unstable and intermittent.

Thessaloniki 360 (www.thessaloniki360.com/en/) provides a virtual guided tour of the city. It was created by "Little Planet Image Services" as a Web guide to the city. The developers' intention was to create an advertising platform with customised configurations to advertise city companies and organisations. One issue that is particularly important is the quality and aesthetic value of the city representations, especially the night panoramic views. There are three applications on the platform: (a) *Address finder and driving directions*, with a usual structure of point of origin and destination, drop down lists, and directions given by car or foot; (b) *Tourist information mapping*, covering the entire city with geo-located information. Places of interest are given in ten categories, from shopping to arts, going out, sightseeing, and life in the city; and (c) *Virtual tour,* with interactive 360 panoramas of the city, with more than 350 locations in Thessaloniki being presented digitally, including city views, shopping, and discovering the city virtually. This allows the visitor to access monuments and landmarks, and to explore the city's history, culture, and highlights.

To support the creation of e-services, the City of Thessaloniki in collaboration with Open Knowledge Foundation (OKFN) and URENIO Research launched the competition "Apps4Thessaloniki" (http://thessaloniki.appsforgreece.eu/), scheduled to run from November 2013 to April 2014. The aim of the competition was to unleash the potential of the city in creating Web and smartphone applications that might improve the workings of the city and offer new e-services to residents,

114 *Planning for intelligent cities*

visitors, and businesses. The competition also aimed to disseminate a culture of open data, either through the opening of available data by public organisations or by the participants in the competition creating open datasets themselves. Available open data relate to city monuments, equipment, hospitality, mobility, government, and emergency issues. Open data were offered in multiple formats (shx, shp, prj, dbf, xml) over the CKAN platform, an open-source data platform that makes data accessible by providing tools to streamline publishing, sharing, finding and the use of data.

Participants in the competition were invited to submit ideas for e-services improving the economy, the quality of life, utilities, and government, and then solutions in the following three categories:

- Development of new applications that will make use of open data provided by the City and other organisations;
- Adaptation of existing open source applications to the environment and needs of Thessaloniki;
- Creation of open data sets.

Apps4Thessaloniki was based on two current trends within smart cities: (1) crowdsourcing of ideas and solutions, mobilizing through the competition a large group of people or the entire community of the city; and (2) open data, where public bodies and agencies provide access to data on cultural, economic, government, and other subjects, which can then be used to create value added applications and e-services. The overall goal of the competition was to create a community of developers, research organisations, companies, and citizens that will permanently work on digital solutions for the benefit of citizens and the city.

5. Planning for smart city-districts

The digital space of Thessaloniki created by broadband networks and city-wide e-services is emerging totally bottom-up. Broadband and e-services development are evolving as parallel, but uncoordinated, digital processes into Thessaloniki's knowledge economy. On the other hand, policies for privatisation and liberalisation of city government and infrastructure are creating pockets of independent control and management in city-districts and utilities and are giving birth to another type of bottom-up process: the regeneration of city-districts via public–private partnerships focusing on smart city solutions.

The development of smart city districts was the main concept behind 'Intelligent Thessaloniki,' a strategic plan for broadband networks, smart environments, and e-services targeted at the needs and functions of the main productive districts of the city. The plan was inspired by intelligent city principles and combines bottom-up regeneration at the level of city districts with top-down coordination of the districts at the level of the entire city.

Intelligent Thessaloniki is a strategy for deploying ICTs and Web-based services with the clear objective of strengthening the innovation ecosystems of the city and new growth sectors of transport, commerce, education, and high-tech

Intelligent cities and the bottom-up regeneration 115

industry. This approach was initiated in 2008, thanks to the collaboration between the Ministry of Development, the Regional Authority of Central Macedonia, and the Aristotle University of Thessaloniki, in the context of the National Strategic Reference Framework 2007–2013. The strategic plan trusts that smart environments can improve the innovation ecosystems of the city, opening the local economy up to global supply chains and markets and enabling participatory innovation processes driven by citizens, employees, and end-users.

Intelligent Thessaloniki is blending ICTs and user-driven innovation at the city-district level through actions such as:

- The creation of connected smart city-districts with strong internal broadband, based on locally open networks, mainly Wi-Fi and Wi-Max, and embedded sensor networks, smart metres, RFID, QR codes, and actuators.
- The development of applications and e-services adapted to each city-district and enhancing its mission, operation, and management.
- The support of district activities through collective intelligence, crowdsourcing, and community engagement for learning, innovation, marketing, and performance benchmarking.

Intelligent Thessaloniki is focusing on the most important districts of innovation and entrepreneurship in Thessaloniki, such as (1) the port of Thessaloniki, (2) the Central Business District and shopping centre of the city, (3) the campus of the Aristotle University of Thessaloniki, (4) the technology district of eastern

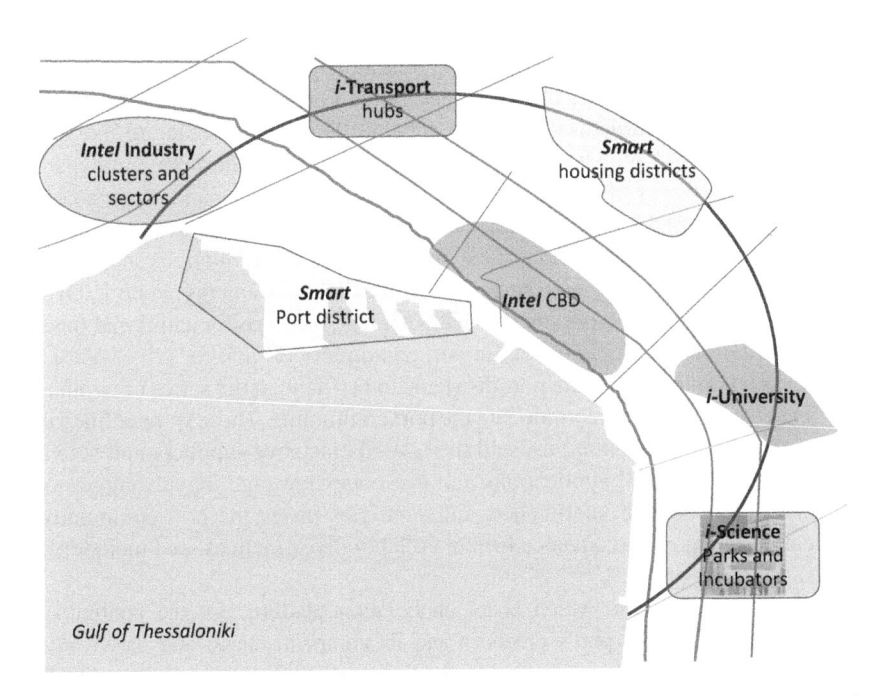

Figure 5.1 Smart city-districts for the regeneration of Thessaloniki

116 Planning for intelligent cities

Thessaloniki, and (5) the airport area (Figure 5.1). In each district, a wide range of digital applications and e-services were designed which can sustain innovation and entrepreneurship, including the development of open wired and wireless broadband networks; the provision of free Internet to businesses, users, and visitors; the development of intelligent environments based on sensors for real-time information processing and alert; the development of e-services suitable to the business community of the district, such as market watch, capacity building and acquisition of technology, new product development, digital marketing, and monitoring and benchmarking; and training services for businesses and organisations in e-content development and use of social media for business purposes.

Applications and e-services are very different from one city-district to the other. In the port area and surrounding cluster, smart environments and intelligent transport systems focus on the competitiveness of the port vis-à-vis other ports of the Mediterranean, lowering operating costs, improving the quality of service, integrating freight transactions, and monitoring and benchmarking the operations of the port. In the Central Business District (CBD), smart spaces focus on attracting and facilitating visitors, improving its competitiveness vis-à-vis the peripheral malls, easing access to the CBD by facilitating mobility and parking, as well as environmental monitoring and alert. At the University campus, smart environments have been designed to facilitate the dissemination of research, the opening up of university infrastructure to the local productive fabric of the city, and to strengthen academic collaboration with enterprises. In the Eastern technology district, smart environments were designed to facilitate the promotion of premises and to attract tenants, to provide online technology services, and to support start-ups and new business incubation.

Thus, the design of networks, smart systems, and applications is specific to the community and the character of the district. In the Port District, for instance, the design of smart infrastructure takes into account the radio coverage of existing networks (Wi-Fi and Wi-Max) inside the port area; the optimisation and expansion of these networks; the need to install new antennas, links, and routers; central management of all wireless and wired links; determination of independent physical subnets and subnet bridges; the design for server installations supporting applications and e-services; and the design of an RFID and cameras network. Over this extended internal network, new services are designed to offer additional functionality and performance to the entire port community (Figure 5.2).

The crucial dimension in the port district is to be found in the series of applications and e-services that accommodate the port community. These were defined in consultation with this community and the related cluster of suppliers and activities around the port. All applications and e-services leverage the advantages of collaboration, collective intelligence, and synergies inside the port community. Applications support and advance further collaborative practices, and include:

- *Strategic intelligence,* which is a collaboration platform for the continuous improvement of the port's practices and its competitiveness, and based on a strengths, weaknesses, opportunities, and threats (SWOT) analysis of the characteristics of the port of Thessaloniki, competition from ports in southern Europe,

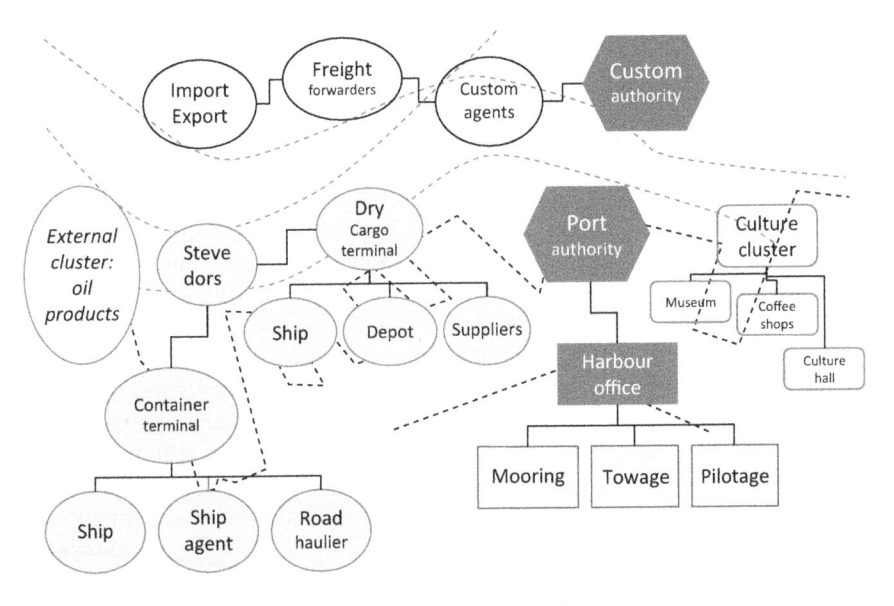

Figure 5.2 Collaboration networks into the Port community

    the creation of a strategic intelligence group by users, employees and partner organisations, crowdsourcing for solutions and improvements of the port infrastructure, and the elaboration of port strategic orientations on a collaborative basis.
- *Port Community – Freight,* which is a system providing communication and cooperation for all members involved in the cargo operations of the port. All parties in the transport chain can cooperate online, including local liner agents, ship operating agents, hauliers, rail operators, tally companies, service providers, repair companies, container terminals, port authorities, administration, customs, and importers and exporters.
- *Intermodal Freight Transportation (IFT),* which is a system covering the transfer of a cargo in a container or vehicle, using multiple modes (rail, ship, truck, etc.) without having to mediate cargo handling when changing vehicle. IFT includes technologies that improve the safety of cruise ships at the port, the approach to port, and technologies that enable efficient tracking and tracing of cargo during transport from the port to the consignee.
- *Port Community – Passenger,* which is a platform that ensures the provision of continuous and adequate information to passengers, offering updates to the travelling public and citizens, allowing online ticketing, monitoring, and cancellation of tickets at the entrance to the ship, and smart safety, as well as e-commerce.
- *Benchmarking performance,* which is an application for comparing the activity of the port with that of competitors or other ports which are considered to be excellent, comparing and assessing services that the port offers, such as pilotage, towage, mooring, loading and unloading, supply, customs clearance, storage and distribution of goods, intermodal transport, and other added value operations.

In all city-districts, the same architecture has been adopted, starting from the creation of a network of actors, the definition of work processes and rules for the delivery of services, smart environments aggregating information from operations, the development of online collaboration platforms, and applications guiding the provision of services. The use of open broadband networks, embedded sensors, and RFIDs also marks a move towards the Internet of Things and the management of innovation with smart collaborative environments. The focus is on communities of users. Higher intelligence is expected to be generated via workflows that combine collaboration, institutional rules, and IT support and coordination. The end result is expected to be the emergence of an intelligent community and better decision-making within each district.

Intelligent Thessaloniki is being implemented in decentralised way and on a per city-district basis. The functionality of collaboration platforms and e-services are to be further elaborated during the tenders to select technology providers. Vendors will be selected on the basis of the solutions they present, and on the basis of development and maintenance costs, and the business models proposed for the sustainability of application and e-services. Beside the coordination provided by the regional authority, the projects are, in fact, progressing primarily based on initiatives being taken by the administration of each district, rather than based on central planning, as was initially planned.

6. Intelligent city planning in old metropolitan areas

The development of broadband networks, e-services, smart districts, and clusters are common elements in smart city initiatives for the regeneration of metropolitan areas in Europe, from north (Manchester) to south (Thessaloniki), and east (Helsinki) to west (Barcelona). Similar processes are taking place in many cities all over the world, combining individual bottom-up initiatives and more organised planning at the level of city-districts by the responsible management authorities. The twin processes of city development – via individual choices and via district planning – are somehow replicated in the creation of the urban digital space and the integration of the digital into the physical and social space of cities. With the mediation of digital solutions, innovative practices make the old metropolitan economies more open and competitive. There are, however, major challenges and barriers to overcome as one advances along this modernisation / regeneration process.

First of all is the creation of a digital space over the pre-existing metropolitan space. This can be conceived as consisting of four concentric rings each one having specific characteristics and a unique functionality (Figure 5.3). At the centre are the broadband networks, wired and wireless infrastructure, and communication protocols that enable communication and the connectivity of various devices. Then comes a ring of Web technologies that enable data protection, processing, exploration, visualisation, and analytics. The third ring is composed of applications for information and Web-based collaboration in different domains of the city. As we have seen, more than 20 different domains of cities can be identified as potential fields of applications related to the economy, city infrastructure and

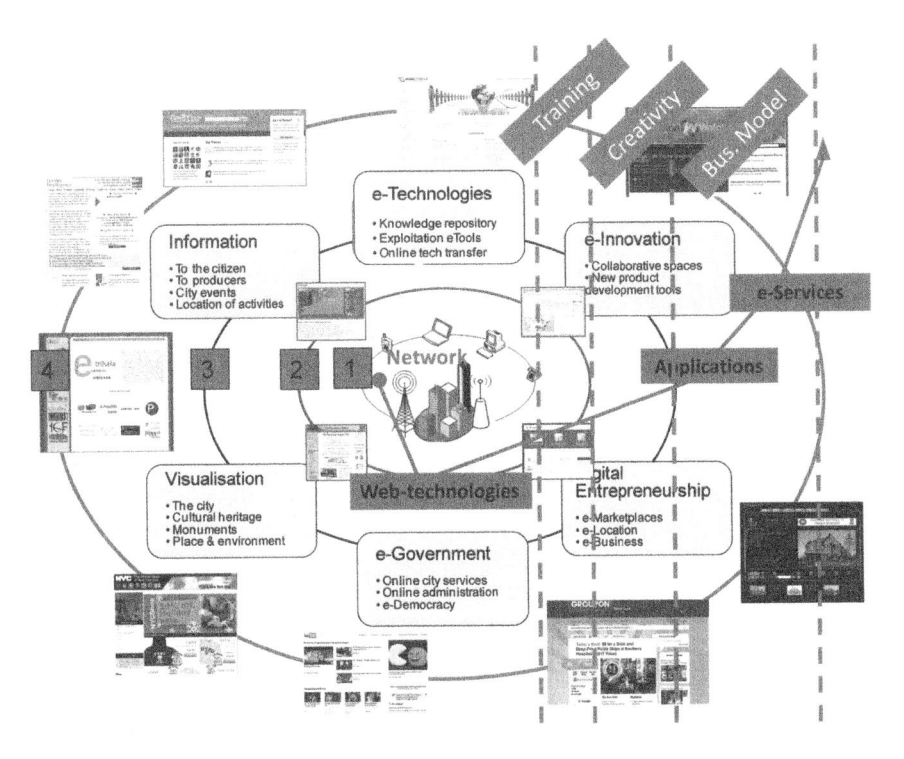

Figure 5.3 Digital space of cities – four rings and three gaps

utilities, quality of citizen life, and city governance. The last and outer ring is composed of e-services, as a few applications manage to be adopted by the market and are offered on a regular basis as a service. Some critical barriers operate in the deployment of this complex digital edifice.

Decisions about the characteristics of the inner ring, the broadband network have to balance performance and cost. All cities would like to have the high bandwidth of a FTTH network, but urban networks always conform to 'traffic' levels and demand. VDSL solutions, for instance, might be more suitable over the medium term, reducing the level of investment in networks required and increasing the effort on applications and e-services. 3G and 4G networks from mobile telecom providers open up large windows of opportunity for broadband connectivity on the move. The critical issue in the field of broadband here is how the networks are used and how they comply with e-services running on different networks, and which is the best distribution of public funds between investments in networks and services. The network is just the beginning. Citizens, companies, and city visitors have to enjoy the services that become available by the networks. To achieve that, three gaps related to skills, creativity, and entrepreneurship must be addressed: the digital skills gap, the creativity gap, and an entrepreneurship gap.

The digital skills gap concerns the ability of citizens and companies to master web-technologies and offer solutions over the net. We have seen in Helsinki, Manchester, Barcelona, and Thessaloniki that important parts of the digital space have been created via bottom-up initiatives. Most applications produced rely on the local capabilities of companies, organisations, and citizens to master Web technologies. The larger the digital skills gap is, the smaller the involvement of citizens in digital, smart, and intelligent city solutions is. It is of primary importance for bridging this gap to promote large-scale IT training. Open-source technologies offer many advantages in this regard, such as easy-to-code, easy-to-deploy Web applications, and low cost and ubiquitous hosting. But, city infrastructure, community centres, and organised training should be provided at large scale.

However, learning and mastering Web-technologies does not spontaneously lead to applications, as a *creativity gap* separates Web technologies from Web applications. Just as learning the grammar and syntax of a language does not make someone a writer, equally so, simply learning programming languages does not make someone a successful application developer. Platforms like the iPhone and Android document this gap, as the same toolbox of technologies has led to thousands of applications with different degrees of complexity, novelty, and success. Bridging the creativity gap between technologies and applications should be a priority for city governance, to take advantage of creativity skills among the city's population. Living Lab methodologies, social experiments, crowdsourcing, apps competitions, and open platforms for creating and promoting applications may offer good solutions to this end, and can mobilise creativity within the entire population of the city.

Only a few digital applications will finally turn into e-services, though, as an *entrepreneurship gap* exists between digital applications and services. Here, the critical issue is to find a viable business model and the initial investment needed to turn an application into e-service and offer it on the market. The question is quite simple: who is going to pay for maintaining the service and at what cost? A survey conducted by Forrester Research identified a series of alternative engagement models that ensure the viability of IT initiatives (Belissent, 2010). Each city has to experiment with such business models and identify which ones are suitable for making each application a successful service.

Creating a digital spatiality is not the only challenge for contemporary city governance. The digital space with all its components and functionalities must integrate into the existing physical and institutional space of metropolitan cities. Integration makes media solutions part of a city's infrastructure and increases the problem-solving capability. Integration is the motor driving the spatial intelligence of cities, combining the strengths of digital spatiality with the communities of the city and its institutional endowments.

The survey and cases analysed reveal two different trajectories leading towards this much-desired integration. At the level of city-districts, integration is taking place as the community of the district starts working more efficiently with Web applications, increasing its competitiveness and the quality of services offered. Digital spaces directly complement the community's activities, improving established processes and workflows. Intelligence and problem-solving are evolving because of more efficient and cost-reducing workflows. On the other hand, we can observe indirect integration also occurring, as knowledge spillovers are disseminating digital learning and know-how within the city. The urban environment becomes a platform for new skills creation and for the digital education of the city's population. Intelligence is evolving because a larger number of people are becoming more aware of and educated in the use of digital technologies.

Impact assessment is another major challenge. The exact impact of digital city spaces on the economy and life of a city is extremely difficult to compute. The literature shows a split between monitoring scoreboards which focus on city systems improved by digital spaces and e-services (Caragliu et al., 2009) and scoreboards which capture the planning efforts made in order to make cities more intelligent (Bell et al., 2009). Both perspectives require an enormous amount of data collection and processing. The first perspective also needs quite good modelling of the urban system in order to separate the impact of digital spaces from the impact produced by other urban processes.

It is certain that smart spaces do have an impact, which is realised by a series of improvements to various city subsystems, infrastructure, and services: the ability to react more quickly in the case of an accident on the road, the option to find the best route for travelling from one place to another, the ability to make a transaction online; the option to pay a parking ticket online, the ability to make a request to a government department online or inform authorities about an accident, the chance to learn about cultural events in the city or find a hotel or a restaurant, the ability to learn the city better or to share a bike or buy something at a great discount, and so on and so forth. These fragmented outcomes are inherent in the way systems and applications have been developed via bottom-up and decentralised actions.

Comprehensive quantitative measurement and impact assessment have not been carried out, except in a few cases only. The assessments we have available to us mainly come from e-service providers and their internal log files and evaluations about the added value of applications. In Thessaloniki for instance, OASTH is extremely satisfied with the investment made in satellite fleet management and bus stop-based information systems. Another source of quantitative data and metrics are global rankings such as Alexa and Google Page Rankings, which indicate a positive diffusion and enlargement of the e-services audience and usage. Web analytics can provide information about the usage of e-services, but cannot describe the impact of e-services on a city's innovation performance and sustainable development.

Interviews with city stakeholders in Thessaloniki reveal a positive and optimistic assessment about e-services. It is considered that a more competitive city with higher information and learning capacity is being created. Digital Thessaloniki, with its hundreds of applications, is sustaining the growth of the ICT sector in the city; new employment and company formation in this sector also profited from demand for digital applications and networks. Online transactions are reducing the need for the physical mobility of inhabitants. Physical mobility is being replaced by online transactions in the relationships of citizens with public authorities, as more and more administration services are offered online. There was less traffic and fewer CO_2 emissions, and less road load gathered on the city's roads because of less mobility. A more visitor-friendly or friendly city is also being created, as much information about the city and its characteristics, monuments, recreation, and cultural resources become available online (Kakderi and Kourtesis, 2009).

These improvements in the urban system come from bottom-up initiatives, such as the expansion of broadband networks by telecom companies, progress in mobile connectivity via 3G and 4G networks, and the large number of applications created by small companies and individual developers. These initiatives are coupled by mid-scale smart environments at the level of city districts. It becomes clear that large-scale master planning has been replaced by strategic planning with flagship projects at the level of city-districts. Relying on bottom-up transformation, intelligent metropolitan areas are emerging spontaneously, in the way Frank Lloyd Wright envisioned future cities throughout America and the world, arguing that, "America will need no help to build a Broadacre City, it will build itself, haphazardly" (McCarter, 2006).

References

Bakici, T., Almirall, E. and Wareham J. (2013). A smart city initiative: The case of Barcelona. *Journal of the Knowledge Economy*, Vol. 4, No. 2, 135–148.

Belissent, J. (2010). *Getting clever about smart cities: New opportunities require new business models*. Forrester for Ventor Strategy Professionals. Retrieved 2 January 2014, from http://goo.gl/hnuuRo.

Bell, R., Jung, J. and Zacharilla, L. (2009). *Broadband economies: Creating the community of the 21st century*. New York, NY: Intelligent Community Forum Publications.

Caragliu, A., Del Bo, C. and Nijkamp, P. (2009). *Smart cities in Europe*. Amsterdam, the Netherlands: VU University Amsterdam, Faculty of Economics, Business Administration and Econometrics.

Carter, D. (2013). Urban regeneration, digital development strategies and the knowledge economy: Manchester case study. *Journal of the Knowledge Economy*, Vol. 4, No. 2, 169–189.

European Commission (2008). *Growing regions, growing Europe: Fifth progress report on economic and social cohesion*. Communication from the Commission to the European Parliament and the Council. Fifth progress report on economic and social cohesion. COM (2008) 371 final. Luxembourg: Office for Official Publications of the European Communities.

Georghiou, C., Komninos N., Martinidies, G., Martzopoulou, N. Sefertzi, E. and Tramantas, K. (2009). *Hybrid innovation and the future of industry in Thessaloniki*. Thessaloniki, Greece: Master Plan Authority & Giahoudis Publications.

Gloor, P. (2006). *Swarm creativity: Competitive advantage through collaborative innovation networks*. Oxford, UK: Oxford University Press.

Hielkema, H. and Hongisto, P. (2013). Developing the Helsinki smart city: The role of competitions for open data applications. *Journal of the Knowledge Economy*, Vol. 4, No. 2, 190–204.

Johnson, S. (2001). *Emergence. The connected lives of ants, brains, cities, and software*. New York, NY: Scribner.

Kakderi, C. and Kourtesis, A. (2009). Local e-governance applications in support of entrepreneurship policy: The case of Thessaloniki metropolitan area. *International Journal of Innovation and Regional Development*, Vol. 1, No. 4, 423–442.

Komninos, N., Pallot, M. and Schaffers, H. (2013). Special issue: Smart cities and the Future Internet in Europe. *Journal of the Knowledge Economy*, Vol. 4, No. 2, 119–231.

Mazower, M. (2004). *Salonica city of ghosts: Christian, Muslims, and Jews 1430–1950*. London, UK: Harper Perennial.

McCarter, R. (2006). *Frank Lloyd Wright*. London, UK: Reaktion Books – Critical Lives.

Pro Inno Europe (2009). *Regional innovation scoreboard 2009*. Pro Inno Europe Paper No. 14. Brussels: European Communities.

6 Top-down planning for new intelligent cities and city-districts

1. Top-down planning for new intelligent cities

Top-down planning represents a very strong tradition in city planning. It appears in any type of planning – strategic, comprehensive, district – when the city is designed centrally by an authority and constructed on the basis of this master plan. As part of this tradition, the city is conceived of as an integrated system which defines all lower-level plans or subsystems. Top-down planning does not leave much room for self-organisation and individual decisions by users or citizens to influence the plan. The city is not produced within a framework that guides individual decisions only, but through the detailed implementation of an initial idea. The whole process resembles the product development of a large and complex object, and product development stages and methodologies can be used. Top-down planning was exercised by various city planning movements, from City Beautiful to Le Corbusier's Radian City and Comprehensive Rational Planning, where most characteristics of urban space were defined centrally by technical and political elites. The top-down approach is commonplace in greenfield projects and new city-district design, where no pre-existing population and social groups are invited to influence the planning process, advocate, or bargain for their interests.

Within the actual intelligent city movement, top-down planning initiatives have appeared in a series of large-scale multibillion projects for the creation of new intelligent city-districts and bright new cities. Well-known cases are New Songdo, an international business district located on the waterfront of Incheon, South Korea; PlanIT Valley in Portugal, a city of 225,000 people to be developed in a series of phases, conceived of as a living laboratory of innovative services, startups, and smart technologies test bed and demonstration; Neapolis SmartEco City in Cyprus, a new mixed-use development including a health park, university campus, theme park, commercial centre, international business centre, and residential neighbourhoods, all designed with green-city principles and supported by centrally run intelligent infrastructure; the New Economic Cities in Saudi Arabia, investing in the creation of high-tech industry and service clusters and designed along smart city principles. These are greenfield projects with well-elaborated master plans that organise construction and the development of high-tech clusters, central city areas with smart infrastructure, embedded sensors and devices to control networks and activities, and turnkey e-services. They are designed and marketed as smart cities and intelligent places offering all the related economic and environmental advantages, in terms of competitiveness, environment, quality of life, and safety.

In this chapter, we focus on such top-down plans for intelligent cities. We discuss four New Economic Cities of Saudi Arabia as representative cases of top-down intelligent city planning, and the challenges and obstacles of centrally organised initiatives that are promising to offer advanced spatial intelligence following the completion of construction.

2. New economic cities in Saudi Arabia

Four new cities are currently being developed in the western part of the Kingdom of Saudi Arabia (KSA) in line with the principles of intelligent city planning:

- Prince Abdul Aziz Bin Mousaed Economic City (PABMEC) near Hail;
- King Abdullah Economic City (KAEC) in Rabigh, northwest of Jeddah;
- Knowledge Economic City (KEC) near Medina; and
- Jazan Economic City (JEC).

Two more were announced, but have not moved forward yet:

- Tabuk Economic City (TEC) and
- Eastern Province Economic City (EPEC).

These mega projects are expected to fulfil the vision of bringing in modern technology and diversifying the country's economy, by focusing growth on energy, transportation, and knowledge-based industries.

Initially, the new cities were overseen by the Saudi Arabian General Investment Authority (SAGIA). SAGIA is a governmental agency established in 2000 to act as a gateway to investment in the KSA. It is responsible for managing the kingdom's investment environment. About a decade ago, the KSA government decided to concentrate efforts on becoming a competitive foreign direct investment (FDI) destination. Thus, in 2006, SAGIA commissioned the "10x10" programme, whose purpose was to enact reforms and promote targeted investments, so as to position the country as one of the world's top ten most-competitive investment destinations by 2010 (Swiss Business Hub GCC and Green Destinations LLC, 2010). By royal decree, in 2010, the Economic Cities Authority (ECA) was spun off from SAGIA as the current regulator and supervisor of the New Economic Cities. The role of ECA is to manage the overall development of the four cities. It works with the individual developers of each city and acts as an intermediary with the relevant government agencies. It is the one-stop governmental agency dealing with all requirements on the side of foreign and local investors (ACN Newswire, 2012). The authority is instrumental in ensuring the creation

126 *Planning for intelligent cities*

of jobs and state-of-the-art infrastructure. It is also in charge of designing next-generation regulatory frameworks to act as a solid backbone for the economic cities (Cadre Economic Cities, 2012).

The Saudi Arabia New Economic Cities follow a general strategy that seeks to accommodate the changing needs of a growing non-oil economy embracing new knowledge-based industries and, at the same time, ensuring balanced regional development, employment opportunities, educational facilities, and housing for a young and growing Saudi population. Three New Economic Cities lie along the Red Sea coast of Saudi Arabia, while the fourth one is located in the hinterland near the city of Hail. Initially, all cities were planned to be completed by 2020. However, their completion dates were extended, as progress has been slower than initially anticipated, due to funding problems and difficulties in attracting private investors.

The project is very ambitious, with a cost exceeding $60 billion. The attempt to create new cities and specialised high-technology poles through top-down planning procedures entails complexities that probably exceed conventional urban planning competency (Komninos, 2006).

King Abdullah Economic City (KAEC)

King Abdullah Economic City (KAEC) is located on the Red Sea coast, about 100 km north of Jeddah, the commercial hub of the kingdom, and approximately one hour away with the new road and rail networks from Mecca and Medina, the two holiest cities of the Islamic religion. It was announced in 2005 by Abdullah bin Abdul Aziz Al Saud, the King of Saudi Arabia, and construction began on the very same day (Foreign Affairs, 2007a). The development area is 168 km^2, and is expected to host a population of 2 million people and 1 million jobs by 2020 (SAGIA, 2013). The development cost is approximately $27 billion, all deriving from private capital (SAGIA, 2013). Its commercial and business amenities will offer businesses that Jeddah currently cannot, and is seen by many as a solution to Jeddah's urban ills (Reisz, 2012). When completed, the city will be the size of Washington, DC.

The vision is to create a "world class fully integrated economic city" (SAGIA, n.d.). KAEC is expected to become an economic powerhouse in the region, with key economic sectors in manufacturing and logistics, shipping, light and processing industry, and financial services (Swiss Business Hub, 2010).

KAEC is privately funded, privately managed, and privately developed; the master developer is 'Emaar, the Economic City' (EEC), a consortium created by Dubai-based Emaar Properties and Saudi investors, also a Tadawul-listed company (Emaar, the Economic City, 2013a). EEC is focused primarily on planning KAEC. It is responsible for a large part of its development, too, such as the recently completed hotel as well as housing areas, and also the primary infrastructure. The rest will be developed by companies that want to operate in KAEC who will buy land, or individuals, who can buy residential plots for development (Construction Week, 2013b). On the governmental side, the ECA is the prime facilitator for the development and acts as the one-stop government servicing centre for the development of the KAEC.

The city's master plan initially had the following components (Swiss Business Hub, 2010):

1. The *Industrial District* covers 63 million m² and is intended to host 2,700 industrial tenants.
2. The *Sea Port* covers 13.8 million m², making it the largest port in the region. The port will have facilities to handle cargo and dry bulk, and will be equipped to receive the world's largest vessels.
3. The *Resorts' Area* includes hotels, shopping centres and other recreational facilities. The number of hotel rooms and suites are estimated to be 11,000 in more than 70 hotels.
4. The *Educational Zone* consists of multi-university campus designed to accommodate 18,000 students.
5. The *Residential Area* is planned to include 260,000 apartments and 56,000 villas. It will be divided into smaller residential, commercial and recreational areas.
6. The *Central Business District* (including the Financial Island) offers 3.8 million m² of office space.

In subsequent revisions to the master plan, the plan for the financial island was abandoned and no longer forms a part of KAEC (Driver, 2013).

King Abdullah Economic City is widely considered the flagship project of Saudi Arabia's economic cities, and its construction, although occasionally delayed, is well under way. It is currently the only economically viable city out of the four New Economic Cities (Wacklin, 2013). The project started in 2006, with a projected completion date in 2020, which was extended to 2025. Its development has not been progressing effortlessly at all times. After a major economic analysis, the master plan was revised in 2011 to better respond to a series of factors and events. The global financial crisis posed serious challenges to the scale of the project. It was thus decided that the city would be constructed in phases, in contrast to the original idea of a single, large project with construction extending across the entire site simultaneously (Construction Week, 2013b). Added to that, since interest on the side of foreign investors was less than expected, the government was repeatedly obliged to step in and fund the development of the city by offering generous loans to EEC (Hall, 2012). On top of that, Jeddah was plagued by massive floods in 2009.

Given the financial crisis, the developers decided to cancel the significant land reclamation project which featured in the original master plan. In the revised master plan, the planners opted for more environmentally friendly solutions, including preservation of the natural lagoon and the construction of a network of canals to provide protection against flooding. In addition, since it was decided that the Haramain High-Speed Rail Line – currently under construction – would pass the outskirts of the city, the highest density residential and commercial cluster will be eventually built adjacent the local station. The tall glass towers of the original plan, intended to attract financial services companies, on the so-called 'Financial Island,' were cancelled (Construction Week, 2013b).

Consequently, the city is currently undergoing progressive development in three phases, with completion earmarked for 2025. At the moment, construction is advancing at several sites, with phases varying, depending on the site. Construction is taking place on the city's port area, while industrial, residential, and commercial buildings are being erected. Many KAEC social and entertainment facilities are up and running, and work is being carried out to finish the remaining development projects. There are numerous restaurants and cafes, as well as hotels. In addition, retail stores have been fully leased and a number of restaurants, cafes, sales outlets and pharmacies are already open (Al-Hamid, 2013).

Although there is a large amount of construction work taking place onsite, the project is so vast that it is progressing slowly overall, giving the impression that "nothing much is happening" (Construction Week, 2013b). One wide-open space follows the other, and the human element seems to be absent. However, Uwe Nienstedt, the head of master planning at EEC, argues that demand is high and that the city will grow as fast as it can deliver the residential units. According to the Oxford Business Group (2013), both industrial and residential settlements have generated a great amount of commercial interest, both from employees of businesses setting up in the city as well as from Jeddah residents in search of more affordable housing. For instance, the first phase of the Al Talah Gardens residential area was sold out in four hours in June 2011, and there is now a waiting list of 2,500 people for plots on phase II.

Prince Abdul Aziz Bin Mousaed Economic City (PABMEC) (Hail)

PABMEC is located 8 km north of Hail city, approximately 700 km northwest of Riyadh, on the crossroads of trade and transportation routes for the Middle East. The initiative was commenced in 2009 and it is expected that by 2025 the city will be fully functional. The development area is 156 km^2, and is expected to host a population of 300,000 people and 55,000 jobs (SAGIA, 2013). The development cost is approximately $8 billion, all deriving from private capital (SAGIA, 2013).

The vision is to create a "new hub for logistics in the region" (SAGIA, n.d.). The city is set to be the largest and most-modern transportation and logistics hub in the Middle East, driving agro-industrial, construction material, and other economic activities. It is located at the crossroads for navigational, trade, and transportation routes between East and West. The focus will be on speedy, comfortable, efficient, and low-cost connections by road, sea, rail, and air, which will attract and encourage logistics companies and travellers to use the PABMEC as a new trans-shipment and transit hub (Emaar, the Economic City, 2013b). The key economic sectors of the city include logistics and transportation, agriculture, minerals, and construction materials (Swiss Business Hub, 2010).

The city is being developed by Rakisa Holding (Oxford Business Group, 2013). The consortium includes key investors from Saudi Arabia, the United Arab

Emirates (UAE), Bahrain, and Kuwait (Foreign Affairs, 2007b). On the governmental side, the ECA is the prime facilitator of the development and acts as the one-stop government servicing centre for the development of the PABMEC. The government will support the development by injecting more than 8 billion SAR (Saudi Arabian Riyal) into roads, railways, and infrastructure.

The main components of PABMEC are (Emaar, the Economic City, 2013b):

1 *Logistics & Transportation:* PABMEC will have its own employment and living facilities, with 30,000 potential employment opportunities supporting demand for up to 15,000 residential units.
2 *Commercial Zone:* High-quality office space will be provided in commercial centres, including PABMEC Downtown, which will also incorporate retail outlets, hotels, entertainment, and civic land-uses.
3 *Entertainment & Tourism Zone:* It is expected to attract domestic tourists, in the form of both pilgrims and business visitors, who will create demand for hospitality, shopping, and entertainment facilities.
4 *An Agro-industrial Zone*, as well as agricultural training and research facilities, will help food processing industries to leverage the region's sizeable agricultural output.
5 *Business Park:* A well-planned business district will offer state-of-the-art technology and reliable infrastructure to allow businesses to take full advantage of their presence in PABMEC.
6 *Recreation Zone:* The provision of large recreation areas, parks, aquatic activities, and entertainment and 'edutainment' facilities will make PABMEC a comfortable and enjoyable place to live in.
7 *Industrial District:* Special focus on the planning of PABMEC's industrial area will ensure the appropriate mix and smooth operation and integration of various industry sectors.
8 *Education District:* An entire area will be dedicated to educational service provision in the form of colleges, research centres, and vocational and training centres, as well as public and private schools.
9 *Infrastructure & Utilities* are envisaged as part of smart city development and PABMEC will incorporate all the necessary infrastructure and utilities required to ensure a high quality urban environment for living and work.

In addition to its industrial zones, the city will also include business, residential, and recreational sectors and a knowledge centre. Well-designed and affordable residential neighbourhoods – supported by conveniently located community facilities, such as schools, mosques, parks and health centres – will ensure the high appeal of PABMEC to prospective residents. A downtown area and secondary business centres will offer the vibrant mix of office, retail, and entertainment activities that is characteristic of many world-class cities. The transportation system is designed to support the heavy demands of a logistics-driven economic city and embed innovations and services, such as intelligent transportation systems and public transit (Emaar, the Economic City, 2013b).

130 *Planning for intelligent cities*

The project was announced in 2009, with a projected completion date of 2020, which was extended to 2025. Construction was planned to take place in three phases (Oxford Business Group, 2008). The first phase was supposed to be completed by 2016 (Foreign Affairs, 2007b). However, PABMEC is currently just an empty plot of land and construction was stopped because the project suffers from inadequate infrastructure and financing. The success of the city is currently strongly tied into the city's ability to attract private investment. In addition, many companies that were involved in the development of the city have been hit by the global economic crisis (Wacklin, 2013).

Knowledge Economic City Al-Madinah (KEC)

The Knowledge Economic City (KEC) is located just outside the holy city of Medina, serving as an alternative Central Business District (CBD) for the existing city. The initiative was launched in 2006, and it is expected that by 2025 the city will be fully completed. The area of 4,8 Km^2 is expected to host a population of 150,000 people and 20,000 jobs. The development cost is approximately $7 billion, all deriving from private capital (SAGIA, 2013). The land for the development was provided by the King Abdullah Foundation. The project is being developed by Knowledge Economic City Developers, a consortium of companies set up for this purpose.

The vision is to "attract Muslims from around the world" (SAGIA, n.d.). KEC will play a crucial role in transforming Saudi Arabia into a global force in the knowledge-based industry. Situated to the east of Medina, KEC will be a cultural landmark for visitors and a national centre for knowledge-based industries with an Islamic focus. Given its proximity to the Holy Mosque in Medina, it is expected to attract huge numbers of visitors from Saudi Arabia and from around the world. It is also expected to attract the best Muslim talent in information and communications technologies from around the world (Foreign Affairs, 2007a). The city's key economic sectors are knowledge-based industries, tourism, and health services (Swiss Business Hub, 2010).

The main components of KEC master plan are (Swiss Business Hub, 2010):

1   *A complex for technology and knowledge-based economy:* supporting technological research and development in the region, the complex has extensive facilities and support services focused on a number of areas including e-government, e-libraries, e-education, Arabic language technologies, and technologies for managing religious tourism.
2   *Technological and administration colleges:* KEC's new technological and administration colleges will offer advanced technical study options and facilities, including scientific research laboratories, IT, software development, automation, multimedia, and business administration.
3   *The Islamic Civilisation Studies Centre:* this centre will be a hub of intellectual activity, focused on collecting, developing and transmitting the knowledge, values and artwork of the Islamic civilisation, as well as finding Islamic solutions to contemporary problems (such as designing Islamic banking products).

4 *A campus for medical studies, biological sciences and health services:* a specialised medical campus will provide medical services to visitors and residents, while the Campus for Biological Sciences will concentrate on fields critical to Saudi Arabia, such as vaccine development, crop engineering, and biotechnologies for waste and water treatment.
5 *Business Centre:* KEC will be equipped with an advanced infrastructure, including conference halls, exhibition centres, and offices accommodating up to 10,000 employees.
6 *Transportation networks* are planned to connect the city to Medina and to other major centres in the country. A central transportation station will connect the city with Prince Mohammed Bin Abdul Aziz International Airport and the city with Mecca, Yanbu, King Abdullah Economic City, and Jeddah.
7 *Lifestyle complexes:* Both tourism and commerce will be supported by planned commercial complexes, residential and hospitality facilities, a theme park ("Seera Land") and a mosque capable of accommodating 10,000 worshippers.
8 *Commercial Plaza:* The main plaza in the centre of KEC will be surrounded by pedestrian passages forming a point of connection between visitors, workers, and residents of Medina, as well as by the hotel towers and residential apartments. These, together with the commercial centres, are designed in the classic style of Medina markets, making it a landmark destination for tourists.
9 *Residential Areas:* In the heart of KEC and on its outskirts there will be residential areas of varying levels, including two villa areas, mid- to high-rise residential buildings, serviced apartments, green spaces, and hospitality facilities providing for 30,000 visitors and 150,000 residents at a time.

In architectural terms, the planners have attempted to retain forms close to traditional settlements, while crafting a more modern high-tech Arabian design, combining tradition and modernity. In order to enhance pedestrian mobility, the plan incorporates several shaded green areas within the built environment which facilitate a walkable, user-friendly city that encourages interaction (Roberts, 2009).

The project was launched in 2006. In June 2008, the master plan was finalised and was reviewed in September 2009. The project will be carried out in three phases. Phase I, which was concluded in 2012, consists of infrastructure works and the construction of 200 villas and 600 apartments in high-rise blocks. Phase II includes the construction of hospitality facilities, more than 220 villas out of 550 villas, and there will also be 600 flats; this phase is expected to be completed by 2016. Phase III is expected to be finished by 2020. Infrastructure work, however, did not begin until 2010 (Whitaker, 2010b) and the time horizon of the project has been extended to 2025 (Whitaker, 2010a).

Jazan Economic City (JEC)

Jazan or Jizan (JEC), the fourth New Economic City is located close to KSA's border with Yemen, 60km northwest of Jazan City, the country's most important port on the Red Sea. The initiative was commenced in 2006 and it is expected to be concluded by 2037 (MMC Corporation, 2006). The development area is 100 km², and is expected to host a population of 300,000 people and 100,000 jobs. The development cost is approximately $27 billion, all deriving from private capital (SAGIA, 2013).

JEC has been designed as state-of-the-art industrial city that is geared to become an important logistics hub, a major destination for regional raw materials, and an export platform for global consumer markets. The main economic sectors in JEC are related to heavy industry and the industrial products of JEC are expected to be exported to Asia, Africa, and Europe. A new seaport and dry dock will be constructed for this purpose (Swiss Business Hub, 2010). The new city is expected to be especially alluring for industries, as it will provide energy at extremely competitive prices; the power plant, which has an integrated desalination facility for the city's vital water supply, will run on Saudi crude oil (Foreign Affairs, 2007b).

The vision is to "Achieve competitiveness on Heavy Industry and Agribusiness" (SAGIA). The key sectors of KEC include heavy and labour intensive industries, agriculture, and energy (Swiss Business Hub, 2010).

JEC's developer is a joint venture of Malaysia's MMC Corporation and the local Saudi Binladin Group (SBG). On the governmental side, the ECA is the prime facilitator of the development and acts as the one-stop government servicing centre for the development of the JEC. The master plan was designed in 2006 by DP Architects (DP Architects, 2013).

Two-thirds of the city will be covered by industrial activities and one-third will be commercial and residential (Foreign Affairs, 2007b). Main components of the heavy industrial area of JEC are (Swiss Business Hub, 2010):

1   The *Power Plant,* located next to the coastline on the south side, consisting of the main power plant, desalination plant, associated balance-of-plant, electrical substation, and fuel storage facilities. Using steam-cycle technology fired on Arabian crude oil, the power plant will be built with sufficient capacity to provide for the demand of JEC with excess capacity to be sold to the grid.
2   The *Water Desalination Plant* will be capable of providing about 50,000 m³ of potable water per day to cater for the internal requirements of JEC, as well as to supply water to the distribution network.
3   The *Industrial Port* will provide an additional terminal on the Red Sea's coast, becoming one of the biggest ports in the region. Through its capability in handling the largest ships and carriers, the port will offer numerous job opportunities in various major industries related to cargo and storage as well as associated logistics and assisting services.
4   The *Aluminium Smelter* with an annual production capacity of 1 million metric tons. This development is a joint venture between the MMC Malaysia Group and the Saudi Binladin Group, and China Aluminium Co. (China's largest aluminium company and second-largest producer of aluminium worldwide). Competitive energy prices at JEC will contribute to minimising production costs, offering a great competitive advantage when it comes to fulfilling the increasing demand for aluminium on the global market.

5   The *Refinery* is one of the Kingdom's projects aimed to develop the Jazan area in economic terms. It is one of the most significant industries, intended to attract more investments to the region with a production capacity of 250,000–400,000 barrels per day.
6   The *Iron Ore Complex* which aims to produce iron ballets with an annual production capacity of 1 million metric tons. In addition, an raw iron trade complex and a raw iron fabrication factory with production capacity of 6 million tons per year will also be developed. Additional developments include an iron plate and fabrication plant with an annual production capacity of 2 million tons.
7   The *Ship Building,* a dry dock will be built next to the main port for the purpose of repairing and maintaining ships and fishing boats. This will position JEC as a leading centre for such industries in the region.

The non-industrial zones will include a CBD, residential areas, a marina, and facilities for education, hospitality, and recreation (MMC Corporation, 2006). Located at the marine cove, a variety of low-rise residential developments will complement the surroundings, combining accessible and contemporary living in a tranquil natural setting.

Construction of the project was planned for the period 2007–2037. The first phase of the project, intended to last 18 months, includes the construction of a number of industrial roads and ancillary works (Construction Week, 2008). The development of JEC has gone through different phases, from the planning, engineering and master planning stages, to checking the financial pieces of the puzzle. The developers are now in the first phase of actual development, with several industrial tenants signing up or starting their operations. They have also started building the infrastructure that is required for existing and future operations (ACN Newswire, 2012). However, the project has not been advancing as initially anticipated. In 2013, the Malaysian construction firm MMC Corp. announced that the Saudi government had terminated the rights of its joint venture with Saudi Binladin Group to develop the JEC (Construction Week, 2013a; TradeArabia, 2013).

3. Setting up smart city complexes in Saudi Arabia

The four ambitious, mixed-use real estate projects are being developed on the basis of the same business model, which is thought to represent an innovation in public–private partnerships (PPPs). In this model, the state provides the land and facilitates the project, and the private sector plans and develops it. In the case of KSA's new economic cities, ECA (and formerly SAGIA) acts on behalf of the state as a land provider, regulator, facilitator, and promoter, while the private sector acts as an investor, builder, and property owner. With ECA streamlining regulations and approvals, the construction of the New Economic Cities is expected to be less time consuming and effort intensive.

Each city is being developed around one or more competitive clusters. They are all seen as satellite cities of already existing cities, complementing the local economies of their regions. They are strategically positioned throughout the country, taking advantage of logistics and religious tourism pathways. SAGIA's vision was about economic growth fuelled by intelligent city principles and drivers: (1) telecom connectivity designed to handle as much information traffic as possible; (2) technology infrastructure built into the groundwork of the cities – whether roads or buildings – allowing for an interconnected communications web to exist that will enhance knowledge sharing, security, and civil service responsiveness; (3) software and content creation by companies, built on top of the technology infrastructure to ensure that the hardware's lifespan is extended by software management; and (4) knowledge generation and sharing built on the technology infrastructure and software management of that infrastructure allowing international virtual knowledge communities to exist within the physical space of the economic city (Interview with Seema Khan at SAGIA).

In matters of their smart city infrastructure, CISCO was first appointed to undertake the design of the network infrastructure and connected city services of KAEC in early 2008. Since then, the company has signed similar agreements with the remaining three cities. In 2010, SAGIA commissioned CISCO to provide strategic advisory services and assess the feasibility of a Smart Cities Operating Company to support the building infrastructure and technology-enabled value-added services to the new economic cities. CISCO's goal is to deliver network-based technologies to help the government and businesses throughout Saudi Arabia to drive national competitiveness and accelerate productivity. This network platform will be crucial for driving growth, innovation, efficiency, and productivity in the public as well as private sectors in the kingdom (Arab News, 2012). The advisory services will encompass project management, market and service analysis, financial model definition, and feasibility analysis. The Smart Cities Operating Company will build and operate the infrastructure and also provide value-added services across all the economic cities. CISCO's Smart+Connected Communities (S+CC) model promises to transform physical communities into connected communities that can help realise sustainable economic growth, deliver environmental sustainability through resource management and operational efficiencies, and enhance the quality of life (CISCO, 2010b).

The solutions will be selected in cooperation with each city's developer, choosing from the array of smart city solutions that CISCO has developed, including the S+CC and 'Connected Real Estate solutions' concepts. Smart data centres and network infrastructures will provide centralised operational management of the city services at reduced operational costs. These networks will facilitate data, voice, video, and mobile communications across commercial buildings, residential buildings, and industrial sectors (CISCO, 2010a). The cities will be managed through integrated operations centres (IOC). These centres are seen as the 'brain of the city,' so as to facilitate automation and interconnection of home and office functions, with the purpose of ensuring quality of life, higher productivity, safety, security, and savings on capital expenditure and operating costs. All these solutions will be realised through high-speed broadband infrastructure, putting the whole city online (Arab News, 2008). In fact, the cities are envisioned by the KSA government as "cities wired from top-to-bottom with IP technology" (CISCO, 2008).

4. A critical appraisal of top-down intelligent city planning

Can these high-profile master plans generate self-sustained complexes of technology and innovation? Do they generate spatial intelligence? If yes, what type of spatial intelligence? And how it is produced?

The concept of intelligent city outlines innovative agglomerations in which different dimensions work together: people, bringing in the intelligence, inventiveness, and creativity of individuals who live in the city; innovation institutions advancing collective intelligence deriving from collaboration and connected variety of knowledge-based activities; and smart environments enhancing communication, knowledge exchange, and co-working (Komninos, 2008). Intelligent cities integrate all these aspects of the physical, institutional, and digital space to increase the efficiency of urban environments. The question is whether the creation of cities from scratch with top-down planning, and the ambition to see them developing in intelligent places, cultivating knowledge, technology, and innovation is compatible with this concept. Equally important is the question whether intelligent cities in greenfield developments, where the human presence and institutions for collaboration are absent, is just a label for marketing purposes and do not report any particular form of spatial intelligence.

To address this key question for intelligent city top-down planning, we will examine how the three building blocks of intelligent cities, namely the 'city,' 'innovation,' and the 'digital' dimensions are formed in Saudi Arabia New Economic Cities.

The urban dimension

There are strong arguments that the primary purpose behind those large-scale projects is capital accumulation, and little else matters besides the business plan (Cugurullo, 2013). These cities strive to attract global capital, by passing as open and modern, in contrast to the conservative culture of the country. Thus, they are designed to resemble Western progressive cities, largely failing to account for local needs, culture, and standards. Replicability is the key attribute here. The absence of past settlements, combined with the daunting scale of the project, point towards the replication of the same design multiple times. Thus, KSA's New Economic Cities stand for 'a solution in a box,' a model city that can be replicated anywhere in the world. "This city can be anywhere because it is everywhere. It heeds to 'international standards'; it promises world-class" (Reisz, 2012).

Thus, a major concern has been about the meaning of social life, culture, and identity in those new economic cities. To counterbalance the absence of identity and history – an inevitable fact due to their birth from scratch – these cities impose a way of living, a specific lifestyle that is to be embraced. Here, "the 'informal sector' is missing; the informal economy, the informal mobility and all of the practices that people use to make life doable, that fall between the cracks of the explicit articulation of how things are done. If you don't have a city with informal activity, you don't have a city at all. If you try to formalize everything in the city, it will break down utterly in very short time" (Greenfield, 2013b).

Culture and community spirit are crafted to accommodate capital inflow and FDI attraction. Criticism about the architectural and aesthetic qualities of these new settlements also points out that "architecturally they couldn't be more dreary and conventional – bloated glass towers encircled by quaint town houses and suburban villas decorated in ersatz historical style," while "the public spaces [in KAEC] are closer in spirit to Las Vegas than to Riyadh" (Ouroussoff, 2010).

The debate goes on to examine the social implications of gated communities, or so-called 'urban fortresses,' including issues such as accessibility, inequality, and social polarisation. The KSA government decided that the residents of the new economic cities will live in gated communities in order to alleviate security concerns, although KSA is a country with low crime rates. Peripheral highways isolate the cities from their neighbouring areas and there is control over who enters and exits the cities, with the option of shutting down the city completely, in case of emergency (Ouroussoff, 2010). As such, these cities may represent middle-class hopes for a better life, but it is highly questionable whether they can nurture a culture of openness and creativity (Reisz, 2012). The development of these new places was negatively criticised, because "the government was pouring billions of dollars into the creation of entire new cities while large areas of existing ones had deteriorated into slums. Jeddah, for example, already has a port in desperate need of upgrading. Its historic center is a medieval slum inhabited by foreign laborers. The city has no sewer system, only septic tanks that regularly spill into the streets. And people who live there will have to continue living by the old rules" (Ouroussoff, 2010).

The management of land uses and zoning, in particular, seems too extremely rigid to accommodate the spirit of open creative communities. The strict zoning principles that prevail in the new cities' plans, disputed in the urban planning practice for decades now, raise questions about the new settlements' viability and success in creating vibrant communities. A close view of the new cities' master plans shows that all cities are planned on the basis of single-purpose zones, comprising industrial areas, residential areas, and CBDs. Most of them also have adjacent educational and recreational districts. This strict segmentation of land uses and urban functions cannot accommodate innovative practices relying on the flexible combination of production, service, and learning practices. Forward-looking master plans increasingly envision communities that encompass a mixture of functions, including diverse housing types, retail shops, restaurants, offices, cultural amenities, and recreational facilities, with the purpose of creating vibrant communities, social interaction, and usability at all hours of the day.

Furthermore, in the development of new top-down smart cities, the risk of slow progression or indefinite suspension is fairly imminent. Such ventures represent complex tasks, highly vulnerable to an array of threats, unforeseen in the initial plan and development progress: global economic downturns, changes in citizens' needs and funding priorities, inadequate legislation, bureaucracy barriers, etc. Top-down interventions point to large-scale infrastructure upgrade, inarguably associated with high requirements in terms of time and funds. Owing to the global economic slowdown, private investment in the New Economic Cities of KSA has been slower than anticipated, which has also damaged the reputation of SAGIA (Driver, 2013; Hall, 2012; Reisz, 2012). The timeframe for construction of most of the new cities has had to be extended (Oxford Business Group, 2013). However, the new cities of KSA are not the only ones to have experienced funding difficulties and delays. New Songdo, for instance, a new smart city in North Korea, has been progressing very slowly compared to the original plan. The economic downturn of 2008 forced Gale International (the developer of Songdo) to change the city plans and reduce the amount of planned office space. Although the initial plan aspired to attract foreign investment, Songdo is today a rich suburb of Incheon city, mostly populated by locals (Shwayri, 2013).

The innovation dimension

The four New Economic Cities plan to create research, technology, and innovation ecosystems, including research centres, incubators, technology networks, industrial liaison centres, and innovation funding institutions. In KEC Medina, that infrastructure includes a technology park, technological and management colleges, a complex for medical studies, bio-sciences and health services, the Islamic Civilisation Studies Centre, and a business centre. These knowledge-intensive entities are expected to collaborate, and to develop complementary functions. Even at Jazan, with a heavy industry focus, the development of the industrial complex is expected to be a hub for management, technology, and related research, and to attract considerable local and international equity capital and venture capital funds.

But, can innovative agglomerations be created by top-down planning, or do they just emerge? Can we plant innovative clusters through central planning and policy-making, or does only the complexity of the market have this privilege? Most planners and policy-makers accept that under certain conditions innovative agglomerations may result from planning. A number of clusters and innovative cities around the globe, mainly planned technology parks and technopoles, sustained these arguments. This was the thinking, however, when technological planning was in its adolescence during the 1980s. Since the 1990s, policy-making has shifted from technopolitan planning to territorial systems of innovation and the management of intangible assets and collaboration networks. It became clear that innovative agglomerations depend more on knowledge-sharing, funding, and technological cooperation institutions than hard infrastructure. If you look today at the indicators of innovation drivers in OECD countries and regions, you will find few areas related to hard infrastructure and heavy capital investment. Theoretical thinking attributes innovation to education, R&D, collaboration, and social capital, branching out from older industries, recombination of know-how of existing industries, valorisation of scientific breakthrough, innovation by small companies, risk capital, and intellectual property.

Most theories of innovation and technological development now recognise the role of community and agglomeration in innovative practices. Technological development and innovation are seen as collaborative processes in which knowledge and insights from different fields of science and technology are combined to create something new. This mainly happens within human communities, in which different skills and competences are pooled together and combined (Boschma 2005; Hargadon, 2003). Innovation is also seen as an uncertain, cumulative, and path-dependent process, based on the transformation of tacit knowledge into explicit knowledge (Nonaka and Takeuchi, 1995). But, tacit knowledge is bound to spatial proximity, as it is not easily communicated other than through personal interaction (Morgan, 2004); clustering becomes inevitable to make the innovative behaviour itself happen. In open innovation, the external environment offered by the agglomeration has become extremely decisive because companies can find locally rich knowledge resources, exceeding their own competences; innovation becomes regulated by this "external selection environment" (Nelson and Winter, 1982) of institutions that switch on–off flows of knowledge and funding. Innovation is a highly systemic phenomenon appearing in innovative clusters, districts, cities, and regions within networks, supply chains, and other forms of collaboration and association.

The emphasis on knowledge, skills, and community marks the actual stage in the thinking about innovative agglomerations. Innovation systems have become extremely glocal, combining local skills and capabilities with global supply chains and distributed product development. Intelligent city strategies must comply with these conditions of innovative agglomerations, global networks, and recombination that sustain innovative behaviour. Can all these be realised by bricks and mortar in the absence of the human presence, communities, and innovation institutions?

The digital dimension

There are many concerns about smart environments and personal data when it comes to the top-down design of smart cities, which are built on proprietary platforms. IBM and CISCO, for example, offer assurances that privacy issues have long been resolved. However, a major discussion on which data should be collected, how, and for how long it should be stored is underway. The greatest concern is about who controls the data, and who has access to it and for what purpose. Could, for example, smart city vendors take advantage of the data for monetary gain? What happens after the data have been collected? Is it wise for public administrations to hand down control and become committed to a smart city vendor? Greenfield (2013b) suggests that citizens ought to have access to the data they generate themselves; they have the right to see how value is created out of it and realise the benefits.

Furthermore, no use of data records can be accounted as completely objective, transparent, and free from politics (Greenfield, 2013a). There is variation in expectations regarding what data can do, depending on the culture and personal preferences of each person, and expectations are, at times, situation specific and context dependent. The proliferation of social networks in everyday life has dynamically changed our perception of privacy and the degree of acceptance towards revealing personal data (Townsend et al., 2010). Consequently, it is expected that successful smart city services will operate within flexible frameworks. They will be required to offer different configuration options, reflecting user expectations and preferences (Batty et al., 2012; Net!Works Expert Working Group, 2011; Townsend et al., 2010).

Another issue is the fact that top-down smart cities dictate a specific solution as optimal, ignoring the wider potential of piecing together elements that give rise to more complex systems. Those smart city visions simply announce how networked technology will regulate daily functions in those cities, leaving no option for discussing how people imagine their everyday life to be. They fail to take advantage of the infinite potential of grass-roots efforts. The creativity and resourcefulness of the populace, underpinned through web spaces of collective intelligence, seems more powerful than any form of digital or artificial intelligence (Komninos, 2011; Ratti and Townsend, 2011). Cities are settlements where complex social and cultural interactions take place, and central operating systems cannot capture those. Consequently, top-down smart city visions present only a very narrow slice of the potential of what a smart city can actually do (Greenfield, 2013a).

Finally, the selection of a conducive business model for the top-down development of new cities may be challenging. Developing a scheme to realise the venture is a complex task, which requires a great deal of funding and a conducive business model. Funding is absolutely critical when it comes to developing wholly new cities, as these kinds of developments require generous investments in all stages, because, in general, greenfield projects have a budget up to many times higher than the budgets of brownfield projects (Alcatel-Lucent, 2011). According to a 2010 report from the Bank of America Merrill Lynch, KSA's new cities rely more on private sector involvement than on government spending. However, there are not enough incentives yet for the private sector to push these projects forward once the basic infrastructure is completed; more must be done to encourage private sector involvement (Sambridge, 2010; TradeArabia, 2010). The public–private partnership model employed is proving less successful than initially expected, even more so due to the recent financial crisis. As a result, KSA's government has repeatedly found itself in a position where it had to step in and provide more subsidies and loans to developers in order to keep things going (Oxford Business Group, 2013; Reisz, 2012). What is more, although SAGIA initiated the New Economic Cities' plan with the intention of developing six new cities, their number was reduced to four very early on (Hall, 2012).

There is vagueness as to the governance model of those cities, if they are to function as smart cities. The Merrill Lynch report mentions that uncertainties regarding the new economic cities' governance and jurisdiction need to be clarified in a long-awaited new piece of legislation: "Given the huge scale of these projects, we believe the involvement of private sector depends on the long-awaited Economic Cities Act, which will clarify the uncertainties regarding city governance, jurisdiction and living standards" the report adds (Sambridge, 2010; TradeArabia, 2010). Furthermore, the issue of who will provide the smart city services musr be clarified. Will these cities host and manage their own city services? Is there a role for external services providers, either managed services providers or the local telecom operators (Belissent, 2010)? It is essential that the awaited governance model will define and describe the roles and responsibilities of each participant / actor of the smart city venture. It will also necessary to clarify the relations between them by setting the ground rules for their co-existence.

The creation of the four New Economic Cities using a top-down approach and the expectation to see them develop into intelligent cities promoting knowledge and innovation is a challenge for any aspect of this mega-project. Since the 1970s, urban planning realised the complexity and risks of creating entirely new cities, and has re-oriented itself towards revitalising and renewing existing places, and introducing new ingredients into them, such as technology districts, smart networks, education and human skills improvement infrastructure, science-industry joint efforts, incubators, centres for innovation, and others. This is not an argument against the endeavour to create new economic cities, but a message for particular attention to be given to intangible assets, knowledge, R&D, education, IT, community, and institution building. Top-down planning must open up opportunities for bottom-up initiatives that nurture spinoffs, spillovers, local networks, and innovative behaviour. New intelligent cities must be seen as agglomerations of countless knowledge-intensive activities, innovative clusters, micro-districts, networks, and joint-ventures, actualised by the active engagement of citizens.

References

ACN Newswire. (2012). Ensuring the long-term viability of Jazan Economic City. *ACN Newswire*. Retrieved 2 January 2014, from www.acnnewswire.com/Article. Asp?Art_ID=9324.

Al-Hamid, F. (2013). KAEC to have 2m people, projects worth $100bn on completion. *Saudi Gazette*. Retrieved 2 January 2014, from www.saudigazette.com.sa/index. cfm?method=home.regcon&contentid=20131125187656.

Alcatel-Lucent. (2011). *Getting smart about smart cities. Understanding the market opportunity in the cities of tomorrow*. Retrieved 2 January 2014, from http://goo.gl/MfdbWO.

Arab News. (2008). Madinah KEC strives to attract investors: Bawazir. *Arab News*. Retrieved 2 January 2014, from www.arabnews.com/node/314638.

Arab News. (2012). Dr. Tarig Enaya: Job creation key element of Cisco's strategy. *Arab News*. Retrieved 2 January 2014, from www.arabnews.com/economy/dr-tarig-enaya-job-creation-key-element-cisco%E2%80%99s-strategy.

Batty, M., Axhausen, K., Fosca, G., Pozdnoukhov, A., Bazzani, A., Wachowicz, M., Ouzounis, G. and Portugali, Y. (2012). *Smart cities of the future*. (Paper 188). Retrieved 2 January 2014, from www.bartlett.ucl.ac.uk/casa/publications/working-paper-188.

Belissent, J. (2010). *30 hours In Saudi Arabia: How "smart" is that?* Forrester. Retrieved 2 January 2014, from http://blogs.forrester.com/jennifer_belissent/10-05-19-30_hours_saudi_arabia_how_smart.

Boschma, R. (2005). Proximity and innovation: A critical assessment. *Regional Studies*, Vol. 39, No. 1, 64–71.

Cadre Economic Cities. (2012). *Cadre overview*. Retrieved 2 January 2014, from www.cadre-ec.com/sagia.html.

CISCO. (2008). *Prince Abdulaziz Bin Musaed Economic City to create quad play infrastructure with CISCO technology*. Press release. Retrieved 2 January 2014, from http://newsroom.cisco.com/press-release-content?articleId=4169015.

CISCO. (2010a). *Jazan Economic City uses CISCO Smart+Connected Communities master plan to develop world-class smart city services in Saudi Arabia*. Press release. Retrieved 2 January 2014, from http://newsroom.cisco.com/press-release-content?articleId=5333927&type=webcontent.

CISCO. (2010b). *Saudi Arabian General Investment Authority chooses CISCO for advisory services*. Press release. Retrieved 2 January 2014, from http://newsroom.cisco.com/press-release-content?type=webcontent&articleId=5412091.

Construction Week. (2008). Infrastructure work to begin in KSA's Jizan Economic City. *Construction Week*. Retrieved 2 January 2014, from www.constructionweekonline.com/article-3765-infrastructure-work-to-begin-in-ksas-jizan-economic-city/.

Construction Week. (2013a). MMC, SBG removed from Jazan Economic City project. *Construction Week*. Retrieved 2 January 2014, from www.constructionweekonline.com/article-21799-mmc-sbg-removed-from-jazan-economic-city-project/.

Construction Week. (2013b). King Abdullah Economic City. *Construction Week*. Retrieved 2 January 2014, from www.constructionweekonline.com/article-23235-site-visit-king-abdullah-economic-city/#.UpMqe-LIdoE.

Cugurullo, F. (2013). How to build a sandcastle: An analysis of the genesis and development of Masdar City. *Journal of Urban Technology*, Vol. 20, No. 1, 23–37.

DP Architects (2013). *Jazan Economic City Masterplan*. Retrieved 2 January 2014, from www.dpa.com.sg/projects/jazan-economic-city/.

Driver, M. (2013). *Saudi Arabia's four New Economic Cities*. The Metropolitan Corporate Counsel. Retrieved 2 January 2014, from www.metrocorpcounsel.com/articles/22205/saudi-arabia%E2%80%99s-four-new-economic-cities.

Emaar, the Economic City. (2013a). *King Abdullah Economic City*. Retrieved 2 January 2014, from www.kaec.net/.

Emaar, the Economic City (2013b). *Prince Abdul Aziz Bin Mousaed Economic City*. Retrieved, 2 January 2014, from www.pabm-ec.com/.

Foreign Affairs. (2007a). The Kingdom of Saudi Arabia. Strategic powerhouse, global strength. Part I. *Foreign Affairs*. Retrieved 2 January 2014, from www.foreignaffairs.com/about-us/sponsors/saudi-arabia-strategic-powerhouse-global-strength.

Foreign Affairs. (2007b). The Kingdom of Saudi Arabia. Strategic powerhouse, global strength. Part II. *Foreign Affairs*. Retrieved 2 January 2014, from www.foreignaffairs.com/about-us/sponsors/saudi-arabia-strategic-powerhouse-global-strength-part-ii.

Greenfield, A. (2013a). *Against the smart city*. Retrieved 2 January 2014, from http://urbanomnibus.net/2013/10/against-the-smart-city/.

Greenfield, A. (2013b). *Interview with Nora Spark: Against the smart city*. Retrieved 2 January 2014, from www.cbc.ca/spark/popupaudio.html?clipIds=2410181330.

Hall, C. (2012). New champion for Saudi's economic cities. *Financial Times*. Retrieved 2 January 2014, from www.ft.com/cms/s/0/6c25a83c-ae25-11e1-b842-00144feabdc0.html#axzz2magRw1d1.

Hargadon, A. (2003). *How breakthroughs happen. The surprising truth about how companies innovate*. Boston, MA: Harvard Business School Press.

Komninos, N. (2006). Technology and intelligent city strategies in Saudi Arabia. *Think: Global Issues in Perspective*, No. 9, 6–13.

Komninos, N. (2008). *Intelligent cities and globalisation of innovation networks.* London and New York: Routledge.
Komninos, N. (2011). Intelligent cities: Variable geometries of spatial intelligence. *Intelligent Buildings International,* No. 3, 172–188.
MMC Corporation (2006). *MMC to develop US$30 b Jizan Economic City in Saudi Arabia.* Retrieved 2 January 2014, from www.mmc.com.my/content.asp?menuid=100042&rootid=100003&PressId=50.
Morgan, K. (2004). The exaggerated death of geography: Localised learning, innovation and uneven development. *Journal of Economic Geography,* Vol. 4, No. 1, 3–21.
Nelson, R. and Winter, S. (1982). *An evolutionary theory of economic change.* Cambridge, MA: The Belknap Press.
Net!Works Expert Working Group. (2011). *Smart cities applications and requirements.* Retrieved 2 January 2014, from www.networks-etp.eu/publications.html.
Nonaka, I. and Takeuchi, H. (1995). *The knowledge-creating company.* Oxford, UK: Oxford University Press.
Ouroussoff, N. (2010). Saudi urban projects are a window to modernity. *The New York Times.* Retrieved 2 January 2014, from www.nytimes.com/2010/12/13/arts/design/13desert.html?pagewanted=all_r=0.
Oxford Business Group (2008). *The report: Saudi Arabia 2008.* Oxford Business Group.
Oxford Business Group (2013). *From the ground up: The new economic cities will provide housing and jobs.* Retrieved 2 January 2014, from www.oxfordbusinessgroup.com/news/ground-new-economic-cities-will-provide-housing-and-jobs.
Ratti, C. and Townsend, A. (2011). Harnessing residents' electronic devices will yield truly smart cities. *Scientific American,* September. Retrieved 2 January 2014, from www.scientificamerican.com/article.cfm?id=the-social-nexus.
Reisz, T. (2012). Pipe dreams and real deals: Building cities in Saudi Arabia. *New Towns & Politics,* 12 November 2012, Almere, the Netherlands: International New Town Institute.
Roberts, J. (2009). The joy of knowledge. *Construction Week Online.* Retrieved 2 January 2014, from www.constructionweekonline.com/article-4242-the_joy_of_knowledge/#.UqrEluLIdoF.
SAGIA. (n.d.). *Saudi Arabia's economic cities. Cities Economic Cities Agency SAGIA.* Retrieved 2 January 2014, from www.oecd.org/mena/investment/38906206.pdf.
SAGIA. (2013). *Interactive map Saudi Arabian General Investment Authority.* Retrieved 2 January 2014, from www.sagia.gov.sa/en/SAGIA/Media-centre/Interactive-map1/.
Sambridge, A. (2010). More incentives needed for KSA economic cities. *Construction Week Online.* Retrieved 2 January 2014, from www.constructionweekonline.com/article-7758-more-incentives-needed-for-ksa-economic-cities/#.UqxUxuLIdoE.
Shwayri, S.T. (2013). A model Korean ubiquitous eco-city? The politics of making Songdo. *Journal of Urban Technology,* Vol. 20, No. 1, 39–55.
Swiss Business Hub GCC & Green Destinations LLC. (2010). *Economic cities Saudi Arabia. Opportunity assessment for cleantech companies.* Retrieved 2 January 2014, from www.green-destinations.com/docs%5Csbasa.pdf.
Townsend, A., Maguire, R., Liebhold, M. and Crawford, M. (2010). *A planet of civic laboratories. The future of cities, information and inclusion.* Palo Alto, CA: Institute for the Future.
TradeArabia. (2010). Saudi set for strong long-term growth. *Trade Arabia.* Retrieved 2 January 2014, from www.tradearabia.com/news/BANK_175883.html.
TradeArabia. (2013). $30bn Jizan Economic City deal terminated. *Trade Arabia.* Retrieved 2 January 2014, from www.tradearabia.com/news/CONS_233675.html.

Wacklin, S. (2013). *Saudi Arabia's economic cities – Big plans, big challenges. Embassy of Finland, Riyadh*. Retrieved 2 January 2014, from http://kauppapolitiikka.fi/Public/default.aspx?contentid=279167&nodeid=41394&contentlan=1&culture=fi-FI.

Whitaker, G. (2010a). Dialogue: Madinah Knowledge Economic City. *Construction Week Online*. Retrieved 2 January 2014, from www.constructionweekonline.com/article-7812-dialogue-madinah-knowledge-economic-city/#.UqxQcuLIdoF.

Whitaker, G. (2010b). Madinah economic city site work set to begin. *Construction Week Online*. Retrieved 2 January 2014, from www.constructionweekonline.com/article-7896-madinah-economic-city-site-work-set-to-begin/#.UqxQcOLIdoF.

7 Strategic planning for intelligent cities
A roadmap across spaces and stages

1. Cities: from masterplans to strategic planning

Traditional city planning methodologies based on master plans and comprehensive planning are inadequate to guide intelligent city planning. This is due to the digital dimension of intelligent cities, which is based on smart infrastructure and e-services, and the need to connect city planning methods, innovation management, and software development. 'Innovation platforms' and 'smart environments' are the fundamental implementation elements of intelligent cities, and end-of-the-day intelligent city planning introduces a group of e-services that enables innovation and better performance to take place.

Also, a major role in the journey towards intelligent cities is played by the co-creation paradigm, which entails the design, development, testing, and implementation of e-services collaboratively by citizens and end-users. The central role of users, producers and consumers in the design and development of e-services is leading intelligent city planning to rely on bottom-up than top-down processes.

Therefore, strategic planning implemented through projects seems the most suitable model of intelligent city planning, with 'e-services' taking the place of 'urban projects.' Even in cases where the term 'master plan' is used in the context of intelligent cities, the perspective is clearly strategic, being closer to corporate strategic planning than traditional city planning.[1]

Actually, there is a strong movement towards strategic city planning. In *Planning through Projects: Moving from Master Planning to Strategic Planning*, Carmona (2009) presents the contemporary shift towards strategic planning in 30 cities from around the world in which urban projects have become the principal mechanism for implementing futuristic visions of city development within the global innovation economy. Some projects are about intelligent cities; others concern innovative clusters, new city-districts, neighbourhood renovation, and advanced urban infrastructure. Overall, the demise of master planning and the shift towards strategic planning highlight a new type of urban governance that does not attempt comprehensive control over the city but inserts innovative elements that enhance the dynamics of urban systems.

Following the discussion about bottom-up and top-down intelligent city planning in the previous two chapters, here we concentrate on connecting these perspectives by proposing a roadmap for intelligent city planning based on strategic planning methodologies. The roadmap uses conventional strategic planning methodologies, such as environmental scanning, foresight and scenario building, balanced scorecards, and measurement and benchmarking, placed under the building blocks of intelligent cities and leading to innovative practices, smart infrastructure, and e-services.

2. Intelligent city planning: a connectionist model

Intelligent cities, in contrast to centrally planned cities, are organised along a decentralised connectionist model in which knowledge functions are distributed among citizens, organisations, software entities, and smart devices. Higher efficiency is structural and system implicit, and often is not apparent.[2] It does not mean that all cities claiming smartness have achieved it, but when collective or distributed intelligence occurs, it should be identified and documented with indexes and scoreboards.

Intelligent city planning relies more on human capabilities and active communities than on property developers. The planning methodologies followed focus on efforts to optimise decision-making and city operations through the use of information technology. For example, Living PlanIT's planning model is based on a four-layer framework connecting urban challenges, people and city functions, software applications, and networks and embedded technologies. An Urban Operating System (UOS) that has been built upon CISCO's infrastructure and Microsoft cloud platforms combines distributed sensing and processing with central command and control. Through this top-down design, the UOS enables real-time control for all buildings and infrastructure by using a common layer of sensing, actuation, network, and computation (LivingPlanIT, 2011). Neapolis Smart Eco-City, Cyprus, has adopted a number of development stages that are very much like strategic planning steps: conception, analysis, planning and design, implementation, launch and operation, and monitoring and control (Abdoullaev, 2011). There is also a great deal of interest about sustainability, and therefore about business models which capture key trends and market opportunities. On the other hand, larger cities such as Amsterdam, Manchester, Stockholm, and Helsinki have moved along a bottom-up path of becoming more 'intelligent' through decentralised initiatives and gradual implementation of successive projects, with each one focusing on a specific objective. Despite these very general orientations, there are very few examples of explicit methodologies that cities have followed when planning intelligent environments.

A rare exemption is New York's *Road Map for the Digital City* (City of New York, 2011), which includes a strategic planning methodology. It is comprised of four separate steps: Internet access, open government, citizen engagement, and digital industry growth. Each step is achieved through a number of initiatives that together achieve the targets set. The strategy was designed after a thorough analysis of the city's digital situation and a consideration of the future needs of citizens and the private sector. Information was derived from public consultation and dialogue with the community of entrepreneurs and developers. The plan is to measure the degree of progress achieved one year after implementation.

146 *Planning for intelligent cities*

Some more integrated insights regarding the planning process can also be found in corporate documents prepared by global technology vendors and infrastructure providers, such as IBM, CISCO, HP, Microsoft, Oracle, and Accenture. A general approach is proposed by IDC Government Insights, which proposes six significant steps in order to build a smart city: (1) defining leadership roles, (2) formalizing innovation as a citywide function, (3) developing an innovation ecosystem to involve the larger urban community, (4) open data and transparency as a citizen engagement and sourcing strategy, (5) next generation non emergency systems, and (6) promoting partnership and vendor engagement models (Clarke, 2013).

Similar to the above, for Accenture (2011), a common path to be followed in intelligent city planning is to assess the city's starting point, based on its unique geographic, economic, and political situation in order to weigh the costs, impacts, and tradeoffs of each development scenario. The company suggests five principles that are important in the whole endeavour. These principles are: (1) encourage and develop new forms of leadership and governance structures, (2) align and engage all relevant stakeholders, (3) assemble the capabilities to drive an open, intelligent infrastructure, (4) extend managers' capabilities in programming management and delivery, and (5) create financial models that are up to the challenges and opportunities ahead.

These are just a few examples that can be found about roadmaps and guides when planning for intelligent cities.

The roadmap we propose adopts a problem-oriented approach, because intelligence is linked to the ability to solve problems and accomplish objectives. The roadmap unfolds in three stages and seven steps, illustrated in Figure 7.1. The first

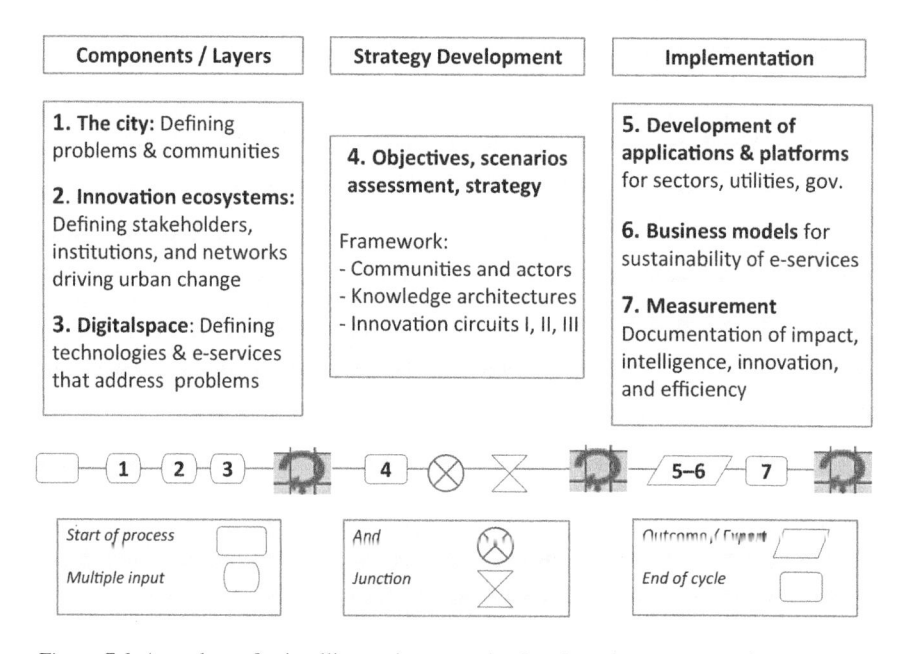

Components / Layers	Strategy Development	Implementation
1. The city: Defining problems & communities	**4. Objectives, scenarios assessment, strategy**	**5. Development of applications & platforms** for sectors, utilities, gov.
2. Innovation ecosystems: Defining stakeholders, institutions, and networks driving urban change	Framework: - Communities and actors - Knowledge architectures - Innovation circuits I, II, III	**6. Business models** for sustainability of e-services
3. Digitalspace: Defining technologies & e-services that address problems		**7. Measurement** Documentation of impact, intelligence, innovation, and efficiency

| Start of process | And | Outcome / Event |
| Multiple input | Junction | End of cycle |

Figure 7.1 A roadmap for intelligent city strategic planning: three stages and seven steps

stage takes into account the main building block of intelligent cities (urban system, innovation system, digital environment). The second is about the integration of those components and elaboration of a strategy of innovation to address the problems initially stated. The third stage concerns the implementation of strategy by developing digital applications and platforms, business models for e-services, and measurement scoreboards.

The rationale behind these stages is to ensure the application of the connectionist model by the interconnection of innovation platforms and e-services with city problems and challenges, the interconnection of e-services to innovation practices and behaviour, and the actualisation of participatory processes among stakeholders, users, organisations, and citizens in order to create smart city solutions and e-services.

3. Step one. The city: defining problems and communities

Intelligent cities as the planning model of today and the urban reality of tomorrow do not modify the very nature and fundamental logic of cities, forged through centuries of urban life. Cities emerge from blind market forces and chaotic individual choices, but also from strategic planning and detailed urban design. Agglomeration is the major driving force of cities and the spatial concentration of population and economic activities creates positive externalities and beneficial systemic effects.

In a well-known essay on Synekism, Soja (2001) outlines the collaborative character of cities with references to Thucydides, who saw the benefits of cities in the physical agglomeration of people and the political unification of the community, and Aristotle, who considered the *polis* to be a social and spatial process that involved political and cultural confederation around a distinctive territorial centre. Today's critical spatial thinking is also attributing to Synekism the seeds of creativity, innovation, territorial identity, political consciousness, and societal development which appear from living together in dense and heterogeneous urban regions.

Cities emerge from numerous uncoordinated individual choices giving birth to environments that are incomplete, driven by conflicts among people, activities, and land uses. Within distributive systems – which is what cities are – even the best individual choices do not lead to optimisation of the system overall. Due to competition, bounded rationality, and class structure, cities suffer from unemployment, marginalisation of weaker social groups, poverty, illegal housing, criminality hidden within large scale agglomerations, and environmental pollution, as well as social and spatial inequality. Beneficial systemic effects due to collaboration are coupled with systemic diseconomies and disequilibria. Dystopian visions of cities and anti-urban movements owe their origin to those dark sides of cities as environments nurturing conflict, degradation, and negative side effects.

Thus, while the spatial agglomeration and co-existence of people within urban systems is beneficial for collaboration, creativity, and innovation, it is also a source of urban problems, diseconomies, conflicts, and social and environmental inequalities. These are two fundamental aspects of every city: (1) the city as community and political association for collaboration and problem-solving; and (2) the city as a framework of divides, inequalities, and problems. As cities grow

148 *Planning for intelligent cities*

and their activities diversify in territorial terms, problems and communities change from one city district to the other; heterogeneous city-districts and urban communities co-exist in larger agglomerations.

Planning for intelligent cities starts from these deep city structures related to challenges and communities, which set out a framework of reference that pre-exists any transformation towards more efficient intelligent environments. City intelligence is intelligence stemming from the very nature of cities: active communities, collaboration, and beneficial systemic effects. Defining challenges and communities that can address those challenges is the starting point of any intelligent city planning process. There is something more, however. Within intelligent cities, the social and physical urban space is enriched by a third digital dimension. The digital space is modifying the dynamic relationship between challenges and communities, between positive and negative urban externalities. From the very beginning, the digital layer of intelligent cities opens a gateway to information and knowledge, and has been strengthening the 'bright' aspects of cities.

Getting down to more practical tasks in this initial step of the roadmap, a series of issues must be taken into account and carefully studied. These fall into two inter-related areas:

- Defining one or more domains for intervention in terms of city sectors, cluster, and utilities, etc., and mainly defining problems to address and objectives to reach within these domains. A good deal of data is needed, both to document problems that need to be solved and to describe the baseline, the actual situation of the city.
- Mapping communities related to challenges and objectives and assessing the governance capacity of those communities. Various actors should be identified within the communities of reference: authorities, organisations, companies, stakeholders, citizens, and users. These actors are expected to contribute in devising solutions to the challenges identified and develop more intelligent behaviour.

As contemporary cities are becoming more and more global, urban communities are connected to external actors spreading out globally. Business communities in manufacturing clusters, technology districts and export-oriented services, for instance, have many members (suppliers, marketers, end users) outside the city. The increased efficiency of an intelligent city depends on the practices of such glocal communities. The digital space is becoming an indispensable condition of global collaboration and synergy. Mapping has to reveal the entire network of relationships, while taking into account how global actors might contribute to more resourceful and effective practices.

4. Step two. Defining innovation ecosystems driving urban change

Within urban agglomerations, city districts with distinctive characteristics are formed and are connected with networks, infrastructure and utilities. Central business districts (CBDs), historic centres, port districts, transport hubs, technology districts, university campuses, hypermalls, industrial estates, business clusters, airport districts, and so on are entities to be found in most developed cities. The 'city of districts over networks' has become a mainstream pattern of urban agglomerations within developed market economies. The reasons for this specialisation are to be found in the ground rent, the different functional needs of urban activities, and the decentralisation of city governance towards semi-autonomous pockets of decision-making. Each district tends to specialise in one set of activities and offer specific products and services to local, national, and global markets. However, behind this apparent structure, we may find an agglomeration of innovation ecosystems, with each city-district having its own ecosystem of stakeholders, suppliers, producers, and users. Such functional innovation ecosystems guide they way in which city districts change, how activities are added or removed, and how the district adapts to changing demand and user needs.

The second step of the roadmap turns towards these fundamental drivers of change of cities, the innovation ecosystems of city-districts, clusters, and utilities. The purpose here is twofold:

- To map innovation ecosystems which are closely connected to urban system(s), by describing their composition, stakeholders, decision-makers, networks of collaboration locally and globally; and
- To understand the forces that introduce innovations in the urban system(s), and define the governance, operation rules, institutions, and decision-making processes of change, and the actors involved in these processes.

With the infusion of digital technologies and smart environments, the innovation ecosystems of cities become more open, global, and people driven, as suppliers and users start providing ideas, creativity, skills, and financial resources. The crowdsourcing paradigm or democratising innovation (Von Hippel, 2005) illustrates this widening of social and spatial collaboration within the innovation ecosystems enabled by Web and Internet technologies.

'Innovation-for-all' is a concept that captures this participatory model of innovation, encompassing not only 'innovation for everyone' but also 'innovation by everyone.' Intelligent cities are expected to enable every citizen or organisation in the city to fulfil his / her / its own personal goals and expectations within environments that enable collaboration and the sharing of resources. They are expected to achieve this vision thanks to innovation ecosystems augmented by smart environments and improved cognitive abilities and resources.

Innovation is not predictable, but intelligent cities set up collaborative platforms and environments that increase the probabilities for innovation. Digital platforms that aggregate a large numbers of efforts and a high degree of experimentation can deal with the uncertainty and serendipity of innovation. The creation of novelties tends to adapt to the logic of complexity, with small changes leading to universal effects, and institutions interacting under conditions of spontaneous self-organisation, feedback, and learning.

150 *Planning for intelligent cities*

Innovation ecosystems of city-districts, clusters, and utilities offer the framework for user-driven innovation and distributed problem-solving. There are many methodologies for involving users, such as Lead-Users, User-Driven Innovation, User-Centred Design, and User-Created Content. Living Labs, Open Innovation, and Web 2.0 product development also promote a more proactive role for users and citizens in innovation. The second step of the roadmap focuses on these innovation ecosystems, charted with respect to recognised urban entities, problems, and communities.

5. Step three. Digital space: horizon scan of technologies and smart environments

The third step of the roadmap focuses on the digital space of cities and performs a horizon scan at local and global levels. In Chapter 5, we gave a description of the digital space of cities as a system composed of four concentric rings. At the centre are broadband networks, wired and wireless infrastructure, and access devices enabling communication, data collection, and data exchange. Then, a second ring includes Web technologies enabling data storage, authentication and processing. The third ring is composed of digital applications in many different domains of the city. The outer ring comprises e-services and a few only applications that work with viable business models and are offered on a regular basis as services.

At the local level, the horizon scan is about mapping all digital solutions that have been implemented within the planning area. At global level, the scan is about finding available technologies, applications, and solutions that can address the problems and challenges defined at the starting point of the roadmap. These tasks require a good understanding of the dynamics and trends of a continuously changing digital landscape.

The creation of the digital space of intelligent cities is guided by two complementary yet distinct processes. Digital planners and IT developers may use existing solutions – off-the-shelf applications – that have already being used in other cities and recognised as good practice for the management, sustainability, and development of cities. Alternatively, they can try to create something from scratch, developing new solutions and applications by using available technologies, research, and the creative communities of the cities concerned. In both cases, the deployment of digital solutions relies on a series of information, communication, and programming technologies, most of which have become available over the last 15 years. These technologies are evolving and changing at an extremely rapid pace, and already within a short period from the mid-1990s until now we can distinguish three consecutive and overlapping waves of Web technologies and corresponding intelligent city solutions that have appeared in succession. These technologies offer different types of spatial intelligence and solutions to urban problems.

Wave 1: The World Wide Web started in 1990, and by the end of that year the fundamental Web architecture had been set, including the HyperText Transfer Protocol (http), HTML syntax, the first Web browser, URL address, Web servers,

Strategic planning for intelligent cities 151

and the first Web pages. A critical step for reaching a wider public was made with the introduction of the Mosaic graphic Web browser in 1993. The following year, in 1994, the first commercial Web browser, Netscape, was developed and the World Wide Web Consortium (W3C) was founded to oversee and spread Web standards. By 1996, the commercial Web was a reality, and companies and public organisations felt the pressure of having a Web presence. The era of digital cities was initiated.

The first digital cities, based on the above set of technologies, were mainly static Web pages providing information about the urban area through the combination of texts, data, maps, events, and information services about commerce, recreation, and city accommodation. Such digital cities were accurately described as mirror-city metaphors, as their design was based on principles of representation and visualisation of the urban environment (Couclelis, 2004). The innovations that they introduced related to certain city activities being substituted by digital elements, new ways of doing things (digital), reinforcing city functions, and leading to reconfiguration of the physical and social space of cities. Ishida (2000) compared four digital cities which were representative of this era: the AOL digital cities, which collected recreation and shopping information of the corresponding city coupled with local advertising and vertical markets; Digital City Amsterdam, which was a platform for various community networks and social interaction among citizens; virtual Helsinki, a 3D reconstruction of the entire city; and Digital City Kyoto, also a 3D virtual space enriched with avatars which offered information related to city traffic, weather, parking, shopping, and sightseeing. He concluded that all digital cities followed a three-tier architecture composed of: (1) a technology for information integration, (2) a technology for public participation with 2D and 3D graphic interfaces, and (3) a technology supported by agents for interaction with citizens. In addition, a technology for information security, which transversely crossed the previous tiers, became important as more people joined digital cities.

The spatial intelligence of cities related to this technology stack was based on advantages of representation and visualisation and reflects the idea that complex urban environments can be described and understood better by maps, images, 2D and 3D designs, icon models, and simulations. Online search in the vertical markets represented also offered additional capabilities for understanding cities.

Wave 2: Increases in communication bandwidth, wider coverage with ADSL connections, and the development of open source Content Management Systems (CMS) marked a radical change in the Web landscape and in digital cities, as well. WordPress, released in 2003, offered a Web publishing platform built on the PHP language and MySQL database. It is an open source CMS, and is actually the most popular globally. Joomla, released in 2005, also offers a free and open source CMS written in PHP, which stores data in a MySQL database. Together with Linux, they formed the dominant technology stack of Web 2.0, the free open-source solution LAMP – from the first letters of Linux, Apache Server, MySQL, and the Perl / PHP / Python programming languages. The ideas behind the rise of

152 *Planning for intelligent cities*

the Web 2.0 were about sharing, both software and content. Web 2.0 introduced this collaborative and sharing perspective, and in many respects it might be considered to be more a social than a technological breakthrough. The Web became a medium via which users interact and collaborate, exchange information, join efforts, and create virtual communities. The transition to the participatory Web was manifest with the proliferation of wikis, blogs, social networking sites, social media, hosting of Web applications, mash-ups, and other collaborative Web applications. The critical change was on the user side, as users became both producers and consumers of content and applications.

Web-based collaboration platforms separated programming language and content and simplified the participation of users. They can contribute with content without being concerned with code and programming. Web 2.0 cities followed these trends and new applications for many domains populated the landscape of digital cities. Good examples are *SeeClickFix* in the area of city governance that enables users to report non-emergency issues for improving their neighbourhood and city; *Madri+d* in the area of research and innovation enabling collaboration among the innovation institutions of the city; *Scoop.it* for collaborative intelligence at targeted subjects; *NYC Simplicity IdeaMarket*, engaging employees' ideas for a more customer-focused, innovative, and efficient city; *Zonability*, leveraging open data for better zoning information; *GoldenDeals* and *Groupon* for marketing and promotion of services locally; and *Localocracy,* which gathers citizens, government officials, and journalists to discuss and learn about local politics and priorities. The Citizens 2.0 report (Barkat et al., 2011) compiled 17 applications of social media that provide inexpensive tools that empower citizens to improve local government responsibility and accountability.

This type of Web applications better simulates the fundamental concept of the city as a social space of collaboration. Web 2.0 enables people to come closer and work together in a digital rather than a physical space. Key concepts for 'digital agglomeration' are those of outsourcing and crowdsourcing, opening and transferring tasks and activities to suppliers and the crowd. The Crowdsourcing Landscape (Dawson and Bynghall, 2011) offers a good overview of tools and concepts and how crowdsourcing "could be applied to anything reducible to bits and bytes" (Howe, 2008, p. ix), from prediction markets, idea generation and assessment, distributed innovation, service marketplaces, competition, allocation of microtasks, and funding.

The spatial intelligence of cities that emerged from this type of collaborative Web platforms built on collective intelligence and social capital. These are fundamental drivers of innovation and problem-solving capability, outlining the intelligence of cities as collective rather than individual achievement. They also paved the way towards Living Labs and other forms of user-driven innovation by introducing the principles of openness, realism, and empowerment of users in the development of new solutions (Bergvall-Kåreborn and Ståhlbröst, 2009).

Wave 3: By 2009, the turn to embedded systems and wireless networks marked a breakthrough in technologies for creating the digital space of cities. It was none other than IBM who captured this shift by stating that, "smarter cities make their systems instrumented, interconnected and intelligent. Pervasive information and communication technology means that there is much greater scope for leveraging technology for the benefit of cities" (IBM, 2010, p. 10). With instrumentation, the working of a city is made measurable by sensors, smart devices, and meters; with interconnection, all parts of a city communicate with wired and wireless networks; and intelligence refers to predictive modelling for forecasting and more informed decisions.

The smart city as a digital spatiality embedded in the physical space of cities, into buildings, roads, bridges, and other infrastructure is based on a new set of technologies, devices, and applications:

- Mobile devices enabling ubiquitous access to data and the Web.
- Real-world user interfaces, QR codes over buildings, RFID, mesh sensor networks, low-energy consumption meters and control devices.
- 3G and 4G wireless networks, next-generation networks, and network interoperability giving 100 percent Internet usage and penetration everywhere.
- Applications for smart phones, iPhones, GPS devices, voice control, augmented reality visualisation.
- Opening of public data over the Web, open access to data from sensors, linked data, and Semantic Web with RDF, SPARQL, OWL and ontoloty languages for M2M communication of embedded devices.

In this wave, smart cities come closer to the Future Internet research and experimental facilities, offering an extensive domain of experimentation for the Internet by and for people, the Internet of Contents and Knowledge, the Internet of Services, and the Internet of Things. Smart cities can be understood as a particular type of intelligent cities, generating spatial intelligence from sensors, large data sets, and real-time information and response.

Again, the drivers of the spatial intelligence of cities have changed. Within this technology stack, intelligence has moved out of Web applications and entered into the domain of data: the meaning of data becomes part of data. Data are provided just-in-time. Real-time data enable real-time response. Data and technologies, however, do not automatically lead to new solutions and new services for the citizen. Urban systems working with open data also require open innovation models and people-driven innovation models to turn the capabilities offered by data into services and solutions. Living Labs and Web 2.0 participatory innovation models retain their value in bridging the gap between the technology push of Future Internet test beds and the application pull of smart cities (Pallot et al., 2011).

The continuous evolution of Web technologies from the static Web to the Social Web, the Real-Time Web, the Semantic Web, and eventually the Intelligent Web in the near future, substantially widens the options for constructing the digital space of cities. There is a stack of available solutions, which any planning attempt has to take into account before creating something new.

Thus, this step of the roadmap is about a horizon scan and search for good practice globally; a scan for applications and solutions which have been implemented successfully and have provided positive results to urban challenges. A very large range of technologies, applications, data, and e-services is now offered. Managing this complexity has become a key issue in intelligent city planning, as well as retaining the value of ICT investments as each new wave of Web technologies eventually makes the previous digital solutions quickly obsolete.

6. Step four. Strategy: communities, knowledge functions, and circuits of innovation

Step 4 of the roadmap is a direct follow-up to the previous steps, focusing on the activation of the 'golden triangle' of intelligent cities: the integration of 'city communities and challenges,' 'innovation processes,' and 'smart environments' into a coherent array that can optimise the functioning and decision-making of the city. Thus, the second stage of the roadmap includes one only – but the most demanding – step: elaborating a strategy of spatial intelligence and innovation to address the challenge(s) initially defined.

A strategy for making a city intelligent can be formulated at the level of the entire city or at the level of the city-districts, clusters, and networks comprising it. As mentioned, each city-district or cluster has to be treated differently, because problems, functions, communities, and governance differ from one to the other. Whatever the level of approach taken, the preparation of an intelligent city strategy must consider several dimensions: the innovation economy; living conditions; the environment and social divides; transport infrastructure and utilities for energy, water and waste; and city governance, management, and operation. Taking into account these domains, the strategy should start by using balances scorecards methods (Kozena et al., 2011) and setting a series of objectives, such as the goal of increasing the competitiveness of economic clusters and sectors, generating new companies and employment, saving resources in energy and transport, protecting the environment, and reducing greenhouse emissions and the built footprint, as well as advancing democracy and participatory decision-making in city governance. Overall, the strategy must pave the way of the innovation-led development of the city.

But how these objectives can be achieved? Which resources can be mobilised? Which actors should take the lead in defining and assessing alternative solutions? To provide an informed answer to these questions, we must take into account contributions from theories on knowledge-based development and the discussion on drivers of spatial intelligence, as presented in Part I of this volume.

The place dependence of knowledge-based development has been clearly corroborated by various theoretical strands, such as local synergies and innovative milieu (Camagni, 1991), embeddedness (Grabher, 1993), knowledge spillovers and regional interconnectedness (Gertler, 1995), untraded interdependencies (Storper, 1997), regional innovation systems (Cooke et al., 1998), institutional thickness (Amin, 1999), regional learning and tacit knowledge clustering (Morgan, 2004), related variety and knowledge proximity between sectors of activity

Strategic planning for intelligent cities 155

(Boschma, 2005). The ability of cities and regions to induce innovation is widely accepted as condition of growth in knowledge-driven economies.

Within these perspectives of place-based innovation and development, the intelligent strategy to be elaborated ought to include a coherent sequence of objectives, scenarios, use cases, applications, outcomes, and impact assessments. Taken together, these elements will establish a solution for making a city intelligent, and describe the projects, platforms, and e-services that will enhance the innovation capacity of city actors and the efficiency of the urban system. We argued that intelligent city strategies, at the level of sectors, clusters, districts, and utilities, deploy multi-level knowledge processes and different types of collective and machine intelligence, which set in motion architectures for distributed problem-solving and innovation. This may seem fairly abstract and its logical coherence must be further explained.

To address their problems, cities should turn to those actors and frameworks that generate solutions. Urban problems are solved within innovation ecosystems (innovation supply chains), since any solution, incremental or radically new, will come from stakeholders of the responsible innovation ecosystem. Here is placed a first circuit of innovation, from the innovation ecosystem towards the smart environments. Stakeholders, producers, external providers, lead users, and citizens design and develop digital spaces and smart environments to improve the working of the city.

However, once digital applications, spaces, and smart environments are in place, they activate two more circuits of innovation (Figure 7.2). These circuits derive from the knowledge functions introduced by the digital application / smart environment related to information gathering, learning and skill development, innovation and making something new, information dissemination, and promotion.

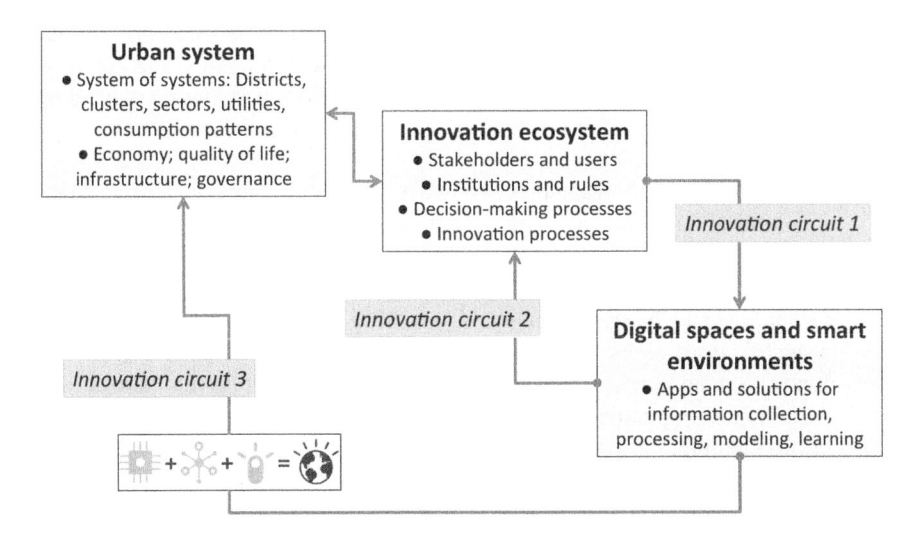

Figure 7.2 Intelligent city strategy – three innovation circuits

In circuit 2, digital spaces improve the decisions and capabilities of innovation actors by making the urban innovation ecosystem more open, user driven, and participatory. In this case, the digital space acts as 'producer service,' offering know-how and resources to improve the city and make its services and products better. The urban system changes and becomes more innovative, competitive, and efficient.

In circuit 3, smart environments improve the decisions and choices of users and consumers about how to use the urban system. In this case, the digital space acts as 'consumer service' offering information and skills that improve the interaction between the user and the city. The behaviour of users change, and the urban system is used in more resource efficient and sustainable way.

To illustrate these processes, we can take the example of urban transportation. To improve transportation, cities should turn to transportation stakeholders, actors, suppliers, users, and their decision-making processes, in other words, to the responsible innovation ecosystem of transportation. Any improvement of transportation will come from this ecosystem and its choices of intelligent transportation systems (ITS) or other solutions. The implementation of ITS corresponds to the first innovation circuit. Once ITS are in place, they introduce two more circuits of innovation. In circuit 2, ITS make the innovation ecosystem of transportation more open and participatory, by enabling the engagement of citizens and users. Decision-making becomes more informed and more aware of user needs. Subsequent changes of transportation are better adapted to user needs. In circuit 3, ITS make the urban transportation system more efficient because they offer real-time data, information processing, and e-services, which improve the way this system is used. The urban transportation system becomes more resource efficient and its functionality improves.

In general, innovation circuit 1 leads to the selection of applications and e-services, making the smart environment operational. Because most applications are narrowly focused, a group of applications is needed to address the range of problems that usually appear in a city district. Once the smart environment is in place, a series of information and knowledge processes start taking place:

- Information collection and processing over digital platforms, involving communities of interest, end users, citizens, and institutions for information management.
- Knowledge transfer and learning, enabling the acquisition of state-of-the art technology and the creation of skills, involving technology-led organisations, academic institutions, and online knowledge-management tools.
- Innovation and new knowledge creation within user-driven innovation, involving communities of users, citizens, institutions for innovation, and crowdsourcing.
- Information dissemination and information marketplaces combining physical spaces of the city, communities of vendors, virtual marketplaces, and the social media.

Innovation circuits 2 and 3 rely on how the above knowledge functions are inserted into innovation ecosystems and the urban system. In Chapter 4, we discussed different architectures of integration that can be used to achieve spatial intelligence. We referred to *agglomeration intelligence* produced by the spatial concentration of digital applications; *orchestration intelligence* based on organised top-down collaboration within a community, connecting people's skills, collective intelligence processes, infrastructure and machine intelligence; *empowerment intelligence* based on people's learning, up-skilling, and talent cultivation over open platforms and infrastructure offered by the city; and *instrumentation intelligence*, based on streams of data generated by sensors and smart meters, that capture the working of cities and enable informed decisions to be taken by citizens and organisations.

Thus, in step 4 of the roadmap, the entire sequence of urban problems, innovation actors, stakeholders and ecosystems, smart environments, and the innovation circuits 1, 2, and 3 must be defined. In particular, it is essential to identify the innovation platforms and e-services to be developed, and the knowledge processes they will introduce into the ecosystems and sub-systems of the city.

Good strategies, however, have also a number of merits. They are evidence based; they provide frameworks for appropriate stakeholder involvement; they set innovation and knowledge-based priorities; they develop roadmaps, actions, and policy mixes to achieve the outlined objectives; they produce synergies and alignment of different actions and funding sources; they set achievable goals and measure progress; and they proceed by cycles and adapt to conclusions from measurement and assessment.

7. Step five. Development of applications and platforms

The third stage of the roadmap includes three steps dealing with strategy implementation: development of innovation platforms and applications, selection of business models for turning applications into e-services, and measurement and assessment. Strategy implementation, however, is not a linear process and circular loops are needed to improve the strategy with respect to implementation solutions and outcomes.

The development of applications should take into consideration issues concerning users, architecture, hardware and software requirements, quality attributes, data, security, licensing, and sustainability. Table 7.1 summarises some key aspects of hardware and software seen from the perspective of application development.

Software development can opt between different solutions of control and collaboration. Control options range from using proprietary software, through a usage permission granted according to a license which describes in detail the usage conditions, to Free Open Source Software (FOSS), which offers full control over the software through an ex-ante agreement about the rights to use, modify, and distribute software. Collaboration options range from full in-house development

Table 7.1 Smart city software development of applications and solutions

Design of architecture	**Users** • Target audience • Target segmentation; target groups • Lead users • Users • Quality attributes: usability, reliability, interoperability, scalability, security	**Application architecture** • Logical architecture • Subsystems • Information flow diagrams, ontologies • Open architecture / open systems • Multichannel approach: Web, mobile, PDA, city displays • Linkages with other software systems
Software development	**Software development** • Service oriented architecture • Modules and modular structure • Open standards / open formats • Web architecture and technology • Development platform • Data layers and database • User interface	**Data requirements** • Data from Web 2.0 and social media • Sensor data • Compliance to W3C / WAI Web content • Accessibility guidelines • Data renewal • Linked data • Open data • Big data
Hardware and networks	**Computing needs** • Servers • Virtualisation, cloud computing • Memory needs • Distributed computing	**Network and access needs** • Broadband, wired and wireless • Bandwidth • Wireless sensor networks • Sensors • Meters and other embedded devices • Multi-touch screens and other access devices
Operation	**Administration** • Administration platform • Control over data • User interface control • Performance metrics and analytics • Risk mitigation plans • Security • Backup / restore • User support	**License** • Proprietary • Open source • Open source license type • Open data licenses

to external collaboration with local or global developers. The collaboration or development model is independent from the software control model, as collaboration can take place both in proprietary software and FOSS (Daffara, 2009).

Developing applications and solutions for smart cities, authorities, or other organisations managing city assets or utilities should take the necessary steps to avoid both unnecessary spending and technology lock-in. They should adopt a long-term perspective about the development and updating of software to cope with a rapidly changing environment that makes solutions obsolete very quickly. Cities should develop a culture of experimentation and openness based on two principles:

1   'Share more – Develop less,' which is about the exchange of applications among cities, the creation of communities of untraded exchanges, and offering applications for free to other cities. This goes together with the use of FOSS and participation in FOSS communities. Open source is ideal for city authorities, because they do not compete on software and do not create advantages over proprietary software.
2   'Spend less,' opt for low-cost solutions, use existing software, re-use software, proceed by small steps, and minimise investments to those that are safer. Radical innovations and most big things start small. Developing applications from scratch should be the last resort, done only in cases when no other solution is available. Standardisation of solutions will accelerate technology diffusion and learning curves as city administrations become aware of their added value.

A major issue in using open source is related to licenses. Open-source licenses allow one to use software without seeking permission to do so. Free software has been described by 'four freedoms' that determine whether a particular software program qualifies as free software: (1) the freedom to run the program for any purpose; (2) the freedom to study how the program works and adapt it to your needs by having access to the source code; (3) the freedom to redistribute copies for dissemination and usage; and (4) the freedom to modify and improve the program, and release the improvements to the public (GNU, n.d.). These freedoms derive from the Open Source definition, based on similar principles, such as free redistribution that does not restrict any party from selling or giving away the software as a component of a compiled solution from different sources, publication of the source code, and permission for modifications and derived works to be distributed under the same terms as the license for the original software.

However, all open-source licenses are not the same and they determine development and distribution rights in many different ways. More than 50 licenses can be identified as open source or free software that fall in three broad categories:

- Licenses that provide credit: use, modification, and redistribution are allowed, but credit to the original author is due, if redistributed (i.e., BSD license, Apache License v2.).
- Licensed that provide fixes: use, modification, and redistribution are allowed, but source code for any changes must be provided to the original author, if redistributed (i.e., Mozilla Public License).
- Licenses that provide all: use, modification, and redistribution are allowed, but source code of any derived product must be provided, if redistributed (i.e., general public license, GPL).

160   *Planning for intelligent cities*

Among all licenses, GPL (general public license) and LGPL (lesser general public license) are most commonly used, both in terms of the number of projects and in terms of the number of lines of code covered.

We estimate that during the current decade, a full range of open source applications for intelligent cities will become available. FOSS communities will provide coding and accompanying activities, such as bug fixing and documentation, creating virtual software houses that share effort and resources. We have already created the ICOS (Intelligent Cities Open Source) community and platform (icos.urenio.org) to host open source solutions under FOSS licenses. ICOS provides overview and guidance to find and use open source applications for intelligent cities/smart cities, while the software is hosted on Github (https://github.com).

Sharing applications, using existing and proven solutions, turning to open source and cloud-based solutions, and adopting a long-term perspective over solutions and data are principles for creating a sustainable digital space of intelligent cities and secure viable solutions over the long run.

8. Step six. Selecting business models of sustainability

The purpose of broadband infrastructure and software applications is to enable e-services to be provided to citizens, organisations, and the city authorities anywhere and anytime. However, there is major discontinuity between applications, solutions, and the provision of e-services. The gap is created by needs for funding and revenue creation that can keep IT infrastructure and applications alive in the long run.

The functionality of business models lies in bridging such gaps by providing solutions for initial funding and financial viability. Business models deal with the financial aspects of smart city strategies and applications. They concern both the sources of the initial investment and the funding of operations. Thus, a business model is much more than a business plan that merely calculates costs and revenues. It is a creative solution for securing the necessary funds for the initial investment and revenue for the long-term operation and maintenance of infrastructure and e-services.

A Forrester Research report on smart cities (Belissent, 2010) described several engagement models that can ensure the viability of smart city initiatives. These financial solutions are based on different funding opportunities and revenue generated from IT infrastructure and e-services, such as:

- *Public funding:* In this business model, funding is provided by national or international funding organisations and investment banks, which undertake the cost of public sector IT initiatives. The EU Structural Funds are a usual line for this kind of funding.
- *Revenue-generating or cost-cutting initiatives* can provide funding and prove appealing for budgetary and political reasons. JESSICA funding instruments in the EU follow this concept of providing funds with a low interest rate which are to be paid back using revenue generated from the funded projects.

Strategic planning for intelligent cities 161

- *PPPs for revenue-sharing:* Public–private partnerships (PPPs) with vendors, service providers, systems integrators, real estate developers, and businesses located in the city, based on a revenue-sharing agreement, can provide funding in advance and sustain an initiative over the long term.
- *Capacity reselling:* Excess capacity from large municipal infrastructure and services from the IT department of a large city can be provided to neighbouring cities and other organisations and can thereby cover operating costs and ensure sustainability.
- *Multi-city collaboration:* This model is based on agreements to pool resources and share infrastructure and costs. It can facilitate larger initiatives.
- *Leasing and financing:* This is the traditional model of financing based on own resources to pay back capital and interest on loans or leasing fees.
- *Barter or in-kind exchange* is about the provision of services and other in-kind payment; it is a way of overcoming budget shortfalls, particularly for organisations that have large human or technological resources.
- *Data monetisation:* This financing model is based on the use of primary data generated by instrumented city infrastructure and sensors, which create a potential revenue source for the data owner.
- *Advertising* is a usual means for funding operating costs. City authorities and utility organisations can offer advertising space on the city's digital space or other public spaces, thereby capitalising on the large number of visitors to these spaces.
- *Crowdfunding* is a new business model with great potential that has emerged within the wider culture of crowdsourcing. People and organisations pool their financial resources in order to pursue a common objective together.

These business models offer different solutions which can work either on their own or in a complimentary manner. The main task of this step of the roadmap is to examine such solutions per application comparatively and select those that best fit the environment and profile of each city. The management capability of the organisation responsible for providing the service must be carefully assessed, as this capability is a precondition for the success of any business model.

Disruptive business models for intelligent city development can be obtained by a combination of open source, open data, and cloud computing. The advantages of open source applications are well known. Additionally, open data offers "data that can be freely used, reused and redistributed by anyone – subject only, at most, to the requirement to attribute and share alike" (OKFN, n.d.). Open data make content available over the Internet and permit free reuse and redistribution without discrimination against fields of endeavour or against persons or groups. On the other hand, cloud computing leads to significant cost reduction, lowering entry costs, scalability of costs, pay-per-use, and costs scaling-up with respect to use and revenue. For instance, the OpenStack software (Nova for computer services; Quantum for networking services; Cinder for storage; Horizon Web front-end; Glance for storing virtual machine images; and Keystone authentication and authorisation) provided under the Apache 2.0 license, offer a free cloud

162 *Planning for intelligent cities*

operating system for computing, storage, and networking, sustained by an active open developer community (OpenStack, n.d.). Open source applications, open data, and cloud-based solutions provide enormous advantages of cost reduction and increased quality of service, with expanding libraries, instant scalability, and trustworthy and reliable complex infrastructure for intelligent city solutions.

9. Step seven. Documenting spatial intelligence

In this final step of the roadmap, the major concern is to document that intelligent city solutions do, in fact, offer higher spatial intelligence and improve the quality and performance of cities. Measurement and assessment of intelligent city performance is about the monitoring of key performance indicators (KPIs), the creation of scoreboards, and the gathering of data and analytics, and about understanding the factors shaping the performance of cities. Measurement is indispensable, as most dimensions of spatial intelligence are usually hidden at first glance.

In the literature, different measurement methodologies can be found, which vary with respect to the perspective and variables that are measured and assessed. Measurement and assessment can focus on urban characteristics, planning efforts, and smart city infrastructure and operation.

Policy focused measurement: The Intelligent Community Forum (ICF) was the first organisation to introduce a methodology for measuring intelligent cities. ICF assesses what a community (region, city, city-district) is doing to sustain spatial intelligence by a set of criteria related to policies from broadband, innovation, and city promotion:

1 Broadband connectivity is measured by the Broadband Performance Index (BPI), which quantifies the relationship between a region's broadband subscriptions per capita and that region's economic and demographic endowments.
2 Knowledge workforce indicators measure how a community equips its workforce to succeed at knowledge-intensive work, and looks at the public sector contribution in education, computer literacy, and skills creation; the public-private sector of universities and NGOs contribution to education and specialised training; and the private sector contribution to the continuing education of employees.
3 Digital inclusion is assessed by indicators capturing efforts for improving IT education in public schools, programmes to subsidise IT and public access to computers and broadband networks, training programmes for all ages in IT and use of the Internet, and e-government for the provision of e-services.
4 Innovation is measured by the effort of communities in creating economic and social environments in which innovation can thrive, the government resources available for innovative local companies, access to risk capital, and e-government programmes that deliver information to companies and organisations.
5 Effective city marketing is measured by indicators capturing investments in professional public relations, hosting of regional and national conferences,

and changes in the public perception of the place. They measure the ability of communities to market their intelligence and put the Intelligent Community strategy at the centre of economic development efforts.

Since 2001, a large number of cities have received ICF awards because they excelled in one or more of the five criteria above. Cities do not need to excel in all criteria. It is clear that the assessment is not a benchmarking exercise for urban environments. The indicators used do not measure the social and physical qualities of a city, but rather policies and planning efforts. They evaluate the commitment and effectiveness of local and regional government in supporting the new innovation economy created on broadband networks and e-services.

City-focused measurement: The European Smart Cities project consortium devised a different methodology for assessing smart cities, based on the characteristics of cities. Data was provided by the Urban Audit database, the most comprehensive list of indicators on cities in Europe (EU27+NO+CH), which covers almost 1,600 cities with comparable data relating to population, employment, age, activity, land use, and many other characteristics.

A city performing well in six areas built on the 'smart' combination of endowments and activities of self-decisive, independent, and aware citizens was defined as a 'Smart City.' Those areas are: (1) smart economy, (2) smart people, (3) smart mobility, (4) smart environment, (5) smart living, and (6) smart governance. Within these areas, 33 factors and 80 indicators were used to capture urban smartness (see Table 1.1). Indicators were aggregated with equal weighting; aggregation was additive, but divided by the number of values added, allowing one to also include cities which do not have metrics for all the indicators (Giffinger, 2007).

Following this methodology, city smartness was assessed in 70 European cities, selected from functional urban areas in Europe with a population between 100,000 and 500,000 (medium-sized cities), having at least one university (to exclude cities with a weak knowledge base), and a catchment area of less than 1,500,000 inhabitants (to exclude cities which are dominated by a larger city). Indicators were rationalised by z-transformations. The assessment produced a ranking of European Smart Cities with Scandinavian cities and cities from the Benelux region and Austria at the top, while cities that ranked lowest were mainly in the new EU member states (Giffinger, 2007).

The measurement concept proposed by Cortright (2007) for assessing four key dimensions of American cities – namely, talent, innovation, connectivity, and distinctiveness – is similar. Twenty indicators were used in this case. Talent was measured by college attainment, creative professionals, the young and the restless, traded sector talent, and international talent. Innovation was measured by patents, venture capital, self-employment, and small business. Connectivity was measured by voting, community involvement, economic integration, transit use, international students, foreign travel, and Internet connectivity. Distinctiveness was measure by the weirdness index, the culture / cable ratio, restaurant variety, and movie variety.

Infrastructure-focused measurement: The IBM smart city model of instrumentation (enabling cities to data using utility meters and sensors), interconnection (creating links between data, systems, and people), and intelligence (enabling predictive modelling) is suitable for urban infrastructure and utilities assessment as it relies on the availability of sensor-based data.

IBM proposes this monitoring system to assess a city's core systems and activities, in areas such as (Dirks et al., 2009):

- City services through e-government and use of ICT for service delivery and management by local government.
- Citizens that use ICT for human and social services related to education, health, housing, and social aspects.
- Businesses that make use of an efficient business system with a high level of innovation and creation.
- Transport systems and the accessibility to and from cities.
- Communication through ICT infrastructures, such as high-speed broadband and Wi-Fi.
- Energy and the presence of smart grids and use of smart metering for energy management.
- Water and the use smart technologies for water management and regulation.

For each of the above core systems, measurements are using indicators related to: (1) prerequisites dealing with the existing situation of the city, (2) management, (3) smarter systems and IT solutions, and (4) outcomes in terms of efficiency and value added. Each city should be measured against appropriate peer cities that share key characteristics, challenges, and priorities, and which highlight best practices. The result is a benchmarking of core city sectors with respect to peer city average and peer city best practice.

These three perspectives represent well-known cases of smart city measurement, assessment, and benchmarking. It is clear that measurement is a much broader exercise than just the selection and use of indicators. The different methodologies described reveal differences in the concept of intelligent cities / smart cities, but also differences in the objectives and methods of measurement.

In our view, a good methodology of measurement and assessment should include a clear statement about the measurable objectives, indicators defined with respect to the drivers of intelligent city development, measurement of efforts, and indicators capturing the outcome of intelligent city planning on critical aspects of the physical, social, and environmental condition of cities. This leads to a merging of policy-focused and city-focused methodologies which can be achieved with balanced scorecard methodologies.

Whatever method of city measurement is adopted, the use of structural KPIs concerning the building blocks of intelligent cities – knowledge skills, innovation ecosystems, and digital spaces – should be present to capture the physical, social, and digital dimensions of intelligent city planning.

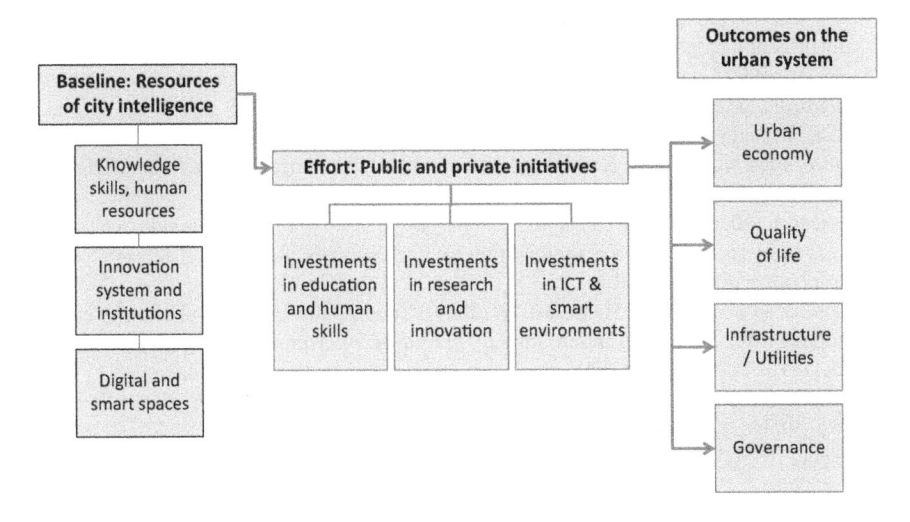

Figure 7.3 Intelligent city scoreboard structure

Furthermore, provision should be made for collecting data and managing records so that the data required are accessible and reliable, and for normalisation of indicators to enable data comparison, and for the creation of composite indexes to capture complex situations (World Bank, 1994). Within this perspective, three sets of indicators should be used to capture available resources of the urban system, efforts in intelligent city initiatives and solutions, and outcomes in the improvement of the urban environment (Figure 7.3.).

Notes

1 "Intelligent Nation 2015 (iN2015) is Singapore's ten-year master plan to help us realise the potential of infocomm over the next decade" (IDA, 2007, p. 1).
2 See the description of intelligent city Cyberjaya by a student in engineering: "For your knowledge, I'm currently studying in Multimedia University and live in a place called Cyberjaya, some sort of an intelligent city. Doesn't make me intelligent in any way. So, the point is, this city is like a desert. It is hot, it has very few people that you can sleep on the road and waking up alive. Not much restaurant or stalls selling food around. It is not like Subang. So thank to the events held since last 3 weeks inviting the vendors to sell food in Misri Plaza. We got Bubble Milk Tea!" (www.fellxion.com/2010/04/bubble-milk-tea-day.html).

References

Abdoullaev, A. (2011). A smart world: A development model for intelligent cities. *11th IEEE International Conference on Computer and Information Technology*. Retrieved 2 January 2014, from www.cs.ucy.ac.cy/CIT2011/files/SMARTWORLD.pdf.

Accenture (2011). *Building and managing an intelligent city*. Retrieved 2 January 2014, from www.accenture.com/SiteCollectionDocuments/PDF/Accenture-Building-Managing-Intelligent-City.pdf.

Amin, A. (1999). An institutionalist perspective on regional development. *International Journal of Urban and Regional Research*, Vol. 23, No. 2, 365–378.

Barkat, H., Jaeggli L. and Dorsaz P. (2011). *Citizen 2.0: 17 examples of social media and government innovation*. Retrieved 2 January 2014, from http://citizen20.redcut.ch/Citizen%202.0%20(EN.pdf).

Belissent, J. (2010). *Getting clever about smart cities: New opportunities require new business models*. Forrester for Ventor Strategy Professionals. Retrieved 2 January 2014, from http://goo.gl/hnuuRo.

Bergvall-Kåreborn, B. and Ståhlbröst, A. (2009). Living Lab: An open and citizen-centric approach for innovation. *International Journal of Innovation and Regional Development*, Vol. 1, No. 4, 356–370.

Boschma, R. (2005). Proximity and innovation: a critical assessment. *Regional Studies*, Vol. 39, No. 1, 64–71.

Camagni, R. (1991) (ed.). *Innovation networks: Spatial perspectives*. London, UK: Belhaven.

Carmona, M. (2009). *Planning through projects: Moving from master planning to strategic planning – 30 cities*. Amsterdam, the Netherlands: Techne Press.

City of New York. (2011). *Road map for the digital city: Achieving New York city's digital future*. Retrieved 2 January 2014, from www.nyc.gov/html/media/media/PDF/90dayreport.pdf.

Clarke, R.Y. (2013). *Business strategy: Smart city essentials – Six ways to drive innovation in your city*. IDC Government Insights report. Retrieved 2 January 2014, from www.idc.com/research/viewtoc.jsp?containerId=GI243301.

Cooke, P., Uranga-Gomez, M. and Extebarria, G. (1998). Regional systems of innovation: an evolutionary perspective. *Environment and Planning A*, Vol. 30, No. 9, 1563–1584.

Cortright, J. (2007) *City vitals*. Impressa Consulting, Chicago, IL: CEOs for Cities.

Couclelis, H. (2004). The construction of the digital city. *Environment and Planning B: Planning and Design*, Vol. 31, No. 1, 5–19.

Daffara, C. (2009). *The SME guide to open source software*. Luxembourg: European Commission, DG Infosoc. Available at http://smeguide.conecta.it/smeguide.pdf.

Dawson, R. and Bynghall, S. (2011). *Getting results from crowds*. San Francisco, CA: Advanced Human Technologies.

Dirks, S., Keeling, M. and Dencik, J. (2009). *How smart is your city? Helping cities measure progress*. Somers, NY: IBM Global Business Services and IBM Institute for Business Value.

Gertler, M. S. (1995). Being there: Proximity, organization, and culture in the development and adoption of advanced manufacturing technologies. *Economic Geography*, Vol. 71, No. 1, 1–26.

Giffinger, R. (2007). *Ranking of European medium-sized cities*. Report of the Centre of Regional Science (SRF), Vienna University of Technology. Retrieved 2 January 2014, from www.smart-cities.eu/download/smart_cities_final_report.pdf.

GNU. (n.d.). *The free software definition*. Retrieved, 2 January 2014, from www.gnu.org/philosophy/free-sw.html.

Grabher, G. (ed.) (1993). *The embedded firm*. London and New York: Routledge.

Howe, J. (2008). *Crowdsourcing: Why the Power of the crowd is driving the future of business*. New York: Three Rivers Press.

IBM. (2010). *A vision of smarter cities: How cities can lead the way into a prosperous and sustainable future*. IBM Institute for Business Value. New York, NY: IBM Global Services.

ICF. (2009). *Intelligent community indicators*. Intelligent Community Forum. Retrieved 2 January 2014, from www.intelligentcommunity.org/index.php?submenu=Research&src=gendocs&ref=Research_Intelligent_Community_Indicators&category=Research.

IDA (2007). *Innovation. Integration. Internationalisation – Singapore: An intelligent nation, a global city, powered by infocomm*. Singapore iN2015 Steering Committee.

Ishida, T. (2000). Understanding digital cities. In T. Ishida and K. Isbister (eds) *Digital cities: Technologies, experiences, and future perspectives* (pp. 7–17). Berlin, Germany: Springer.

Kozena., M., Striteska, M. and Svoboda, O. (2011). Balanced scorecard for sustainable regional development. *Recent Researches in Environment, Energy Planning and Pollution* (pp. 146–151). Proceedings of the 5th WSEAS International Conference on Renewable Energy. Iasi, Romania: WSEAS Press.

LivingPlanIT (2011). *Cities in the cloud. A Living PlanIT introduction to future city technologies*. LivingPlant IT. Retrieved 2 January 2014, from www.cisco.com/web/about/ac78/docs/Living_PlanIT_SA_Cities_iWhitepaper.pdf.

Morgan, K. (2004). The exaggerated death of geography: Localised learning, innovation and uneven development. *Journal of Economic Geography*, Vol. 4, No. 1, 3–21.

OKFN. (n.d.). *Open data definition*. Open Knowledge Foundation. Retrieved 30 November 2013, from http://okfn.org/opendata/.

OpenStack. (n.d.). *Open source software for building private and public clouds*. Retrieved 2 January 2014, from www.openstack.org/.

Pallot, M., Trousse, B., Senach, B., Shaffers, H. and Komninos, N. (2011). Future Internet and Living Lab research domain landscapes: Filling the gap between technology push and application pull in the context of smart cities. *eChallenges e-2011 Conference Proceedings* (pp.1–8). IIMC International Information Management Corporation.

Soja, E. W. (2001). Writing the city spatially. *International Conference on Writing the City: Urban Life in the Era of Globalisation*. Dublin, Ireland: Dublin Business School, School of Arts (LSB College).

Storper, M. (1997). *The regional world*. London and New York: The Guilford Press.

Von Hippel, E. (2005). *Democratizing innovation*. Cambridge, MA: MIT Press.

World Bank (1994). *Building evaluation capacity lessons & practices N4*. Washington, DC: DV Operation Evaluation Department World Bank.

Part III
Strategies and governance
Innovation-for-all into smart environments

8 Toward intelligent clusters and city-districts

Platforms for self-organising growth

Cities are full of clusters. Most urban economic activities take place in different types of clusters: in industrial parks, industrial districts, science and technology parks, technology districts, transport hubs, port clusters, central business districts, shopping streets, and shopping malls. The European Cluster Observatory lists various types of organisations and institutions as clusters or related to cluster development: business incubators, cluster organisations, professional organisations, regional agencies, science parks, universities, research organisations, technology brokers, and university transfer offices, as well as venture capital firms. This large collection of entities illustrates the variety of cluster forms and types and the multiple purposes for which clusters are established and what they are mandated to do. The city itself is a cluster of clusters, a system of systems. Furthermore, from a network perspective, the city is an agglomeration of polarised networks (clusters) over city-wide networks and utilities. Making clusters intelligent is a fundamental strategy for all these spaces.

1. New growth conditions

In recent years, the growth dynamic has developed and changed rapidly. Globalisation and new information and communication technologies (ICTs) radically changed production processes and contributed to a drop in manufacturing's share of GDP in old industrial centres. It is now almost a rule that industrial production is being shifted to the dynamic-growth countries of SE Asia and China. The financial crisis changed development conditions even more, putting an end to debt-based and consumer-fuelled growth. The real economy and real production capacity came to the fore again. Countries, regions, cities, and businesses in the developed world faced competition on new terms with a turn towards new sectors and the adoption of knowledge-based development strategies.

Today, manufacturing is no longer at the heart of high-growth sectors in the European Union. The shift in employment and added value presented in the *5th Progress Report on Economic and Social Cohesion* (European Commission, 2008) shows that high-growth sectors in the EU have altered significantly and include:

- Two service sectors with high productivity levels: business services and financial services.

172 Strategies and governance

- Three service sectors with a major increase in employment or added value but average productivity: trade, hotels and restaurants, and transport and communications.
- The construction sector, marked by major changes in employment, coupled with a significant increase, but below average, in added value.
- Three manufacturing sectors with a major increase in added value, but a drop in employment, which are high- and medium-tech sectors: chemicals and artificial fibres, electrical and optical equipment, and transport equipment.

Despite these changes, manufacturing remains an important production sector in Europe, given that it accounts for 20 percent of overall gross added value (GAV) and 18 percent of employment. However, following 2000, the total rise in manufacturing GAV was slow and employment went into decline. Productivity in manufacturing is higher than average compared to all sectors (112 percent), but around half the figure for financial and business services (192 percent), and higher than productivity in construction, trade and transport (85 percent) (European Commission, 2008). The EU's high-growth manufacturing sectors (transportation, chemicals, electrical equipment, optical devices) are technology-, research-, and innovation-intensive sectors. These features support their competitiveness in the international market. Sectors in decline or in crisis are traditional labour-intensive sectors which are vulnerable to international competition from low-labour-cost countries, such as textiles, clothing, leather, footwear, and furniture (Kourtesis, 2008).

Efforts to foster European high-growth sectors, which show above-average employment or GVA growth, is a permanent concern of the European Union and the member states since 2000. These sectors offer a better global perspective to Europe, while they can also sustain the convergence within the Union. Advanced and convergence regions in the EU support a shift towards knowledge-based manufacturing and services to address the competition from Chinese and other Asian countries. Actually, most EU policies facilitate the progressive reorientation of the industry to avoid specialisation and lock-in in sectors strongly exposed to international competition with poor growth potential. The turn to knowledge-based development can relax competition from large Asian countries which exhibit strong advantages in terms of cost and manpower.

However, the shift towards the knowledge economy is a complex challenge. In the theory of development, a group of complementary approaches have emerged that have become known as 'new institutional economics,' 'new growth theory,' and 'evolutionary economics' which radically reformulate growth models by placing knowledge, technology, and innovation at the core of the forces that drive growth.

In these perspectives, a key factor which is today shaping growth is not capital accumulation, but rather knowledge – coupled with research and innovation. Knowledge and technology lead to increasing returns and create opportunities for almost unlimited growth. In contrast with neoclassical economic theory that focuses on markets, individuals, and businesses that supposedly act rationally in relation to price mechanisms to maximise use and returns on the economic resources of capital and labour, *innovation economics* focus on the ways in which economic agents – small and large businesses, multinationals, industrial sectors, cities, and regions – create new products, develop new knowledge, innovate, and become more productive and competitive.

New Growth Theory, in particular, approaches economic activity from two different starting points. First, it considers that technological progress is the result of economic activity and that it is an endogenous feature of how markets operate. Second, it considers that knowledge and technology are characterized by increasing returns, and that these increasing returns sustain a continuous process of growth. New Growth Theory was developed as a critique of neoclassical economics and its inability to fully explain growth in relation to changes in capital and labour factors of production (known as the residual problem, the un-interpretable part of growth). In contrast to economic factors of growth under neoclassical theory which are consumed when used, knowledge can be shared and reused indefinitely, and can also be improved and increased with use. Knowledge is based on itself, resulting in the generation of wealth and an increase in its own value with use over time (Romer, 1990; Romer, 1994).

The subversive element that New Growth Theory introduces is that it rejects the cornerstone of traditional economic growth models, the decreasing return on investments. In microeconomic neoclassical theory, the 'law' of decreasing returns argues that we receive less extra product when we add additional inputs in instalments. As a production process grows, the same input of capital resources and labour leads to lower returns compared to previous inputs. This declining return results in an increase in the marginal cost of production; economic growth becomes increasingly slower, and might even stop.

However, this tendency for decreasing returns does not apply in the knowledge economy. As Romer states, "The physical world is characterized by diminishing returns. Diminishing returns are a result of the scarcity of physical objects. One of the most important differences between objects and ideas, the kinds of differences that I alluded to before, is that ideas are not scarce and the process of discovery in the realm of ideas does not suffer from diminishing returns" (Paul Romer interview, Kurtzman, 2001). In effect, New Growth Theory describes the dynamic of economic relations that develop in the context of the knowledge economy, where intangible goods, increasing returns, and the cumulative effectiveness of knowledge predominate. These new conditions radically transform competition and highlight the history, geography, and institutions as main forces shaping the growth of knowledge-based economies:

> History matters because increasing returns generate positive feedbacks that tend to cause economies to 'lock in' to particular technologies and locations. Development is in part chaotic because small events at critical times can have persistent, long term impacts on patterns of economic activity. Institutions matter because they shape the environment for the production and

employment of new knowledge. Societies that generate and tolerate new ideas, and that continuously adapt to changing economic and technological circumstances are a precondition to sustained economic growth. Geography matters because knowledge doesn't move frictionlessly among economic actors. Important parts of knowledge are tacit, and embedded in the routines of individuals and organizations in different places.

(Cortright, 2001, p. ii)

The logic of competitiveness is radically changing in the knowledge-economy. Competition develops in stages, in quasi-monopolistic markets with products constantly being replaced and often being cannibalised. Companies renew constantly their own products, long before they become technologically obsolete, so that its competitors cannot introduce them into its own products in the market and replace it totally. Competition occurs by introducing new products – which is the most radical form of innovation – rather than by changing production cost and product price. Technological paths are affected in a definitive manner by chance, coincidence, and serendipity.

Overall, knowledge-based growth will tend to adapt to the logic of complexity and chaos, where small changes tend to lead to global results, and the economic actors interact in conditions of spontaneous self-organisation, feedback loops, and learning. The future becomes exceptionally complex and uncertain. There is no innate equilibrium in the market; there is, in fact, no optimal solution, since all probabilities of generating new knowledge and new products are open and potentially feasible. Increasing returns, quasi-monopolistic competition, imperfect markets, and multiple equilibria are key principles in New Growth Theory, which are defined by the reduction in the marginal cost of intangible goods and increasing economic returns (Cortright, 2001).

Today, the majority of knowledge-creating enterprises are small and medium-sized companies. On the other hand, the large and dynamic markets of innovation are global. Due to size, available funds, and organisational structure, smaller organisations face particularly pronounced challenges in competing in global markets. They are unable to identify global market opportunities, achieve economies of scale in the purchase of materials and equipment, comply with varied national standards and regulations, and secure a flow of technology inputs and other specialised knowledge. Price is not the only factor affecting competitiveness. Neither is it even the most decisive one. More important are continuous market presence, scalability, working within different cultural and linguistic contexts, and ubiquitous access to companies' products and services. All these constraints make competition of innovative products in global markets extremely difficult for smaller companies.

Achieving access to international markets is a top priority for any company, and innovation led-companies in particular. However, those selling end products and services on international markets should have advanced capabilities in many different areas of production and marketing. A simultaneous presence in many national markets is necessary. Brand name is important. They also need capability to scale-up production and product delivery in many different forms. After-sales support and services are necessary. In fact, it is even difficult for larger companies to meet all these conditions. Size vs. global market presence is a major challenge of the knowledge economy, and clustering has become a mainstream practice for effectively addressing it.

2. Clustering for growth

Clusters represent an established solution for addressing the above challenges of new growth sectors, knowledge-based development, and access to global markets. Michael Porter (1990), introducing the term and reviving the discussion on the economics of agglomeration, defined clusters as geographic concentrations of interconnected companies, specialised suppliers, service providers, firms in related industries, and associated institutions (i.e., universities, standardisation agencies, trade associations, chambers of commerce, and industry) in a particular sector of the economy, which compete with each other but also cooperate among themselves. A few years later, he defined a cluster "as [a] geographically proximate group of interconnected companies, suppliers, service providers and associated institutions in a particular field, linked by externalities of various types" (Porter, 2003, p. 562). A cluster became equivalent to 'geographic agglomeration' plus 'sectoral specialisation' plus 'value chain.'

The expression 'geographically proximate group of interconnected companies' is of prime importance, since it makes it clear that clusters are localised systems emerging from proximity and networking, and that both those factors offer competitive advantages. Spatial proximity and networking are *sine-qua-non* drivers of clusters; however, institutional factors related to policy and governance, and social factors related to trust, social capital, association, and risk-sharing also sustain clustering, as well. Thus, mere collaboration and networking between organisations should not be taken as a cluster unless spatial proximity of organisations or a common spatial base – such as location, common infrastructure, city district, or other area – is also present.

Localised production systems and clusters of interconnected activities create competitive advantages of cost and innovation. The popularity of clusters as development instruments is largely due to structural relationships between the underlying shared factors:

- *Cost-related advantages* are created because of risk-sharing, common infrastructure, external economies, and cooperation in production and markets among the organisations constituting the cluster.
- *Innovation advantages* are created because of specialisation, collaborative learning and competence development, tacit knowledge flows, and knowledge spillovers, which takes place between the organisations in the cluster.

Both types of advantages benefit from proximity, locality, and geographic agglomeration that enable external economies and knowledge-sharing. Such competitive advantages lead companies and regions into a development spiral in which clustering is the propulsive force: company competitiveness is propelled by clusters, and flourishing clusters sustain the competitiveness of cities and regions.

Porter proposed a universal explanation of how clusters contribute to competitiveness and innovation. "Recent academic and practitioner literature has placed increasing emphasis on industry clustering as a basic feature of regional and national economies, with an important influence on innovation, competitiveness and economic performance" (Porter, 2003, p. 562). His 'Diamond Model' described the favourable environment that companies find within clusters: a synergetic convergence of demand and supply conditions, knowledge flows and strategy. The five elements of the 'diamond' outline a system that sustains competitive advantages due to collaboration: (1) factor conditions refer to external inputs such as labour, land, natural resources, capital, information, and infrastructure; (2) sophisticated domestic market provides the primary driver of growth, helping companies to evolve from startups to bigger organisations; (3) related and supporting industries include suppliers and upstream and downstream industries, and offer cost-effective and innovation inputs; (4) strategy, management styles, and rivalry spur innovation; and (5) the government's role, as a catalyst and supporter, encourages companies to raise their expectations and move towards higher levels of competitiveness and performance (Porter, 1990).

However, this is a rather simplified explanation of competitive advantage created within clusters, which does not take into consideration the diversity of cluster forms and types. The five elements of the 'diamond' can be traced in any cluster, but competitive advantages differ substantially from one type of cluster to another. It is, therefore, more accurate to refine innovation advantages with respect to cluster type and collaboration network (He and Fallah, 2011).

Different types of clusters actualise different enablers of competition and innovation:

- *Marshallian clusters* are characterised by dense company networks, mostly among small companies in traditional industry sectors. Companies cluster to profit from external economies. Co-location produces plenty of production linkages and advantages of specialisation, reduced transaction costs, and strong information flow (Marshall, 1920).
- *Innovative milieu, system-areas, or industrial districts* are bottom-up agglomerations of manufacturing companies specialised in different segments of the same production sector. Supported by trading associations and strong social relationships of collaboration, companies form flexible production networks after receiving a contract or market order. Advantages emerge from company specialisation, flexible production chains, and leading organisations (buyers) opening markets and initiating production activities (Becatinni, 1989).
- *New industrial districts* are agglomerations of high-tech industry, a mixture of smaller and larger companies with advanced technological capability,

competitive producer-supplier relationships, specialised business services, and venture capital organisations. Advantages spring from non-traded interdependencies and input-output relations at the local level, knowledge spillovers, and risk-capital funding (Storper, 1997).

- *Star-type clusters* are created by a leading company which links other companies and organisations around its activity through subcontracting and technology agreements. Advantages stem from the technological and organisational leadership of core companies which are transferred to subcontractors and cooperating companies (Sefertzi, 1996).
- *Satellite districts* are mainly created by multinational companies establishing branch plants in offshore locations around which local networks of subcontracting companies and service providers flourish (Markusen, 1996). Advantages are based on subcontracting networks, know-how, and market access provided by the multinationals.
- *Institutional or state-led clusters* are created by public initiatives for setting up science and technology parks, business networks around research institutions, and other forms of technopoles and top-down clusters (Komninos, 1993). Public institutions and infrastructures offer the platform for R&D, networking, collaboration, capacity building, and innovation.

All these types of clustering and competitive advantage have been discussed extensively in the literature. With the rise of the paradigm of core competences in the 1980s, interest in clustering and networking rose geometrically. Williamson had already presented his theory on transaction costs (structural model, efficient boundaries, governance, role of power) by making transaction costs rather than commodities the basic unit of analysis, and by assessing governance structures, such as firms and markets, in terms of their capacity to economise on transaction costs (Williamson, 1981). The interest in the literature on transactions, together with the shift from make-or-buy to co-production, and advances in computer integrated manufacturing and intelligent manufacturing systems highlight the move towards a wider landscape of interconnected and network-type production.

However, for clusters operating in global knowledge-intensive markets, new questions have been raised about the character of locally created advantages and their persistence within a landscape of global markets and digital networks. Do locally created advantages of competitiveness and innovation retain their value within global production and innovation environments? How do clusters change because of globally scattered resources and capabilities? How do clusters enrich their endowments by online commons, real-time communication, social media, sensor networks, and digital platforms for open innovation?

No doubt, clusters in the second decade of the twenty-first century are not the same as those of the 1980s (industrial districts), 1990s (technology districts), and early 2000s (innovative clusters). The trend is now towards more open, global, and intelligent clusters. These clusters are born 'global' within international markets and global resources, and are IT enabled, while preserving the advantages of proximity and locality for knowledge-sharing, trust, and face-to-face communication. All these new qualities of clustering highlight a trend towards smart and intelligent clusters, in which external economies and innovation capabilities are further enhanced by digital networks, smart environments, Web applications, and hybrid products and services.

3. Toward smart clusters: top-down thrust from smart specialisation

Strong pressures on clusters and localised industry sectors to develop functions of intelligence and learning are to be found in the EU 2020 strategy for smart growth and smart specialisation. In smart specialisation, cities and regions are invited to go through an entrepreneurial discovery process and invest in technologies that modernise and diversify their industries and clusters towards new production activities for global niche markets.

The EU 2020 strategy appeared in a period of profound changes that challenge the strengths of the European economy and the welfare state which was created over the last 50 years. The financial – and underlying competitiveness – crisis has drained away years of economic and social progress and reversed convergence between the less-favoured and most-developed regions of Europe. Given these conditions, EU 2020 outlines a vision of development and cohesion in Europe with three priority objectives: (1) smart growth, with an economy based on knowledge and innovation; (2) sustainable growth, with a resource-efficient and greener economy; and (3) inclusive growth, with high employment ensuring social and territorial cohesion. Seven flagship initiatives have been developed to turn these priorities into reality (European Commission, 2010).

Smart growth, the first pillar of the strategy, means that knowledge and innovation will drive future European growth. R&D and innovation, education and life-long learning, and the digital society are expected to cross-fertilise each other and create a globally competitive knowledge economy. The strategy starts with the quantitative target of spending 3 percent of GDP investment on R&D. Objectives related to university education – the spread of the digital society and online dissemination of knowledge – have also been set. Three of the seven EU 2020 flagship initiatives focus on smart growth:

- 'Innovation Union' to improve framework conditions and access to finance for research and innovation to ensure that innovative ideas can be turned into products and services that create growth and jobs.
- 'Youth on the move' to enhance the performance of education systems and to facilitate young people entering the labour market.
- 'A digital agenda for Europe' to speed up the roll-out of high-speed Internet and reap the benefits of a digital single market for households and firms.

The initial budget proposal for the EU 2020 strategy was €1,083 billion, which corresponds to 1.11 percent of Europe's Gross National Income. Smart growth accounts for the lion's share, making up more than 45 percent of the total budget (European Commission, 2011). After months of complex negotiations, the European Parliament finally approved, on November 2013, a budget of €960 billion, and for the first time in the history of the Union a real spending cut was included in a long-term budget. However, important parts of the strategy will be implemented with national funds and much higher national budgets. Member states will be ultimately responsible for achieving the strategy's objectives. Each member state must prepare a National Reform Programme (NRP), putting in place development and cohesion policies. Many NRPs give higher priority to measures for economic growth at the expense of policies for social inclusion and sustainability. This is, however, in line with the overall philosophy of EU 2020 regarding the importance of smart growth.

'Smart specialisation' is the territorial arm of the smart growth strategy. It is driving new EU regional policy towards research and innovation strategies for smart specialisation (RIS3). RIS3 calls for intelligence and insight in order to identify a region's competitive advantages and unique strengths and potential, to 'discover' technologies and innovation where a region can benefit from specialisation, and to align regional stakeholders for a shared vision of innovation-led development (Foray et al., 2012). Smart specialisation also paves the way to new territorial systems of innovation, in which networking, collaboration, and mobilisation of creativity take place in selected clusters and fields of technology.

Table 8.1 Key elements of smart specialisation strategy

Smart is about	Specialisation is about
• *An evidence-based approach,* which entails considering all assets and problems in a region, including external and internal perspectives, global markets, and assessing critical mass, opportunities, excellence, cooperation, and value chains. • *No top-down decisions,* but rather a dynamic entrepreneurial discovery process uniting key stakeholders around a shared vision. • *Mobilising investments and synergies* across different departments and governance levels (EU-national-regional). • *All forms of innovation* and not only technology-driven innovation.	• *Differentiation*: All types of assets, competitive advantages, the potential for excellence and global opportunities. • *Concentrating resources* on thematic priorities, problems, and core needs. Do not adopt a 'sprinkler principle,' supporting many small projects or just picking the winners. • *Place-based economic transformation:* rejuvenating traditional sectors through higher value-added activities, cross-sectoral links; new market niches by sourcing-in and disseminating new technologies rather than re-inventing the wheel; exploiting new forms of innovation.

Source: Landabaso, 2012

The theoretical foundations of smart specialisation are at the intersection of 'intelligence as raw material of growth,' 'related variety,' and 'place-based interventions,'

> One simple and interesting argument in favour of this consideration revolves around the nature of the new knowledge-based economy in the making, with intelligence as the key raw material of economic activity and regional competitiveness. Fortunately, and in contrast with the type of raw materials on which past industrial revolutions depended on, intelligence is the one economic resource that is geographically evenly distributed. Therefore it might be safe to assume that regional differences will progressively rest in the future on the way this intelligence is valorized or left idle. In other words regional differences will depend more and more on regions having the infrastructures (schools, vocational training centres, universities and technology centres and R&D laboratories), policies and business environment to effectively transform and exploit intelligence in the form of innovation, and which are capable of attracting more talent from elsewhere.
>
> Grillo and Landabaso (2011, p. 4)

'Related variety' has been also an influential concept in innovation-led regional development more than 20 years, sustained by studies on industrial districts attributing their innovation potential to the presence of many and diverse skills covering various fields of knowledge, changing collaborations, and catalysts that facilitate combinations among skills; on high technology regions in which a variety of machinery and knowledge infrastructure becomes available; and on the variety of science and technology fields in world-class research institutes or universities to be found in innovative cities. Industrial variety is expected to increase innovation because of knowledge spillovers that take place between industries that have complementary knowledge bases. According to Boschma and Frenken (2011, p. 67), "It is the related variety in a region that feeds the branching out of new activities from technologically related activities, not regional diversity nor regional specialisation *per se.*"

This new territorial development paradigm is supported by strategic planning agreements and a sound system for monitoring, measuring, and assessing results. Within the smart specialisation perspective, innovation is an overall priority, but each region must focus on and invest in selected clusters, technology areas, and digital agendas where innovation can readily occur and a competitive knowledge base can build-up. Clusters and local productive systems are invited to develop functions of intelligence, market and technology scan, foresight, and self-assessment.

4. Cluster needs for intelligence: bottom-up demand

A bottom-up pull toward intelligent clusters emerges from cluster managers and experts assessing a cluster's needs in areas such as strategy, technology, and market. Evidence for such needs has been documented in the survey of cluster training needs in the regions of southern and central Europe, in Spain, Italy, Austria, Bulgaria, and Greece in the context of the InnoSee project (2012–2013). Cluster managers and cluster experts were asked to provide information about the most important needs in terms of knowledge skills, methods, and technologies for managing research-driven and innovative clusters, today and in the near future. These surveys followed a common methodology that made it possible to synthesise results and conclusions.

In Catalonia, Spain, the survey was focused on the BioRegión of Catalonia. The cluster was established in 2006 and now consists of nearly 1,000 stakeholders that cover the entire value chain, from cutting-edge research agencies in innovative areas, like nanomedicine or bioinformatics, to traditional pharmaceutical or medical technology companies currently undergoing the process of modernisation. It involves more than 350 companies and a significant number of universities, ten of which offer studies in the life sciences.

In Tuscany, Italy, the survey focused on the technology districts of Tuscany, the "territorial-based aggregations of enterprises, universities and research institutions, focused on a number of defined scientific areas and strategic technologies, designed to develop and strengthen the competitiveness of territories and settlements" (ASEV, 2013). Tuscany's clusters have a relatively high proportion of high-tech enterprises, compared to the rest of the country. Companies with tertiary activity outnumber those in manufacturing by almost two to one. Four sectors provide most of the jobs: the mechanical sector, pharmaceuticals, electronic elaboration of data, and medical and optical instruments. Priority areas for strengthening and reorganising the technology districts are based on their current industrial excellence, and mainly on the clusters of ICT, life sciences, cultural heritage, energy efficiency, renewable energy, and high-speed railways.

In Austria, 21 clusters were identified both in traditional industry sectors, in newly emerged market niches and high-tech sectors. Most cluster initiatives were introduced by regional public authorities and are owned by public agencies, with the goal of strengthening the competiveness of the respective regions. Many clusters are integrated into competence centres, where joint research activities take place. In Styria, the survey focused on the Styrian Business Promotion Agency (SFG), an agency of the federal government which is responsible for setting up clusters throughout the region. In Upper Austria, the policy for economic development and technology is strongly cluster and network oriented. Inter-branch networks have been set up in the fields of human resources, design and media, logistics and energy efficiency. In the region of Tyrol, the Standortagentur Tirol is the cluster-promoting agency owned by the Tyrolean government. Among its key priorities are the establishment of clusters, leading to an increased cross-linking of Tyrolean businesses, and intense knowledge and technology transfer between business and research organisations.

Following a rather late and hesitant start, cluster development in Bulgaria has accelerated since 2007. Regions are still lagging, though, in terms of cluster creation and cluster participation. Recently, groupings of enterprises were formed in some of the most dynamic sectors of the Bulgarian economy, such as IT, wood processing, tourism, clothing and textiles, and wine. The first cluster organisation was registered in 2004, and almost 30 clusters in different industries have been established since then. With respect to cluster development, policy in Bulgaria is rather heterogeneous with many initiatives facilitating and promoting cluster-related activities without them being formally labelled as 'cluster-specific.' The state recently recognised clusters as an instrument for promoting economic development and defined a national policy for financial and technical support for existing and emerging clusters. In 2009, the Bulgarian Association of Business Clusters (ABC) was established with the aim of promoting cluster development and disseminating good practices.

Cluster development in Greece is also a long-term priority. Existing clusters operate in diverse industrial and service sectors, including traditional sectors, such as food, wine, and furniture, as well as technology-intensive sectors, such as ICT, microelectronics, bio-science, and solar energy systems. Although several attempts to create clusters have been made since the 1990s, mainly through EU regional programmes for innovation, innovative clusters emerged only recently in Athens and Thessaloniki. At present, prominent innovative clusters include the Hellenic Bio Cluster (HBio, Athens), the Hellenic Nano-Microelectronics and Embedded Systems Cluster (mi-Cluster, Athens), the Space Industries Cluster (si-Cluster, Attica), the Organic Product Cluster (Bio-cluster, Northern Greece), and Technopolis (ICT cluster, Thessaloniki).

These cluster surveys document an impressive convergence of needs related to knowledge and innovation. Table 8.2 shows that most sought-after skills and competences are those related to strategy development, market intelligence and technology watch, knowledge transfer, international collaboration, and access to global markets.

Cluster management and strategy elaboration was a common point of reference for cluster growth in all the above surveys. Understanding of members' needs and creating trust are essential characteristics of successful cluster objectives. The surveys have shown that the profile of a cluster manager should correspond to a trade-off between an innovation and a marketing manager, to identify factors of success and failure and adjust resources to market opportunities. This is a clear orientation both in Tuscany and south Austria, where many successful clusters hire experts for strategy and advice, thus enhancing the longevity and professionalism of the cluster. Cluster companies expect their network to be managed neutrally, but there is no shared view on who should assume this role: a partner company, a cluster manager, or a technology centre. Technology centres and specialised consultancies comply well with demands for neutrality, as far as they remain outside of the cluster's value chain. While both may have specific interests, they do not conflict with the competition-oriented goals of the cluster's members. Important competences in this area are leadership and strategy development skills, knowledge management, communication and IT skills, customer and public relationships, and business and financial planning.

Cluster strategy depends heavily on the cluster typology. Different clusters have different requirements and mix of leadership and management practices.

Table 8.2 Most-sought-after competences for cluster development

	Strategy and management	Intelligence, watch, and foresight	Knowledge sharing, learning, and innovation	Access to markets, internationalization
Tuscany, Italy	Follow-up new research ideas. Stimulate Creativity	Market analysis. Future trends analysis	Establishing IPR agreements. Patent management	International cooperation and networking
Catalonia Spain	Research management	Competitive business intelligence	Technology transfer inside and outside the cluster	Identification of niche markets. Market research
Thessaloniki Greece	Leadership and management	Foresight and futures tools	Dissemination of good practice among cluster members	Cluster branding and promotion
Sofia, Bulgaria	Strengthen trust	Market and technology watch	Establishing IPR agreements	Market research
South Austria	Professional cluster management	Competitive business intelligence	Commercialisation of research. Collaboration with research centres	International co-operation and networking

Source: InnoSee cluster survey, 2013

All successful clusters have some kind of a hub or anchor. The leader can be the largest enterprise in the value chain, an organisation owner of infrastructure, a research or rechnology organisation.

Cluster strategy differs significantly by their stage of development. Different phases of cluster evolution are associated with variations in knowledge-intensity, inter-firm relations, objectives and determinants of success. Network management, for instance, is more needed in established than in emerging clusters. The latter are more likely to require conditions in which new companies can evolve, as entrepreneurs need funds and market access to move from an idea to a product or service to be offered in non-local markets. Life cycles can be defined with respect to investments or maturity stages. Cluster life cycle drives strategy, which adapts to phases of emergence, growth, maturity and decline.

Trust and stakeholders engagement are also key determinants of cluster strategy. In the networked model, sound cluster management is supposed to offer platforms for discussion and joint action across members. Collaboration and participation are entirely voluntary and the cluster organisation should offer an environment enabling trust and a shared vision about the direction to be followed together.

184 *Strategies and governance*

Intelligence, market watch and foresight on technologies, innovations, and market opportunities are key areas of cluster growth. The surveys clearly indicate that innovative clusters continuously seek out new ideas and intelligence. They search for more-efficient production processes, and new products and markets. Greek cluster practices for information and market intelligence are instrumented through training, participation of members in conferences and seminars, online newsletters, online information about technologies and market opportunities, and collaboration with research organisations. Austrian clusters employ experienced staff with skills to anticipate emerging technologies and market opportunities. Innovation, new product development, and IPR management are practiced widely in the majority of clusters in Austria. Needs in this area are related to strong knowledge of the cluster's industry or sector, innovation management methodologies, new product development roadmaps, market and technology watch, patent analysis, and assistance with IPR agreements.

Knowledge development, learning, and innovation through collaboration have also appeared as a key pillar of cluster competitiveness. Without common practices for networking, individual initiatives risk remaining isolated and failing. Although R&D at universities and research centres attract much of the resources and attention of governments, many valuable innovations come from improvements in business and production routines devised by employees. Cluster development in Bulgaria shows that collaboration network building is indispensable, as individual members are usually not closely associated. There is a need to ensure the continuous flow of information, and for communication and coordination of activities with respect to cluster member interests. Without effective coordination, transaction costs remain too high for individual partners, and clusters start collapsing. The same practices are highlighted in Tuscany: exchange of information and communication, balance of interests and conflict settlement, building trust between network partners, collaboration in decision-making, and strengthening of common interests. In Greek clusters, efforts to support product development and innovation were mainly realised by promoting collaboration between the members of the cluster for joint activities, establishing collaborations with international and national research centres, technology transfer between industry and academia, and assistance in IPR management. Overall, needs for knowledge inputs focus on sharing technology, opening up information channels, building trust, and developing collaboration and joint ventures with research organisations.

Internationalisation and access to global markets were highlighted as priority areas related to the setting up of global networks, participation in international brokerage events, promotion of members' activities through online platforms, and attracting foreign investments for research and innovation. Global market promotion and internationalisation of sales are key issues in Austrian clusters. The automotive cluster, for instance, continuously faces this challenge, as many of its companies operate in international rather than national markets. Other clusters in the fields of materials and renewable energy need know-how and expertise which is gained through the opening up to global technology providers.

In the Spanish BioRegión, 34 percent of companies have explicitly tried increasing their international presence, and internationalisation is an important goal of the BioRegión overall. The cluster maintains close knowledge ties to companies and organisations worldwide, with scientific exchanges, business partnering, and commercial promotion.

Overall, these surveys focused on research-driven clusters showed that cluster knowledge development, internationalisation, and collaboration across regional or national borders are difficult to achieve, for several reasons. Numerous practical impediments arise that are linked to differences in legislation and administrative systems, cultural differences, and language barriers, which make internationalisation extremely complex. Clusters tend to consider themselves as fully autonomous in their everyday operations and business activities, often regarding other clusters as direct competitors, particularly those belonging to the same industry. Cross-border cluster development usually fails to be systematically supported by policies, which have national or regional priorities. Despite these impediments, the advantages of collaboration are significant. Networking facilitates the exchange of information and expertise, acting as a bridge across clusters and companies. This is particularly significant for smaller companies of clusters that have limited human and financial resources but wish to work in international markets and adopt global marketing and product placement practices. Digital networks, digital commons and platforms, and smart environments have much to offer to this end.

5. A strategy for intelligent clusters

Both top-down and bottom-up trends reflect the need for advanced intelligence, information, and knowledge functions in clusters. Any localised grouping of companies can turn into an intelligent cluster by enriching its founding conditions through digital technology, namely: the spatial agglomeration of companies, operation into the same or connected sectors, and collaboration over vertical or horizontal value chains.

This transformation can be achieved through a process of ICT-based re-organisation; the use of Web and communication technologies to improve collaboration in knowledge and innovation, and strengthening of cluster mechanisms that create competitive advantages and knowledge externalities. These mechanisms fall into three categories:

- Community building. Clusters enable collaboration and complementarity in skills and innovation capabilities. Innovation is a collaborative process in which knowledge and insights from different fields of science and technology are combined to create something new. A critical factor in connecting different knowledge fields is the community in which skills and competences are pooled together.
- Building endowments and digital commons for knowledge flows and common technology efforts. Nonaka and Tackeuchi (1995) described innovation as tacit knowledge being transformed into explicit knowledge. They explained

186 *Strategies and governance*

the enormous organisational effort that is needed to convert atypical and personalised knowledge into explicit modelled know-how and engineering. But, tacit knowledge is spatially 'sticky' and, despite the growth of knowledge management tools, is not easily communicated other than through personal interaction (Morgan, 2004). Collaboration, proximity, and commons are beneficial to innovative practices, not only for reducing transaction costs, but also for encouraging innovative behaviour to happen.
- Creating externalities and generating economies of scale and scope. Both types of external economies make cluster members more resource-efficient and transactions less costly. ICTs, together with geographical clustering, can save transport, communication, energy, and infrastructure costs if provided in organised way.

Intelligent clusters can emerge from these mechanisms through new knowledge functions based on collective intelligence, co-learning, and collaborative innovation. External economies can be enhanced by real-time communication, data and information processing, automation based on machine intelligence, and machine-to-machine communication. Collaboration scales-up into hybrid physical and digital spaces and can take on global dimensions. Such improvements are feasible in all clusters, in traditional or high-tech sectors. This is an 'innovation for-all clusters' perspective based on the infusion of information technology and machine intelligence into spatial groupings of companies. The transformation towards intelligent clusters can be achieved by (1) the building of a consensus space, (2) deployment of digital platforms for self-organising innovation, and (3) the use of ICTs for resource-efficient solutions.

6. Consensus space: foundations of an innovation community

'Consensus space' is a fundamental element towards an intelligent cluster community. It can be created as a digital space hosting the cluster community or social media-based community of interest (Passiante and Secundo, 2002). Such a digital space is easy to build, but its operation demands a culture of sharing and practices of networking and collaboration which go far beyond the digital dimension. In the activation of the consensus space, the digital and institutional dimensions of the cluster activity converge.

The importance of the consensus space for innovation was analysed in the 'consensus-knowledge-innovation' triptych proposed by Etzkowitz (2002) as guiding creative interactions within triple-helix associations:

- The creation of a 'consensus space' is based on networking, communication, existing forms of collaboration, and on the trust which links individuals and organisations in common initiatives.
- The development of a 'knowledge space' is based on the concentration of research and technology activities via the collaboration network and the shared geographical location. The existence of a critical mass of research and innovative undertakings creates the conditions for this space forming.

- The creation of an 'innovation space' is based on concentrating resources and skills, on utilising research, on open innovation, and collaboration for new product and service development.

No aspect of this triptych takes precedence or overlaps the other. Each one offers the basis for the growth of the others and fully developed triple-helix requires a combination of the three aspects of collaboration in the knowledge economy. A digital consensus space can promote such collaboration and extend its boundaries, multiply the actors, and amplify information, knowledge, and innovation functions.

The specific form of the 'consensus space' depends on the type cluster and the way competitive advantages are built within the cluster. Virtual spaces offer limit-less possibilities of networking and collaboration. Collaborative networks can be defined as

> consisting of a variety of entities (e.g., organisations, people, or intelligent machines) that are largely autonomous, geographically distributed, and heterogeneous in terms of their operating environment, culture, social capital and goals, but that collaborate to better achieve common or compatible goals, and whose interactions are supported by computer network.
> (Camarinha-Matos and Afsarmanesh, 2012, p. 8)

The above authors also presented a typology of 26 different forms of collaborative networks, with a major split between long-term strategic networks and goal-oriented networks, founded on consensus and collaboration spaces.

The consensus space of clusters contributes to the foundation of an intelligent community, which uses digital technology to advance information sharing and collaboration in innovation. It is a space of social life within the cluster, upon which trust, synergies, and external economies are formed.

7. Digital platforms for self-organising innovation

Platforms are externalities that enable cluster members to move forward in technology and innovation by pooling and sharing resources and efforts. Digital platforms are commons based on the Web, intranet, and Internet networks that facilitate the collaborative creation of knowledge and the development of innovation by the community of the cluster. Through digital platforms, the cluster community is self-organised to the extent that participants become aware of the capabilities of and contributions made by other members. Various forms of collaboration can start to take place on digital platforms; and many different platforms can be used to coordinate collective action without the need for a coordinator.

Knowledge-sharing platforms can be developed into clusters to be used for collaboration in fundamental knowledge processes and innovation, such as information gathering and intelligence, technology learning and acquisition, new product development, information dissemination, and marketing and e-commerce platforms. Such platforms can be built with Web 2.0 and Web 3.0 technologies and be used by all members of the cluster. Table 8.3 shows a

Table 8.3 Knowledge-sharing platforms and Web-based innovation tools

	INFORMATION INTELLIGENCE — The Web as source of information, insight, and foresight	TECHNOLOGY LEARNING — The Web as medium for technology acquisition, learning, and up-skilling	NEW PRODUCT DEVELOPMENT — The Web as medium for collaboration and people-driven involvement	INNOVATION PROMOTION — The Web as medium for dissemination, marketing, and promotion
INNOVATION PLATFORMS FOR COMPANIES AND CLUSTER MEMBERS — *Standalone organisations creating and offering new products or services*	Tools and applications for business intelligence Visualisation Customer immersion labs Patent analysis Foresight, forecasting, data mining, predictive modelling at company level.	Learning tools and Web-applications for intra-company training and up-skilling Virtual demos and demonstration	Intra-company new product development Web-based tools and applications Web-based stage-gate NPD models Collaborative environments and co-design tools Digital prototyping	e-commerce Company based product marketing and promotion applications and tools Product sales simulation Social media applications for marketing
INNOVATION PLATFORMS FOR CLUSTERS AND CLUSTER-TYPE INNOVATION ECOSYSTEMS — *Groups of companies, and organisations, such as R&D, funding, and marketing working together: Clusters, technology districts, incubators, triple helix alliances, supply chains.*	Technologies, tools, and applications for collaborative data collection, processing and interpretation Cluster intelligence Platform-based data mining, forecasting, and predictive markets	E-learning for groups of companies sharing common technologies and business processes E-learning along supply chains Learning tools and technologies provided by the platform Experimental environments for learning and training	Collaboration Web tools Applications and technologies for network-based NPD Crowdsourcing apps at different NPD stages Internet-based Living Labs environments New product testing and experimental facilities in real life conditions Simulation environments	Technologies and tools for new collaborative product marketing and promotion Social media for marketing and product promotion Geo-spatial product marketing for mobile apps Technologies and marketing platforms for new product aggregators

collection of digital tools to populate such platforms for knowledge-sharing and innovation at the level of individual organisations making up a cluster or groups of organisations.

Living Lab platforms may be extremely useful for clusters producing and testing consumer goods. Living Labs create innovation ecosystems via user driven-innovation and crowdsourcing, and via experimentation and testing within real-life environments. End users are placed at the centre of the LL innovation ecosystem and contribute with their own experiences. They contribute by selecting solutions from hundreds of alternatives, by validating and refining solutions in real-life environments. It should be expected that the contribution from end users is significant at specific stages of new product development, such as the idea generation stage, the assessment and selection of the most suitable solutions with respect to user needs, beta- and market testing of new products. In other stages, such as the business case analysis, prototype development and drafting technical specifications for production, user involvement is less significant and solutions rely more on technical and expert knowledge.

The contribution of users with ideas and experiences becomes feasible within physical, virtual, or hybrid environments. The initial conception of Living Labs was about physical environments, which allowed the observation of users' behaviour and practices. Experiments within physical spaces are usual in the case of mobile devices, sensors, and other instruments for data collection and communication.

New product development platforms: The involvement of users has also been extremely widespread with the help of virtual environments and Web-based applications. Dion Hinchcliffe (2009) used the term 'Product Development 2.0' to describe the innovation process that embodies the contribution of users and the use of Web 2.0 collaboration for new product development, such as harnessing collective intelligence, users as co-creators, and turning applications into platforms and into product development. Hinchcliffe (2009) outlined 50 strategies for creating a successful product based on Web 2.0 concepts. Some of these were: create prototypes as early as possible; get people on the network to work with the product prototype rapidly and often; release early and release often; gather usage data from your users and input it back into product design as often as possible; choose the technologies later, and think carefully about what your product will do first; when you do select technologies, consider current skill sets and staff availability; plan for testing to be a larger part of software development process than non-Web applications; have an open source strategy; whenever users can provide data to your product, enable them to do so; make sure your product can be spread around the Web by users; create an online user community for your product and nurture it; user experience should follow a 'complexity gradient'; go to the user, don't only make them come to you; know the popular Web standards and use them; build on the shoulders of giants, don't recreate what you can source from elsewhere; explicitly enable your users to co-develop the product; design your product to build a strong network effect; know your Web 2.0 design patterns and business models; and integrate a coherent social experience into your product.

Pallot (2009) described four types of innovation processes engaging users into research and innovation, which can lead to equivalent platforms:

- Co-creation, bringing together technology push and application pull (i.e., crowdsourcing, crowdcasting);
- Exploration, engaging all stakeholders, especially user communities, at the earlier stage of the co-creation process;
- Experimentation, implementing the proper level of technological artefacts to experience live scenarios with a large number of users; and
- Evaluation of new ideas and innovative concepts as well as related technological artefacts in real life situations.

User-driven new product development can sustain innovation in any sector of economic activity: traditional manufacturing sectors (food, clothing, building materials), new high-tech sectors (telecom, ICTs, mobile devices, creative industries), energy and the environment, old and new services, and social and public sectors. However, telecommunications, mobile devices, Web products, ICT services, and media remain predominant sectors for this form of innovation.

With crowdsourcing platforms, clusters can open up their collaboration networks to larger audiences. In this case, crowdsourcing becomes an additional source for competences. Crowdsourcing platforms can be used for collaboration with large audiences (crowds) in many diverse fields, such as knowledge-sharing, ideas management, design, marketing, citizen engagement, service supply, microtask processing, labour pools, equity crowdfunding, and business models (Dawson and Bynghall, 2011). Each platform combines an objective with a roadmap for achieving it. The crowd – a community of users – must follow the roadmap on the platform to generate solutions, prioritise them, and aggregate skills and resources to implement the desired objective. As crowdsourcing rises in popularity and use, platforms have evolved and are specialising.

Large companies have also extensively practiced crowdsourcing in their own clusters of suppliers and customers. For instance, Dell, IBM, and CISCO practice crowdsourcing in very different ways. Dell primarily uses an open forum (IdeaStorm) to collect ideas from a wide array of clients. The site has been in operation for just over two years and has collected over 11,000 ideas, of which more than 300 have been implemented by Dell. IBM's application (Idea Jam) follows a slightly different model, using an event-driven and topic-driven approach to generate ideas. The application is used internally and the 'Jam' becomes more of a conversation thread than a true idea-generation technique. In one 'Jam,' thousands of ideas were generated and over 36,000 comments attached to those ideas. CISCO sustains communities and discussion forums, and aims to assess the will of the crowd by the feedback and comments within these communities and forums (Phillips, 2009). However, it is questionable whether user-driven innovation can lead to radical / disruptive innovation. It is more likely that users can sustain a flow of incremental innovations framed by the technological boundaries set by experts.

Sensor network platforms and test-bed environments can also contribute to knowledge-sharing within clusters. Such platforms provide support for organising data from devices and meters embedded into the physical space, infrastructure, and facilities within which the cluster operates. Cluster-based operating systems for the Internet of Things can be used in a wide variety of sensor-based solutions, such as streetlights, networked electrical power meters, industrial monitoring, radiation monitoring, alarm systems, and security and remote monitoring. Sensor network platforms within clusters can offer real-time information, alert, technology hazard management, resource management and power savings. Open data and sensor-based data may also offer opportunities for new services and ventures.

All of the above platforms encourage knowledge-based collaboration and open innovation in clusters. However, the precise way they should be deployed is a question specific to each cluster and the strategy chosen for creating competitive advantages. Chesbrough et al. (2006, p. vii) defined open innovation as "the use of purposive inflows and outflows of knowledge to accelerate internal innovation, and expand the markets for external use of innovation, respectively," and described nine different perspectives or paths of open innovation towards: (1) spatial extension of innovation networks combining proximity to centres of excellence and global research, technology, and product development networks in a more global and flat world; (2) deepening of work division in innovation and greater specialisation needed for more complex technologies and product systems; (3) user participation in early phases of innovation in order to understand customers' latent requirements and to take advantage of users' hidden application knowledge; (4) suppliers' early integration into the innovation process that can increase innovation performance; (5) commercialisation of existing technology and intellectual property in future fields with high potential; (6) combining core processes of innovation, such as outside-in, inside-out, and coupled; (7) using tools and instruments that enable customers to create or configure their own product or companies to integrate external problem-solvers and innovators; (8) free revealing of inventions, discoveries, and knowledge that intensify technology spillovers without compensation in open source initiatives; and (9) creating a culture that values outside competence and know-how influenced by concrete artefacts such as incentive systems, management information systems, communication platforms, and others (Gassmann et al., 2010). Platforms and commons can be built in all the above orientations of open innovation.

Digital platforms for knowledge sharing, Living Labs, Web 2.0 product development, crowdsourcing, sensor networks, and open data can push forward open innovation and learning initiatives thought self-organising processes. Each platform can work as the 'giant' that enables clusters members to stand on its 'shoulders and see farther.'[1]

8. Resource efficiency innovations: green clusters and eco-districts

Environmental management of the physical space of clusters is a separate aspect of innovation and is vital in the self-organisation of clusters. It is activated through the initiatives of members of the cluster who seek out eco-innovation. In this way, they can address environmental problems and issues, such as materials recycling, energy savings, waste management, risk management, and other forms of eco-innovation, while achieving major benefits in terms of reduced operating costs and fewer environmental impacts.

The concept of eco-innovation refers to all forms of innovation in productive activities that seek to improve the level of environmental protection. It includes new production processes, new products or services, and new business management methods; and implementing these could prevent or significantly reduce environmental risks, pollution, and other negative environmental impacts.

Collective initiatives that promote eco-innovation within clusters foster a culture of environmental awareness and offer advantages in terms of reduced production costs, eco-brand name, and competitiveness. Some illustrative examples of eco-innovation which can transform a cluster include:

- Manufacturing eco-districts. These are districts that upgrade areas of spontaneous industrial location with the redesign of networks, built spaces, infrastructure, while promoting environmental protection and reviving of natural ecosystems. The creation of manufacturing eco-districts requires a comprehensive strategy for intervening in existing areas of industrial location, re-organising land uses, and the planning scheme for the area.
- Eco-clusters for managing green energy. These install and operate renewable energy sources (RES) such as photovoltaics, wind generators, use of biodiesel, geothermal facilities, and biomass incinerators. The cluster brings together a number of energy consumers to use renewable energy. In doing so, it can achieve better prices per energy unit and also increases bargaining power with energy suppliers in the context of a free energy market.
- Heating and cooling eco-districts. These districts have central production and heating and cooling distribution systems, pumped geothermal energy, and cogeneration of energy from alternative fuels which have been proven to lead to a major reduction in energy spending.
- Smart eco-districts. These are districts that have installed automated energy-saving and optimisation devices, sensors, actuators, control devices, and and smart measuring systems which can combine environmental comfort conditions with energy consumption reduction.
- Local green production chains, that adapt to environmental regulations, use network analysis methodologies to identify traces of CO_2 emissions, rationalise reserves and storage facilities, reduce energy consumption, and select suppliers based on green strategies.

Eco-innovation and eco-district initiatives within clusters can radically change the landscape of traditional clusters, from environmentally harmful and land-intensive activities into areas of better quality and higher aesthetic value. Clusters and city districts such as 22@barcelona offer examples of best practices along these lines, having regenerated old industrial areas and transformed them into environmental and energy-efficient districts that host knowledge-based activities.

9. The G component

The governance needed to set in motion the key components of this strategy towards intelligent clusters – consensus space, digital platforms and commons, and eco-innovation – rely on internal forces of the cluster. What is needed is little top-down effort and much more bottom-up initiative undertaken by cluster members.

Once the consensus space has been put in place and the cluster's value chains identified, leadership and governance become the decisive factors for setting up common platforms for innovation and undertaking resource-efficient practices. Leadership has to emerge from within the consensus space with respect to members' contributions and stewardship of the cluster's growth.

Knowledge commons and platforms should be operated as neutral organisations, ensuring the motivation of members and their willingness to continuously contribute data, information, knowledge, and other resources. Rules of participation, members' rights and obligations, and the intranet and extranet parts of communication should be defined at the outset, when such commons are established. Platforms should also be managed as independent business ventures relying on their own business model. Public–private partnership (PPP) is a good solution in the case of public support to build the platform. It has been observed that PPPs offer longer sustainability to support mechanisms, especially when they are based on viable business models. Top-down efforts for setting up and managing platforms should be kept to a minimum. Large-scale commons usually fail to ensure the sustainability of collaboration after the period of public finance has ended.

However, the content and added value of these platforms for self-organising innovation and growth is a function of the motivation and contribution of the cluster members, and the cluster itself as a conscious community of producers.

Note

1 Bernard de Chartres saying, *"nanos, gigantium humeris insidentes, ut possimus plura eis et remotiora videre, non utique proprii visus acumine, aut eminentia corporis, sed quia in altum subvenimur et extollimur magnitudine gigantea"* ("dwarfs on the shoulders of giants can see more than they, and things at a greater distance, not by virtue of any sharpness of sight, or any physical distinction, but because they are carried high and raised up by their giant size") reflects the idea that progress in knowledge is based on prior knowledge. The metaphor was used by Sir Isaac Newton in his letter to Robert Hooke (1676): "If I have seen further it is by standing on the shoulders of Giants." It appears also on the homepage of Google Scholar as, "Stand on the shoulders of giants."

References

ASEV (2013). Analysis of the research driven clusters in Tuscany, Italy. Retrieved 2 January 2014, from http://goo.gl/WbsuwR.

Becattini, G. (1989). Le district industriel: milieu creative. *Espaces et Societes, Revue Scientifique Internationale*, No. 66–67, 147–163.

Boschma, R. and Frenken, K. (2011). Technological relatedness and regional branching. In H. Bathelt, M.P. Feldman, and D.F. Kogler (eds), *Beyond territory: Dynamic geographies of knowledge creation, diffusion, and innovation* (pp. 64–81). London, UK: Routledge.

Camarinha-Matos, L. M. and Afsarmanesh, H. (2012). *Taxonomy of collaborative networks forms' Future Internet Enterprise Systems (FInES)*. Task Force on Collaborative Networks. Retrieved 2 January 2014, from http://goo.gl/yCWF3H.

Chesbrough, H., Vanhaverbeke, W., and West, J. (eds) (2006). *Open innovation: Researching a new paradigm*. Oxford: Oxford University Press.

Cortright, J. (2001). New growth theory. technology and learning. *Reviews of economic development literature and practice, no. 4*. Portland, OR: Impresa, Inc.

Dawson, R. and Bynghall, S. (2011). *Getting results from crowds: The definitive guide to using crowdsourcing to grow your business*. San Francisco, CA: Advanced Human Technologies.

Etzkowitz, H. (2002). *The triple helix of university – industry – government. Implications for policy and evaluation*. Working paper 2002–11, Science Policy Institute. Retrieved 2 January 2014, from www.sister.nu/pdf/wp_11.pdf.

European Commission. (2008). *Growing regions, growing Europe*. Communication from the Commmission to the European Parliament and the Council. Fifth progress report on economic and social cohesion. COM(2008) 371 final. Luxembourg: Office for Official Publications of the European Communities.

European Commission. (2010). *Europe 2020. A strategy for smart, sustainable and inclusive growth*. COM (2010) 2020 final.

European Commission. (2011). *A budget for Europe 2020*. COM (2011) 500 final.

Foray, D., Goddard, J., Goenaga Beldarrain, X., Landabaso, M., McCann, P., Morgan, K., Nauwelaers, C. and Ortega-Argilés, R. (2012). *Guide to research and innovation strategies for smart specialisation (RIS^3)*. European Commission, Smart Specialisation Platform. Retrieved 2 January 2014, from http://s3platform.jrc.ec.europa.eu/en/c/document_library/get_file?uuid= e50397e3-f2b1-4086-8608-7b86e69e8553.

Gassmann, O., Enkel, E. and Chesbrough, H. (2010). The future of open innovation. *R&D Management*, Vol. 40, No. 3, 213–214.

Grillo, F. and Landabaso, M. (2011). Merits, problems and paradoxes of regional innovation policies. *Local Economy*, Vol. 26, No. 6–7, 544–561.

He, J. and Hosein Fallah, M. (2011). The typology of technology clusters and its evolution – Evidence from the hi-tech industries. *Technological Forecasting a Social Change*, Vol. 78, No. 6, 945–952.

Hinchcliffe, D. (2009). 50 strategies for creating a successful Web 2.0 product. Retrieved 2 January 2014, from http://dionhinchcliffe.com/2009/01/29/50-essential-strategies-for-creating-a-successful-web-2-0-product/.

Komninos, N. (1993). *Technopoles and development strategies in Europe*. Athens, Greece: Gutenberg.

Kourtesis, A. (2008). Creative cities and Thessaloniki. In G. Kafkalas, L. Lambrianidis and N. Papamichos (eds), *Thessaloniki on the verge: The city as process of change* (pp. 265–293). Athens, Greece: Kritiki.

Kurtzman, J. (2001). Interview with Paul M. Romer. *Strategy + Business*, No. 6, 20 November.

Landabaso, M. (2012). *Research and innovation strategies for smart specialization (RIS³)*. DG Regio, Thematic Coordination and Innovation. Retrieved 2 January 2014, from http://goo.gl/Ex4b6u.

Markusen, A. (1996). Sticky places in slippery spaces: A typology of industrial districts. *Economic Geography*, No. 72, No. 3, 293–313.

Marshall, A. (1920). *Principles of Economics*. London, UK: Macmillan.

Morgan, K. (2004). The exaggerated death of geography: Localised learning, innovation and uneven development. *Journal of Economic Geography*, Vol. 4, No. 1, 3–21.

Nonaka, I. and Takeuchi, H. (1995). *The knowledge-creating company*. Oxford, UK: Oxford University Press.

Pallot, M. (2009). *Engaging users into research and innovation: The Living Lab approach as a user centred open innovation ecosystem*. Retrieved 2 January 2014, from www.cwe-projects.eu/pub/bscw.cgi/1760838?id=715404_1760838.

Passiante, G. and Secundo, G. (2002). From geographical innovation clusters towards virtual innovation clusters: The innovation virtual system. Paper presented in the 42nd ERSA Congress, *From Industry to Advanced Services – Perspectives of European Metropolitan Region*, Dortmund, 27–31 August.

Phillips, J. (2009). *What do the crowds know about innovation?* Retrieved 2 January 2014, from http://innovateonpurpose.blogspot.com/2009/04/what-do-crowds-know-about-innovation.html.

Porter, M. E. (1990). *The competitive advantage of nations*. New York, NY: Free Press.

Porter, M. E. (2003). The economic performance of regions. *Regional Studies*, Vol. 37, No. 6 & 7, 549–578.

Romer, P. M. (1990). Endogenous Technological Change. *Journal of Political Economy*, Vol. 98, No. 5, 71–102.

Romer, P. M. (1994). The origins of endogenous growth. *The Journal of Economic Perspectives*, Vol. 8, No. 1, 3–22.

Sefertzi, E. (1996). Flexibility and alternative corporate strategies. *Industrial Relations*, Vol. 51, No. 1, 97–119.

Storper, M. (1997). *The regional world*. London and New York: The Guilford Press.

Williamson, O. E. (1981). The Economics of organization: The Transaction cost approach. *American Journal of Sociology*, Vol. 87, No. 3, 548–577.

9 Toward smarter companies

Building innovation ecosystems with smart environments

Digital spaces and smart environments within intelligent cities enable companies to build their own innovation ecosystems (BOWIE). BOWIEs are custom ecosystems of innovation created by communities and virtually connected actors around the value chain of a company. They can assist an innovation-driven company to manage information intelligence, to discover new markets, to find external knowledge and technology resources to improve its capabilities, and to redefine the business model in collaboration and partnership with other organisations.

We call these companies 'smart' because they use smart environments to set up their own innovation ecosystems. The spatial agglomeration of smart companies leads intelligent cities to emerge, as spatial intelligence is produced by the juxtaposition and interconnection of individual Internet-enabled innovation ecosystems.

In this chapter, we describe how BOWIEs are set up with respect to lessons learnt from three pilot projects dealing with open innovation and smart environments. *CROSS-INNO-CUT* was an Interreg project about the use of ICTs to reduce costs in 15 areas of business activity, including the use of social media for marketing and market creation (www.cost-cutting.eu/crossinnocut). *INTERVALUE* was a southeast Europe project about the valorisation of academic R&D and use of Web-based repositories for technology acquisition and innovation (www.urenio.org/intervalue). *PEOPLE* was a project of the EU Competitiveness and Innovation Programme (CIP) about the making of smart city ecosystems by user-driven innovation (www.people-pilot.eu).

These projects highlight how companies can create their own innovation ecosystems using digital spaces and smart environments, which enable them to harness external resources and discover markets, technologies, and new business models.

1. New trends: indivual empowerment and big data

The Research Triangle Foundation and the Institute for the Future (IFTF) organised workshops in 2008 and 2009 with the participation of experts from different countries and professions to brainstorm about important trends in technology-led economic development for the next 20 years. The White Paper produced entitled "Future

Knowledge Ecosystems" describes 14 emerging trends in economy and society, science and technology, R&D models, and places of innovation, which will broadly set the context for technology-based economic development in the coming decades (Townsend et al., 2009). Most of these emerging trends (eight out of fourteen) outline key characteristics related to the three building blocks of intelligent cities:

Agglomeration

- Regional knowledge ecosystems emerging as a new strategic framework that provides scale, efficiency, and global platforms for economic development.
- Group economy, with new tools for cooperation that drive down the cost of forming groups around any shared interest, identity, or activity, and new models for creating wealth at the intersection of the social web and grass-roots movements.
- The social life of small research spaces creating dynamic, transdisciplinary places that bring virtual networks to ground.

Digital space

- Spread of ubiquitous computing, creating massive new streams of research data, while simultaneously providing new tools for scientific collaboration in the lab.
- Social networks where people and computers work together to make sense of data will enable a shift from artificial intelligence to hybrid sense-making.

Innovation

- New models of lightweight innovation seeking to do more, faster, with less, and cast a broader net for ideas.
- Economic development practice shifting from trying to copy the success of others to building sticky know-how and tacit knowledge on local cultural and industrial resources.
- Universities continuing their transformation from ivory tower to economic engines with expanding roles in economic development. In time, this could become their primary function, trumping education.

These upcoming trends – which revolve around collaboration and social networks, machine intelligence and sense-making, and innovation – are expected to endow communities located in metropolitan areas with know-how that has high economic value and is difficult to copy. The report concludes with three scenarios, which combine these trends in different ways and define alternative futures. The first scenario is a continuation of current trends with incremental changes that add up to spaces of innovation. In the second scenario, entirely new networks of R&D emerge in a 'research cloud' of small facilities, which combine existing innovation districts with small, Web-enhanced, social collaborative research spaces. In the third scenario, the dematerialisation of innovation expands, most innovations come from research teams that are highly virtualised, and only the last stage of product development involves face-to-face collaboration. In this case, "Universities have become nothing more than very expensive coffee shops. Much of what they provide can be replicated in other places or online through new platforms" (Townsend et al., 2009, p. 36).

There are, however, other foresight exercises which point towards complementary directions. The report from the National Intelligence Council (2012), *Global Trends 2030: Alternative Worlds*, mainly emphasises 'individual empowerment' and 'big data' as megatrends and game-changers that will alter the world of megacities.

Individual empowerment is expected to accelerate because of a huge growth in the global middle class, and greater educational attainment. "The growth of the global middle class constitutes a tectonic shift: for the first time, a majority of the world's population will not be impoverished, and the middle classes will be the most important social and economic sector in the vast majority of countries around the world. Individual empowerment is the most important megatrend because it is both a cause and effect of most other trends – including the expanding global economy, rapid growth of the developing countries, and widespread exploitation of new communications and manufacturing technologies" (National Intelligence Council, 2012, p. iii).

On the other hand, 'big data' figures among the technology arenas that are expected to shape future economic development (information technologies, new manufacturing and automation technologies, technologies to meet food, water, and energy needs, and health technologies). ICTs are entering the big-data era, as computing power and data storage are becoming almost free and broadband networks and the cloud provide global access and pervasive services. "Information technology-based solutions to maximise citizens' economic productivity and quality of life while minimising resource consumption and environmental degradation will be critical to ensuring the viability of megacities. Some of the world's future megacities will essentially be built from scratch, enabling a blank-slate approach to infrastructure design and implementation that could allow for the most effective possible deployment of new urban technologies- or create urban nightmares, if such new technologies are not deployed effectively" (p. ix).

The messages from these foresight exercises are that in future cities, companies and individual entrepreneurs are more and more able to work within rich digital–physical environments and deploy their activity using big data from social media, sensing environments, smart objects, semantic meaning tools, and other smart technologies. Innovation capabilities are expected to increase as small-scale collaboration networks and ecosystems (one producer, a few suppliers, one-two funding institutions, one major market, etc.) are placed into smart environments and smart cities, the vastness of the Internet, global collaboration networks, and virtual worlds. These world-changing trends are already in place.

2. Innovation-for-all companies into smart environments: building own innovation ecosystems

In *Democratising Innovation,* Von Hippel (2005) accurately described the convergence of innovation and ICTs, pointing out,

> Innovation is rapidly becoming democratised. Users, aided by improvements in computer and communications technology, increasingly can develop their own new products and services. These innovating users—both individuals and firms—often freely share their innovations with others, creating user-innovation communities and a rich intellectual commons.
>
> (p. 13)

Empowering users, he argues, bringing lead users into the innovation process, and adopting a user-centric innovation approach offers significant advantages over manufacturer-centric innovation. The latter has been the norm for hundreds of years, but now innovation can happen in a more decentralised way from the bottom up. In the same direction, Bingham and Spradlin (2011), drawing on their experiences from building InnoCentive, described how over the Web, global research networks can be created that connect knowledge from virtually any source, integrate multiple innovation channels in one framework, and transform knowledge into innovation.

Bauwens et al. (2012) identified two other drivers of innovation in the rising collaborative economy. The first is related to inter-networked economic actors that characterise productive communities. The second is about the individual and corporate privatisation of intellectual property, which becomes, if not untenable, surely more difficult in a world of extended digital reproduction of ideas and collaborative creation of value.

All these new trends that are actually taking place are aspects of a more central tendency related to the placement of innovation ecosystems into the Internet. Those innovation ecosystems that connect their operation with the World Wide Web see their capabilities amplify and their reach expand: co-creation communities and Living Labs turn consumers into producers; digital identities of products are marketed globally over the Web; and value is generated via open intellectual property, free software, shared design, and open hardware models. Innovation stands on new pillars, becoming available to all and attainable by all.

With online crowdsourcing marketplaces for micro- and macro-tasks, the nodes of innovation ecosystems somehow 'explode.' The number of participants in the ecosystem multiplies geometrically, as large numbers of suppliers and users are involved and undertake innovation tasks. The social media help orchestrate the engagement of even larger communities; marketplaces start by registering users and informing them about offers; ideas and skills are offered for free. Participants submit ideas, write reviews and interact, solutions are assessed, and providers are selected.

With co-creation and virtual Living Lab environments, consumers become co-producers of innovation. Co-creation is the logical outcome of open innovation, a collective creativity practiced jointly by many people. Pater (2009) defined four different types of co-creation: (1) the 'club of experts,' which is best for very specific challenges that demand expertise and breakthrough ideas and contributors that meet specific qualifications found through an active selection process; (2) crowdsourcing, which plays with the rule of big numbers, bets on the power of the masses, uses online platforms that anyone can join, and allows people to rate and respond to ideas and suggestions from others; (3) the 'coalition of parties' that team up to share ideas and investments, while each participant brings in specific assets or skills; and (4) the 'community of kindred spirits,' in which groups of people with similar interests and goals come together and create commons.

Collaborative Web platforms and digital commons of information, knowledge, and infrastructure create new advantages. Companies that work on such platforms make their products on top of those commons. Platforms are materialising in online environments of open, flexible workplaces that use networking technologies to orchestrate a broad range of resources, from product design to innovation funding and market placement. There are 'commons-oriented' platforms in which the collaborative infrastructure is often under the governance of a non-profit organisation, and corporate platforms, in which users share their own creative work, but no common knowledge base is created and working rules and benefits are established by the corporate owners.

With the spread of augmented reality solutions and the Internet of Things, all objects become hybrid, combining a physical and a virtual identity. The generation of a sea of digital identities is redefining markets and marketing. Using the web, companies and advertisers are attempting to insert themselves into the flow of interactions by understanding and practicing digital marketing techniques. 'Intention markets' are created where buyers notify the market of the intent to buy, and sellers compete for the buyer's purchases. Such markets grow around buyers, not sellers. Marketing is not needed because buyers pre-order goods that are not yet on the market. Potential sellers, even those that are not on the market, can capture these signs and contract production before it is being produced.

In such collaborative smart environments closed intellectual property (IP) and individual appropriation of IP is often a burden rather than an advantage. Innovation without IP is gaining ground via free and open licenses. Commons-oriented licenses create goods that can be used universally, sharing licenses define individual control over the use, and quasi-closed IP models aggregate ownership on corporate platforms for whatever is placed on the platforms. Bosserman (2008) presents this diversity with a quadrant formed by two axes of IP: open vs. closed, and paid vs. free. Four IP models are defined: closed IP for paid assets; closed IP for a free portfolio; open IP for paid practices; and open free IP.

All these changes are taking place because innovation networks and ecosystems are placed into the Internet and the World Wide Web. They indicate a new potential: an *innovation-for-all into smart environments* model which becomes possible thanks to smart technologies, social media, and software platforms and applications, customised to the needs of each company and organisation.

Smart environments enable companies to reconsider their innovation supply chain and build their own innovation ecosystem (BOWIE). Such individual solutions restructure their entire innovation supply chain, from R&D, to production, marketing, and funding. In this sense, smart environments offer each company the possibility of renewing its innovation ecosystem and redefining:

- The market, in the context of Internet-enabled global markets, semantically tagged products, uniquely addressable and interconnected objects, and social media operated by customers and users.
- The knowledge base, by combining sector-specific technologies pertaining to its sector of production and Internet technologies for discovering fields of unexploited knowledge and by acquiring technology from external providers.
- The business model, by using cloud-based services, open platforms, and collaborative funding, which offer cost reduction advantages due to virtualisation, self service on demand, metered use, scalability of costs and charging, as well as low entry costs.

'Innovation-for-all into smart environments' is a model that corresponds to a cultural and psychological shift towards 'less-materialist' practices, hybrid identities, and empowered users and customers who get satisfaction from having access rather than owing products. At the heart of the model is the increasing importance of collaborative practices enabled by the Internet and an economy driven by knowledge and innovation assets.

3. Market discovery using smart environments

Market intelligence and market discovery are timeless landmarks of innovation. Innovative companies are in a continuous process of changing products, markets, and supporting technologies, transforming ideas into new products, sustaining innovation with next-generation products that replace older portfolios, and making products more efficient and affordable.

Market discovery goes hand-in-hand with product discovery and development. In well-established markets with a number of producers offering quasi-similar products, market discovery is 'obvious' and 'fast-follower' strategies prevail, especially in cases where there is no proprietary ecosystem, brand name, or significant economies of scale. But in many cases, the market is unrecognised and product intelligence and discovery can reveal new opportunities for innovation. Product discovery is a responsibility of the product manager and requires collaboration between product managers, engineers, suppliers, customers, and end users. It is a never-ending process and companies can always come up with great products to serve unmet needs in existing markets.

Mainstream market discovery follows a 'push perspective' of gathering and analysing information, and adapting the marketing and product placement accordingly. The goal is to introduce a product into the market by collecting information about competitors and existing and potential customers, and then starting the marketing 'push' campaign. Such 'market discovery' can be frustrating, but the results compensate for the effort involved. The consecutive steps to be followed include:

- Products and services review: outline the products / services offered; determine key product benefits and competitive differentiators; examine product documentation and identify top profitable products.
- Sales review: lead sales sources; lead Return on Investment; examine sales documentation; look at pricing rationale as well as incentives and discounts, and sales statistics.
- Existing customers review: look at customer database and the distribution per industry code, as well as customer profiles and motivations.
- Competitor review: look at top competitors, competitors' strengths and weaknesses and their marketing strategy, offline and online, as well as their ranking in the market.
- Generate the customer database: market research; marketing library; trade shows and events; ROI information.
- Marketing design, implementation of marketing campaign, and product push.

The rise of the Internet-based collaborative economy marks a profound change in such market-making practices. In smart environments, the expert-based collaboration for product and market discovery is placed under communities of users, consumers, and technology providers. Larger populations are asked to provide data, preferences, demands, and likes. Interactions within connected and collaborative environments in which business operate can capture information via online communities and generate new business practices. Smart technologies and applications can capture insights by users and consumers and turn them into market strategy and discovery. Bauwens et al. (2012, pp. 25–34) outline three interrelated trends that are changing the rules of the game in the collaborative economy.

First is the rise of the 'Intention Economy,' which refers to the active role of customers and the ability to declare and discuss intentions. Expressions of intent that correlate to purchase or other money-based transactions are extremely valuable for producers that can fulfil these needs. The intention economy grows around buyers and users. It is about markets and not about marketing. The buyer notifies the market of the intention to buy, and the market responds to intentions. This becomes feasible because of interconnected audiences that can declare and discuss intentions. Digital environments enable the expression of intent, replacing push with pull dynamics.

Second is the rise of the 'Pull Economy' and the ability to have demand instead of supply as the main driver of growth. In push economies, producers anticipate customers' needs, and consumers are pushed to like the products they offer. On the contrary, a "pull economy – the kind that appears to be materialising in online environments – is based on open, flexible production platforms that use networking technologies to orchestrate a broad range of resources. The networked environment radically empowers individuals, and communities of like-minded individuals, to pull the products and services that they want, on their own terms and time requirements" (Bollier D. cited by Bauwens et al., 2012, p. 30).

Third is the rise of the 'Attention Economy,' and the significance for producers of capturing the attention of actors. Here, critical factor is the user and managing his attention within environments of overabundant information. The 'attention' and 'time' the user offers become scarce resources. By putting the user in control, the attention economy has to manage a series of services (info, news, alerts, and search), store information (repositories), and record attention (devices). A precondition for this is working within smart environments offering the necessary connectivity, infrastructure, and instrumentation everywhere, at any time, and in real-time. The smart city environments described by IBM as interconnected, instrumented, and intelligent become the proper environment for the combined rise of intention, pull, and attention economies.

Placing the market discovery process into such Internet-based economies means that extended collaboration, and user-driven and community-based information are reshaping the market discovery process. Smart technologies and Web applications can capture information from users and consumers and turn them into market strategy and discovery. A series of e-tools have become available to trace down customer needs and preferences:

- Search Engine Optimisation (SEO) and Search Engine Marketing (SEM) enable one to obtain higher Google Rankings and Higher Search Engine Rankings.
- Google adwords, pay-per-click campaigns, and conversion tracking for enhanced monitoring. These involve keyword optimisation and creating lists of keywords relevant to a company's products or services.
- Email marketing for targeted, low cost–high value marketing enable one to create email campaigns and send them to targeted customers and target markets.
- Market intelligence dashboards that fit a whole visual display of most important market segments and trends entirely onto a single computer screen.
- e-commerce websites, online shops, and sales solutions for business-to-consumer and business-to-business sales of products and services.
- Product Feed Manager Systems and Web applications enabling to benefit from large-scale online shopping and mass product uploads to big digital marketplaces such as eBay, Amazon, and Google Merchant.

However, the most widely used tools are those related to social media. Online market discovery is the kingdom of the social media, enabling one to better understand information and signs coming from users. The social media – a democratisation of information – are changing people from content readers into content creators, and are opening up many different forms of content creation,

204 Strategies and governance

communication, and exchange. The usual types of social media include blogs, perhaps the best known form of social media; microblogging, based on small batches of words that are distributed online and through the mobile phone network; wikis, applications that allow people to add content to or edit the information on them and formulate content collaboratively; podcasts, audio and video files that become available by subscription; forums, applications for online discussion around specific topics of interests in online communities; and content communities, for organising and sharing particular types of content, photos, bookmarks, and videos.

For market search, intelligence, and market discovery, the social media are channels that allow one to reach consumers in both ways: exploring needs and intentions, understanding markets, and informing them with messages tailored to customer interests and social interactions. A survey prepared by the Social Media Examiner (2011) showed that 88 percent of all marketers indicated that their social media efforts have generated more exposure for their businesses. Improving traffic and subscribers was the second major benefit, with 72 percent reporting positive results. Nearly two-thirds indicated a rise in search engine rankings thanks to social media marketing. Slightly more than half of marketers found that social media generated qualified leads.

A number of social media techniques that may be useful in product discovery include:

Social media analytics: Companies marketing via social media have discovered that social media analytics is crucial, especially for customer feedback. Such social analytics include listening platforms from companies (such as General Sentiment social analytics, Attensity, Telligent) that are used by advertising agencies, corporate marketing departments, and call centres to scan popular social media networks. Analytics enable companies to understand their customers and identify trends in order to respond to their needs better.

Social bookmarking and tagging analysis: Social bookmarking is the Web equivalent of sharing references. Social bookmarking services such as Delicious or Diigo allow people to store their favourite sites online and share them with others who have similar interests. Tagging is a way of categorising online content using keywords that describe what can be found at a website, bookmark, photo, or blog post.

Viral marketing campaigns: Entail the planned promotion of a product, brand, or service through a process of creating interest in actual or potential customers by disseminating information to friends, family, and colleagues. This word-of-mouth advertising is accomplished by the creative use of social media and other non-traditional marketing channels. The most usual viral campaign is the viral video and refers to video clip content which gains popularity through emails, blogs, and other media-sharing websites.

These methods were used in CROSS-INNO-CUT in different tracks, such as social tactics, to find out the best and newest ways to market products with social media; social strategy, to discover new strategies that will draw in customers, using social media profiles and measuring social activities and organisational trends; community management, to build communities around products; and unveiling markets by social media and social content. Social media marketing was the methodology most sought after of all cost cutting technologies and solutions that were proposed to 100 companies in this pilot project, and presented the highest value for money in respect to the savings generated (Zygiaris and Sefertzi, 2012).

4. Technology discovery using smart environments

On the other side of markets, companies are using technology to create new products, reduce production costs and materials, and create competitive advantages. Internal company R&D and technology investment have been fundamental pillars of their competitiveness and growth. Recently, movements towards more open and sometimes free use of technology have been multiplying with open knowledge initiatives, R&D licensed under a Creative Commons license, free open source software under GPL, DSB, and LGPL licenses, open initiatives to consult for free published journal articles, open conference presentations, and open R&D policies, such as the UK policy to make publicly funded scientific research immediately available for anyone to read for free by 2014, or European Union research policy that encourages publishing in open access journals and developing software under free licenses.

Academic research as source of disruptive innovation

Within the open innovation landscape, universities have become an important and yet underutilised source of new knowledge and technology. The valorisation of university research is now a major topic in both literatures of university reform and innovation development. Especially in the literature of innovation, university R&D is considered to be a major and unexploited source of technology and innovation. About 40 percent of global R&D spending takes place within universities and public R&D centres (Jaruzelski and Dehoff, 2008), while university R&D is considered to be a primary source for radical innovations generated by academic breakthroughs in science and technology.

A series of academic papers focus on models that describe the processes of university-to-industry collaboration and knowledge transfer as well as the relative importance of different channels of research dissemination and diffusion (Cohen et al., 2002; Brennenraedts et al., 2006). Initially, this literature outlined a linear sequence of technology transfer (Szulanski, 2000), but also highlighted interpersonal networks and established relationships for knowledge sharing and learning (Reagans and McEvily, 2003). Since 2000, however, open innovation perspectives have come to prevail, placing university–industry collaboration into more complex alliances and innovation environments supported by information technologies and Internet-based marketplaces. The bond between academic R&D and innovation has been analysed in depth, documenting the transition from linear towards systemic and open models (Chesbrough, 2003; Chiesa et al., 2004; Godin, 2006), triple-helix (Etzkowitz, 2002), and quadruple-helix collaboration (Stewart and Carayannis, 2013).

The shift towards knowledge-based development, the increasing importance of science and technology in sustaining innovation and competitiveness, and the limitless growth that knowledge can generate made universities more sensitive to valorisation of their intellectual capital and the intellectual property deriving from the research activity. Commercialisation of research gave birth to university-based innovation ecosystems with institutions for research–industry intermediation, liaison offices, triple-helix alliances, and campuses expanding to host research and science parks. University cities connecting education, research, innovation, and commercialisation strongly encouraged this orientation and financially contributed to the development of infrastructure sustaining such university-based innovation ecosystems. Apart from the main players at the two ends of this process (universities and enterprises), the web of interactions also involves technology transfer and liaison offices, financial institutions, technology consultants and advisors, marketers, and governmental policy institutions. Within such open ecosystems, companies can identify and acquire technologies that complement their internal knowledge and technology base.

Potential paths through which academic knowledge and research are being transferred to companies include publications, recruiting cooperation in R&D, joint ventures, contract-based research, and consulting. Next to these, individual mobility, personnel exchanges, and participation in conferences and workshops create collaboration networks and generate knowledge spillovers. A lot of attention has also been devoted to intellectual property rights in the form of patenting, co-patenting, and licenses. Spinoffs also represent a popular mechanism for introducing a new technology into the market. However, the digital dimension is gaining momentum, and more and more technology absorption is practiced within hybrid physical–virtual environments.

From an operational point of view, it is also important to underline the difference between 'contractual' or formal procedures of valorisation, such as research contracts, patents, licenses, buy-sell transactions between academic institutions and companies, and 'collaborative' or emerging relationships between universities and firms (Harmon et al., 1997). In the former case, valorisation is seen as a process resulting from a contract between technology supply and demand, where suppliers and users of technology operate independently, and the gap between them is bridged by a licensing contract. In the latter, valorisation of academic R&D relies on interdependence and interactive learning.

Another meaningful distinction is made with respect to policies that shape this relationship. Goldfarb and Henrekson (2003) identified two central policy models – bottom-up vs. top-down policies of university intellectual property (IP) commercialisation – which are formed by incentives for universities to commercialise their research and by governments directly creating mechanisms that facilitate commercialisation. In the former case, which is common in US universities, intellectual property from R&D is awarded to universities. The Bayh-Dole Act adopted in 1980 allowed universities to appropriate the property rights resulting from university research that was funded by federal grants. This has encouraged universities to create technology transfer offices and cover the expenses associated with marketing, patenting, and license negotiation. The organised promotion of IP and the availability of funds for this purpose make commercialisation more likely when IP rights belong to universities.

In the second case, which is common in Sweden and many EU countries, IP rights stemming from R&D are awarded (fully or partly) to inventors. A result of faculty ownership of property rights is that universities have little incentive in technology transfer, which discourages the systematic pursuit of research valorisation. This barrier, combined with constraints on the entrepreneurial activity of academics, leads to very low level of research commercialisation. "In a system that discourages faculty involvement with industry beyond consulting and where the property rights rest with the researcher, there is a lower likelihood that the commercial benefits of academic research will be reaped" (Goldfarb and Henrekson, 2003, p. 647). This is a great challenge in Europe, known as 'the European paradox' of high-level academic research and low-level resultant innovation (Dosi et al., 2006).

Still, knowledge exchange between academia and industry is a highly complex and risky process that often fails, for many reasons. These factors can be attributed to the particular properties of the knowledge exchanged (tacit–explicit, interdisciplinary, fuzzy) or to the specific context in which the knowledge is developed and transferred, such as the institutional structures (legal framework) or the individual (culture, habits) and organisational (norms, regimes) characteristics of the stakeholders involved (Dasgupta and David, 1994). Contextual characteristics influence the ability of companies to learn and utilise externally generated knowledge, such as the level of 'connectedness,' or the firm's absorptive capacity (Cohen and Levinthal, 1989).

In the open innovation / democratising innovation perspectives, one of the most important developments has been the appearance of technology platforms and virtual environments for the valorisation and global offering of academic research (Komninos et al., 2006). Such open platforms make it possible to transform high-level scientific research into commercial products.

Intervalue: a digital platform for getting technology from academia

INTERVALUE was an experiment to make academic research widely available to companies. The main objective was to bridge the gap between R&D creators and producers by creating a trans-national mechanism that facilitated the valorisation and eventually commercialisation of academic research. INTERVALUE followed an integrated approach for strengthening the linkages between university R&D, companies, and funding organisations through the involvement of experts in the evaluation and valorisation of R&D results. It is based on a collaborative Web platform enabling research teams to reach potential users through a process of selection and promotion of research results to relevant audiences. The

208 *Strategies and governance*

platform combines a repository of R&D outcomes set up by research communities, researchers, and laboratories; an experts' pool that facilitates the valorisation of research results through drafting technology exploitation plans to be used by companies and other potential users; and a collaboration space for IPR agreement between laboratories and companies. A central assumption was that an open digital platform and a virtual marketplace would substantially improve the use of academic R&D, while minimising operation and technology transfer costs (Komninos et al., 2010).

The collaborative Web platform for R&D valorisation has been organised into three types of spaces (Figure 9.1):

- *The repository space:* Research teams and technology providers from universities and research institutions upload research outcomes that can lead to new products, production processes, and services.
- *The valorisation space:* Experts help researchers to draft valorisation plans for their R&D results, addressing issues such as technical feasibility, IP protection, market potential, and funding.
- *The IP agreements space:* Research outcomes and valorisation plans are promoted to selected markets and brokerage events with a view to achieving different forms of commercialisation agreements: new contracts, licenses, or equity. Online learning roadmaps, newsletters, models of IP agreements, and pilot applications create a learning environment guiding research commercialisation.

Key component of the platform is the middle block of valorisation plans (VPs), which bridge the knowledge and communication gap between research and business communities. Experts, technology, and innovation intermediary

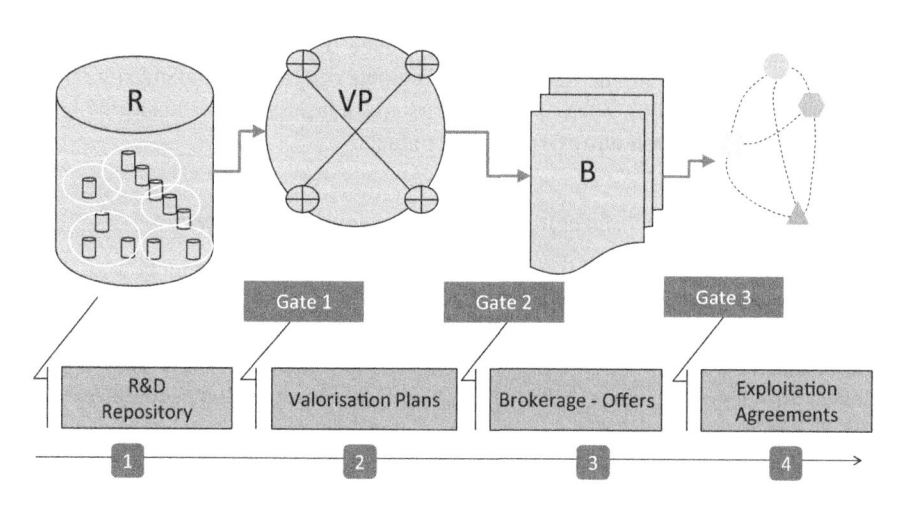

Figure 9.1 Components and gates of the INTERVALUE platform

organisations (i.e., liaison offices and knowledge transfer offices within universities) can identify potentially marketable R&D and then create VPs that facilitate the step from research to the market. VPs are based on detailed examination of research with regard to (1) technical feasibility, (2) scientific relevance and IP protection, (3) market potential, and (4) investment and funding opportunities.

The *Technical Feasibility* aspect of the VPs focuses on the technical maturity of research as a potential source of new products or services. The expert team is asked to cooperate with the research team in order to explore features of the research result: Has the result being tested and at which level? Is it tested as a prototype? Is there a pilot application or have alpha / beta tests been done? What were the results of this testing and based on them, what further testing needs to be done? What would be a realistic timeframe for these further tests and what would be the costs associated with them? To what extent does the research team have the technical resources to support production of a new product, in terms of human resources, knowledge, hardware, etc.? What are the technical issues that need to be tackled for full deployment of the product or service? What additional technical resources are needed to produce this new product? What are the materials, tools, technologies, and staff effort that are necessary for full-scale production of the new product? At the end of the technical feasibility assessment, the expert team is able to give a clear picture of all technical issues needed to bring the research result to the market.

The *Scientific Relevance* aspect of the VP is concerned with the originality and intellectual property futures of each research outcome. Here, the expert team attempts to position the research done within contemporary technology trends, and research and define possible ways to defend the underlying know-how. The following issues are examined: How does the result fit with the-state-of-the-art in its scientific field? What is the problem or need that the research result responds to? How was it addressed before and what is the approach that makes the result unique and valuable? What is the potential for further research? What is the potential of the research result for synergy with other research areas either in the same or in a different discipline? What is the proposed method of IP protection (patent, license, trademark, etc.)? What are the steps that need to be taken in order to secure IP protection and what are the associated costs? Based on the above, the expert team is able to assess the scientific maturity of the research result, the optimum way to secure its IP, and the potential for further research either in the same direction that was followed up until now or in other related research fields.

The *Market Potential* aspect explores the market (existing or potential) for the new product or service that can be developed from the research being examined. This part of the VP focuses on market analysis in order to define: What is the Unique Sales Proposition of the potential product? Is this related to a technology-driven innovation or a market-driven innovation? What would be the added value for end users be? Would this added value be based on higher quality or better technical characteristics? What is the target market for the product? Can this market go beyond the national level to global markets? Will the product or service address existing demand, or future and latent demand? Are there any existing or potential strategic partnerships that can be used for marketing the new product or service? What is the current level of competition within the target market and what competitive advantages will the introduction of the new product entail? Will the potential products be marketed to regulated or open markets? And finally, what is the estimated cost of new product development, the expected sales volume, and the expected market share? By answering these questions, the expert team formulates the seed of a market analysis and the market potential that could yield revenues from the new product or service.

The *Investment and Funding Potential* aspect draws on the suggestions of all the previous parts of the VP (Technical Feasibility, Scientific Relevance, Market Potential) in order to develop a summary version of a cost-benefit analysis illustrating the projected costs (fixed costs, personnel costs, other running costs, marketing costs), expected sales, and revenues for a three- to five-year period. It also includes an evaluation of the financial risks associated with further investment in exploitation of the research result. Finally, having assessed the level of investment required to develop the new product, the expert team provides an assessment of suitable funding sources (i.e., EU funding, national and regional funding, private funding from venture capital, business angels or other sources). At the end of the investment analysis, a full version of the technology valorisation business plan for a new product or service is produced.

This four-way assessment provides different insights to the stakeholders involved. For the research team, the VP offers a roadmap that defines the main parameters at play in commercial exploitation and the best solutions for exploitation through licensing, patenting, or the creation of spinoffs. For the potential user, the VP provides a clear picture of the new product or service development and an initial estimation of costs, risks, and revenues that should be expected. VPs address the gap in information, knowledge, and communication between researchers and entrepreneurs, by removing communication barriers, by translating academic research into a language that companies can understand, and by simplifying the procedures involved in getting to an agreement.

The INTERVALUE Platform was developed in line with Web 2.0 principles, with a view to facilitating the creation of such content by multiple users. WordPress Multi-User (http://mu.wordpress.org) was used as the basic content management system, which was customised according to the needs of the experiment. WordPress Multi-User is ideal for cases that run multiple content applications or in cases of multiple users hosting services. Development of the platform also followed the principles of service-oriented architecture, in terms of reuse, granularity, modularity, composability, componentisation, and interoperability, and service identification categorisation, delivery, monitoring, and tracking. Each space within the platform was organised along a three-tier architecture: (1) the presentation tier, which is the topmost level of the application and displays information related to services such as browsing item, detail reading, and content selection; (2) the applications tier, which controls an application's functionality by performing detailed processing; and (3) the data tier, which consists of databases in which information is stored and retrieved. This tier keeps data neutral and

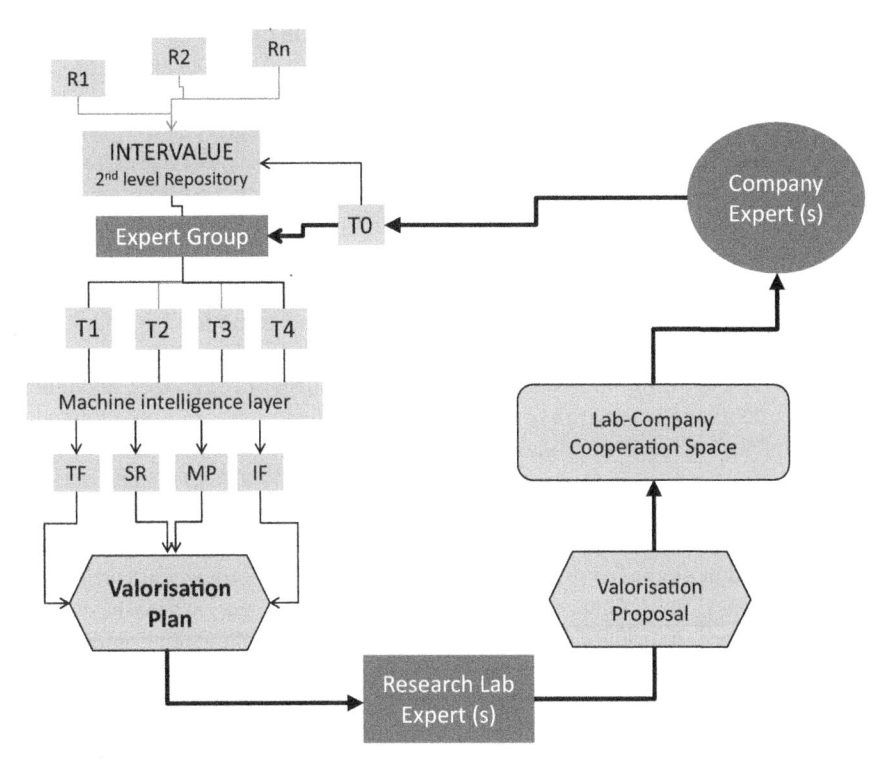

Figure 9.2 INTERVALUE technology exploitation process

independent from application servers or business logic. Giving data its own tier also improves scalability and performance.

The operation of the INTERVALUE Platform is presented in Figure 9.2. University labs, experts, companies and other interested users work into a virtual environment for efficient R&D valorisation.

- Initially, labs and research teams upload content onto the platform using a predefined template (T0) that allows them to describe the R&D. Universities that initiated the experiment started feeding in R&D data, but as the platform was open, other universities and research institutes followed in the collective gathering and upload of research.
- Experts create valorisation plans based on four predefined templates (T1, T2, T3, and T4). Four methodologies and a learning roadmap assist them in preparing the reports on technical feasibility (TF), scientific relevance (SR) and IP protection, potential market analysis (MP), and investment and funding opportunities (IF). The collaborative work of experts and researchers is disseminated at brokerage events and communicated via newsletters.

- The platform assists all these procedures: the repository of R&D in the beginning, the drafting of valorisation plans based on the four templates, the dissemination of information to potential users and brokerage events.
- The IP agreement space facilitates different forms of commercialisation agreements, ranging from new research contracts to equity in new business creation. Here, additional tools offered bring intelligence to the user, in terms of visualisation, popularity of entries, similar content, and Web analytics. The platform offers an integrated smart environment to be used by academic R&D labs, companies, and technology transfer organisations.

Researchers, experts, users, and the platform tools set in motion a collaborative system, which combines knowledge from research labs and individual researchers, experts in drafting valorisation plans, a large number of companies, and other users for data retrieval and analysis. It is a smart platform sustaining an intelligent community of technology producers and users.

During the first two years of operation (2011–2012), INTERVALUE gathered 850 research offers for commercialisation, created 250 valorisation plans, and achieved 39 research exploitation agreements. A network of 210 university and research labs was involved in producing this content. An impact analysis survey was carried out in five regions of Italy, Greece, Bulgaria, Romania, and Hungary where the experiment took place. It revealed that major scientific areas for commercialisation were ICTs, engineering, and biological sciences, while the sectors of potential use of this research were computer and related activities, environmental management, health and social work, and manufacture of machinery and equipment. The scientific areas were region-agnostic, but potential commercialisation of research depended on the production specialisation of the regions. Most research was about improving existing products and only a few outcomes focused on services and processes. In most cases, additional development and testing were needed to translate research into products. Research results were mainly aimed at global and highly competitive markets. Therefore, the existence of affordable services related to marketing and product placement were of crucial importance. However, usual mechanisms of intermediation – such as technology transfer and liaison offices – may be ineffective in the transfer of such research to the market, given the fact that they primarily work on a regional scale. The main added value of the research offered was related to improvement of the technical characteristics of products, while the most important contribution made by valorisation plans were market analysis and marketing strategy, product improvement, and consultation for funding.

INTERVALUE documented the fact that major technology barriers are related to understanding the potential of research for generating innovation and can be removed by information and communication platforms. Research on entrepreneurial universities indicates that most academics naively presume that a discovery will somehow automatically produce financial rewards. However, it is the existence of dedicated institutions, such as university technology transfer, liaison, and marketing offices, that substantially increase the level of research valorisation. Waugaman and Tornatzky (2001, p. 29) accurately argue, "we are witnessing a phenomenon wherein universities that are reactive in technology transfer will respond to the rare entrepreneurs and faculty members who wish to 'pull' inventions or technologies out of the institution. As these institutions become proactive, their mix of licenses becomes more balanced as more out-of-state deals appear with larger, established licensees."

The experiment also revealed the barriers of technology acquisition. At the side of the researchers, the main barriers of valorisation were about the lack of understanding of the business environment, a tendency to either overestimate or underestimate the commercial potential of their research, a sense of insecurity regarding relations with companies, a tendency to focus on a single set of questions and interests that does not allow crossovers to other disciplines and exploitation of knowledge in non-conventional ways, isolation that leads to failure to meet a critical mass of R&D, and lack of clear IP policy at the institutional level that defines rules and incentives.

At the side of the companies, the obstacles were about investments risks; too much focusing on numbers leading to them systematically underestimate the new market potential coming from research ideas; failure to realise the potential of research for innovation; the lack of technical and scientific skills and awareness of research-based new product development; focusing on short-term results and quick yields on investments; and an inability to fund the commercial exploitation of research.

There are, however, a number of gates to open to make this collaboration environment functional and the transition from one stage to the other smooth. First, an institutional gate between the R&D repository and valorisation plans, to make data from R&D results available, identify promising technologies and to draft valorisation plans. Second, a market gate between valorisation plans and brokerage events in order to reach innovation funding and business angel communities that might understand the potential of research for innovation. Third, a legal or support gate between research offers and exploitation agreements in order to select the best IP protection mode and provide specialised services for IP exploitation contracts (Figure 9.1, gates 1, 2, and 3).

These gates can open within a wider favourable environment of valorisation created by relevant policies and institutions. Apart of research, production, funding actors, a fourth type of actor at play should be considered: policy-makers, who should offer this external favourable environment that can smooth the overall valorisation process. National or regional research and innovation systems have to bring together researchers and business people and achieve a common language and understanding, which, in turn, will offer companies the possibility to enrich and extend their know-how through academic research. By opening these gates, a quadruple innovation model into smart environments becomes operational and effective.

5. Business model re-discovery using smart environments

Business models serve two important objectives: they create value by defining the flow of activities from raw materials to final products, and they help capture a portion of this value by establishing a unique resource, bottleneck, or position

214 *Strategies and governance*

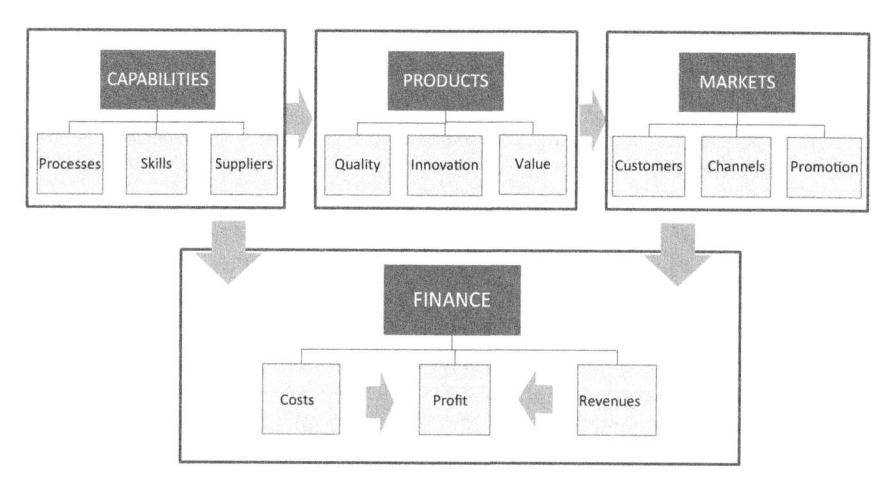

Figure 9.3 Business models building blocks
Source: Adapted from Global Cloud Business

within this flow of activities in which the company holds an advantage. Figure 9.3 presents the main building blocks of a business model, including the internal capabilities and the external know-how provided by partners and suppliers; products and services and their value proposition; markets and distribution channels; and the block of finance with costs, revenues, and profit.

More specific functions to be found in a business model are: (1) articulating the value proposition, (2) identifying a market segment, (3) defining the structure of the value chain required to create and distribute the product or service, (4) specifying the revenue generation mechanisms and estimating the cost structure and profit, (5) describing the position of the firm within the value network or ecosystem linking suppliers and customers, and (6) formulating a competitive strategy for innovating firms in order to gain and retain advantage over rivals (Chesbrough, 2006).

Smart environments and intelligent city infrastructure disrupt the established business model by introducing significant changes into all those building blocks, from capabilities to funding. The changes are towards the gradual substitution of 'undifferentiated,' 'differentiated,' and 'segmented' business models, characterised by limited scalability and internal focus, with 'externally aware' business models that harness external sources of knowledge to complement internal capabilities, 'integrated' business models that bring together internal and external technologies, and finally 'platform-based' business models that bring in third-party investments on the platform and create collaborative innovation ecosystems (Chesbrough, 2006, 2008). Cloud computing enables further changes. Changes start with companies that began to grow their cloud storage and use cloud-computing services leveraging internal Web-based infrastructure, and redefining hosting, cloud-based offerings, and SaaS markets. Developing a cloud strategy is potentially more important for small to medium-sized companies, because

Table 9.1 Changing business models by using smart environments

Business model block	Potential changes	Advantages
Capabilities: partners and suppliers	• Crowdsourcing for skills, ideas, and competences over platforms and virtual networks	• Increase in the skill base and innovation capability of the company
Products and services: value proposition	• Turning products into smart objects • Using smart object-components • Turning products into hybrid objects • Managing hybrid identities	• Connects products to the Internet of Things • Traces components on the Web • Access products during real-time operation
Customers: channels and market segments	• Using other companies' distribution channels • Creating collaborative marketplaces • Turning customers into producers of services for company products	• Increases customer base • Increases customer loyalty • Scales down marketing and distribution costs
Funding: costs and funding	• Infrastructure and services leased from the cloud • Maintaining data and services on the cloud • Using collaborative funding	• Reduces initial investments • Reduces operational costs • Scales up service with minimum hardware investment

they have smaller data needs and often work with one server closet in one location (Crump, 2013). The question is, how does cloud computing disrupt existing business models? And this question is part of a wider transformation that future Internet technologies (IoT, Semantic Web, smart objects) and smart environments bring into business models.

Thus, smart environments offer each company the possibility of re-defining its business model by moving towards an open and platform-based model and a radical re-organisation of the company's building blocks (Table 9.1). This is done:

- In the sphere of capabilities, by enhancing technology collaboration, R&D absorption, crowdsourcing of every kind of input, ideas, designs, knowledge, skills, and services.
- In the sphere of products and services, by making it possible to make all products 'smart' by combining a physical and digital identity and linking it to the Internet of Things, with all the advantages that this transformation brings in terms of management, marketing, maintenance, repair, and operation.
- In the sphere of customers and markets, by creating virtual identities for all products and by placing them into large-scale virtual marketplaces, which

can actualise promotion networks, engage customers in market making and marketing, and utilise the creative skills of customers to enrich products and services with content, applications, and ideas.
- In the sphere of finance, by opening up through smart environments new forms of funding, such as crowdfunding, social lending, equity-based crowdfunding, online payments, and introduce cloud-type payment of infrastructure and services with high scalability and pay-per-use.

The key issue for this transformation is the pooling of resources with other companies and the creation of commons and collaborative platforms. In the PEOPLE project, for instance, the creation of a marketplace was made possible by companies pooling resources and preparing a business model to run a collective marketplace. A SWOT analysis helped describe the pros and cons of different funding solutions per platform.

Business models for commons and open innovation platforms can be made sustainable by combining internal company's resources with external resources from:

- Advertising: For commercially oriented services or services raising funds from advertising, this may be a sound solution. Possible marketing opportunities for individuals or companies include displaying advertisement banners and video commercials. Advertising fees can then cover all or part of the platform's operating costs.
- Sponsorship: Likewise, sponsorship derives from individuals or companies who wish to offer an amount of money to be commercially promoted via the service. Sponsorship overlaps considerably with advertising, but differs in the terms of the scope of how an organisation and its operations are endorsed and supported.
- Free Core Service & Paying for Additional Features: In this solution, the core service is open to the public and provided without any charge. However, when the user pays a fee, additional features are made available (i.e., option to select various templates, increased hosting space, support for users).
- Data Monetisation: This is based on the idea of offering data collected and analysed through the various tools of the platform. If the data are not sensitive and do not contain personal information, then selling them also becomes an option.
- Crowdfunding: This particular option has emerged over recent years and shows great potential. It may be possible for a service to be funded by raising capital through crowdfunding platforms. This kind of funding is actually a collective form of cooperation and is based on trust by people who pool money via the Internet to support efforts and initiatives by other people and organisations.

Overall, the platform-based business model is a further step towards the collaborative knowledge economy, combining commons and custom solutions to match individual company needs. The PEOPLE pilot and the virtual marketplace created showed that collaborative business models and platforms rely more on (1) cultural views and digital skills than on heavy investments in capital and hard infrastructure, and (2) the efforts of companies within smart environments and digital commons collaboratively started.

6. BOWIE: an individual innovation trajectory

Smart environments enabling market, technology, and business model discovery create custom and individualised ecosystem settings suitable for each company. The three building blocks of smart companies described – market discovery, technology discovery, and platform-based business model discovery – involve different levels of difficulty and complexity, with platform-making being the most demanding. They can be deployed at basic and more advanced levels depending on the digital skills of each company.

However, in all cases, commitment, the desire for learning and experimentation, and the will to collaborate are more important factors of successful BOWIEs than funds and investments. Companies cannot 'subcontract' and buy turnkey solutions to make their own innovation ecosystem; they have to build it. In this sense, a BOWIE is a cultural turn and individual discovery process for each organisation, but one that is feasible with the assistance of virtual identities and smart environments only.

References

Bauwens, M., Iacomella F., Mendoza, N., Burke, J., Pinchen, C., Léonard, A. and Mootoosamy, E. (2012). *Synthetic overview of the collaborative economy*. Amsterdam, the Netherlands: P2P Foundation. Available at http://p2p.coop/files/reports/collaborative-economy-2012.pdf.

Bingham, A. and Spradlin, D. (2011). *The open innovation marketplace: Creating value in the challenge driven enterprise.* Upper Saddle River, NJ: FT Press.

Bosserman, S. (2008). *P2P foundation, open business models.* Retrieved 2 January 2014, from http://p2pfoundation.net/images/Open-free-quadrant.svg.

Brennenraedts, R. M., Bekkers, R. and Verspagen, B. (2006). *The different channels of university – industry knowledge transfer: Empirical evidence from biomedical engineering.* Eindhoven, the Netherlands: Eindhoven Centre for Innovation Studies.

Chesbrough, H. (2003). *Open innovation: The new imperative for creating and profiting from technology.* Boston, MA: Harvard Business School Press.

Chesbrough, H. (2006). *Open business models: How to thrive in the new innovation landscape.* Boston, MA: Harvard Business School.

Chesbrough, H. (2008). Business model innovation: The next frontier of innovation. Slideshare. Retrieved 25 January 2014, from www.slideshare.net/SiliconValleyST/business-model-innovation-by-h-chesbrough?from_search=3.

Chiesa, V., Manzini, R. and Pizzurno, E. (2004). The externalisation of R&D activities and the growing market of product development services. *R&D Management*, Vol. 34, No. 1, 65–75.

Cohen, W. and Levinthal, D.A. (1989). Innovation and learning: The two faces of R&D. *The Economic Journal*, Vol. 99, No. 397, 569–596.

218 Strategies and governance

Cohen, W. M., Florida, R., Randazzese, L. and Walsh, J. (1998). Industry and the academy: Uneasy partners in the cause of technological advance. In Noll, R. G. (ed.), *Challenges to Research Universities* (pp. 171–199). Washington, DC: Brookings Institute Press.

Crump, G. (2013). *A cloud strategy for small and medium-sized businesses.* Retrieved 2 January 2014, from www.storage-switzerland.com/Articles/Entries/2013/3/20_A_Cloud_Storage_Strategy_For_The_SMB.html

Dasgupta P. and David, P. A. (1994). Towards a new economics of science. *Research Policy*, Vol. 23, No. 5, 487–521.

Dosi, G., Llerena, P. and Labini, M. S. (2006). The relationships between science, technologies and their industrial exploitation: An illustration through the myths and realities of the so-called 'European Paradox'. *Research Policy*, 35, 1450–1464.

Etzkowitz, H. (2002). *The triple helix of university – industry – government. Implications for policy and evaluation.* Working paper 2002–11. Stockholm, Sweden: Science Policy Institute.

Godin, B. (2006). The Linear model of innovation: The historical construction of an analytical framework. *Science, Technology & Human Values*, Vol. 31, No. 6, 639–667.

Goldfarb, B. and Henrekson, M. (2003). Bottom-up versus top-down policies towards the commercialization of university intellectual property. *Research Policy*, Vol. 32, No. 4, 639–658.

Harmon, B., Ardishvili, A., Cardoso, R., Elder, T., Leuthold, J., Parshall, J., Raghian, and M., Smith, D. (1997). Mapping the university technology transfer process. *Journal of Business Venturing*, Vol. 12, No. 6, 423–434.

Jaruzelski, B. and Dehoff, K. (2008). Beyond borders: The global innovation 1000. *Strategy and Business*, Vol. 53, Winter.

Komninos, N., Miariti, C., Milossis, D., Tsarchopoulos, P. and Zaharis, N. (2010). Valorisation of academic R&D: The INTERVALUE platform. *Proceedings of the 3rd International Conference on Entrepreneurship, Innovation and Regional Development* (pp. 404–411). Novi Sad, Serbia: ICEIRD.

Komninos, N., Sefertzi, E. and Tsarchopoulos P. (2006). Virtual innovation environment for the exploitation of R&D (Vol. 2, pp. 95–104). *Intelligent Environments 06 Conference*. Athens, Greece: Institution of Engineering and Technology.

National Intelligence Council. (2012). *Global trends 2030: Alternative worlds.* Retrieved 2 January 2014, from www.dni.gov/nic/globaltrends.

Pater, M. (2009). *Co-creation's 5 guiding principles.* White Paper No 1, Fronteer Strategy, Retrieved 2 January 2014, from www.fronteerstrategy.com/uploads/files/FS_Whitepaper1-Co-creation_5_Guiding_Principles-April2009.pdf.

Reagans, R. and McEvily, B. (2003). Network structure and knowledge transfer: The effects of cohesion and range. *Administrative Science Quarterly*, Vol. 48, No. 2, 240–267.

Social Media Examiner (2011). *How marketers are using social media to grow their businesses. Social media marketing report.* Retrieved 2 January 2014, from http://issuu.com/bepperiva/docs/socialmedia_marketingreport_2011

Stewart, M. D. and Carayannis, E. (2013). Dystechnia: a model of technology deficiency and implications for entrepreneurial opportunity. *Journal of Innovation and Entrepreneurship*, Vol. 2, No. 1. Retrieved 2 January 2014, from www.innovation-entr.epreneurship.com/content/2/1/1.

Szulanski, G. (2000). The process of knowledge transfer: A diachronic analysis of stickiness. *Organizational Behavior and Human Decision Processes,* Vol. 82, No. 3, 9–27.

Townsend, A., Soojung-Kim Pang, A. and Weddle R. (2009). *Future knowledge ecosystems: The next twenty years of technology-led economic development.* IFTF Report Number SR-1236. Research Triangle Park, NC: Research Triangle Foundation.

Von Hippel, E. (2005). *Democratizing innovation.* Cambridge, MA: MIT Press.

Waugaman, P. G. and Tornatzky, L. G. (2001). *Benchmarking university-industry technology transfer in the south and the EPSCoR states.* Research Triangle Park, NC: Southern Technology Council.

Zygiaris, S. and Sefertzi, E. (eds) (2012). *Cost cutting innovative technologies.* Thessaloniki, Greece: Aristotle University of Thessaloniki, URENIO Research.

10 Smart city infrastructure

Applications and solutions every city should have

1. Infrastructure and applications every city should have

As happens in early stages of any industry, the landscape of smart cities is chaotic, with many competing products, devices, and services; little standardisation; and the dominant players competing over imposing their solutions in this rising market. On the other hand, cities and city authorities are looking for proven solutions, promising technologies and applications, and solutions that guarantee a positive impact and that are sustainable in the long run.

The applications and smart solutions that every city should have are a concern for all actors involved in smart city development, in academia, consulting, and planning, and for technology providers and city leaders. Blogs and company websites often outline portfolios of solutions that cities should implement (City 2.0, n.d.; Libelium, n.d.; Mashable, n.d.). In this chapter, we present a group of 15 solutions that all cities should implement. This portfolio of solutions is based on two sources: on the one hand, the outcomes of surveys prepared in the context of the FIREBALL project, and on the other hand, the smart cities survey realised by the Committee of Digital and Knowledge-based Cities of UCLG (CDK-UCLG, 2013).

FIREBALL was a Coordination Action within the 7th Framework Programme (FP7) for ICT that ran in the period 2010–2012. The aim of this project was to bring together communities and stakeholders who are active in three areas for making smart cities, namely: research and experimentation on the Future Internet (FIRE), open and user-driven innovation (Living Labs), and city development. The goal was to develop a common vision of how the different approaches, methodologies, and policies in these communities can be aligned to boost innovation and the socio-economic development of smart cities and to establish a network of smart cities across Europe by adopting user-driven innovation to explore the opportunities offered by the Future Internet. The outcomes of the project can be found in the FIREBALL White Paper (2012), and the special issue of the *Journal of Knowledge Economy on Smart Cities and the Future Internet in Europe* (Komninos et al., 2013).

The CDK-UCLG (2013) survey offers an overview of the current situation of smart cities around the world, in terms of applications and solutions in the fields of smart economy, smart people, smart governance, smart mobility, smart environment, and smart living. In total, 28 cities – from Europe (13), Africa (5), Asia

Table 10.1 Applications and solutions every city should have

Domain	Solutions and applications
Broadband City	1. Broadband networks 2. Sensors networks 3. Open data – big data
Smart Economy	4. City branding and promotion 5. Online community marketplaces 6. Crowdfunding
Quality of Life	7. Monitoring environmental pollution 8. Safety in public spaces 9. Health advisor
Smart City Networks and Utilities	10. Smart metering for energy savings 11. Multimodal trip planner 12. Smart parking
Intelligent City Governance	13. Public services to citizens 14. Improve-my-City 15. e-Democracy

(1), and Latin America (9) – contributed to this survey by giving information and describing practices for smart city development. All city sizes were represented in the survey: small and medium-sized cities with a population of less than 100,000 (32 percent), larger cities from 100,000 to 1 million inhabitants (36 percent), and agglomerations with more than 1 million people (32 percent).

Thus, the FIREBALL survey focused on in-depth case studies in the cities of Barcelona, Helsinki, Lisbon, Manchester, Oulu, and Thessaloniki. The CDK-UCLG survey presented key performance indicators in the six areas of smart cities that were mentioned. Both surveys allow identification of experiences, practices and solutions, and lessons learnt. Based on these surveys, we propose a group of 15 solutions and applications that should be adopted by all cities (Table 10.1). Among them, some concern specific applications which we name, while in other cases the logic and functionality of solutions are described.

This portfolio of solutions does not include simple websites providing information in various fields, such as development incentives, government information, or advertising websites, but it does gather together more advanced solutions and applications, which create a basic smart infrastructure suitable for and adaptable to any type and size of city. Each solution is not about software only, but provides a combination of communities, hardware–software, information processes, and regulations for learning and improving the practices targeted.

2. Broadband city: networks, sensors, and open data

Broadband networks, sensors of various types – active, passive, human sensors – and open data offer the fundamental layer that every smart city should have, over which applications and e-services are deployed to optimise city activities, decision-making, and performance.

Broadband networks

In OECD countries, broadband network coverage varies considerably, among counties, cities, and access technologies. In fixed wired connections, Switzerland is at the top, with 41.6 subscriptions per 100 inhabitants (sp100i), including DSL, cable and fibre-LAN connections, and Turkey at the bottom, with 10.4 sp100i. Most EU countries are between 20 and 35 sp100i, while the average OECD figure is 26 subscriptions per 100 inhabitants (OECD, 2012a). The top technology in wired subscriptions is DSL (54.8 percent of total broadband subscriptions), followed by cable modem (30.4 percent) and fibre-LAN (14.2 percent). Fibre broadband connections are generally low, with the exception of five countries (Japan, Korea, Sweden, Slovakia, and Norway) in which the percentage of fibre connections in terms of total broadband is more than 20 percent. However, in the majority of OECD countries, fibre connections are below 3 percent of total wired broadband.

In wireless connections, Korea holds the top position, with 104 subscriptions per 100 inhabitants – including satellite, terrestrial fixed-wireless, and standard and data-dedicated mobile – and Mexico is in the lowest position, with 9.8 sp100i. In the EU, Sweden, Finland, and Denmark are at the top with about 100 sp100i, while most EU countries have coverage between 60 and 40 sp100i. The OECD average is 56.6 subscriptions per 100 inhabitants, more than double the figure for fixed-wired connections (OECD, 2012b). In wireless broadband, the top technology is mobile, in which standard and data-dedicated subscriptions account for 99.1 percent of all wireless connections. The fact that mobile has become the major broadband access technology enables smart city services on the move, and location-based services offered while citizens are engaging in activities in the physical space of cities.

Broadband through Wi-Fi hotspots is another important technology for smart cities. This type of access is not measured in broadband statistics. More and more cities, however, are developing networks of Wi-Fi hotspots with the aim of providing Internet access to citizens. The CDK-UCLG study shows that among the 27 cities that participated in the survey, 62 percent offer Wi-Fi hotspots. This percentage is higher in Europe, with 85 percent of cities having developed such infrastructure. The number of hotspots varies considerably, up to 25 hotspots in 54 percent of cities, between 26 and 50 in 15 percent of cities, and more than 500 hotspots in another 15 percent. The survey sample is very small, but nevertheless it is indicative of the trend towards local Wi-Fi networks deployment and the number of hotspots per city. A case of wide city coverage is 'Wireless Taipei – Taipei Infinity' which covers more than 90 percent of the city's areas serving a population of 2.3 million inhabitants and offering Internet access to citizens and visitors free of charge and without limit.

The wireless technologies used in smart cities vary in terms of bandwidth and range: near-frequency communication (NFC) works in low bandwidth and a very close range; GSM, 3G, and 4G have variable bandwidth between 100 Kb and 6Mb and range up to 10km; Wi-Fi and Wi-Max work at 10Mb max and with a range of between 50 m and 10Km; and wireless ultrawideband works at 1Gb but at a very short distance of a few meters (Tsarchopoulos, 2013). The juxtaposition of different networking technologies make the broadband networks of smart cities heterogeneous, consisting of a variety of communication modes and technologies. A 'heterogeneous network' is a network which provides communication to its subscribers using many different access technologies and a common core (typically a packet) which interconnects with and obtains the cooperation of all heterogeneous technologies. For instance, a heterogeneous network can include wired and wireless access technologies, such as GSM, Universal Mobile Telecommunications System (UMTS), and WLAN, and users enjoy services regardless of the access technology employed. Instead of relying on a single large network, the area is covered with many smaller networks (cells), each of which offers better performance to its users.

Sensor networks

Over broadband networks, a layer of sensors and measurement devices connected to wired, wireless, and Wi-Fi networks can collect data about the functioning of the city. Data about the city, generated while it is working, creates gigabit datasets and 'gigabit cities.' The 'Internet of Things' (IoT) is the term used to denote the recent most important technological development in smart cities, based on the use of sensors, actuators, and RFID tags to identify and control the activities and infrastructure of cities. The IoT becomes possible through sensor networks, which collect streams of information from smart objects, city activities, and utility networks. According to Gartner, "The Internet of Things is the network of physical objects that contain embedded technology to communicate and sense or interact with their internal states or the external environment" (Gartner, n.d.). A large variety of sensors is already on the market. Libelium, for instance, offer sensors which can record information and support services in various domains of city life, such as smart parking assistance and parking space availability in the city; structural health – monitoring vibrations and material conditions in buildings; urban noise – sound monitoring in central city zones; electromagnetic fields – measurement of energy radiated by cell stations and Wi-Fi routers; traffic congestion – monitoring vehicles and pedestrian movement to optimise driving and walking routes; smart lighting – weather-adaptive lighting in streetlights; waste management – detection of rubbish levels in containers to optimise trash collection routes; and intelligent highways with warning messages and diversions according to conditions en route and unexpected events or traffic jams (Libelium, n.d.).

Open data – big data

Many cities offer data collected from sensor networks and from transactions between citizens and the public administration as open data. Sensor data, government data, and data provided by citizens on social media are the main sources of open data in cities. The Open Knowledge Foundation (OKF) uses the Open Data Index to assess the offer of open government data around the world, in fields such as transport timetables, government budget, government spending, election results, company register, national map, national statistics, legislation, postcodes, and emissions of pollutants (OKF, n.d.).

224 *Strategies and governance*

Open data can be freely used, reused, and redistributed by anyone, provided that reference is made to the authors, and datasets are further available under the same conditions (Open Definition, n.d.). There are no restrictions arising from copyright, patents, or other mechanisms of control. An Open License (i.e., CC0, PDDL, CC-BY-4.0, CC-BY or other) ensures that information is freely available from the 'producer.' However, such license does not guarantee the absence of defects or irregularities that may be contained in the information. The 'reuser' is solely responsible for the reuse of information for reproduction, copying, publication and transmission purposes. The reuser is authorised to adapt, modify, extract, and transform information to create derived information without misleading third parties as to the content of the information. The reuser may also use the information for commercial, provided that he includes a citation indicating the information's authors.

Tim Berners-Lee proposed a five-star assessment scale for Open Data indicating different stages of 'openness': 1 star, make data available on the Web (whatever the format) under an open license; 2 stars, make data available in structured and machine-readable format (e.g., Excel instead of image scan of a table); 3 stars, use non-proprietary formats (e.g., CSV, instead of Excel); 4 stars, use a Uniform Resource Identifier (URI) to denote things; and 5 stars, link data to other data, presenting its networks relationships and providing meaning and context (EPSI Platform, 2013).

In smart cities, open data from various sources (sensors, citizens and businesses, public administration) create opportunities for advanced analytics, visualisation, and intelligence – allowing patterns to be detected, alerts generated, and information depicted on the physical space of cities through augmented reality applications. In the near future, media research and technology are expected to offer new solutions that might work in parallel with the IoT and embedded systems, providing new opportunities for content management (European Commission, 2010a). Technologies, such as content and context fusion, immersive multi-sensory environments, location-based content dependent on user location and context, augmented reality applications, open and federated platforms for content storage and distribution, are expected to offer new ground for e-services within the ecosystems of cities (European Commission, 2010b).

3. Smart economy: city branding, marketplaces, and crowdfunding

Smart economy is the first area that the CDK-UCLG survey examined and refers to the contribution of 'smart' industries and the use of ICTs to improve production processes and the economic competitiveness of cities. For the cities that took part in the survey, smart economy is related to: Internet usage in enterprises; financial promotion through collaborative and participatory strategy design; retaining and attracting talent through support programmes for creative businesses; entrepreneurship and startup support; development of business spaces; and international promotion and positioning plans and strategies. A great variety of digital spaces and applications are used to serve these objectives. Here, we will focus on

Smart city infrastructure 225

three areas – branding, marketplaces, and funding – which can be implemented in any city and provide economic advantages through innovation and smart environments.

City branding

'Destination branding' is another term to denote the promotion of a place's identity using marketing and communications means. Most authors agree that destination branding is the total perception of a place as shaped by ideas, images, and assessments of consumers (Anholt, 2007; Baker, 2007; Moilanen and Rainistro, 2008). Cities that have a branding strategy disseminate an articulated concept, such as the brand of Barcelona as a global trademark for refined urban life and advanced design; the brand of Bilbao as a trademark for art, eco-technology, and design; and the brand of Languedoc-Roussillon as a place where true luxury is simply 'being there.' As part of an intelligent city strategy, city branding is the collaborative formation of an identity and promotion of that identity using digital means, the Web, and smart technologies. It includes a sequence of three interlinked stages: (1) core values formulation, (2) development of communication strategy, and (3) digital dissemination–implementation.

Core values

Initially, the community – the living city – through a participatory process and open consultation, has to define the identity that it wishes to promote and the concept, signs, and symbols that express this identity. Elements of identity can be found in its history, nature, culture, events, tradition, people, customs, entertainment, and luxury. Each city has to bring together a unique combination of such values under a coherent narrative and produce visualisations with signs, images, designs, logos, colours, and aesthetic means. Since city branding aims to sustain the competitive advantage of cities, it should be expected that selected identities will reflect local production capabilities, products, and services in an all-inclusive perspective. This is extremely difficult to achieve, given the diversity of cities. Each city is a locus of a large and complex group of products, services and producers, which is heterogeneous and pluralistic. The collaborative approach and open consultation have to narrow down this diversity, select a promotion concept, and build the city brand on this.

Promotion strategy

This is then followed by identifying the promotion strategy and practices, such as setting of objectives, selecting target groups and the physical and digital means to be used, and selecting communication channels, available resources, measurement, and adjustments. It is the equivalent of a large-scale marketing and promotion plan deployed on a global scale, in diverse cultural environments, languages, and contexts. Again, collaboration is important and branding authorities should seek partners from the public, private, and voluntary sectors and encourage them to become brand adopters (Heeley, 2011). Creating local communities of practice to sustain different aspects of the brand is a usual practice.

Digital implementation

The last stage is deployment of the city branding digital implementation, with an array of instruments for reaching global audiences. A complex and wide digital platform is needed to support and integrate all functionalities and technologies, Web, smartphones, virtual city and monument tours, search engine optimisation, use of social media, content management systems, analytics, and more specialised applications, such as destination hopping and hospitality services. Deployment of the branding portal includes applications and support, data updates, maintenance of social media pages, and constant communication with city companies and services, as well as the use of analytics and brand strategy adjustments. Content analysis of tourist portals in southern European destinations shows large differences in their online presence, due not only to the changing philosophy of Web promotion at various destinations, but also to different territorial characteristics, especially in terms of facilities and services that cities offer (Koutoulas, 2011).

Online community marketplaces

e-commerce is far beyond the reach of most small companies located in cities. Due to the low skills level and IT literacy, fear of e-banking and credit card transactions, limited turnover and financial resources, trading on the Internet, and e-sales and e-purchases is very limited. According to Eurostat 2010 data, the main factors inhibiting the buying and selling of goods online are related to the security of payments (11 percent), privacy (10 percent), receiving or returning goods and getting redress (9 percent), access to payment card (4 percent), delivery (3 percent), difficulty in finding relevant information on the website (3 percent), and other reasons (3 percent) (European Consumer Centre, 2012). Overall in the EU, e-commerce is fairly low, with average e-sales practiced by 15 percent of enterprises only, while e-purchasing is more advanced, being practiced by 20–60 percent of enterprises (Eurostat, 2010). Community marketplaces offer a good solution to this gap, enabling small companies to be actively involved in e-sales, keeping development and maintenance costs down, while assuring technical support and high capability of customer reach. Online city marketplaces are the digital equivalent of contemporary malls, grand bazaars, and the covered markets of the Ottoman and Middle East cities that house hundreds of small merchants.

Such e-marketplaces are created by communities of merchants. The community is the founding institution, as well as the management and development agency of the e-marketplace. The community settles the market, gathers a critical mass of merchants, offers training, supports the initiation of individual e-stores on the market, promotes the market, and offers the necessary trust and social capital for collaboration. As the community grows, other categories of actors – citizens, customers, trade associations – start participating more actively. Apart from initiating the marketplace, the role of the community is to guarantee and implement the rules of good operation, regulating complaints and dispute management, and other issues of transactions concerning prices, unsolicited goods and inertia selling, hidden costs, secure transactions, and delivery.

Every individual e-shop in the e-marketplace maintains full control over merchandise, e-content, transactions, and the continuous update of the shop. Marketing practices are placed under the regulation of the e-marketplace community, in terms of product categories, practices, and marketing ethos. The collective character of the marketplace offers higher levels of trust, restricting the factors that inhibit online commerce, such as security of payments, returning goods, payments by credit cards, fraud, and fake traders. Within the marketplace, even the smaller e-shop works under the high-quality standards that only big trading companies can traditionally offer.

Many different Web solutions and applications are available for marketplaces and e-shops, such as the Columbia Heights, Ujamaa Collective, Blink, and others. Usually the e-marketplace is a common platform on which e-shops are created and function as separate entities. It appears as an agglomeration of e-shops accessible via the Web or smart phones. Use of open source platforms for e-marketplaces is a good starting point for every city.

In the context of the CIP PEOPLE project, we developed an open source solution for a virtual city marketplace, which is composed of five interrelated subsystems: a business directory with descriptions and locations of businesses on the map, a virtual marketplace with e-shops, product promotion and offers, customer assessment of e-shops, and a shopping optimisation engine for best product baskets creation. E-shops are presented by categories on a list and on the map. They are managed at multiple levels, with different access rights to each level. Shopkeepers can create, modify, and manage their stores, create e-content, upload photos and videos, and publish promotions. Content automatically feeds the social media pages of the shop. Users can create accounts, register, review articles, and give assessments and comments. The marketplace administrator oversees the proper functioning of the system overall. Customer assessments are published with the option of having been validated by the administrator. The system generates a QR code for each e-shop, which can be placed on the entrance of the shop and give access to promotions via smart phone scans. Analytics are provided by the system offering data on e-shop frequency, items views, and customer assessments. This is an open source solution under GPLv3, and users can download the application from the Github (https://github.com/icos-urenio/virtual-city-market).

Crowdfunding

Crowdfunding is a form of resources pooling and collaborative funding, enabling a community to select between alternative investments offered, and to raise funds for those given the highest priority. Collaborative funding is considered as the next frontier in the shareable economy, and with the rise of crowdfunding platforms it has become a mainstream method for gathering financial resources for social, community, and creative projects. Crowdfunding has helped cover a specific funding gap. UK crowdfunding, for instance, complements and covers equity gaps in innovation funding between £0.5 and £2 million, which are not covered by personal savings, venture capital, and other forms of equity funding (Pierrakis, 2012).

Many alternative forms of crowdfunding are possible, such as donations and philanthropy, individuals pre-ordering a product, equity funding in exchange for a share of future profits, and public funding in which the community contributes when individuals have already covered a part of the investment. Other definitions are narrower and cover some of the above funding types only, for instance crowdfunding as "the provision of financial resources either in form of donation or in exchange for the future product or some form of reward and/or voting rights" (Belleflamme et al., 2012, p. 7). The benefits of crowdfunding are multiple: pooling money; raises visibility on key issues and projects; increases collaborative learning; gives access to an array of opinions; and links to the local, national, or even global, finding of resources.

In crowdfunding, making the selection between the alternative funding options offered is influenced by peers more than externalities. The study by Ward and Ramachandran (2011) shows that investors are more influenced by information aggregating devices, such as popularity lists, and by the information provided by projects in blog updates than by more granular information sources. They are also influenced by the success or failure of related projects, and use other similar investments to guide funding decisions. However, projects can quickly go out of favour in the investment community unless their managers achieve and maintain momentum in their funding drive.

In every city, a crowdfunding platform can be created to offer opportunities for raising funds and implementing projects, whether they are individual or community projects, for which the usual funding channels would be ineffective. The basic idea is to raise external finance from a large pool of participants, where each one contributes with some amount. Social networks and Internet platforms enable them to gather attention and funds.

Wordpress, the leading open source content management system, presented a plugin for crowdfunding developed by Astoundify for WordPress. It is an extension that seamlessly integrates with Easy Digital Downloads. The plugin allows one to crowdsource a large variety of projects from films, games, and music to art, design, and technology. The Astoundify Crowdfunding plugin is designed to work alongside PayPal Adaptive Payments or the Stripe gateway so that pledges are collected but no funds are taken until the campaign reaches its goal (http://wordpress.org/plugins/appthemer-crowdfunding/).

Kim (2012) compiled a list of crowdfunding platforms and presented 41 different types of such funding: general crowdfunding platforms; crowdfunding for social causes, for health and medical, for small and local businesses, for science, for music, for education, and for gaming and apps; and crowdfunding for startups and companies. Two types of innovation funding are supported on these platforms. Innovators can pledge support for an idea or project as a donation or in exchange of some kind of reward or use value. On the other hand, innovations can ask for crowdinvesting. However, the latter requires that funding regulations be loosened to permit more people to take part and invest in what they consider a promising venture. Good examples for cities and community funding are Fundrazr (https://fundrazr.com/), which allows money to be raised for group, political, and non-profit causes; Causes (www.causes.com/); Causevox (www.causevox.com/) for social fundraising campaigns; Kickstarter, the largest fund for creative projects; Petridish, to support scientists for research projects and expeditions; and Public Interest Projects (www.publicinterestprojects.org/), which strengthens the work of philanthropic institutions, non-profit groups, and other public-interest organisations.

4. Quality of life: environment, safety, and health care

The city is a place for living and a world of consumption. Quality of life is an important driver of urbanisation and the degradation of living conditions, during periods of crisis and restructuring, is a central concern for all cities. Quality of life problems arise from inequality, poverty, pollution, segregation, and crime. Smart city solutions are available to confront those challenges and improve the environment, safety in public spaces, and health conditions.

Monitoring environmental pollution

Most cities suffer from environmental pollution due to use of fossil fuels in industry, transport, and housing. Statistics have shown that air pollution in the cities of developed and developing countries is a great threat to public health. Small airborne particles and toxic components of urban air are drivers of disease and mortality (Samet et al., 2000). It is a high priority for cities to monitor and regulate the maximum levels allowable in a 24-hour period, rather than on an annual basis. Sensor-based solutions are available to this end. They can help with monitoring air pollutants and micro-particles, and can alert city authorities and citizens about the quality of the environment round the clock.

A low-cost solution that we have tested successfully is based on Libelium devices. It uses four types of elements (Libelium, n.d.):

- Waspmote hardware, which offers 8 different wireless communication interfaces including long range (3G / GPRS), medium range (802.15.4, ZigBee, WiFi), and short range (Bluetooth, RFID, NFC), and is designed for extremely low energy consumption.
- The sensor board with sockets for placing sensors, which is connected to Waspmote. Many different sensors are available to measure carbon monoxide, carbon dioxide, oxygen, methane, hydrogen, ammonia, isobutane, ethanol, toulene, hydrogen sulphide, nitrogen dioxide, ozone, hydrocarbons, temperature, humidity, and atmospheric pressure.
- Meshlium, a Linux router and the gateway to the sensors. It contains five different radio interfaces, WiFi 2.4GHz, WiFi 5GHz, 3G / GPRS, Bluetooth, and ZigBee. Meshlium communicates with the sensor board, receives data that is stored locally, and sends it to the database at the central server.

230 *Strategies and governance*

- The applications, which take data from the router (Meshlium or other) and present it on the PC or smartphone. The Waspmote API is available as an open source Web application on the Github. Applications for iPhone and Android are also available from the respective download centres.

This solution allows data on environmental conditions to be collected from monitoring stations, driven to a central hub, measurements presented on PCs and smart phones, and alerts generated in cases where pollutants go beyond established limits. Data can also be offered as open data in csv format.

Safety in public spaces

Risk of crime and actual crime is another area of increasing concern, influencing the selection of location for living and the management of housing neighbourhoods. This is particularly true for developing counties, where urban development is taking place in a spontaneous and in a less coordinated manner. But in developed countries, as well, crime is unevenly distributed geographically and the increase of suburban wealth is frequently accompanied by shoplifting, drug abuse and aggravated assault.

The CDK-UCLG survey shows that the majority of cities (61 percent) have implemented ICT systems to improve public safety. Measures taken include the provision of portable equipment to municipal police officers (Barcelona), giving access to police online information systems, and accident and emergency handling systems; use of surveillance cameras in vital city areas and districts (Bilbao, Katowice), allowing people and objects to be identified; emergency buttons and speaking stands in the city (Mexico); as well as sensor-based devices to capture drivers violating red lights at locations with high accident rates.

The urban tradition, however, is to address crime through community and environmental design. The ideas of Elizabeth Wood, the first Executive Director of the Chicago Housing Authority; Jane Jacobs' 'eyes on the street' described in *The Death and Life of Great American Cities* (Jacobs, 1992); and design principles that increase socialisation can lead to a reduction of fear and crime incidence in cities (Crowe, 2000). Continuing this tradition in the age of intelligent cities means empowering the citizen and the community with information, alert, and quick response to prevent criminal behaviour.

Crime mapping is an important step towards a more secure urban environment. Data and applications are needed to implement crime mapping. For the US, applications are available for computer notebooks and smart phones. The 'Crime-Mapping' app, for instance (www.crimemapping.com/), for the Web and mobiles helps to sustain law enforcement and reduce crime through a better-informed citizenry. The application maps recent crime activity at the city neighbourhood level, covering 16 types of crimes, such as assault, theft, robbery, vandalism, car break-ins, and others. 'Neighbourhood-Scouts' helps assess the level of safety in neighbourhoods, aggregate crime data from various sources, and provide information about safe or dangerous neighbourhoods and cities across the US, (www.neighborhoodscout.com).

Some cities are also developing their own applications and solutions. The city of Wylie, Texas, for, instance, announced the launch of Regional Analysis and Information Data Sharing Online, an iPhone application that helps residents search for criminal activity in their neighbourhood, report crime anonymously, and get alerts and neighbourhood watch reports.

It is a priority for every city to open crime data up to the public and to develop a city portal and applications that inform citizens and ask for engagement with information and ideas about crime prevention, risk avoidance, and risk reduction. In developing such dedicated content management systems, the social media can significantly contribute, with communities and interest groups to identify criminal activity, notify the public, and ensure outreach action (see also, Backgroundcheck, n.d.).

E-health advisor

E-health is defined as "patients and the public using the Internet or other e-media to disseminate or provide access to health and lifestyle information or services" and it is currently provided to citizens in emergency cases, neither on a large scale nor for everyday treatment (Stamatelatos et al., 2012, p. 311). According to the CDK-UCLG survey, the most usual e-health solutions in smart cities are: electronic health cards; online medical services such as online appointments, electronic prescriptions, and digital dossiers; and remote control and alarm systems. The most technologically advanced are telemonitoring applications providing real-time medical services to people with disabilities or chronic diseases. They can offer continuous monitoring, detection, and alert for critical events and delivery of preventive and corrective actions. Systems are partly automated with data being collected by sensors, but information is processed and response actions are designed by trained professionals. Home remote control and alarm systems for patients work in the same way, which include home access services, tele-alarm, TV patient monitoring, and video-to-video over the Internet. They can help citizens to act more effectively in various circumstances, such as real-time support, medical advice, unforeseen events, and patient requests. They are offered in a few cities only (Bilbao, Havre, Malmo), and in many cases on an experimental basis.

To be effective, such platforms and electronic applications should be integrated into the medical system and services of each city and offered systematically and professionally. However, the role of citizens is rather passive in defining a demand and receiving a service remotely via the Internet. But, a smart city is a place of collective intelligence, where solutions are produced collaboratively with the engagement of citizens and users. From a collective intelligence perspective, e-health in smart cities should be based on collaborative solutions, with the active involvement of citizens in content and solutions creation. A city-wide 'e-health advisor' is an application that would move us in this direction.

Available e-health advisors are based on the combination of expert and content management systems and locally available medical services. They are offered as applications for medical assistance, ranging from low to almost fully automated systems. From a software perspective, the 'advisor' starts with various responses given by the user and produces a report suggesting a roadmap for professional medical advice, based on the input given. Using an expert roadmap, the system refers the patient to appropriate medical support services available in the city. Functionalities of the application include access over the Internet; user registration; online maintenance of health records; online advice and referrals to local health professionals and hospitals; user upload of personal experiences; user review and rating of medical services; disease databases and alternative treatment methods; and similar cases; as well as self-diagnostic tools. A trusted city authority can guarantee data privacy and system neutrality as far as the professional advice is concerned. Users should also be able to make their own choices for medical support, based on content and ratings by other users.

5. Smart city networks and utilities

Cities are systems of activities, districts, and clusters over networks. Networks – transport, energy, water, waste, and communication – make up the backbone of the urban system over which city ecosystems city-districts are placed and connected. Networks and government are key elements which integrate production and consumption activities and make cities work as a coordinated whole.

In smart city planning and development, networks offer a primary field for implementing smart environments, smart grids and metering, sensor-based solutions, and intelligence from big data sets. Usually, the objective of these systems is optimisation: to improve the efficiency of operation and economise resources without compromising the quality of the service offered. From an extremely large field of potential applications, we focus on three solutions for energy savings and green mobility which can be easily implemented in any city.

Smart metering for energy saving

This solution is based on smart meters embedded into a city district – housing, commercial, office, or other district – to monitor energy consumption and help define energy-saving behaviour. There is no single definition for a smart meter, but the most common interpretation implies that the meter supports two-way communication, enabling measurements to be taken and the device to be switched on–off (Haney at al., 2009). Apart from energy monitoring and savings, smart energy metering introduces a cultural change in pursuit of energy efficiency, the most important strategic choice to achieve CO_2 reduction targets. It is estimated that energy savings of between 5 percent and 15 percent can be obtained with the extended use of smart meters throughout Europe (Haney et al., 2009).

Such solutions have already been tested in many cities in Europe, with the best-known cases being those of Geuzenveld Sustainable Neighbourhood, Energy Management Haarlem, and West Orange in Amsterdam Smart City. They can also be part of more-complex smart grid systems which offer continuous monitoring of energy flows, coordination between energy demand and supply, opportunities to send consumer-produced electricity back to the grid, and optimisation of green energy use. Smart energy solutions directed towards the interior of buildings can help smooth out energy consumption peaks and create enormous savings in energy production.

The starting point for smart energy metering is a community, a group of users, or a cluster of activities whose intention is to adopt energy optimisation and saving practices. Implementing the solution includes a series of activities, such providing smart meters and installing them, connecting the meters to the local broadband network, meter reading and data visualisation, and collaborating in focus groups and benchmarking energy optimisation practices.

The hardware architecture includes a central smart meter hub, smart meters connected to various appliances, WiFi or ZigBee adapters over plugs, real-time portable displays, a LAN that gathers information from smart meters, and a district-wide area network connected to a central data system which integrates information from all local LANs. Software allows users to remotely turn appliances on or off, to programme periods of work and pause, to chart and compare live and historical data at local and district levels, and to analyse data and estimate future energy consumption.

Energy optimisation practices start at the level of each housing or working location, by reading and understanding where, how, and why energy is consumed, scheduling the switching of devices on and off, and reducing energy consumption, where appropriate. Focus groups can provide additional intelligence by analysing and comparing individual practices and consumption patterns. At the district level, the functioning of the entire district is monitored, and information can be transmitted to power generators for increased network functionality and overall improvement of the supplier's services. By identifying energy-spending patterns, the city-district can improve its overall environmental performance. Spending patterns can structure relations between users and suppliers, and provide different types of environmental benefits (Marvin et al., 1999).

Multimodal trip planner

This is also a fundamental application for every city. Transit information is usually complex, and citizens or city visitors are increasingly demanding information that will facilitate their journey and mobility in cities. In metropolitan areas and larger cities, it is important that users are informed about alternative routes and can choose between different transportation means. OpenTripPlanner (OTP) responds to these needs via a user-friendly Web application.

OTP is an open source multi-modal trip planner, which allows one to schedule city trips by combining information about pedestrian, bike, car, and public transportation on a Web-based interface. Some key characteristics of the application are: (1) detailed step-by-step directions alongside an interactive map showing the route, services the user can use, and where transfers should be made; (2) accessibility data can be used to make fixed-route plans easier; (3) transit information is offered for trips across all modes of transit, but walking and biking directions are also provided; (4) the user interface can be customised to match the agency's Web presence and brand; and (5) English is the default language but it is has been translated into Spanish and Polish, and translation in other languages is a matter of 500 words only (http://opentripplanner.com/).

The application runs on Linux and Windows, and potentially any platform using a Java virtual machine. OTP is released under the LGPL license, which allows developers to use and integrate LGPL code into their own software without being required to publish the source code of their own software. The code is being continuously developed, with many working demos all over the world. The actual current version 0.9.1 will be the final major one prior to the 1.0 release of OTP. This release will be a milestone and is expected to include support for real-time planning and the new mobile-optimised user interface developed for bikeplanner.org. The development of OpenTripPlanner started in 2009 as a collaboration between TriMet, OpenPlans, and other developers. Since then, an international community of users and developers has been involved. The code is hosted on the Github (Github-OTP, n.d.).

OTP has already been used for demonstration and testing purposes in several cities, including adaptation of the New York City subway map to OTP, and Portland, Oregon; Poznan and Lublin in Poland; Trento in Italy; Bilbao and Granada in Spain; Tel Aviv, in Israel; Pune in India; and Adelaide in Australia.

Overall, OPT offers a good solution compared to expensive custom trip planners, old scheduling software, or online transit information services offered by large companies.

Smart parking

A major problem in cities – specifically in the city centre, the historic centre, and the central business districts – is finding a parking place quickly and easily. High densities, large number of cars entering these zones, traffic regulations and restrictions, and roads given over to pedestrian use only make city parking difficult and costly. Several smart city solutions are available to facilitate parking with real-time information and within a reasonable range of the preferred location. They differ with respect to the technology used, the type of parking places proposed – on-street and off-street, parking garage – and payment modes. Every city can choose to implement a solution with respect to its needs and the budget available.

Search-engine-based solutions collect information from parking garages and offer information and services with respect to the position of the user. The driver can select the cheapest and most convenient parking place. BestParking is one such solution used in 90 cities and at 115 airports throughout North America (BestParking, n.d.). It includes a wide range of information, such as hours of operation for indoor parking spaces and on-street regulations for downtown areas. ParkMe is available for iPhones and helps users find parking by showing real-time availability, parking rates, hours of operation, payment types, and total free spots per parking garage. ParkMe is available in 28,000 locations, 1,800 cities, and 32 countries around the world (ParkMe, n.d.).

Sensor-based solutions rely on a network of sensors placed in parking spaces that inform drivers about real-time parking availability. The information from sensors (on–off) enables the creation of real-time parking maps in city areas covered with sensor networks. Users can select and pay for a parking space using a smart phone application. PayByPhone has been implemented in New York, San

Francisco, Miami, and London. It uses wireless sensors and drivers can find and pay for parking using a smartphone (PaybyPhone, n.d.).

Crowdsourcing-based solutions use information provided by users. Drivers are asked to announce that they have occupied a parking place and then their intent to pull out. iSpotSwap is one such application working with crowdsourcing and encouraging users to tag parking spots: "Tagging Spots is equal to Finding Spots" (iSpotSwap, n.d.). When a driver parks, the application asks him to enter the location and when he / she is planning on leaving, so that other drivers can be alerted to when the spot will be available. Similarly, the Waze application supports finding the best available route to a city destination, on the basis of real-time data from crowdsourcing traffic information offered by users (Waze, n.d.).

Apart from helping drivers in city centres and high-density areas, an additional value of such applications is their contribution to easing congestion. Drivers looking for a place to park often drive round and round in circles, thereby significantly increasing traffic congestion and air pollution. This environmental value of smart parking is equally important as its value in helping drivers find parking places.

6. Intelligent city governance

Intelligent city governance is about a set of electronic applications and solutions that enhance good government, political awareness, responsible citizenship, citizen participation in decision-making, and the provision of public services. It is a domain wider than the use of ICTs in government, entailing the redefinition of communication and interaction between citizens and government. It implies the redesign of the public administration's internal procedures to allow it to put a more open transparent, collaborative, and efficient administration in place. Governance is different from planning – the organised making of cities. It is about the framework conditions that define how cities are managed day-by-day and the infrastructure and services provided to enable such management. Usual solutions for governance include e-democracy, online administration services to citizens, emergency management, police and security, natural and technological risks management, and local digital agendas.

The CDK-UCLG survey places a series of services under the rubric 'smart city governance,' such as local public spending on ICT, website availability, strategic planning for e-government and ICT, online public services, electronic signatures, transparent governance, and e-democracy and electronic voting, as well as promoting ICT and innovation. This domain is the oldest and most developed in the digital-intelligent-smart city movement, and all cities have already developed some kinds of e-governance, ranging from online services to citizens to more advanced and interactive intelligent systems. Here, we present three solutions that are becoming more and more available to cities and citizens.

Public services to citizens

Applications for public services to citizens concern the administrative relationships between citizens and public authorities and allow digital transactions with the authorities. Objectives underpinning the use of digital transactions are gains

236 *Strategies and governance*

in time, effort, and distance as exchanges are carried out over a digital space. Citizens or companies can submit requests for various types of certificates, permits, payments, and other services offered by the public administration and conclude the transaction electronically. For every city, the goal is to increase the number of digital transactions between citizens and administrative services.

The CDK-UCLG survey shows that among online services offered by cities the most frequent is the lodging of complaints and claims. This is a service offered by 68 percent of the cities that took part in the survey. This is followed by requests for certificates and reports and by payments and debits made online, with 57 percent and 50 percent, respectively.

Applications that support electronic transactions in those domains rely on a combination of content management systems and electronic signatures. The content management system makes the administration services available to citizens by category or type of service. The electronic signature is legally equivalent to a handwritten signature and works with digital certificates. The electronic or digital certificate includes data that is used to identify the certificate holder, to exchange information with other entities, and to sign data being sent electronically.

Improve-my-City: citizens requests and participation

Improve my City (ImyC) is an application for participatory planning offered to residents of a municipality to go online and report local problems or place requests with the public administration. The application also allows them to make suggestions about how to improve the urban space and infrastructure in their area. Users can precisely pinpoint the location of the problem on a map and attach photographs. All reports appear on the map of the city, indicating areas that need more attention and support. Requests and problems that have been solved are presented separately. The application allows users to view updates about the progress in addressing the problems they reported.

Requests, reporting options, and suggestions are listed in 25 categories related to improvement of the city. Specific features of the application are that it allows reports to be pinpointed on the map of the area as icons, and to be viewed by category. Users can also access reports and comments from other users, vote about how important each request is, monitor progress in addressing requests, and apply various filters to requests. Following the notification case, the public administration undertakes to resolve the issues reported (Figure 10.1).

To ensure that the application runs more effectively, it is managed in a decentralised way by various departments of the city administration, and authorised officials handle the entries made and monitor requests in each category. How the public administration responds is the most important aspect of the application, since it records efficiency and effectiveness in resolving the problems reported. Innovation is based on a combination of crowdsourcing about city problems and the solutions suggested, while implementation relies on institutional action by the local authority and other public agencies.

ImyC is an open source application under the GPLv3 license. The code is on GitHub and supported by a community of developers. Because it is an open

Smart city infrastructure 237

| Web based front-end for citizens requests | Mobile apps for citizens requests |
| Web based back-end for resolving requests | Web analytics for understanding requests |

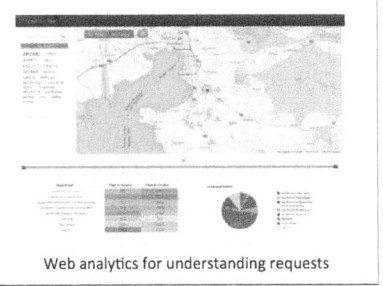

Figure 10.1 Improve-my-City application
Source: icos.urenio.org

source application developed on a well-known platform (Joomla), it was quickly adopted and now is offered in 25 different languages, with many implementations all over the world (GitHub-ImC, n.d.).

e-Democracy

e-democracy is a way for governments and citizens to interact using the Internet, mobile phones, and other communications equipment, which complements traditional methods of democratic governance. The normal objectives of e-democracy are to encourage citizen involvement in decision-making, to introduce forms of direct democracy, to develop more cohesive societies, and to encourage participation in public consultations and information distribution.

So far, only a small number of cities have installed e-democracy and voting applications. The CDK-UCLG survey estimates that only 15 percent of the cities surveyed have electronic voting systems in place.

There is no universal standard specifying the functions of e-democracy, and how it complements representative democracy, neither is there a standard form of the relevant electronic application. Coleman and Gotze (2002) identified four e-democracy scenarios: (1) technology supporting direct democracy, (2) encompassing online grass-roots civic communities of interest, (3) online surveys and opinion polls, and (4) technology as a way to engage citizens in policy deliberation. The Institute for Electronic Government (IEG) proposed a more elaborated model both for the purpose of defining and of implementing e-democracy. The IEG model is not limited to the citizen-to-government relationship, but also maps the progression from an informed to an engaged citizenry, and how successfully a government entity interprets and responds to the digital world. It is based on two axes, 'engagement' and 'influence,' whose intersection define four quadrants and types of e-democracy (Caldow, 2004):

- Q1 is passive, one-way, asynchronous, based on information search, legislation tracking, and Web casts.
- Q2 is two-way, asynchronous, tactical, based on email, online opinion polls, online surveys, and electronic voting.
- Q3 is collaborative, interactive participation, using dynamic monitoring of news and media, volunteer recruitment, fundraising, and online forums.
- Q4 is interactive, strategic, using e-petitions, e-consultation, e-policy, and e-diplomacy.

In the solution we have developed at URENIO, the e-democracy application consists of three modules. The first provides access to municipal council meetings, enabling citizens to watch current and past meetings of the municipal council and learn about decisions taken. The second is a public forum for debate which has been organised around dynamic topic categories. The third is e-referendums, which allows citizens to participate in remote voting via the web or smart phone.

7. Optimising smart city infrasructure

The continuous evolution of Web technologies and the large number of applications and solutions offered, has substantially widened the options for constructing the digital space of cities. An increasingly complex landscape of technologies, applications, data, and e-services is now offered. How to manage this complexity and retain the value of this soft infrastructure in the long run have become key concerns for most city authorities. A good combination, in terms of value for money and sustainability, is based on open source and cloud computing.

Open source software for intelligent cities is a valuable source of applications and solutions offered within a culture of sharing and reusing software. This goes together with the use of free open source software and participation in FOSS communities. Open source is ideal for city authorities and organisations that do not compete on software development and sales. Use existing software, re-use software, spend less and proceed by small steps, and minimise investments are safe ways to deal with smart city software infrastructure. To develop applications from scratch should be the last resort, in the case that no other solution is available.

With this philosophy in mind, we created ICOS, an intelligent cities open source community for sharing, re-using, and adapting software for intelligent cities (ICOS, n.d.). ICOS is a meta-repository of open source applications and solutions. Each application is categorised by the city function it serves, the type of software, its technical characteristics, and license type. ICOS is also a community of developers, planners, engineers, and users working in the field of intelligent / smart cities. It is addressed to anyone interested in intelligent / smart city

Smart city infrastructure 239

development looking for open source applications and solutions that have been successfully implemented in cities. On the technology supply side, it is aimed at developers wishing to disseminate applications and solutions they have created. On the demand side, ICOS is aimed at city authorities, infrastructure and utilities operators, and stakeholders wishing to use smart city solutions in order to increase the competitiveness, cohesion, and sustainability of the city. There is a stack of available technologies and open source solutions for intelligent cities, which any city planning authority has to take into account (Figure 10.2).

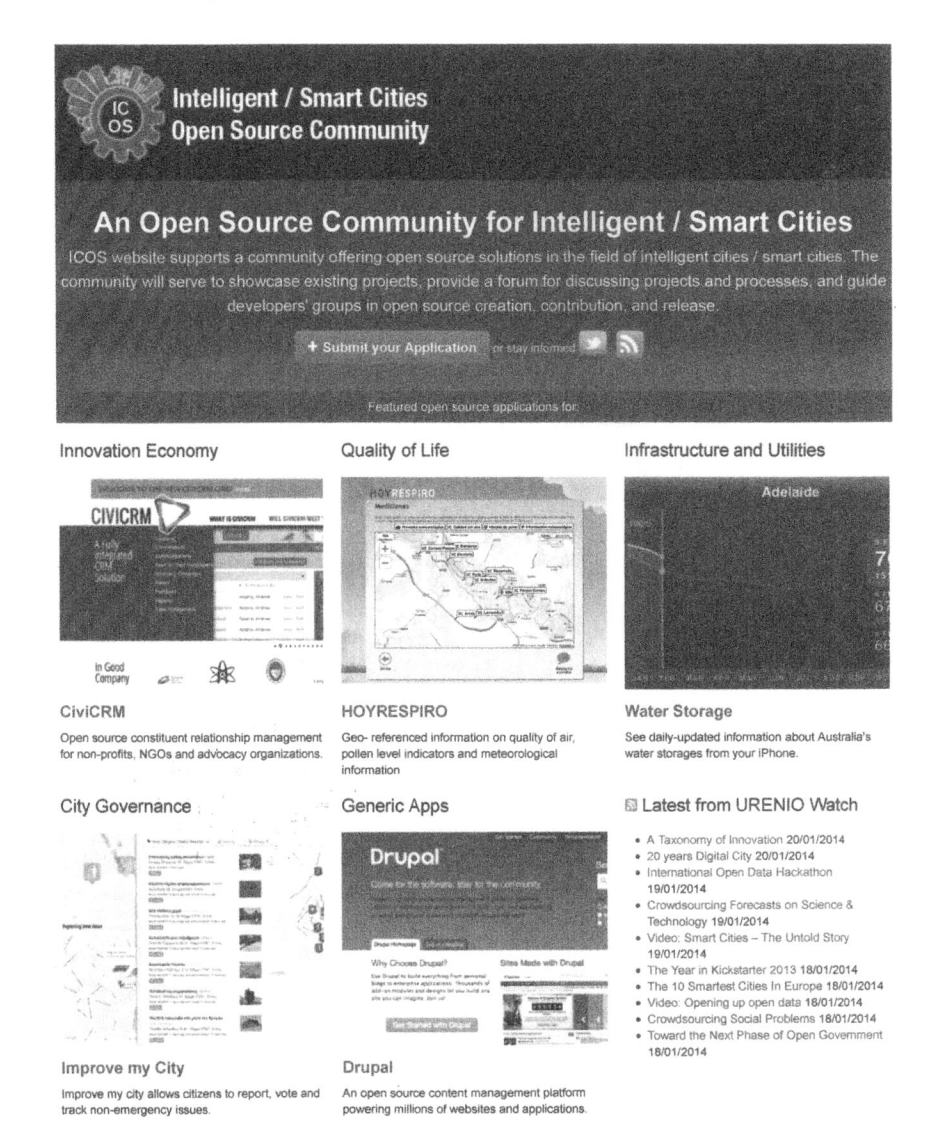

Figure 10.2 ICOS – Intelligent Cities Open Source Community

Source: www.urenio.icos.org

On ICOS, developers can present open source applications for intelligent cities in five categories serving:

- *The economy of cities:* Applications that support the operation of economic sectors, such as manufacturing, business services, financial services, commerce, tourism, education, research, recreation, health, etc.
- *Living in the city:* Applications that improve the quality of life, environmental monitoring and alert, social care, social services, social divides, and safety in the public spaces of cities.
- *City infrastructure and utilities:* Applications for optimising transport and mobility, energy, water, communication, and the corresponding utilities.
- *City governance:* Applications facilitating the provision of administration services to citizens, decision-making and democracy, participatory planning, and monitoring and measurement of city performance.
- *Generic platforms,* which can be used to create any kind of application or solutions in the previous four categories.

Cloud computing also emerges as a key enabling opportunity, allowing one to optimise service provisioning by automatically and seamlessly adjusting resources (bandwidth, infrastructures, data, etc.) to real-time demand, and therefore minimising infrastructure and computing costs. It creates a new momentum about accessing services and information anytime, anywhere, and from any device, and therefore improves the efficiency of operations. It helps increase the reliability of access to updated services and data, while at the same time offering new horizons for security. Finally, it allows for easier and more flexible cooperation and interchange between stakeholders, businesses, and citizens in global economies and societies.

Cities have much to gain by taking a cloud-computing approach to service delivery in their smart environments. However, they must have confidence that the benefits can be achieved without compromising core requirements and institutional values. Several issues may arise when public sector organisations are considering a transition to cloud computing. Some prominent concerns are related to assuring control of ICT systems by public managers and quality of service; ownership and liability issues; security and privacy; trust in the reliability and resilience of infrastructures and services; interoperability and standards; potential dependencies with vendors; regulation; and risk management; as well as governance and culture. Some of these challenges – like trust, reliability, and liability – can be addressed by the city cloud strategy and the choices made concerning technologies and providers. Others need to be approached by small steps, using proven solutions and taking stock of learning by doing.

A combination of open source with cloud-based solutions can offer enormous advantages by keeping cost down, due to non-propriety software, scalability, and the standardisation of solutions. Disruptive innovations in smart city environments become possible by minimising development costs and maximising the quality of services. These two technologies (open source and cloud) actually indicate the most important and urgent directions related to how digital technologies can support economic regeneration, social inclusion, smart energy efficiency, and the sustainable development of cities.

References

Anholt, S. (2007). *Competitive identity: The new brand management for nations, cities and regions*. Basingstoke, UK: Palgrave Macmillan.

Backgroundcheck. (n.d.). *Solving crime with social media*. Retrieved 2 January 2014, from www.backgroundcheck.org/solving-crime-with-social-media/.

Baker, B. (2007). *Destination branding for small cities: The essentials for successful place branding*. Portland, OR: Creative Leap Books.

Belleflamme, P., Lambert, T. and Schwienbacher, A. (2012). *Crowdfunding: Tapping the right crowd. CORE Discussion Paper No. 2011/32*. Retrieved 2 January 2014, from http://ssrn.com/abstract=1578175 or http://dx.doi.org/10.2139/ssrn.1578175.

BestParking. (n.d.). Website. Retrieved 2 January 2014, from www.bestparking.com/.

Caldow, J. (2004). *e-Democracy: Putting down global roots*. Washington, DC: Institute for Electronic Government, IBM.

CDK-UCLG. (2013). *Smart cities study: International study on the situation of ICT, innovation and knowledge in cities*. Bilbao, Spain: The Committee of Digital and Knowledge-Based Cities of UCLG. Retrieved 2 January 2014, from www.uclg.org/en/media/news/smart-cities-study-situation-ict-innovation-and-knowledge-cities.

City 2.0. (n.d.) *A gathering place for urban citizens to share innovations and inspire actions*. Retrieved 2 January 2014, from www.thecity2.org/.

Coleman, S. and Gotze, J. (2002). *Bowling together: Online public engagement in policy deliberation*, London, UK: Hansard Society

Crowe, T. (2000). *Crime prevention through environmental design*. Boston, MA: Butterworth-Heinemann.

EPSI Platform (2013). *Simple five level open data API evaluation model*. Retrieved 2 January 2014, from www.epsiplatform.eu/content/simple-five-level-open-data-api-evaluation-model.

European Commission. (2010a). *Future media Internet: Research challenges and road ahead*. DG Information Society and Media. Luxembourg: Publications Office of the European Union.

European Commission. (2010b). *Future media networks: Research challenges*. DG Information Society and Media. Luxembourg: Publications Office of the European Union.

European Consumer Centre. (2012). The European online marketplace consumer complaints 2010–2011. Retrieved 2 January 2014, from http://ec.europa.eu/consumers/ecc/docs/e-commerce-report-2012_en.pdf.

Eurostat. (2010). E-*commerce sales and purchases in the EU*. Retrieved 2 January 2014, from http://epp.eurostat.ec.europa.eu/statistics_explained/index.php/E-commerce_statistics.

FIREBALL White Paper. (2012). *Smart cities as innovation ecosystems sustained by the future Internet*. Retrieved 2 January 2014 from www.urenio.org/2012/04/23/smart-cities-fireball-white-paper.

Gartner. (n.d.). *Internet of Things. IT glossary*. Retrieved 2 January 2014, from www.gartner.com/it-glossary/internet-of-things.

GitHub-ImC, GitHub. (n.d.). *Improve my city*. Retrieved 2 January 2014, from https://github.com/icos-urenio/Improve-my-city.

GitHub-OTP. (n.d.). *GitHub open trip planner*. Retrieved 2 January 2014, from https://github.com/opentripplanner/OpenTripPlanner.

Haney, A. B., Janasb, T. and Pollitt, M. G. (2009) Smart metering and electricity demand: Technology, economics and international experience. *Working Paper, Energy Policy Research Group.* Cambridge, UK: University of Cambridge, Faculty of Economics. Retrieved 2 January 2014, from www.econ.cam.ac.uk/dae/repec/cam/pdf/cwpe0905.pdf.

Heeley, J. (2011). *City branding in western Europe.* Woodeaton, Oxford: Goodfellow Publishers Limited.

ICOS. (n.d.). *Intelligent cities open source community.* Retrieved 2 January 2014, from http://icos.urenio.org/.

iSpotSwap. (n.d.). Website. Retrieved 2 January 2014, from http://ispotswap.blogspot.gr/.

Jacobs, J. (1992). *The death and life of great American cities.* New York, NY: Vintage.

Kim, R. (2012). *A gigaOM guide to Kickstarter wannabes.* Retrieved 2 January 2014, from http://gigaom.com/2012/11/28/kickstarter-copycats/.

Komninos, N., Pallot, M. and Schaffers, H. (2013). Smart cities and the future Internet in Europe. *Special issue, Journal of Knowledge Economy*, Vol. 4, No. 2, 149–231.

Koutoulas, D. (2011). *Tourist marketing of southern Aegean.* Report to the Regional Authority of Southern Aegean.

Libelium. (n.d.). *50 sensor applications for a smarter world.* Retrieved 2 January 2014, from www.libelium.com/top_50_iot_sensor_applications_ranking.

Mashable. (n.d.). *25 technologies every smart city should have.* Retrieved 2 January 2014, from http://mashable.com/2012/12/26/urban-tech-wish-list/.

Marvin, S., Chappells, H. and Guy, S. (1999). Pathways of smart metering development: Shaping environmental innovation. *Computers, Environment and Urban Systems*, Vol. 23, No. 2, 109–126.

Moilanen T. and Rainistro, S. (2008). *How to brand nations, cities and destinations: A planning book for place branding.* Basingstoke, UK: Palgrave Macmillan.

OECD. (2012a). *Fixed wired broadband subscriptions per 100 inhabitants.* Broadband Portal. Retrieved 2 January 2014, from www.oecd.org/sti/broadband/oecdbroadbandportal.htm.

OECD. (2012b). *Wireless broadband subscriptions per 100 inhabitants*, June 2012. Broadband Portal. Retrieved 2 January 2014, from www.oecd.org/sti/broadband/oecdbroadbandportal.htm.

OKF.(n.d.). *Open data index.* Retrieved 2 January 2014, from https://index.okfn.org/.

Open Definition (n.d.). *Open definition.* Retrieved 2 January 2014, from http://opendefinition.org/.

ParkMe. (n.d.). Website. Retrieved 2 January 2014, from www.parkme.com.

PaybyPhone. (n.d.). Website. Retrieved 2 January 2014, from http://paybyphone.com/.

Pierrakis, Y. (2012). Financing university entrepreneurial ventures: Evidence from the UK. *Innopolis Final Conference.* Retrieved 2 January 2014, from http://conference.knowledgecities.eu/conference-organisation/papers-presentations/.

Samet, J. M., Domicini, F., Curriero, F. C., Coursac, I. and Zeger, S. (2000). Fine particulate air pollution and mortality in 20 US Cities 1987–1994, *The New England Journal of Medicine*, Vol. 343–24, 1742–1749.

Stamatelatos, M. et al. (2012). Video-to-video for e-health: Use case, concepts and pilot plan. *IFIP Advances in Information and Communication Technology*, Vol. 382, 311–321.

Tsarchopoulos, P. (2013). *Intelligent cities. Technologies, architectures and the governance of the digital space.* PhD dissertation. Thessaloniki: Aristotle University of Thessaloniki.

Ward, C. and Ramachandran, V. (2011). *Crowdfunding the next hit: Microfunding online experience goods.* Department of Operations and Information Systems, University of Utah. Retrieved 2 January 2014, from http://people.cs.umass.edu/~wallach/workshops/nips2010css/papers/ward.pdf.

Waze. (n.d.). Website. Retrieved 2 January 2014, from www.waze.com/.

11 The governance of intelligent city ecosystems

Communities, knowledge architectures, and innovation cycles

1. Toward a generic model of intelligent city governance

In the previous chapters, we discussed top-down and bottom-up planning for intelligent cities and strategies for intelligent clusters and districts, custom innovation ecosystems created by companies with the use of smart environments, and solutions for smart infrastructure that city authorities should implement. In this last chapter, we will attempt to define a generic *model of intelligent city governance* and how it adapts to the horizon of current trends in open innovation, smart systems, and big data. Our focus is the continuous enrichment of the spatial intelligence of cities thanks to the ceaseless contribution of urban communities, smart environments, and innovation processes. The main questions we address regard how to model key instances of governance for the transformation of urban systems into intelligent city entities, and how the governance model is affected by large-scale data provided by smart urban systems and the deepening of distributed knowledge patterns within cities.

We have described the *standard model of intelligent city structure* as composed of three fundamental layers, those of 'city,' 'innovation ecosystem,' and 'digital space' (Komninos, 2008). These layers composing intelligent cities comprise elements which appear in multiple forms (Table 11.1). This variety of forms and combinations lead to multiple configurations and forms of appearance of intelligent cities. For instance, over the last ten years, we have witnessed the rise of three successive innovation paradigms and three successive waves of digital technologies. In the field of innovation, the 'institutional paradigm' (national and regional systems, incubators, liaison offices, technology intermediary organisations, triple helix alliances) was followed by 'user-driven innovation,' democratising innovation and living labs, and recently, 'innovation through smart specialisation' has captured the interest of the European innovation community. In the sphere of the Web, Web 1.0 technologies using representation tools and one-way communication were succeeded by Web 2.0, the interactive Web of participatory content management systems, social media, and crowdsourcing, and now interest has turned towards embedded systems, the Internet of Things (IoT), sensor networks, machine-to-machine (M2M) communication, the Semantic Web, and cloud computing (Schaffers et al., 2012).

Table 11.1 Intelligent cities structural layers and elements

Layers	Elements within each layer				
City: urban system and subsystems	Agglomeration of population, activities, and externalities	Social space of cities: Sectors and districts of activities and uses	Physical space of cities: Buildings and infrastructure	Challenges: Conflicts and problems to resolve	Governance: Representation, administration and city management
Innovation ecosystems	Innovation actors and networks. Commercialisation of R&D. Linear innovation.	Innovation systems, clusters, technology districts. Innovation chains, triple and quadruple helix	Open innovation. Innovation platforms. Democratising innovation. Smart innovation systems	User-driven innovation. Living labs, experience design. Innovation competitions	Smart specialisation. Technology-driven innovation. Innovation branching
Digital spaces and smart environments	Communication: xDSL, FTTH, 3G and 4G, Wi-Fi, Wi-Max, Satellite	Embedded sensor networks, actuators, smart objects, smart meters	Access devices: PCS, iPads, smartphones, augmented-reality readers	Applications and platforms: dedicated and generic software and cloud	Various e-services for knowledge-based practices
Outcomes	Increased competitiveness of city clusters and sectors	Increased competitiveness of of individual companies	Better quality of life; inclusion; safety in the city	Efficiency and saving in city infrastructure and utilities	Better city government; services to citizens

The governance of intelligent city ecosystems 245

The question that immediately comes to mind is why these layers make up the fundamental blocks of intelligent cities. And if the presence of the 'city' layer and the elements comprising it are somehow self-explained (we are dealing with cities and city intelligence), then we should turn to definitions and understandings of intelligence to justify the presence of the other two layers of the standard model?

Legg and Hutter's (2007) comparative review of the concept of intelligence can shed light on these key questions. They analysed 71 definitions of intelligence given by organisations, psychology scholars, and researchers of artificial intelligence, and found that the main attributes of intelligence are, on the one hand, the ability to collect, process, and exchange information through perceiving, storing, retrieving information, calculating, reasoning, and learning; and on the other hand, the ability to find solutions, apply knowledge to practice, solve new problems, innovate, and adapt to objectives and achieving goals in complex environments. Understanding 'intelligence' with respect to those attributes of 'information gathering and processing' and 'problem solving' justifies the presence of the 'digital' and the 'innovation' layers in the intelligent cities structure model. If cities are to become intelligent, they should develop communication and information-processing capabilities (through digital and smart systems) and distributive problem-solving capability to address urban challenges and implement planning visions (through communities and innovation ecosystems).

We have also described the *model of intelligent city functioning* as composed of three innovation circuits generating digital spaces, improvements in decision-making, and better city working. The city is an agglomeration of multiple smaller areas and subsystems: production and services clusters, city-districts, communities, housing districts, utility networks, administration districts, and other areas. Overall, the city is a system composed of such subsystems working interdependently and interacting. Furthermore, each urban subsystem operates in collaboration with an innovation ecosystem, which guides the subsystem's change and evolution. This 'DNA' of urban sub-systems is a governance structure composed of stakeholders, advisory groups, research and intelligence teams, institutions and regulations, decision-making processes, objectives, and practices and assessment modes. Typically, it is an open innovation ecosystem. Digital spaces, Web 1.0 and Web 2.0, and smart environments improve both the decision-making capabilities of these innovation ecosystems and the efficiency of urban sub-systems.

The three fundamental layers of intelligent cities have different roles in the operation of intelligent places. Their interconnection and integration are based on these complementary contributions:

- Cities and urban subsystems offer *communities of practice*, skills, resources, infrastructure for human action, and capacities for governance and management. But cities are also fields of conflict, and of differing visions and objectives, problems to solve, and challenges to address.
- Innovation ecosystems and networks define *how solutions to city challenges are produced*; how communities, citizens, and city-based organisations work together and respond to challenges; how they create new products and

246 *Strategies and governance*

services individually or collaboratively; how they adapt through innovation to changing external conditions.
• The Internet and the Web enable collaborative solutions, offer *capabilities for communication and information processing,* integrate distributed competences, and make cities interactive, capable of gathering, storing, processing, and disseminating information and know-how.

City authorities are increasingly becoming aware of the 'intelligent city' and 'smart city' concepts and are implementing initiatives to create digital spaces and smart environments to improve decision-making processes and the efficiency of city's resources and infrastructure. However, cities have to prove this higher intelligence and efficiency, instead of taking them for granted. Many cities make use of ICTs and Web applications for image building and proof of status – without any real improvement in capabilities and efficiency. Other cities deploy strategies by copying best practices, which do not meet the needs of the area, or the requirements of the specific institutional context in which they operate. In many cases, initiatives are top-down only and do not involve citizens, stakeholders, and communities in order to benefit from collaborative efforts and collective intelligence. Therefore, it is not only the differences in the understanding of what constitutes an intelligent city, but also the complexity of achieving such environments and managing the array of elements that make them emerge that makes it extremely difficult to make intelligent cities a reality. Understanding the building blocks and functioning of the intelligent city model is a prerequisite and constant point of reference.

Making cities smart or intelligent is now a priority for all cities. Through distributed spatial intelligence, cities can cope with economic and environmental challenges, and the rising needs for energy and resources, as well as demands for social justice and cohesion. Cities can achieve these goals by applying adopting the structure and functioning models of intelligent city planning and infusing innovation and ICTs in all sectors of economic activity, in the creation of businesses and employment, in the management of the environment and living conditions, and in city governance. An intelligent or smart city emerges from local development trajectories fuelled by user-driven innovations and facilitated by information and communication technologies and smart environments. But above all, it is an environment of innovation open to everyone, giving the opportunity to every person living in the city, every citizen, and every company and organisation to find resources – through collaboration, Web platforms and other externalities – and fulfil individual needs and objectives.

2. A step forward: insights from big data

Intelligent cities are more and more frequently working with smart environments of high-speed broadband communication, sensor networks, ubiquitous computing, and rich interactions among users over social media. The amount of data and information generated and exchanged over this infrastructure is enormous. By

2012, about 2.5 exabytes of data were being created every day. Forecasts for the near future foresee an increase of the daily amount to about 10 exabytes.[1] Taking into account the expansion of smart city and IoT solutions, this figure will go even higher. In smart cities, large datasets are generated by various sources: sensors that capture the working of the city and conditions in the environment, users uploading posts, content and images on the social media, purchase transaction records, mobile phone geo-location and GPS data, email traffic, public administration data and transactions, and many others. This type of data is 'big data' and cannot be processed with the usual database management tools and traditional data analysis software. Big-data processing includes capture, storage, search, sharing, transfer, analysis, visualisation, forecasting, and predictive modelling. In Gartner's definition, "Big data are high volume, high velocity, and / or high variety information assets that require new forms of processing to enable enhanced decision-making, insight, discovery and process optimisation" (Beyer and Laney, 2012). In a more stylised description, 'big data' is equal to 'transaction data' plus 'interaction data' plus 'observations data' (Tuikka and Ervasti, 2013).

Smart city solutions related to the IoT – with all the connected devices, tagging, and sensing, embedded things and smart phone communications – will be a major source of big data. The machine-to-machine market is expected to be the largest submarket within the IoT solutions; it will be composed of several vertical sectors (automotive, healthcare, consumer electronics, utilities) of which automotive, consumer, health care, intelligent buildings, and utilities are the most rapidly developing (Tuikka and Ervasti, 2013).

The main challenges related to big data concern access to large data sets; how open and available big data is; which organisations can provide big data; how to process big data sets; and what kind of added value they can offer.

The open data movement for making big data available for public use is gaining momentum. Such initiatives consist of opening and sharing data from public organisations and the public administration which hold data from their transactions with citizens, public registries, and city networks. Large data sets are necessary for accomplishing the mission of public authorities and services, but they also have value *per se* in measuring and documenting the operation of the city and the activities of citizens. Cities can open data related to urban infrastructure; geo-spatial data of housing, property, and land use; transit data from transportation means; operational data from transactions with citizens; performance data for various domains of the city economy; public safety and crime; environmental conditions; and pollution. These datasets form the raw material for new services and city functionalities. Opening and sharing data is an invitation to Web and mobile applications developers to make them accessible, readable, visual, and meaningful.

How to process big data is a more-complex question, especially if the problem being addressed requires a real-time response. The MapReduce programming model, for instance, is suitable for processing multi-terabyte data across huge datasets, using a large number of computers in a cluster or a grid of heterogeneous pieces of hardware. MapReduce divides the input into smaller sub-problems and distributes them to computer nodes. It then collects the processed data and recombines it. The system provides automatic parallelisation and distribution, fault tolerance, communications and data transfers between the various parts of the dataset, and management of the whole process (Prabakaran, 2010).

The added value of big data is that it can lead to more informed and accurate decisions in large-scale complex systems, like cities. A McKinsey report (Manyika et al., 2011) identified five broad ways in which big data is being used:

- Big data can make information transparent and usable at higher frequency.
- Big data from transactions can offer more accurate and detailed performance information, expose variability and boost performance.
- Big data allows a narrower segmentation of customers and therefore much more precisely tailored products or services.
- Big data can support sophisticated analytics that improve decision-making.
- Big data can be used to forecast needs and improve the development of the next generation of products and services.

In cities, priority domains for using big data are urban networks for energy and transportation, where considerable savings in resources and investments can be achieved. The operation of these networks and utilities can be substantially optimised, and the quality of service improved, by deploying smart environments and sensor networks parallel to utility networks. A smart grid over every urban infrastructure would allow data to be collected and information about patterns of operation to emerge. However, all city subsystems can benefit from big data making evident the patterns of their operation and enabling better decision by the respective stakeholders and innovation chain.

Intelligent transportation systems are one domain that well illustrates the additional functionalities at the level of infrastructure that become possible thanks to big data, with e-services for arterial management; traffic incident management; traveller information; intermodal freight; highway management; roadway operations and maintenance; emergency management; crash prevention and safety; transit management; and electronic payment and pricing; as well as commercial vehicle operations (RITA, n.d.).

The smart city energy grid is another domain which can profit enormously from big data. Cities are confronted with intense challenges for energy savings and energy optimisation in the case of using renewable energy sources. Smart grid solutions can help distributors to manage energy more efficiently, offer services that save energy on the demand side, and support the use of smart buildings and smart lighting infrastructure in the service of citizens and public authorities. Four key areas of improvement become feasible by deploying smart energy grids in cities.

- First, the smart grid offers a continuous measurement of demand and supply and provides awareness to enable the energy network to be controlled and automated. The significance of observation increases with the complexity of the grid and the variable energy resources placed on it.

- Second, awareness of the grid's state enables energy suppliers and utility organisations to control it better, combine better different energy sources, and waste less energy input.
- Third, better automation of grid functions becomes possible as controls are distributed closer to faults or outages.
- Fourth, the integration of grid devices, systems, and business processes unleash the added value of the grid (Tips, 2011).

Thus, in smart cities, big data combined with analytics can offer understanding and insights about usage patterns of infrastructure and public spaces and can optimise the use of city infrastructure and networks; calculate more accurately future needs for services and infrastructure; and substantiate development strategies based on real data and user behaviour. What really happens is that big data enable new innovation circuits for improvement of urban infrastructure and the operation of city. These innovation circuits are additional to user-driven participatory innovation based on Web 2.0 applications.

3. Governance of intelligent city ecosystems

Processes of spatial intelligence take place in all subsystems of cities, districts, clusters, infrastructure, or utilities. Spatial intelligence – as the capability of using locally distributed knowledge for innovation and problem solving – is an inherent property of urbanisation, due to factors such as the division of labour and specialisation. Purposeful or *de facto* collaboration among citizens, the presence of neighbours and various types of external economies created by proximity, and large-scale infrastructure and accumulation of know-how and technology are all drivers of spatial intelligence. But, the spatial intelligence of cities existed far before the era of the Internet and the current advances in telecommunications and Web technologies.

In contrast to traditional spatial intelligence due to proximity and face-to-face collaboration, which appears spontaneously in urban agglomerations, novel forms of spatial intelligence enabled by the Internet demand a specific type of infrastructure. Digital spaces and smart environments – as empowerment mechanisms – need continuous maintenance, information updates, and system upgrades. The success of intelligent cities is bound into efficient governance in the long run.

Governance is the framework of strategic planning. It consists of principles and rules that sustain and ensure strategy and the successful pursuit of objectives in the long run. Governance principles are somehow canonical and define the conditions for leadership, strategy, monitoring, and continual improvement. It is about the control of dynamics created by strategic planning and implementation of solutions with the continuous engagement of communities in intelligent city development. It is more effective than planning, correcting planning failures, and – above all – bad initial planning setup.

As the Internet-supported spatial intelligence of cities is gaining ground over pre-existing forms of spatial intelligence stemming from agglomeration and collaboration, governance has to organise traditional and novel spatial intelligence into a coherent whole. Therefore, intelligent cities, intelligent districts, and other urban ecosystems demand a strong and sophisticated form of governance, an 'XXXL G' (Extremely Extra Extra Large Governance), that will enable these ecosystems to be transformed into intelligent places of higher innovation capability through digital communication and knowledge.

To shed light on the governance guiding intelligent city strategies, we will refer to experiences gained in the context of the PEOPLE project, a smart city CIP-ICT-PSP project. PEOPLE initiated a series of pilots to develop smart environments and e-services in city-districts in Bilbao (Spain), Bremen (Germany), Virty-sur-Seine (France), and Thermi in Thessaloniki (Greece). The pilots, beside their different strategies, followed the same model of governance, driven by current trends of smart cities, such as sustaining Internet communities with social media, defining knowledge architectures that combine collective intelligence and data from sensors, user-driven innovation and collaborative product development, innovation cycles and feedback, and monitoring and measurement systems. This case study shows how different smart city strategies can be deployed under the same governance principles. This is particularly important for cities, because they are composed of many urban ecosystems with their own characteristics, operations, and planning objectives.

4. Learning from the PEOPLE smart city pilots

The PEOPLE project was a social experiment to test a governance model in different smart city districts, implemented over the 2010–2013 period. The applications and e-services created are still running in the cities involved. The main objective of the project was the rapid uptake of smart city solutions through the implementation and deployment of innovative Internet-based services and smart environments. This aim was pursued with the deployment of smart environments and user-driven innovation in four urban areas: (1) the cultural district of Bilbao, (2) the university campus and technology park of Bremen, (3) the central commercial district of Thermi, and (4) the housing district of Vitry-sur-Seine.

The Bilbao pilot was realised in the district of Abando, which covers an area of 100 hectares in the city centre. The district of Abando (also known as San Vicente of Abando) has a population of 51,875 inhabitants and is divided in two neighbourhoods, Abando and Indautxu to the west of the Plaza Moyúa. At present, Abando is the wealthiest district of the city and hosts most of the offices and commerce, as well as a large number of companies (around 24,000). It is also a district with outstanding public spaces and buildings – such as the Guggenheim Museum, Albia Gardens, Deusto University, the Maritime Museum at Bilbao´s Estuary, and the train station – attracting most of the touristic activity of Bilbao. Inside this district is located the station of Santander, the walk areas of Uribiarte and Abandoibarra, and it is crossed by the ecological electrical streetcar that leads to the Guggenheim Museum. Next to it is the Zubiarte Mall, with shopping, restaurants, and cinemas. Thereafter are the Euskalduna Palace and the Maritime Museum Ría de Bilbao, with exhibitions on the history of Bilbao. Optimising public transport and information systems related to security, leisure, and tourism

The governance of intelligent city ecosystems 251

are among the most important challenges and needs of this area. In Abando three new applications and e-services were developed in the context of the Bilbao pilot:

- Environmental information about air quality, pollen levels, and meteorological information.
- Virtual tours, a service based on 3D representations of Abando and walking itineraries around the Abandoibarra City area, providing information and showing the significant buildings and monuments that can be found in this area.
- The GEOCUR service, which provides information related to education and training activities available in Bilbao.

The Bremen Technology Park is a special city district in the eastern part of the city of Bremen. It covers an area of 170 hectares housing research and education facilities and technology companies. Bremen University is also located in the area. There are more than 400 small and medium-sized companies around the main campus and 20 research institutes, specialising in aerospace, logistics, material sciences, and nanotechnology. There is no residential, commercial, or industrial activity. The Bremen Technology Park is well serviced by the city's transportation networks. A tramway connects this district to the city centre and the airport. In addition, Autobahn 27 and Autobahn 1 can be easily accessed. Three new e-services were developed in the Bremen pilot focusing on the population of the university campus:

- A location-based service, providing information about facilities on the campus, with opening and closing times, meals in the student restaurant, schedules of buses and trams, and other location-finding data.
- The Stud.IP extension, with a messaging OS application for the local Stud. IP platform, allowing courses to be managed, communication with other students, and meetings to be organised among students.
- A student guide module, which makes it possible to manage bachelors and masters courses.

Vitry-sur-Seine is located in a southeastern suburb of Paris, around 7.5 km from the centre of Paris. It is mainly a residential area with a young population, the majority of whom are under 30 years of age, and a secondary city centre. For many years, the municipality implemented a policy to attract higher education facilities, social services, and cultural activities. The university campus hosts two technology institutes in chemical engineering and telecommunications, and the LISSI research lab. Vitry-sur-Seine also hosts the Val-de-Marne Museum of Contemporary Art, which offers workshops in the plastic arts, an auditorium, and a cinema for art and experimental movies. It is among the cities that contributed to the development of the hip-hop movement in France. Urban art has an eminent position in local politics. Apart from the focus on education and arts, Vitry, as National High Interest Zone, is renovating the public transportation infrastructure

252 *Strategies and governance*

in collaboration with the transport management authority for the region of Paris. Social cohesion and integration are among the main challenges the city faces.

The Vitry pilot focused on LISSI's experimental facilities in the area near the town hall. In a second stage, the services will be offered at tramway stops along the new line under construction linking the Metro Station of Villejuif and Orly Airport. The e-services developed focus on social information offered at bus stops with location-based technologies, including:

- A local information service, which provides user-directed information related to the location of the user. When connected, the service provides local only information with respect to the position of the user.
- VitryHub, a social network service, which allows one to create, display, and edit the user's profile and listing of friends' profiles, location, and context (available, online, etc.).
- An Interactive search service for people and facilities. The search is semantic and search requests are analysed to understand the goal and meaning of requests, and to fine-tune and adapt them interactively.
- An immersive instant messaging service, allowing one person to communicate with others in real-time and in private.
- The Improve-my-City application in Vitry, allowing citizens to report and track non-emergency issues about public spaces to the municipality.

The Thermi pilot was implemented in an area of $31.5 km^2$ on the east side of metropolitan Thessaloniki. Thermi is one of the most rapidly growing municipalities of Thessaloniki with 16,014 residents in 2001, a number that doubled over the last few years by attracting industrial and tertiary activities, most of which are of supra-local importance. Apart from housing, the city gathers commercial, administrative, academic, and cultural activities, combined with recreational and sports facilities, R&D and innovative entrepreneurship in the Technology Park, and the Museum of Science and Technology. Despite the large volume of people inflow, local businesses are losing market share, to the benefit of nearby markets and hyper malls. It has been observed that even Thermi's residents do not regularly shop in the local market or use the services offered locally. This problem of weak competitiveness of the central market area is further worsened by traffic congestion in the city's central area where the heart of the local market is located, the poor quality of the physical environment in some areas of the centre, and the limited availability of parking spaces.

The core scenario of the Thermi pilot focuses on these interrelated challenges of competitiveness and environment, with the aim of bolstering the attractiveness, accessibility, and environmental conditions of the central city district. A portfolio of applications and e-services was selected through open innovation cycles, stakeholder and user suggestions, assessment of the expected value added, development costs, content and data input, and business models for sustainability (Figure 11.1). These choices were influenced by a wide-ranging and recursive process of public consultation and user involvement. The e-services selected combine one core

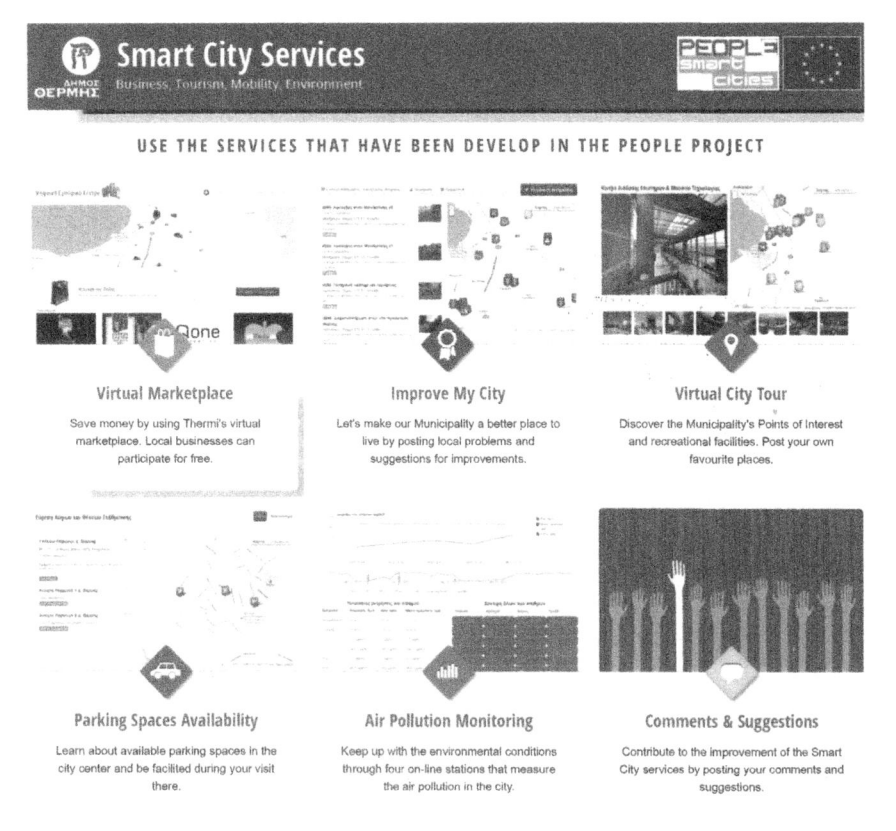

Figure 11.1 Thermi pilot: a portfolio of smart city applications
Source: http://smartcity.thermi.gov.gr/index_en.html

service – to sustain the commercial activity of the city's centre, and four complementary services – to facilitate accessibility in the area and improve the urban environment. The five e-services developed and offered to citizens, businesses, and visitors are:

A Smart Marketplace which includes commercial shops located in the city centre and professionals of the city. It includes five subsystems or applications:

- A business directory to present local businesses and professionals on the city map. The information is classified by category (i.e., hotels, restaurants, clothing stores, real estate, doctors, lawyers, and others). Each entry starts with minimum information about the specific store or professional, but the owners can add detailed information about products and services.
- A virtual marketplace with e-shops where local storekeepers are able to create and present their stores using text, photos, and video about their products.
- A coupon site containing promotional codes from local retailers and professionals, offering discounts for specific products and services. The visitors

can print the coupons or store them on their mobile phones and get discounts from shops.
- A purchase-optimisation engine, based on open data available from the national price observatory, which enables users to compare consumer goods from local supermarkets and create personal baskets of goods with the better prices.
- A review engine that assists customers in gathering shopping information, posting reviews and opinions about local shops, and related content. This component allows users to contribute different kinds of content, including reviews, photos, votes, quick tips, and more. The result is the creation of a local social shopping network.

City Tour 360: This application supports the creation of virtual tours of recreation facilities using interactive maps, 360° panoramas, video, and images. The promotion of recreational facilities is based on an interactive map of the city indicating points of interest, such as public buildings, monuments, museums, parks, and open-space activities. Each location, building, or area is described with text and media. Users can upload content or comment on content created by other users.

A Parking Assistance application, which provides real-time information about the exact number of places available in the underground parking facility situated in the city centre and information about the two other peripheral parking areas that are located at the outskirts of the city centre.

Air Pollution Monitoring which provides online measurement of atmospheric conditions via a wireless sensor network. The latter consists of four stations placed throughout the area of Thermi and a group of sensors connected to each station. The sensors measure CO_2, micro-particles, and other pollutants and the information is displayed on the Web, smartphones, and public screens.

An Environmental Request and Reporting application which enables residents to report local problems, such as discarded trash, burned lighting, broken tiles on sidewalks, illegal advertising boards, etc. The issues submitted are displayed on a map. Users may add comments, suggest solutions for improving the environment of their neighbourhood, or add video and pictures. They are informed about the current state of resolution of the reported problem by the responsible public authority and the municipality.

All of the above applications and e-services have been developed with open source software (PHP application language, MySQL database server, and Apache Web server), HTML5, and CSS3, and are offered as open source under the GLPv3 license. All applications follow a service-oriented architecture where services are autonomous reusable components. Services are self-contained and loosely coupled, meaning that dependencies between services are kept to a minimum. Instead of one service depending on another, coordination services are provided in situations in which multiple services must be accessed, and access to them must be sequenced.

With the above four pilots in Bilbao, Bremen, Vitry, and Thermi, the PEOPLE project was a test bed of governance practices in different collaborative environments enabled by Internet technologies. Existing city-districts and activities were sustained by user-driven innovation and smart environments. Some solutions and e-services proved to be very successful (Lakavicius, 2013). The pilots were implemented with a common governance model with three major instances: (1) mobilisation of communities, actors, and users; (2) setting-up knowledge architectures; and (3) realisation of innovation cycles to define smart city solutions for better city management and operation.

5. Governance of actors: the art of community

City ecosystems are created spontaneously or through planning; they progress with good governance, leadership, informed decision-making, monitoring, and assessment. Top-down and bottom-up processes, as well as external and internal dynamics, complement each other and control the structuring of urban ecosystems and the ways things happen within them. Usual city ecosystems are:

- City-districts, such as central business districts (CBDs), downtowns, historic centres, commercial districts, industrial districts, technology districts, port districts, and university campuses, in which the physical proximity, the common function, and the managing bodies define their relative autonomy within the city;
- Clusters of activities connected by vertical supply chains, horizontal collaboration networks, producers alliances, and associations;
- Sectors of similar economic activities located into the city, in which co-location and competition make them acting like a structured entity or a swarm;
- Utility networks and infrastructure management organisations, providing services to households and producers, such as energy, transportation, water, and waste management;
- Transport hubs and large-scale transport infrastructures, ports, and airports, which operate as autonomous cities within cities.
- Residential districts, such as housing districts and neighbourhoods, which include urban residential, single family residential areas, and garden apartments, where common concerns prevail about the maintenance and protection of housing, safety, and the quality of the environment.

These city ecosystems host communities composed of stakeholders, producers, citizens, and users. Each community with its members, activities, infrastructure, leadership, and external environment is a structured entity guided by networks of interactions and relationships of co-existence. Actors for novel solutions in city ecosystems are primarily the members of the respective community. Any novel solution ultimately comes from a member of the community, but it becomes possible because of the presence and collaboration with other members. On the

256 *Strategies and governance*

one hand, members bring in smart environments and e-services, and on the other hand, use those smart environments and e-services to improve decision-making about the ecosystem and the functioning of the city. Mobilising the community and its members is the starting point of effective governance toward intelligent ecosystems.

The PEOPLE project pilots offered key conclusions about the role and contribution of communities, their members, and actors in smart city solutions. The pilots worked with a common methodology based on the actualisation of local communities in consecutive innovation cycles promoting the design, deployment, and use of e-services. The whole process progressed in four steps, including the identification of communities, mobilisation, contribution, and assessment.

Identification of communities occurred with respect to the city-district in which the pilot took place, and the services deployed per district. Somehow, these are common sense principles, because communities and actors are district-specific and services were designed with respect to user needs and participation. In each pilot, communities, stakeholders, and lead users were identified, and information was collected about active members, the contact person or coordinator, the motivation to participate, the engagement strategy, ethics, and confidentiality. Many different communities were selected for each pilot: professionals, service producers, merchants, public administration personnel, non-profit and cultural organisation representatives, students, researchers, software developers, and citizens in the area of the pilot. The large diversity was justified by the number of applications and e-services deployed per district. In principle, three different types of communities were chosen per application or e-service: those sustaining the offer of the service, those creating the demand, and those sustaining the marketing and dissemination of the service.

The *mobilisation of communities* has been achieved mainly through key individuals and community leaders. A great deal has been written about the role of social media, Facebook, Twitter, YouTube, Linkedin, and others, in creating and mobilising communities online. In the case of the PEOPLE pilots, the contribution of social media to creating and mobilising communities has been rather marginal. The main impact came from stakeholders and lead users who spread the word and convinced members of the targeted communities to get involved. Regular meetings and face-to-face communication were more effective than were online communication and online community building. The sole exception was with online surveys, which offered real value in gathering user's opinions and feedback during the design of services. Open source communities and infrastructures, such as the Github, Sourceforge, and Joomla, have also proven to be very effective in mobilising developers' communities. All pilots followed the same strategy for the release of services: use of open source solutions, storing applications on Github, and inviting developers to contribute.

The *contribution* of communities to pilots took place bottom-up by their members. In non, were communities presented as organised groups in a coordinated manner. On the contrary, members, users, producers, and citizens contributed individually in many different ways and assumed different roles:

- Giving feedback to applications and e-services, improving the concept and design, validating solutions and services;
- Taking part in the implementation of services as producers, users, or consumers;
- Providing data, information, requests, and other digital content necessary for the uptake of services;
- Sustaining e-services in the long run with skills, effort, and resources, thereby taking part in implementation of the business model to promote their economic viability.

The same communities and members were invited to contribute to successive stages of the pilots, from design to development and operation. As happens with traditional city infrastructure, the participation of users is permanent and users take on different roles during the lifecycle of infrastructure.

In the *assessment* stage, the added value of applications and e-services has been directly proportional to the communities and users involved. Improve-my-City, which has been by far the most successful application and service, was based on the contribution of many different communities, active lead-users locally, the public administration community, the academic community, open source Joomla developers, and citizens. Among the most important lessons learnt for the PEOPLE pilots were that smart city added value depends on the mobilisation of communities and users. Their involvement makes the difference. Software and applications are means to make user involvement happen.

In *The Art of Community*, Jono Bacon (2012) offers a detailed framework about the setting up and governance of communities. He discusses topics for empowering and leading communities to success, such as building an effective community strategy that meets stakeholder requirements, creating excitement and participation to motivate about the goals of the community, using social media to grow awareness and active involvement; organising community events, governing infrastructure, selecting community managers, and learning from the best-established community leaders. Starting from a bird's-eye view on communities, he gradually zooms in closer, down to the day-to-day management and operation details, and from personal experiences to generic community management ideas, best practices, and approaches.

Communities are fundamentally organised by non-profit practices and their participants build up social capital via contributions, social interaction, and trust (Bacon, 2012). The sense of 'belonging' is critical in keeping people in communities. Belonging is the goal of community building and measure of social capital that keeps it alive (pp. 5–7). Creating and sustaining such communities should start from solid foundations about the mission and goals, opportunities for success, areas of collaboration, and the skills and needs required. Opportunities

258 Strategies and governance

codify the desired impact if the goals of the community are met, such as improving the quality of life for homeless people, producing revolutionary software, improving skills, etc. Areas of collaboration are fields in which the community members can work together, organising events, performing advocacy, writing software, etc. (pp. 44–45). A part of these initial steps, communities need continuous governance – which is to lead, initiate, and engage the members on activities that affect the community as a whole. Governance is more necessary when the community exceeds a certain size in order to resolve issues of conflict when multiple people are involved and factions develop, to manage the resources which the community relies on, to handle commercial interests, and to stand up against any improper requests that may come from commercial sponsors (pp. 315–316).

Overall, the experience from running the Ubuntu community and interviews with leaders of other well-known communities – such as Linux, MySQL and Eucalyptus, Creative Commons, O'Reilly Media, PayPal and eBay, Humble Indie Bundle, Mozilla and Drupal – led Bacon to the conclusion that structuring and running communities of interest and practice is close to social economies and commons built around social capital, trust, and communication.

6. Governance of assets: knowledge architectures

The contribution of communities and their members is codified into distributed knowledge architectures specific to the district, application, and e-service. E-services offered in intelligent city ecosystems stand over distributed knowledge architectures that create information intelligence, empower citizens and companies, and offer new ways of working and living in the city. Distributed knowledge architectures represent networks and flows of data and information. They connect different components of intelligent ecosystems, traversing the layers of the structure model.

The main elements connected over distributed knowledge architectures are citizens, producers, and users; elements of city infrastructure and physical space; software applications; and embedded devices such as sensors and actuators; as well as city operators and utility organisations. Knowledge architectures define how these instances are organised, how information moves from one element to the other, and how information is transformed by the presence of other elements into knowledge. Information going through knowledge architecture undergoes significant changes, in the first place by upgrading its content, in the second place by improving skills and competences, and in the third place by being used in the physical and social environment of cities. Every e-service offered in smart cities relies on a specific knowledge architecture, which determines data flows, transformation, and information generation.

In the case of the PEOPLE project, two main modelling tools were used to define data models and data flows: UML Graph design and the RDF/S ontology design. Unified Modelling Language (UML) is a standardised general-purpose modelling language in the field of object-oriented software engineering. UML includes a set of graphic notation techniques to create visual models of object-oriented software-intensive systems. UML combines techniques from data modelling (entity relationship diagrams), business modelling (work flows), object modelling, and component modelling. It has proven to be an efficient tool for handling complex data models and data warehouses (Prat et al., 2006). The UML diagram is a partial graphic representation of a system's model, while the UML model also contains documentation that drives the model elements and diagrams, such as written-use cases. In a complementary way, the RDF/S ontology design was only used to describe the metadata that are associated with the data classes defined in UML. The classes were later transformed in SQL Tables. The models were easily understandable between the pilots and could be reused or modified without important issues. The pilots mostly used PhpMyAdmin Data Base Design Application to create all the data models represented in UML and RDF. The information flow schema was represented by the combination of the processing stages connected by directed information channels. Once the flow model has been constructed, names were assigned to each of the stages and channels. The main modelling stages included data provisioning; data collection from external suppliers; data internal creation; data processing with input acceptation, output, and effects generation; data packaging, storage, aggregation, summarising, and reporting; decision-making; decision implementation; data delivery; and data use.

Most e-services from the pilots stand on knowledge architectures producing information intelligence, which at the end of the process offer a better understanding of the urban environment, the needs, demands, and requests of citizens. In fewer cases, architectures for up-skilling and competence creation were implemented.

Knowledge architectures start from communities, linking members and information objects, and at the end of the journey knowledge transformations occur, measurable in terms of time required for the task to be accomplished, the cost of operations, resources used, and the quality of service provided. Since these are measurable effects, alternative architectures can be evaluated and selected with respect to their effectiveness, performance, cost efficiency, and quality of service.

Because knowledge architectures involve users and knowledge transformations, they conclude with cognition changes. Thus, we can speak about cognitive architectures or cognition-centric systems that include human beings and other cognitive entities with sufficient awareness, learning, language, autonomy, and cooperation capability (Mitola, 2009; Sheard and Mostashari, 2009). They allow one to describe the standard problem-solving model, introduced by John Dewey and revised by George Polya, from a distributed intelligence perspective, in which the six stages of the problem-solving process[2] do not appear as constructions of the individual mind, but as constructions of thought distributed in the environment, the tools, and other persons in collaborative activities (Pea, 1993). Pea showed how these stages are influenced and capabilities augmented by distributed networks, such as computing, guided participation, collaborative inscriptional systems, situated cognition in environments, and designed artefacts that play important roles in human activities.

7. Governance of activities: collaborative innovation cycles

Collaborative innovation is the third and final stage of the governance model tested and comprises all those activities that allow a community or group of actors to engage in knowledge transformation and offer a better solution to a defined challenge. What really happens in collaborative innovation is that groups of users set in motion knowledge architectures, and the knowledge flow generated drives more efficient solutions.

The foundations of collaborative innovation are in the open innovation paradigm. Open innovation is defined as "the use of purposive inflows and outflows of knowledge to accelerate internal innovation and expand the markets. It combines internal and external ideas into architectures and systems and treats innovation as an open system. Open innovation means that valuable ideas can come from inside or outside the company, placing external ideas and at the same level of importance as internal ideas" (Chesbrough, 2006, p. 3).

The open innovation paradigm (Chesbrough, 2003; Enkel et al., 2009; Fredberg et al., 2007; Pénin et al., 2011; Von Hippel, 1986) acknowledges that in a worldwide economy, technologies are becoming more and more complex, and external knowledge is richer and more important than internal. The same holds true for user-driven approaches. User-driven innovation implies that the source of innovation is in the profound understanding of customer needs, as well as in the ability to translate customer knowledge into unique products and experiences. User-driven innovation has an important focus on user pull instead of technology push. It promotes the direct involvement of users (consumers or businesses) in the innovation process through observation processes, toolkits, user panels, and Living Labs in an open collaborative environment that is flexibly structured (Pallot et al., 2011). With user-driven innovation, ideas and concept generation tap into participants' creativity. Three different levels of contribution from users to innovation processes can be defined – namely, information, decision, and creation. And four different kinds of users can be also identified: intuitive, professional, freshman, and nerd, based on their familiarity with application and object knowledge (Reichwald et al., 2004).

Collaborative innovation takes place in very diverse environments: supply chains linking suppliers and producers, clusters, networks set by intermediary organisations, open innovation platforms, digital and smart environment of collaboration, and crowdsourcing. While the initial focus of open innovation was primarily R&D, a number of new areas have grown out of this perspective towards more collaborative environments. These include the spatial extension of innovation networks in a more global world; deepening of the work division in innovation and greater specialisation; user participation in early phases of innovation; suppliers' early integration in the innovation process; commercialisation of existing technology and intellectual property; use of instruments that enable customers to create or configure their own product; and free revealing of inventions, discoveries, and knowledge that intensify technology spillovers without compensation in open source initiatives (Grassmann et al., 2010).

Working with such open and user-driven innovation perspectives, the PEOPLE pilots deployed activities for user engagement in successive 'innovation cycles,' where the design of e-services were carried out by users in all stages of solutions development. These cycles are illustrated in Figure 11.2. Ideas from users and

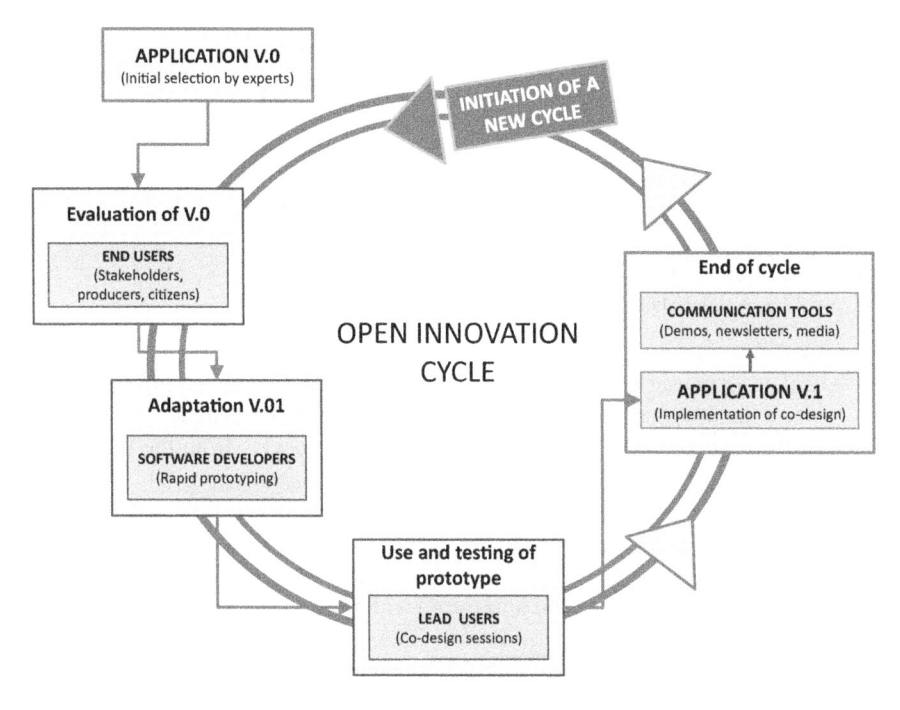

Figure 11.2 User involvement into innovation cycles

stakeholders were taken into account when defining the solutions and services to be deployed. Use cases were identified with respect to citizens and companies. Prototypes were tested by lead users in early stages, allowing iterative modifications of the prototype until it converged on an accepted and validated solution.

The concept of innovation cycles linking theory and practice in cyclical itineraries that bring understanding, insights, and new knowledge has been taken from the action research literature (Baskerville, 1999). In particular, it comes from open user-driven innovation perspective that show situations of openness and cooperation, complex social processes, and introduce changes into these processes while observing their effects (Schaffers et al., 2008).

Four innovation cycles were implemented per the PEOPLE pilot and application. All cycles had the same structure, with the exception of the first 'Preparation Cycle' that focused more on the definition of use cases. Following the 'Preparation Cycle,' the subsequent cycles decreased in duration, due to repetition of the same tasks. As participatory activities evolved, the applications deployed converged around a validated solution. The main steps of each innovation cycle were:

- Definition: In this step, based on users' feedback carried out at the end of the previous cycle, each application had to define what kind modifications should be introduced during the current cycle.
- Modification and deployment of applications: This step was about the implementation of modifications and new version of applications to be deployed.

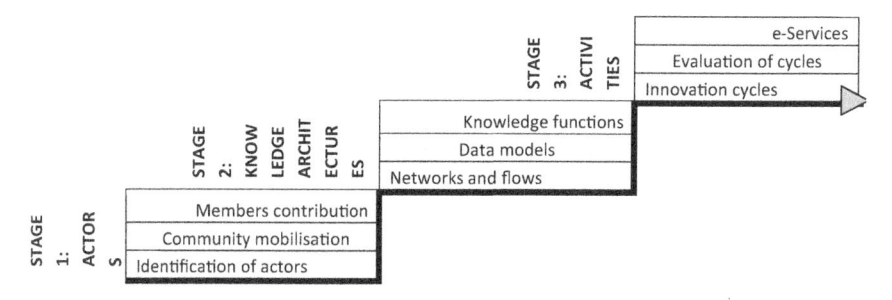

Figure 11.3 A three-stage governance model

- Gathering of user feedback: After the deployment of modifications, users had to test the new version of application and give their assessment.
- Analysis of user feedback: This step draws conclusions from the modifications that were introduced to applications and the users' appraisal.
- Evaluation of the cycle: This is not a step but a milestone; at the end of every cycle an evaluation of the cycle took place.

Two types of innovations were introduced with the mobilisation of users during the innovation cycles. First, innovations related to new electronic services introduced in various city systems and services. Collaborative innovation in this case is about the involvement of users in the design and deployment of applications and e-services. Second, innovations related to better functioning of urban systems because of the introduction of new e-services. Collaborative innovation in this case is about new practices for more efficient networking, co-working, complementarities of actors, and various types of external economies created.

The overall governance model tested in the PEOPLE pilots is illustrated in Figure 11.3, with three stages (Actors—Architectures—Activities) and the corresponding steps per stage. It has proven very efficient in sustaining smart city strategies implemented in different environments and city districts.

8. Intelligent ecosystems in the near future

The most distinctive feature of urban ecosystems is that solutions to problems and challenges are devised by active members, either by direct collaboration among members or by indirect externalities due to the presence of other members in the ecosystem. This is a fundamental feature of any ecosystem – the creation of mutual advantages due to voluntary collaboration or interaction among members living in close physical association, referred to also as 'symbiosis.' In intelligent urban ecosystems, traditional solutions of collaboration or symbiosis are further enhanced by broadband infrastructure, digital spaces, e-services, and online knowledge management.

During the actual technology wave, smart environments and big datasets complement user-driven setting of intelligent cities with real-time information gathered by sensors, location-aware applications, Internet of Things solutions, and social media.

IDC Government Insights prediction on the potential state of play for smart cities in 2014 point out at a series of trends. Smart cities are at an inflection point and will need to focus on mission-driven technology solutions; mashups of many technologies centred on a core mission will drive those efforts. The IoT mobile will be a big driver for smart cities growth. Innovation around 311 services, for non-emergency government issues accessible via call centres or the Web, will continue to grow and include more powerful analytics. Big data, open data, and analytics will continue to drive policy decisions and smart cities spending. More city and government functions will move to the cloud. Overall, according to the authors of the report (R. Y. Clarke, A. Brooks, and M. Chulani), 2014 is going to be a big year for smart cities. Cities will move more quickly from research and evaluation to investment in pilots and the organisational structures to support smart city initiatives (McCann, 2014).

Medium-term trends in the future Internet technologies also point towards the availability of Semantic Web services over cloud-based platforms. Semantic Web applications and e-services utilise ontologies in their data modelling in order to support semantic interoperability between applications and take advantage of automated mechanisms for discovery, selection, and execution of e-services. "The introduction of semantics as an extension of Service-Oriented Architectures, and thus the creation of Semantically Enabled Service Oriented Architectures (SESAs), provides for next generation of service-oriented computing based on machine-processable semantics" (Charalabidis, 2011, p. 17). Semantic Web, speech recognition, and the use of smartphones can extend the provision of the smart city services on the move in almost all sectors, from transport, security, emergency management to trade and the public administration.

However, technology is not the only driver of change. Urban and innovation dynamics, beside their longer cycles compared to ICTs, contribute to the evolution of intelligent city ecosystems. Urban change follows a 30–40 year cycle of spatial renewal. Actually, the objectives of a knowledge economy, environmental sustainability, and climate change are shaping a quantitative city-planning model that optimises the use of resources and minimises the impact on the environment.

New trends in innovation dynamics point towards connected knowledge and specialisation. Already in the EU, smart specialisation is endorsed as a core driver of innovation in the 2020 EU strategy. Smart specialisation strategies and digital agendas are expected to strengthen the competitiveness of European industries and drive state aids towards selected industries and activities (Foray et al., 2012). But specialisation also needs co-ordination to achieve higher efficiency. Distributed knowledge and connected knowledge can reveal new capabilities and sustain new dynamics of innovation. In distributed knowledge and learning architectures, problem-solving and innovation capabilities arise from specialised and yet complementary skills. Orchestration is the suitable architecture for combining those skills in the pursuit of common objectives. Permanent questions within distributed knowledge architectures are about what is distributed (the components of the problem-solving process or the product), and the constraints that govern the dynamics of distributed systems over different time scales (Pea, 1993).

If one were to draw a conclusion from these trends, it is that intelligent ecosystems rely on and will continue to rely on distributed bottom-up and community-based efforts, and cannot be created by large-scale top-down projects. The fundamentals of intelligent cities – the structural model, the functioning model, the planning model, and the governance model – are all bottom-up models. They rely on contributions by active communities, small-scale urban ecosystems around enterprises located in the city, multiple applications and e-services created by the city administration, and the contribution of citizens and informed users. All these efforts enter into a cumulative process of spatial intelligence and innovation from below. Even the largest ICT providers and multinationals and the wealthiest state authorities cannot build turnkey intelligent city ecosystems. But they can greatly contribute to the standardisation of solutions, creation of state-of-the-art monitoring and assessment systems, and setting cloud-based infrastructure to ease the starting stage of intelligent city initiatives.

Notes

1 An exabyte (EB) is equal to 10^{18} bytes or 1 billion gigabytes. The number of all words ever spoken by human beings is estimated at 5 exabytes. According to CISCO, by 2016, global Internet traffic is expected to reach 1,300 exabytes annually (www.pcmag.com/article2/0,2817,2405038,00.asp). The journal *Science* estimated the amount of data stored in the world by 2007 at 295 exabytes (www.bbc.co.uk/news/technology-12419672), while the digital universe of 2009 was estimated at 0.8 ZB and is projected to rise to 35 ZB by 2020.
2 The stages are: (1) finding the problem, (2) representing the problem, (3) planning a problem solution, (4) executing the plan, (5) checking the solution, and (6) reflecting to consolidate learning. These are not linear stages in a top-down process, but rather represent moments of a more-cyclic system in which each next stage exploits opportunities created during the problem-solving process (Pea 1993, p. 66).

References

Bacon, J. (2012). *The art of community*. 2nd edition. Sebastopole, CA: O'Reilley Media.
Baskerville, Richard L. (1999). Investigating information systems with action research. *Communications of the Association for Information Systems*, Vol. 2, No. 19. Retrieved 2 January 2014, from http://aisel.aisnet.org/cais/vol2/iss1/19.
Beyer, M. A. and Laney, D. (2012). *The importance of 'big data': A definition*. Gartner. Retrieved 2 January 2014, from www.gartner.com/DisplayDocument?id=2057415&ref=clientFriendlyUrl.
Charalabidis, Y. (2011). *ISU business models in e-government*. A COIN project White Paper. Retrieved 2 January 2014, from http://goo.gl/Cl4iYt.
Chesbrough, H. (2003). *Open innovation: The new imperative for creating and profiting from technology*. Boston, MA: Harvard Business School Publishing.
Chesbrough, H. (2006). *Open innovation: Researching a new paradigm*. Oxford, UK: Oxford University Press.
Enkel, E., Grassmann, O. and Chesbrough, H. (2009). Open R&D and open innovation: Exploring the phenomenon. *R&D Management*, Vol. 39, No. 4, 311–316.

Foray, D., Goddard, J., Goenaga Beldarrain, X., Landabaso, M., McCann, P., Morgan, K., Nauwelaers, C. and Ortega-Argilés, R. (2012). *Guide to research and innovation strategies for smart specialisation (RIS3)*. European Commission, Smart Specialisation Platform. Retrieved 2 January 2014, from http://s3platform.jrc.ec.europa.eu/en/c/document_library/get_file?uuid=e50397e3-f2b1-4086-8608-7b86e69e8553.

Fredberg, T., Elmquist, M. and Ollila, S. (2007). *Managing open innovation: Present findings and future directions.* VINNOVA 02204, 45. Retrieved 2 January 2014, from http://goo.gl/2r3Mu4.

Grassmann, O., Enkel, E. and H. Chesbrough (2010). The future of open innovation. *R&D Management*. Vol. 40, No. 3, 213–221.

Komninos, N. (2008). *Intelligent cities and globalisation of innovation networks* London and New York: Routledge.

Lakavicius, R. (2013). *Improve my City. Digital Agenda for Europe.* Retrieved 2 January 2014, from http://ec.europa.eu/digital-agenda/en/blog/improve-my-city.

Legg, S. and Hutter, M. (2007). A collection of definitions of intelligence. In B. Goertzel and P. Wang (eds), *Advances in Artificial General Intelligence: Concepts, Architectures and Aglorithms*, Amsterdam, the Netherlands: IOS Press.

Manyika, J., Chui, M., Brown, B., Bughin, J., Dobbs, R., Roxburgh, C. and Hung Byers, A. (2011). *Big data: The next frontier for innovation, competition, and productivity.* McKinsey Global Institute. Retrieved 2 January 2014, from http://goo.gl/RQdzh.

McCann, B. (2014). *IDC releases 10 predictions for smart cities in 2014.* Retrieved 25 January 2014, from http://civsourceonline.com/2014/01/24/idc-releases-10-predictions-for-smart-cities-in-2014/.

Mitola, J. (2009). Cognitive radio architecture evolution. *Proceedings of the IEEE 97*, No. 4: 626–641. Retrieved 2 January 2014, from http://ieeexplore.ieee.org/xpls/abs_all.jsp?arnumber=4814771.

Pallot, M., Trousse, B., Senach, B., Shaffers, H. and Komninos, N. (2011). Future Internet and Living Lab research domain landscapes: Filling the gap between technology push and application pull in the context of smart cities. *eChallenges e-2011 Conference Proceedings* (pp.1–8). IIMC International Information Management Corporation.

Pea, R. D. (1993). Practices of distributed intelligence and designs for education. In G. Salomon (Ed.). *Distributed cognitions* (pp. 47–87). New York, NY: Cambridge University Press.

Pénin, J., Hussler, C. and Burger-Helmchen, T. (2011). New shapes and new stakes: A portrait of open innovation as a promising phenomenon. *Journal of Innovation Economics*, Vol. 1, No. 7, 11–29.

Prabakaran, I. (2010). Large-scale data processing and storage. *International Conference on Advanced and Emerging Technologies, ICAET 2010.* Retrieved 2 January 2014, from http://goo.gl/JeHZC.

Prat, N., Akoka, J. and Comyn-Wattiau, I. (2006). A UML-based data warehouse design method. *Decision Support Systems*. Vol. 42, No. 3, 1449–1473.

Reichwald, R., Seifert, S., Walcher, D. and Piller, F. (2004). Customers as part of value webs: Towards a framework for webbed customer innovation tools. *Proceedings of 2004 Hawaii International Conference on Computer Sciences (HICSS)*, Hawaii. Retrieved 2 January 2014, from http://goo.gl/qrkdSa.

RITA. (n.d.). *Intelligent transportation systems.* Retrieved 2 January 2014, from www.itsoverview.its.dot.gov/.

Schaffers, H., Guzman, G. and Merz, C. (2008). An action research approach to rural living labs innovation. In P. Cunningham and M. Cunningham (eds), *Collaboration and the knowledge economy: Issues, applications, case Studies* (pp. 617–624). Amsterdam, Netherlands: IOS Press.

Schaffers, H., Komninos, N. and Pallot, M. (eds) (2012). *Smart cities as innovation ecosystems sustained by the future Internet.* FIREBALL White Paper. Retrieved 2 January 2014, from www.urenio.org/wp-content/uploads/2012/04/2012-FIREBALL-White-Paper-Final.pdf.

Sheard, S.A. and Mostashari, A. (2009).Principles of complex systems for systems engineering. *Systems Engineering*, Vol.12, No. 4, 295–311.

Tips, B. (2011). Distributed intelligence: The path to a smarter grid. *UTC Journal*, 3rd Quarter, 29–35.

Tuikka, T. and Ervasti, M. (2013). *Technical foresight report. Crowd-based services for digital cities.* EIT ICT Labs. Retrieved 2 January 2014, from www.eitictlabs.eu/news-events/publications/.

Von Hippel, E. (1986). Lead users: A source of novel product concepts. *Management Science*, Vol. 32, No. 7, 791–805.

Index

Page numbers in *italics* indicate tables and figures.

Abando, district of 250–1
ABI Research reports 75–6
absorptive capacity (AC) 53
academic research 16, 205–7
Accenture 63, 64–5, 146
ADSL connections 107
advertising funding model 161
Affero General Public Licence (AGPL) V3 license 73
Against the Smart City (Greenfield and Kim) 15
ageing city infrastructure 64–5
agglomeration: of innovation ecosystems 149–50; innovative 137–8; intelligent cities building block 197; as major driving force 147; of smart ecosystems 49–51
agglomeration intelligence though connected variety 83–4
air pollution 229–30
Al Talah Gardens residential area 128
ambient sensor networks 69
American smart cities assessment 163
Amsterdam, digital city 151
Amsterdam Smart City 92–3
analytics, social media 204
AOL digital cities 151
A Planet of Civic Laboratories: The Future of Cities, Information and Inclusion (report) 67
application domains and metrics *29, 31*
applications and solutions: development of 157–60; taxonomy of *28, 30*
Apps4Finland 105
Apps for Smart Cities 29
architectures of cooperation 84
Aristotle, on cities 147
artificial intelligence 20, 39–40

The Art of Community (Bacon) 257
Asia, innovation spending and performance 43
assets, governance of 258–9
'attention economy' 203
augmented reality 68
Aurigi (2005) 14
Austria, clusters in 181

Bacon, Jono 257, 258
Bangalore City 18
Bangalore Intelligent Urbanisation initiative 64
Barcelona Smart City 16–17, 102–3
Bario, Malaysia 17
barter model 161
Bayh-Dole Act (1980) 206–7
Berners-Lee, Tim 224
BestParking 234
big data (megatrend) 198, 223–4, 246–9
Bilbao pilot project 250–1
Birmingham, England 18
Bletchley Park, England 85–7
bookmarking and tagging analysis 204
bottom-up demand 180–5
bottom-up initiatives 109, 114, 118, 122
BOWIEs 196, 199–201, 217
Bremen (Germany) pilot 251
British Bombe 85–7
Broadband Economies (Bell et al.) 15
broadband networks: benefits of 63; European smart cities, intelligent city planning in 107–9; inadequacy of 41; infrastructure 17, 27; Intelligent Urbanisation initiative 64; private sector operators 107; smart city infrastructure and 222–3
Broadband Performance Index (BPI) 162

Building and Managing an Intelligent City (Accenture) 29
building *vs.* city duality 109
Bulgaria, clusters in 181–2
bus fleet management 112
business intelligence 52
business mobility 64–5
business models: alternative engagement 120; building blocks of *214*; capacity reselling 161; cost-cutting 160; embedded spatial intelligence 76; innovation into smart environments 200–1; of intellectual property 200; objectives of 213–14; platform-based 216–17; re-discovery using smart environments 213–17; specific functions of 214; sustainable 160–2, 216
business startups 43

Catalonia, Spain 181
CDK-UCLG survey 220–1, 230, 231
cell phones 76
Centre for Advanced Spatial Analysis (CASA) 16
Centre for Learning Communities 16
Centre for Urban Science and Progress reports 75–6
Centre of Regional Science 16
change: architectures of cooperation 84; drivers of 263; in intelligent cities 61
China, R&D collaboration and expenditure 42, 43
Cinder storage 161
CIP-ICT-PSP (Policy Support Program) 66, 73
circuits of innovation 155–7
CISCO: crowdsourcing 190; global 'Intelligent Urbanisation' initiative 18; innovation facilities 42; Intelligent Urbanisation initiative 64; Smart Cities Operating Company 134; smart city agenda 63; Smart + Connected Communities (S+CC) initiative 29, 64, 134; unified network architecture 75
cities: as clusters of clusters 171; collaborative character of 147; distributive systems 147; fundamental aspects of 148; negative aspects of 147
city branding 225–6
city development, twin processes of 118
city-district design 31, 124
city ecosystems, governance of 255
city-focused measurement 163

city governance: domains 31; e-Democracy 237–8; Improve my City (ImyC) 236–7; public services to citizens 235–6; unified architecture 75
city infrastructure/utilities domains 30
city intelligence 82, 148
city marketing, effective 162–3
'city of districts over networks' 148–50
city planning 16, 144
city-related applications and e-services 109, *110, 111*
City Tour 360 254
closed intellectual property 200
cloud computing: changing business models and 214–15; city governance and 240; five essential characteristics of 70; metaphor for Internet-based services 26; smart cities and 70–2
'club of experts' 200
clusters: bottom-up demand 180–5; in Catalonia, Spain 181; competitiveness and innovation 176; competitiveness of 184; defined 175; development competences *183*; diamond model of 176; drivers of 175; global 177–8; for growth 175–8; growth areas 184; of innovation 42, 88, 105, 137; management and strategy elaboration 182; over time 177–8; smart specialisation 178–80; strategies 46–7, 133–4; in Tuscany, Italy 181; types of 176–7; *see also* intelligent city clusters
'coalition of parties' 200
co-creation, four types of 200
cohesion clusters 88
collaboration, multi-city 161
collaborative economy, Internet-based 202
collaborative innovation cycles 260–2
collaborative innovation network 55
collaborative knowledge work 85–7
collective creativity 200
collective information intelligence 52–3
collective intelligence: competitive advantages of 40; of institutions 14, 26; and spatial intelligence of cities 62, 80–1, 82
Colossus 85–7
Committee of Digital and Knowledge-based Cities of UCLG 220
commons-oriented licenses and platforms 200
communication barriers 108–9
community, the art of 255–8
community empowerment 15

'community of kindred spirits' 200
competition 65, 105
competitive advantage 40
competitive clusters 133–4
Competitiveness and Innovation Programme (CIP) 17, 66
Computer Aided Design (CAD) 26
Congress for the New Urbanism (CNU) 21
Connected Real Estate solutions concepts 134
consensus space 186–7
construction sector growth 172
consumer-fueled growth 171
content management systems (CMS) 151, 210
contract R&D labs 43
conversion tracking 203
corporate strategic planning: master plans and 144; *see also* intelligent city strategies; strategic planning
Corridor 'Living Lab NGA' pilot project 103–4
cost-cutting business model 160
creativity gap 120
crime mapping 230
CROSS-INNO-CUT (Interreg project) 196, 204–5
crowdfunding 161, 227–9
crowdsourcing: co-creation and 200; in collaboration environment 56; digital agglomeration and 152; innovation explosions 199; Living Lab platforms 189; NYC Simplicity Idea Market 72–3; paradigm 149; platforms 190
Crowdsourcing Landscape 152
Crowdspirit 56
cryptanalysis 85–7
culture and community spirit 136
customer relationship management (CRM) 52
cyber cities 19, 20
The Cybercities Reader (Graham) 14
cyber-intelligence 81
Cyberjaya project 51
Cyberport, Hong Kong 88–91
Cyberport Institute 91

data *see* big data (megatrend)
data integration, challenges of 75
data monetisation 161
The Death and Life of Great American Cities (Jacobs) 230
debt-based growth 171
decision-making, decentralised 75

Dell 56, 190
Democratising Innovation (Von Hippel) 199
Dense Wavelength Division Multiplexing (DWDM) technology 108
development theory 172
Dewey, John 259
Diamond Model of clustering 176
digital agenda for Europe 103, 178
digital agglomeration 152
digital cities: defined 20; as metaphor of the city 82; symposium series 14; three-tier architecture of 151; Web technologies and 150–2
Digital Cities II (Tanabe et al.) 14
Digital Cities III (Van den Besselaar and Koizumi) 14
Digital City Amsterdam 151
Digital City Kyoto 151
digital collaboration 31
digital commons 200
digital democracy 17
digital dimension, of top-down planning 138
Digital Entertainment Incubation and Training Programme 90
digital inclusion 162
digital innovation tools 41
digital intelligence 39–40
digital interaction 84
digital marketing 200
digital marketplaces 57
digital media and entertainment (DME) sector 46
Digital Media Centre 90
digital platforms: crowdsourcing 190; knowledge sharing 187–9; Living Labs 189–90; self-organising innovation 187–91; sensor network and test-bed environments 191
digital skills gap 120
digital space: development processes 150; four concentric rings of 118, *119,* 150; information dissemination and product promotion *57*; intelligent cities building block 197; intersection with physical environments 15; knowledge creation and collaborative innovation *55*; strategic planning and 148; technology learning and absorption *54*
digital strategy 103
Digital Strategy for Manchester 103
Digital Thessaloniki 121
disruptive innovation 205–7, 240–1

270 *Index*

distributed intelligence 40
distributed knowledge architectures 263–4
distributed problem-solving 150
distributed spatial intelligence 246
district-focused strategies 46–7
DP Architects 132

Eastern Ring Road Information System (e-service) 112–13
East Manchester Regeneration Project 104
Eastserve community network 104
eco-districts innovation 191–3
Economic Cities Act 139
Economic Cities Authority (ECA) 125
The Economies of Cities (Jacobs) 83
e-Democracy 237–8
e-health advisor 231–2
El Nasser, Haya 13
Emaar, the Economic City (EEC) 126
email marketing 203
embedded spatial intelligence: business models 76; capabilities 74–5; cloud computing 70–2; innovation ecosystems of 73–7; Internet of Things 67–9; milestones 63–7; Semantic Web 69–70; smart environments and 61–3; smart products–smart objects 74–5; technology markets size estimates 75–6; user-driven innovation 72–3; *see also* spatial intelligence of cities
'embedded tacit knowledge' thesis 42
emergence, state of 49–50
empowered users 199
empowerment intelligence 83, 88–91
Energy Management Haarlem 232
energy optimisation practices 233
Enigma machines 85–7
enterprise resource planning (ERP) 52
entrepreneurial universities 212
entrepreneurship gap 120
environmental pollution 229–30
environmental request and reporting application 254
Equal Partnership labs 43
EU 2020 strategy for smart growth 178–80
European Cluster Observatory 171
European Commission activity 65
European Initiative on Smart Cities 66
European Innovation Partnership (EIP) on Smart Cities and Communities 22, 66
European Network of Living Labs (ENoLL) 17, 47
European paradox 207

European smart cities: Barcelona 102–3; broadband networks 107–9; city-wide applications and e-services 109–14; Competitiveness and Innovation Programme (CIP) 196; defined 22; Digital Agenda for Europe 103; district-focused strategies 46–7; FP7 research 62, 63; Helsinki 104–5; high-growth sectors in 171–2; Horizon 2020 programme 17; intellectual property rights 207; islands of innovation 41–2; Manchester 103–4; metropolitan regeneration processes 118–22; new planning paradigm 14; R&D expenditure 43; smart city-districts 114–18; Smart City stakeholders platform 30; smart metering 232–3; smart specialisation strategies 263–4; Thessaloniki (Greece) 105–7; Wi-Fi hotspots 222; wireless broadband connections 222
European Smart Cities project consortium 163
evolutionary economics 172
extended digital space 15
external actors, urban communities and 148

FIREBALL project 65, 101, 109, 220
FIREBALL Smart Cities white paper (2012) 23, 220–1
fleet management 112
Florida knowledge-based profile 50
foreign direct investment (FDI) attraction 43
foresight exercises 198
Forrester Research 22
Forum Virium Helsinki 47
FOSS communities 159, 160
4G broadband connections 108
four freedoms of open-source software 159
FP7-ICT projects 65, 92, 220
FP7 research 62
free wireless broadband connections 108
FTTH networks 119
Future Internet: business models 76; cloud computing 70–2; Internet of Things (IoT) 67–9; new services and solutions 76–7; OECD policy recommendations 77; policy recommendations 77; Semantic Web 69–70; smart products–smart objects 74–5; technologies, devices, and applications 153; user-driven innovation 72–3

Index

Future Internet Research and Experimental (FIRE) action line 65
"Future Knowledge Ecosystems" 67, 197
Future Media: Internet technologies 62; research and technologies 70; smart cities and 69–70

Gale International 137
gated communities 136
the G component 193
GÉANT (pan-European communications infrastructure) 108
generative design tools 15
generic architectures 69
Geographical Information Systems (GIS) 26
geographically proximate group of interconnected companies 175
Geuzenveld Sustainable Neighbourhood 232
Glance virtual machine images 161
global collaboration, large-scale 56
global economic slowdown 136–7
globalisation and growth 171
global knowledge flows 42
global market presence, size *vs.* 174–5
global promotion 57
Global Trends 2030: Alternative Worlds (2012) 198
GoldenDeals (collaboration platform) 152
golden triangle of intelligent cities 153
Good-Relations annotator tool 69–70
Google adwords 203
governance model, three-stage *262*
governance principles 249
GPL (general public license) 160
Greece, clusters in 182
Greek Research and Technology Network (GRNET) 107–8
green clusters 191–3
greenfield projects 124–5
GRNET network 107–8
gross added value (GAV), employment and 172
Groupon (collaboration platform) 152
growth dynamic, changing nature of 171–5

Haramain High-Speed Rail Line 126–7
heating and cooling eco-districts 192
Helsinki 3D digital city 151
Helsinki smart city initiatives 47, 104–5, 145
holy triad of synergies 84
home R&D 43

Hong Kong Cyberport Management Company Limited 88–91
Horizon 2020 programme 66
Horizon Web front-end 161
HTML5 70
human intelligence of the population 14
hybrid sensemaking and identities 67
Hype Cycles 63, 67–8, 70

IBM: crowdsourcing 190; digital cities and 152–3; Idea Jam 190; Institute for Business Value analysis 28; smart cities agenda 63; Smart Cities project 21–2, 91–2; smart city model of instrumentation 164; *Smarter Cities* programme 19; Smart Planet Initiative 22
ICF awards 163
ICOS (intelligent cities open source) community 160, 238–41
IDC Government Insights prediction 263
Idea Jam (IBM) 190
IdeaStorm (Dell) 56, 190
identification of communities 256
impact assessment, challenge of 121
Improve my City (ImyC) 73, 236–7, *237*
iN2015 strategy 45
Incheon, South Korea 124
India, R&D in 42, 43
individual empowerment (megatrend) 198
industrial districts (clusters) 88, 176–7
industrial production 171
information and communication technologies (ICTs) 45, 171, 199
information dissemination 57, *57*
information processing 85–7
Infrastructure as a Service (IaSS) 28
infrastructure-focused measurement 164
in-kind exchange model 161
InnoCentive 56
innovation: building blocks of 73–4; capabilities 198; clustering of activities 41–2; collaborative 260; consumers as co-creators of 200; crowdsourcing paradigm 149; democratising 149; glocalisation of 41; intelligent cities and 40–1; intelligent cities building blocks 197; Intelligent Community Forum (ICF) 17; measurement of 162; participatory model of 149; policy-making shifts 137–8; spatial polarisation of 42; supply chain 201; theories of 137–8; through smart specialisation 243; two ways to achieve 51; universal

Index

availability 199; user-driven 72–3, 150; without IP 200
innovation circuits *155*, 155–7
innovation clusters 105
innovation cycles 260–2, *261*, 261–2
innovation economy 30, 173
innovation ecosystems: agglomeration of 149–50; BOWIEs 196; business models 76; capabilities 74; crowdsourcing paradigm 149; driving urban change 148–50; Internet and 199; smart products–smart objects 74–6; strategies 41–4, 73–7; urban problem solving within 155
innovation-for-all environments 89, 149
'innovation into smart environments' model 201
innovation networks, globalisation of 42
innovation offshoring 42, 43
innovation planning paradigm 39
innovation spending and performance 43
innovation systems 25
Innovation Union, smart growth and 178–80
Innovation Union Scoreboard 43
innovative agglomerations 137–8
innovative milieu (clusters) 88, 176
Institute for the Future (IFTF): foresight exercises 63; foresight reports 67; workshops 196–7
institutional clusters 177
institutional paradigm 243
institutional space *54, 55, 57*
institutional thickness 25
instrumentation intelligence 83, 91–3
Integrated Urban Infrastructure 74–5
intellectual capital 40
intellectual property (IP) models 200, 206–7
intellectual property rights (IPR) 55
intelligence: main attributes of 20, 245; as raw material of growth 180; three types of 14
intelligence into data 82–3
intelligent cities: application domains 30–1; applications *34*; Bletchley Park 85–7; building blocks of 135–40; characteristics of 87; circuits of innovation 155–6; co-creation paradigm 144; complementary contributions 245–6; concept and structure *32*; criteria of excellence 17; energy savings and CO_2 reduction 88; fundamental implementation elements of 144; gateway to information and knowledge 148; golden triangle of 153; innovation and 40–1; innovation ecosystems *32*; key characteristics 65; knowledge ecosystems 88; knowledge operation layers 57–8; literature review 13–15, 19–21, 39–41; measurement and assessment of 162–5; multiple concepts of 20; opensource applications 238–41; scoreboard structure *165*; smart environments *33*; spatial structure of 88; strategies and planning *33*; structural layers and elements 243–6, *244*; structure 24–7; technological construction origins 39; top-down planning, critical appraisal 135–40; *see also* smart cities
Intelligent Cities: Innovation, Knowledge Systems and Digital Spaces (Komninos) 14
intelligent city clusters: bottom-up demand 180–5; clustering for growth 175–8; consensus space 186–7; digital platforms for self-organising innovation 187–91; the G component 193; new growth conditions 171–5; resource efficiency innovations 191–3; smart specialisation 178–80; strategy for 185–6
intelligent city functioning, model of 245
intelligent city governance: of activities 259–62; art of community 255–8; of assets 258–9; ecosystems and 249–50; future ecosystems 262–4; generic model of 243–6; insights from big data 246–9; pilot projects 250–5
intelligent city paradigm: academic research 16; city planning initiatives 16; international organizations and 17; landscape 31–4; literature review 13–15, 19–21; movements shaping 15–19; multinational companies 18; multiple concepts of 19–24; outcomes 27–31; standardisation of building blocks 28; structure 24–7
intelligent city planning *see* strategic planning
Intelligent City Proof of Concept 18
intelligent city strategies: agglomeration of smart ecosystems 49–51; cluster or district-focused 46–7; critiques of 51; innovation ecosystems 41–4; literatures shaping 39–41; multi-layer knowledge functions 51–7; overview

38–9, 44; sector-focused 44–6; smart infrastructure-focused 47–9; strategies for 44–51; *see also* strategic planning
intelligent city structure 24–7, 243
Intelligent Community Forum (ICF) 15, 17, 162
intelligent infrastructure 65
intelligent islands 45
Intelligent Planet (IBM) 19
Intelligent Thessaloniki 105–7, 109–14, 114–18, 121
intelligent transportation systems (ITS) 156, 248
Intelligent Urbanisation initiative 18, 64
Intelligent X platform 29–30, 64
intention economy 202
intention markets 200
interaction data *see* big data (megatrend)
inter-city competition 65
international organizations 17
international relationships 42
Internet micro-payment systemsIT identity profile 50
Internet of Things (IoT) 21, 24, 67–9, 223
inter-protocol communication 69
INTERVALUE (academic R&D project) 196, 207–13, *208, 211*
investment and funding potential 210
IP agreements space 208
iResource Centre 90
Isbister, K. 13
Ishida, T. 13
islands of innovation 41–2, 88

Jacobs, Jane 230
Japan, R&D expenditure 43
Jazan Economic City (JEC) 131–3
Jeddah, Saudi Arabia 136
Joomla 151
Journal of Knowledge Economy on Smart Cities and the Future Internet in Europe (Komninos et al.) 220

Keystone authentication and authorisation 161
King Abdullah Economic City (KAEC) 126–8
Kingdom of Saudi Arabia (KSA) 125
Kista Science City 48
knowledge architectures 258–9
knowledge-based development and growth 154–5, 172–4
knowledge-based profile 50
knowledge cities 82

knowledge creation and innovation 55–7, 174
Knowledge Economic City Al-Madinah (KEC) 130–1
knowledge economy, complex challenges of 172–3
knowledge ecosystems 88
knowledge exchange 43
knowledge functions, fundamental 51
knowledge precincts 88
knowledge-sharing platforms 187–91
knowledge spillovers 121
knowledge workforce 17, 162
Kyoto, 3D virtual space 151

Laguerre, M. (2006) 14
LAMP (open source solution) 151–2
land use management 136
leasing and financing model 161
LGPL (lesser general public license) 160
LGPL code 234
Libelium devices 223, 229
Linux 151
literature review 13–15, 19–21, 162
Living Labs (LLs): cluster strategies 46–7; creativity gap 120; crowdsourcing 56; defined 17–18; in Finland 105; innovation processes 190; platforms 189; user involvement 88
Living PlanIT planning model 145
local–global innovation dynamics 44
Localocracy (collaboration platform) 152
location-aware applications 68
Lorenz machines 87

M2M communication 69
machine intelligence 14
machine-to-machine market 247
Madri+d (collaboration platform) 152
Malaysia Multimedia Super Corridor (MSC) 17, 51
Manchester, England: knowledge-based profile 50; smart city initiatives 103–4; strategic planning 145
manufacturing eco-districts 192
manufacturing sector growth 172
MapReduce programming model 247–8
market discovery, smart environments and 201–5
market intelligence dashboards 203
market potential 209–10
markets and marketing 17, 162–3, 200
Marshallian clusters 176

master planning 144; *see also* intelligent city planning; strategic planning
Mazower, Mark 105
megatrends 198
Melbourne 2030 Plan 88
metropolitan regeneration processes 118–22
Microsoft 18, 63
mirror-city metaphors 151
Mishlium 229
Mitchell, William 16
MIT Smart Cities Group 16, 21
MMC Corporation 132, 133
Mobile Applications Cluster 105
mobile communication devices statistics 69
mobile phones 76
mobile telecommunications service providers 108
Mosaic graphic Web browser 151
multi-city collaboration 161
multimodal trip planning 233–4
multinational companies 18
mutual knowledge exchange 43

National Building Museum 17
National Institute for Standards and Technology (NIST) 71
National Intelligence Council report 198
National Reform Programme (NRP) 179
Neapolis Smart Eco-City (Cyprus) 124, 145
near-field communication 68
Netscape 151
network interoperability 76–7
networks and utilities 232–5; *see also* broadband networks
New Economic Cities of Saudi Arabia *see* Saudi Arabia New Economic Cities
New Growth Theory 173
new institutional economics 172
New Songdo (North Korea) 17, 137
New Urbanism 13
New York City: digital city 17; knowledge-based profile 50; Simplicity Idea Market 72–3, 152; strategic planning 145
next-generation information and services 68
Nokia 42
non-equity R&D collaboration 42
Normandy LL 46–7
North American R&D expenditure 43
Nova computer services 161
NYC Simplicity Idea Market 72–3, 152

OASTH (Organisation of Urban Transportation of Thessaloniki) 112, 121
observations data *see* big data (megatrend)
OECD reports and governmental papers 62
online analytical processing (OLAP) 52
online community marketplaces 226–7
online transactions, physical mobility and 121–2
open data 70, 223–4
Open Data Index 223
open innovation: co-creation and 200; defined 191; models of 153; paradigm 260
Open Knowledge Foundation (OKFN) 223
open-source licenses 159–60, 200
open-source routing solutions 109
open-source software communities 28
OpenStack software 161
OpenTripPlanner (OTP) 233–4
operating systems, advantages of common 75
orchestration intelligence 83
Organisation for Economic Co-operation and Development (OECD) 17
Organisation of Urban Transportation of Thessaloniki (OASTH) 112
OSWINDS Group 92
OTE Bit Stream Network 107
outsourcing 152
Ovun research reports 75–6

parametric design 15
parking solutions 234–5, 254
participatory Web 152
PayByPhone 234–5
pay-per-click campaigns 203
Peak of Inflated Expectations 67, *68*
people-driven innovation models 153
people-led urban planning 15
PEOPLE project 196, 216, 250–6
physical mobility, online transactions and 121–2
physical-virtual communities of innovation 56
Pike Research reports 75–6
pilot projects, smart technology 66, 250–5, 256
Pirai, Brazil 17
place-based interventions 180
PlanIT Valley (Portugal) 124
planned technology parks 88
Planning through Projects (Carmona) 144
Plateau of Productivity 68

platforms, collaborative Web 200
Point-to-Multipoint (PMP) and Point-to-Point (P2P) links 108
policy focused measurement 162
pollution monitoring 254
Polya, George 259
population mobility 64–5
Portugal 50
Prince Abdul Aziz Bin Mousaed Economic City (PABMEC) 128–30
problem-solving, distributed 150
Product Development 2.0 189
product discovery and development 189, 201
product feed manager systems 203
Progress Report on Economic and Social Cohesion (2008) 171–2
public digital marketplaces 57
public funding business model 160
public–private partnerships (PPPs) 133, 139, 161, 193
public safety 230–1
'pull economy' 202–3
Putrajaya project 51

quality of life domains: e-health advisor 231–2; environmental pollution 229–30; safety in public spaces 230–1; smart city applications 30
Quantum networking services 161

Rakisa Holding 128–9
R&D (research and development): collaboration 42; databases 54; expenditure 43–4; exploitation 53; spending 205; trends 25
RDF/S ontology design 258–9
R&D valorisation: investment and funding potential 210; investment risks 213; market potential 209–10; scientific relevance 209; technical feasibility 209; technology barriers 213; virtual environment for 211–12
real-time spatial intelligence 69, 153
regeneration projects 104
Regional Analysis and Information Data Sharing Online 231
'related variety' concept 84, 180
renewable energy sources (RES) 192
repository space 208
representational intelligence 81–2
Research Triangle Foundation workshops 196–7
research valorisation *see* R&D valorisation

resource efficiency innovations 191–3
revenue-generating business model 160
Road Map for the Digital City (City of New York) 145–6
Rockefeller Foundation 17

safety in public spaces 230–1
Salonica City of Ghosts (Mazower) 105
Santander, Spain 91–2
San Vicente of Abando 250–1
satellite districts (clusters) 177
satellite fleet management 112
Satellite R&D labs 43
Saudi Arabia New Economic Cities: critical appraisal of top-down planning 134–40; Economic Cities Act 139; greenfield projects 124–5; Jazan Economic City (JEC) 131–3; King Abdullah Economic City (KAEC) 126–8; Knowledge Economic City Al-Madinah (KEC) 130–1; planning initiatives 17; Prince Abdul Aziz Bin Mousaed Economic City (PABMEC) 128–30; smart city complexes in 133–4; urban dimension 135–7
Saudi Arabian General Investment Authority (SAGIA) 125
Saudi Binladin Group (SBG) 132, 133
scientific relevance 209
scoreboards, monitoring 121
search engine optimisation (SEO) and marketing (SEM) 203
sector-focused strategies 44–6
Secure Electronic Transactions Competitiveness Cluster (TES) 46–7
Security Operations Centre 18
SeeClickFix (collaboration platform) 152
'Seeker' companies 56
self-organising innovation 187–91
Semantically Enabled Service Oriented Architectures (SESAs) 263
semantic M2M communication 69
semantic sensing 70
Semantic Web 69–70, 263
SEN2SOC experiment 92
Senseable City Lab 16
sensor communication 69
sensor network platforms and test-bed environments 191
sensor networks 223
Seoul Digital Media City (DMC) 17
Seoul IT identity profile 50
Serendipity project 70
service sector growth 171–2

276 *Index*

SETIS (SET Information System) 66
7th Frame Programme for Research and Technological Development (FP7) 17
share more–develop less principle 159
Singapore 17, 45
single-purpose zones 136
Slope of Enlightenment 68
Smart21 cities 17
Smart Amsterdam 16
smart cities: agenda 63; applications and solutions 157–60; background paper 22; big data (megatrend) 246–9; building blocks/layers of 23; business models 76, 160–2; capabilities 74–5; challenges of 27; culture of experimentation and openness 159; defined 21, *23*; as digital spatiality 153; early chaos 220; IBM model for 63–4; infrastructure-focused measurement 163; measurement, assessment, and benchmarking 164; multiple concepts of 20; portfolios of solutions 220; six characteristics of 22; six steps to building 146; smart products–smart objects 74–5; software development 157–60; technologies, devices, and applications 153; technology markets, size estimates 75–6; wireless technologies used in 222–3; *see also* intelligent cities
Smart Cities Operating Company 134
Smart Cities Research Group 16
Smart Cities Stakeholders Platform 66
Smart City endowments 163
smart city energy grid 248–9
smart city infrastructure: branding, marketplaces, crowdfunding 224–9; broadband 221–4; CISCO and 134; essential applications and solutions 220–1; governance 235–8; ICOS 238–41; networks and utilities 232–5; quality of life 229–32
smart community concept 41
smart companies: big data empowerment 196–8; BOWIEs 196, 199–201, 217; business model re-discovery 213–17; market discovery 201–5; technology discovery 205–13
Smart + Connected Communities (S+CC) initiative 29, 64, 134
smart eco-districts 192
smart economy: city branding 225–6; crowdfunding 227–9; online community marketplaces 226–7
smart ecosystems, agglomeration of 49–51

smart environments: business model re-discovery 213–17, *215*; horizon scan of 150–4; innovation ecosystem renewal 201; INTERVALUE 207–13; market discovery and 201–5; R&D valorisation 207–13; technology discovery using 205–13; three layers of 25
Smarter Cities Challenge 19
Smarter Planet – Smarter Cities (SP-SC) initiative 63–4, 91–2
smart growth: defined 21; end of life of 13; EU 2020 strategy for 178–80; new planning paradigm of 13
Smart Helsinki 104–5
smart infrastructure-focused strategies 47–9, 88
smart marketplace 253–4
smart metering projects 91–2, 232–3
smart parking 234–5
smart products–smart objects 74–5
Smart Santander test bed facility 16, 65, 91–2
smart specialisation strategy: European competitiveness and 263–4; intelligent city clusters 178–80; key elements of *179*; theoretical foundations of 180
smart technology pilot projects 66
social capital 40
social media: collaboration platforms 152; market discovery and 203–5; spatial intelligence of cities driver 62
Social Media Examiner (2011) survey 204
Software as a Service (SaaS) 28
software for control and collaboration solutions 157–60
software stack 26
'Solver'scientists 56
South Korea 43, 50
spatial intelligence of cities: agglomeration intelligence 83–4; Amsterdam Smart City 92–3; Bletchley Park 85–7; collective intelligence 82; concept 62; cyber intelligence 81; Cyberport, Hong Kong 88–91; documentation of 162–5; drivers of 153; empowerment intelligence 88–91; generic dimensions of *94*; instrumentation intelligence 91–3; intelligence into data 82–3; literature review 79–81; novel Internet-enabled 249; orchestration intelligence 85–7; representational intelligence 81–2; representation and visualisation 151; smart metering projects 91–2;

Smart Santander 92–3; universal architecture of 93–5; *see also* embedded spatial intelligence
spatial proximity of clusters 175
speech recognition 68
'spend less' principle 159
SP–SC initiative 63–4, 91–2
standardisation of platforms and applications 70–1
startup businesses 43
star-type clusters 177
state-led clusters 177
Stockholm: city planning initiatives 17; innovation accomplishments 47–9; knowledge-based profile 50; strategic planning 145; Vision 2030 88
Stokab 48–9
strategic planning: Accenture 146; applications and solutions 157–60; balances scorecard methods 154; communities, knowledge functions, and circuits of innovation 154–7; a connectionist model 145–7; conventional methodologies for 145; digital space 150–4; dimensions of 154; five principles in 146; governance as framework for 249; human capabilities and 145; IDC Government Insights 146; innovation ecosystems for urban change 148–50; from master plans to 144–5; merits of good 157; New York 145; problem and community definition 147–8; problem-oriented approach 146; roadmap for *146*; spatial intelligence 162–5; sustainable business models 160–2; *see also* intelligent city strategies
strategy implementation 157–60
sustainable growth 13
Switzerland 222
Synekism 147
synergies, holy triad of 84
system-areas (clusters) 176
system of innovation concept 25

tacit knowledge networks 42, 138
tag parking 235
Taipei 50
'Taipei Infinity' 222
taxonomy of domains of applications and solutions 28
technical feasibility 209
technological advancement 63
technological construction origins 39

technology: acquisition barriers 213; collaboration spaces 54; emerging 67; horizon scan of 150–4; learning and absorption 53–5
technology discovery: academic research 205–7; disruptive innovation and 205–7; European Union research policy 205; investment and funding potential 210; market potential 209–10; R&D valorisation 206–7, 207–13, *208*; scientific relevance 209; technical feasibility 209
technology transfer 53–4
Technology Trigger 67, *68*
10x10 programme 125
territorial knowledge and creativity 40
test-bed environments 191
Testing and Certification of Wireless Communication Platform 90
Thermi pilot (Greece) 252–3
Thessaloniki (Greece) 105–7, 109–14, 114–18, 121, 182, 252–3
Thessaloniki 360 (virtual guided tour) 113
3G and 4G networks 108, 119
Thucydides, on cities 147
Tianjin, China 17
Top7 cities 17
top-down planning: business model challenges 139; critical appraisal of 135–40; the digital dimension 138–40; the innovation dimension 137–8; within intelligent city-districts 124–5; public–private partnerships (PPPs) model 133–4; Saudi Arabia New Economic Cities 125–33; the urban dimension 135–7
Toyota 42
traditional city planning methodologies 144
transaction data *see* big data (megatrend)
transportation improvement 156, 251–2
trends: hybrid sensemaking and identities 67; innovation networks, globalisation of 42; intelligent cities building blocks 197–8; R&D spending per sale 43–4; Semantic Web services availability 263; ubiquitous computing 67
triple helix innovation model 48
trip planning, multimodal 233–4
Trough of Disillusionment 68
Turkey 222
Tuscany, Italy 181
22@Barcelona 102, 192–3

ubiquitous connectivity 67, 69, 70
Unified Modelling Language (UML) 258–9
United Nations Conference on Trade and Development (UNCTAD) survey 42
United States R&D expenditure 43
universal ubiquitous sensor network architectures 69
university–industry collaboration 205–6
university R&D, valorisation of 205–7
up-skilling strategies 88, 89
Urban Audit database 163
urban change drivers 148–50, 263
urban communities, external actors and 148
urban development planning paradigm 39
urban dimension, replicability of 135–7
urban economic activities, building blocks of 74
urban fortresses 136
urban governance, new type of 144
urban infrastructure networks 62
urbanisation and data integration challenges 75
Urban Operating Systems (UOS) 74–5, 145
urban operating system 47
urban problems 147–8, 155
urban renewal 13
urban space 54, 55, 57
urban sub-systems 245
urban transportation improvement 156
URENIO Research 16, 21, 26, 73, 238
user-centric innovation ecosystems 88
user-driven innovation 72–3, 150, 189, 203, 243, 260

valorisation plans (VPs) 208
valorisation plan templates 211–12
VDSL solutions 119
venture capital funds 43
Very-High-Bit-Rate Digital Subscriber Lines (VDSL) 107

Vienna Centre for Regional Science 28
virtual collaboration 55–6
virtual Helsinki 151
virtual marketing campaigns 204
virtual technology learning 54
Vision 2030 88
Vitry-sur-Seine (France) pilot 251–2
VoD (Video on Demand) 108
VoIP (Voice over Internet Protocol) 108

Waspmote hardware 229
Wavelength Division Multiplexing – WDM technology 108
Web 2.0 concepts 151–2, 189, 210, 243
Web-based collaboration 28, 152, 200
Web technologies, three waves of 150–3
West Orange in Amsterdam Smart City 232
Wi-Fi hotspots 222
"Will 'intelligent cities' put an end to suburban sprawl?" (El Nasser) 13
wireless broadband 108, 222; see also broadband networks
Wireless Taipei – Taipei Infinity 222
Wood, Elizabeth 230
WordPress 151
WordPress Multi-User 210
World Bank 17
World Foundation for Smart Communities 21
World Wide Web 16, 150–1
World Wide Web Consortium (W3C) 151
Wylie, Texas 231

XXXL G (extremely extra extra large governance) 249

Yet2com 54
youth on the move, smart growth and 178

Zaragoza 17
Zonability (collaboration platform) 152
zoning principles 136